SMALL
BUSINESS
MANAGEMENT
FUNDAMENTALS

McGraw-Hill Series in Management

Keith Davis and Fred Luthans, *Consulting Editors*

SMALL BUSINESS MANAGEMENT FUNDAMENTALS

THIRD EDITION

Dan Steinhoff, D.S.Sc.

Professor of Business Management
University of Miami

McGRAW-HILL BOOK COMPANY

New York   St. Louis   San Francisco   Auckland   Bogotá
Hamburg   Johannesburg   London   Madrid   Mexico   Montreal   New Delhi
Panama   Paris   São Paulo   Singapore   Sydney   Tokyo   Toronto

This book was set in Times Roman by The Total Book (ECU/BD).
The editor was Kathi A. Benson;
the production supervisor was John Mancia.
The cover was designed by Janice Noto;
the cover photograph was taken by Adrian Buckmaster.
R. R. Donnelley & Sons Company was printer and binder.

SMALL BUSINESS MANAGEMENT FUNDAMENTALS

5 6 7 8 9 0 DODO 8 9 8 7 6 5 4

ISBN 0-07-061146-7

Library of Congress Cataloging in Publication Data
Steinhoff, Dan.
   Small business management fundamentals.

   (McGraw-Hill series in management)
   Includes bibliographies and index.
   1. Small business—United States—Management.
2. New business enterprises—United States—Management. I. Title. II Series.
HD62.7.S8 1982   658'.022   81-8412
ISBN 0-07-061146-7   AACR2

ABOUT THE AUTHOR

Dr. Dan Steinhoff is a senior professor of Business Management at the University of Miami. His name has become well known in academic circles since the publication of the first edition of *Small Business Management Fundamentals* almost 10 years ago. He is also the author of more than 10 other books and new editions in the field of business. *Small Business Management Fundamentals* is used in more than 400 colleges in the United States and abroad. It has been translated into Japanese and has a special Canadian edition.

The winner of the outstanding professor award in three different years at the University of Miami and the award for research and writing in two different years, Dr. Steinhoff has presented seminars on business subjects on every continent of the world. His academic achievements have resulted in his inclusion in *Who's Who in the World,* and *Who's Who in America.* He has been a leader in national, state, and regional organizations devoted to advancing the welfare of small business. He is Director of the Small Business Development Center and the Small Business Institute which operate on the University of Miami campus.

TO MY DEAR WIFE JILL

CONTENTS

PREFACE

This third edition of *Small Business Management fundamentals* reflects many of the suggestions from instructors and reviewers in the more than 400 educational institutions–junior colleges through graduate schools–that have ordered previous editions.

Significant additions include:

1 New chapter on Computers and Electronic Data Processing for small firms
2 A new chapter on Franchising
3 A new chapter on Importing and Exporting
4 A new chapter on Small Business and the Law
5 A new continuing problem through the first 22 chapters
6 Additional case studies in Part 7

Every effort has been made to maintain the text's readability in a straightforward, fundamental approach to planning and operating a small firm. The language is planned to be easily understood by college students at all levels. The much applauded logical sequence of the steps in planning a new small business is maintained. After an introduction in the early chapters to the small business world and a review of the basic accounting statements, Chapter 4 presents a comprehensive business plan that involves 14 basic steps in planning a new business firm. These steps are then reviewed in logical sequence with a full chapter devoted to each.

Later chapters discuss other methods of becoming small business owners. Full chapters are devoted to Franchising and to Buying an Existing Business. Other aspects of small firm management, including electronic data processing, importing and exporting, small business and the law, and simplified accounting systems, are detailed in Part 6.

The author is satisfied that the approach and format have been effective in student accomplishment. Large classes each semester have demonstrated student appreciation of the approach and the grasp of the total management area. Planning chapters can be studied in sequence or in isolation but it is believed that the total sequence is most valuable to students.

TO THE INSTRUCTOR

Much effort has been devoted to assisting busy instructors who often need more time to prepare quizzes or develop good class discussion material. Each chapter provides a set of questions for class discussion, suggested projects for class or for homework, essay quizzes, and in chapters, through 21, assignments for the continuing problem. All exercises are designed to stimulate good ideas and student discussion. Fifteen case studies, which can be used as desired by the instructor, are included in Part 7.

The Late Lerner is a fictional character created to be the source of quotations at the beginning of each chapter. Many of the quotes originate in real life, as experienced instructors will vouch. It is hoped that these quotes will prove stimulating to students or at least bring an occasional smile to them as they dig into their study.

The continuing problem extends through the first 21 chapters. Some instructors find it valuable in enabling students to follow a single firm through the entire planning process. Its use should always depend upon the total teaching plan of the individual instructor. That plan, of course, will vary with the makeup of the particular class.

The extensive Instructor's Manual provides comments for the instructor for each chapter and answers to the various types of quizzes. Most instructors will not conduct quizzes after each chapter but those provided can assist in developing periodic examinations as desired.

While responsibility for the final writing must be mine, I wish to thank the following whose advice, suggestions, encouragement, and review of specific chapters were so helpful: Dr. Henry King Stanford, President of the University of Miami, Professors Manuel Zaiac, Carl McKenry, and Donald Johnson of the Business School at Miami, Professor Keith Davis of Arizona State University, Kurt Fabian SBA Officer, of the Coral Gables, Florida office, Gustavo Agusti, Director, Cybernetics Systems International Corp., Professor Rudolph L. Kagerer, University of Georgia, Professor William M. Smith, University of Miami, Professor Jeffrey Turnbull, Pasadena City College, Professor Robert Swindle, Glendale Communnity College, Professor R. B. Keusch, East Carolina University, Dr. F. E. Hartzler, Emporia State College, Professor Charles B. Prentiss, Phoenix College, Professor Charles Downing, Massasoit Community College, and Professor George Solomon, George Washington University. Cooperation of the Small Business Administration officials both in Washington, D.C. and in Florida could not have been greater.

Dan Steinhoff

INTRODUCTION

SMALL BUSINESS IN THE UNITED STATES

I always thought that small business meant the neighborhood druggist, the Mom and Pop fruit stand, and an occasional service station. Gosh, what a different small business world I have discovered.

The Late Learner

When we speak of small business in the United States we are referring to more than 10.5 million small firms, exclusive of approximately 2.7 million small farmers. The total number of small farmers has declined in recent years, but the number of small nonfarm business firms continues to grow each year. There are more than 11 million nonfarm businesses of all sizes in the country. All studies of these statistics show that at least 95 percent of these firms are "small" regardless of which measure of smallness is applied. We will review the more prominent measures of size in this chapter. Meanwhile, we can recognize now that the small business scene in this country comprises more than 95 percent of all the nonfarm businesses in the country—and a total of more than 10.5 million firms.[1]

It is important to note at this early point that in the decade of the 1970s, small firms provided more than 85 percent of the new jobs created in the country.[2] More than 500,000 new small firms are started in our country each year. Unfortunately, more than half are out of business within 18 months. This book is

---

[1]These figures are taken from the proceedings and papers of The White House Conference on Small Business held in Washington, D.C. in January 1980.
[2]Ibid.

dedicated to lowering that percentage of failures by teaching the basic fundamentals of planning, organizing, and operating a small firm.

These small firms have been established to manufacture, distribute, finance,
and retail the innumerable goods and services desired or needed for our
population at home and to export products as well. The vast majority of these
firms concentrate on selling material products, but an increasing number of firms
provide a service. Although most service firms operate for local markets,
services, too, are exported. Recent years have seen a great increase in the export
of services, such as management consulting, and medical and technological
services.

The truth of these statements often comes as a surprise to those who have the
impression that the world of business consists chiefly, or only, of business giants.
It is true that we do have many giant corporations in our country and that they
are essential in order to make economies possible through mass production and
mass distribution. Without these mass facilities, the present standard of living in
the United States could not have been reached. Many small firms are dependent
on larger firms for raw materials or finished products, which would be much
more costly without the economies of mass production or not even available
without the larger business firms that produce and distribute them.

But large firms are likewise dependent upon small firms. Mass-production
industries recognize that they could not distribute their goods and services
without the hundreds of small firms that do that job. It has been estimated that
an average of 500 small suppliers and 3,000 retailers support every major
manufacturing firm in the country. Big business appreciates this interdepen-
dence of large and small firms and, as we shall see, actively promotes the welfare
of small firms (see Figure 1-1).

To understand the small business scene, we must recognize that of the more
than 11 million business firms in the United States, fewer than ½ of 1 percent
employ as many as 2,500 people. Among manufacturing firms, more than 90
percent employ fewer than 100 people, and 66 percent employ fewer than 20
people. When we look at distributors, retailers, and service firms, these
percentages are even more surprising in demonstrating the numerical preponderance of small firms.

The great majority of American business firms are small, and independently
owned and operated by small business proprietors. Numerical evidence is
available to support this fact, both in the United States and in most other
countries of the Western world. Study of this evidence makes it clear that small
business firms actually constitute the backbone of the free enterprise economies.

THE IMPORTANCE OF A STRONG SMALL BUSINESS
COMMUNITY TO THE NATION

The existence of a strong, healthy small business community has always been
recognized as the best way to preserve competition in our capitalistic society,
prevent monopolistic control of any industries, and thus assure the population of
the benefits of competition through better prices and quality products. Since the

FIGURE 1-1
Big business does support small business. The cover of the McDonnell Douglas Corporation's *Small Business Newsletter* shows the interest of a large firm in aiding small firms. This company regularly reports that more than 60 percent of its purchase orders and more than 20 percent of its dollar purchases are placed with small firms.

passage of our first antimonopoly laws in 1898 (The Sherman Act), our government has advocated policies aimed at maintaining competition and a healthy, competitive business community. Incentives have been provided to assist small firms. These have included lower rates of federal income taxes on lower incomes, special forms of legal organizations, and, more recently, an insistence that more large government contracts provide for subcontracting to small suppliers, thus increasing their part of the total job. All government agencies are now required to make more purchases from smaller firms when possible. The government created the Small Business Administration (SBA) in 1954 to provide financial, management, and procurement assistance for small firms.

Despite these developments, the clamor for more relief for small firms became louder and louder in the country. As a result, President Jimmy Carter called for a White House Conference on Small Business, which was held in Washington, D.C. in January 1980. At that time he issued the following statement:

> The small business community constitutes the single most important segment of our free enterprise system. It accounts for forty-eight percent of our gross national product, more than half of the American labor force, and continues to be the major source of inventions and new jobs. Small business is truly the backbone of the American economy.

More than 2,400 elected and appointed delegates from every segment of the small business world were invited to attend. They aired their complaints and presented to the President their requests for further legislation to aid the preservation, profitability, and public-service aspects of their endeavors.

The final report of that conference centered on greater ability for capital formation, fewer regulations, less paper work by innumerable agencies of the government, and a general approval of the work being done by government agencies like the SBA to assist new and ailing small firms. The President promised to submit legislation to Congress on these matters.

TREND OF SMALL FIRM GROWTH

Some critics of the Establishment are surprised to know that there are more small firms per 1,000 population in the United States today than at any other time in our history. Although the rate of growth has not always been uniform, the long-term trend of business history has shown a healthy continuation of the importance, strength, and numbers of small firms. This growth has continued despite the serious failure rate among new firms that are improperly planned, financed, and managed.

Today there are more than 26 small business firms for every 1,000 persons in our total population. This is a somewhat higher ratio than existed in the depression years of the 1930s or the war years of the 1940s. It compares significantly with the fact that at the turn of the century there were about 18 firms per 1,000 population. Such figures indicate that opportunities for small business firms have kept pace with the growth in population. The net growth rate for new small businesses in recent years has been about 100,000 per year. We should never assume that the small business firm is losing its importance in the development and maintenance of a healthy, competitive economic society.

Small firms, as defined by the SBA, employ more than 40 million people and produce almost 45 percent of the total gross national product. They employ 50 percent of the total work force. They produce goods and services with a value in excess of $500 billion each year.[3]

Simultaneously, however, we can recognize that the few firms of giant size—those employing 1,000 or more people—provide approximately 40 percent of the total paid employment in the United States. Even so, we must not minimize the fact that more than one-third of this total paid employment is provided by small firms—firms employing fewer than 50 people. More than 20 percent of our paid employment in manufacturing, 70 percent in whole-saling, and 65 percent in retailing exists in companies employing fewer than 100 people. Thus, despite the importance of our giant corporations, which play an essential role in our total economy, in terms of the number of business units, the volume of business, and the percentage of paid employment, the small firm remains the dominant factor in the United States and most of the Western world.

HOW IS A SMALL BUSINESS DEFINED?

This perfectly normal question does not have a precise answer. It depends upon what definition is used; but two answers remain the most widely used today. These are the definition of the Small Business Administration and that of the Committee For Economic Development (CED). Following is a close look at each.

Small Business Administration Measures of a Small Business

In evaluating small firms for eligibility for financial assistance, managerial assistance, or assistance in procuring government contracts, the SBA uses measures of the firm's total sales or total employment. The measures vary with the type of industry. Over the years these measures have been increased to reflect inflation and other factors in the business economy. The measures currently in effect are:

For retailers The firm is considered small if its annual sales do not exceed $2 million. However, in some industries this total may reach $7.5 million.

For service firms The firm is considered small if its annual receipts do not exceed $2 million. Certain firms may go up to $8 million.

---

[3]*Annual Reports,* Small Business Administration.

For wholesalers The firm is considered small if its annual sales do not exceed $9.5 million. Certain types of firms may go as high as $22 million.

For manufacturers The firm is considered small if it does not have more than 1,500 employees. Again, some industry variations exist.

For transportation and warehousing companies The firm is considered small if its annual receipts do not exceed $1 million.

For construction firms The firm is considered small when its annual income does not exceed $9.5 million for the immediately preceding 3 years. Exceptions can be made for certain types of trade construction.

Special circumstances may justify variations from these limits at the discretion of the SBA.

It should be quickly added that all of these measures are subject to frequent change. They do not, for example, fully reflect the inflationary trends of the decade of the seventies which have continued into the eighties. Each year most of the size limits for eligibility for SBA services change, some several times. Firms that plan to seek SBA assistance with financing, management, or procuring government contracts should always check with their nearest SBA office (a listing of which appears in Appendix B) for current rulings on size.

Committee For Economic Development Measures of a Small Business

This significant research organization (CED) developed the following definition of a small business some years ago. It is based upon a cross section of characteristics of the individual firm. That definition says:

> A small business is one which possesses at least two of the following four characteristics:
>
> **1** Management of the firm is independent. Usually the managers are also the owners.
> **2** Capital is supplied and the ownership is held by an individual or a small group.
> **3** The area of operations is mainly local, with the workers and owners living in one home community. However, the markets need·not be local.
> **4** The relative size of the firm within its industry must be small when compared with the biggest units in its field. This measure can be in terms of sales volume, number of employees, or other significant comparisions.

Of the characteristics cited, most scholars believe that the fourth, relative size, is the most important. Under this relative size concept, a small chain of men's shops would still be small compared to a major national clothier's chain of outlets.

It will be obvious that our definitions of a small firm encompass a wide range, from Mom and Pop stores to substantial manufacturing plants, distributors, retailers, and service firms.

Another excellent definition of a small business is contained in the Small

Business Act of 1934 passed by the United States Congress. It says "a small business is one which is independently owned and operated and not dominant in its field." The feature of dominance has come to be of greatest importance in most attempts to specifically define any small firm.

The emphasis in this text will be on firms that desire to grow. We will find that management principles are common to all types and sizes of business firms. With a thorough review of all steps in planning and organizing, we will bring all phases of management into a cohesive whole.

ADAPTING VERSUS ADOPTING MANAGEMENT PRINCIPLES

An important observation can be made with regard to size: The same principles of business management apply to the largest firms in the country as well as to the smallest. This does not mean that a principle should be *adopted* uniformly in all cases, but that principles should be *adapted* to the particular needs of the firm. Nevertheless, the fundamental truths of business management must be recognized regardless of size. Division of labor and the ability to delegate responsibility are cases in point.

TYPES OF ACTIVITY OF SMALL BUSINESS

The areas of activity for most small firms can be classified as follows:

Manufacturing
Mining
Wholesaling
Retailing
Service
Finance

Manufacturing   Manufacturing firms engage in the gathering of raw materials necessary for the creation of consumer and industrial products and in giving them useful form through their manufacturing processes. Most small manufacturing firms then pass their finished products on to wholesalers or other distributors (jobbers, sales agents, brokers, commission merchants, or manufacturers' agents) who handle their further distribution to the eventual users of the products. The use of manufacturers' agents to represent small factories in this process seems to be on the increase. This is particularly true in the machinery and heavy industrial goods industries. Very few small manufacturers of home-consumer products engage in the distribution process beyond normal wholesale channels.

Mining   Mining firms engage in gathering raw materials from the bowels of the earth. They either process the raw materials into consumer goods as part of their normal operation or sell them to other firms which convert them into usable form. An example of the former is the small salt mine where the salt is

FIGURE 1-2
Small businesses are prominent in manufacturing, mining, wholesaling, retailing, and service-oriented firms.

Arthur Tress/Photo Researchers, Inc.

Owen Franken/Stock, Boston

Daniel S. Brody/Stock, Boston

FIGURE 1-2 (Continued).

gathered and packaged in its own operation. The latter is exemplified by the small oil-well operator who drills for a product but sells it to a refinery. Many people would be surprised to know that small mining companies form a large part of the total mining activity in the United States and abroad. In many product areas, more than 50 percent of the mined products come from small firms.

Wholesaling   Wholesaling for the distribution of both consumer and industrial goods is a large part of the small business scene. For most consumer goods, marketing experience in business has demonstrated the economic benefits of using established wholesale channels of distribution. Let us consider a pork-and-beans cannery attempting to distribute its product to all the individual stores that would like to have it on their shelves. By using wholesalers, the cannery can greatly reduce the costs of distribution. In addition, one wholesaler handles many other products in a particular area of activity—in this case, groceries—providing further benefits to the individual stores, which can obtain other products at the same time from the same source.

Retailing   Retailing represents the largest percentage of all small firms. Small retailers are to be found in every area of products and services we can imagine. Perhaps this is because more people feel competent to attempt independent firm ownership in this field. All retail firms buy their products from wholesalers, jobbers, or other distributors in final form for use by the consumer. The function of retailers is to give these products *place utility,* that is, to make them available to consumers where they desire them. Creation of this place utility and provision of other services for the consumer are the economic justification of the retailers' profits.

Service   Service firms are numerous and varied. They are engaged in rendering an essential service to their customers. Pure services are not tangible products that may be inventoried, but they are in great demand by many people in many areas. Doctors and dentists provide services. Consultants and accountants provide services. Many common types of services are supplied by firms which do work on products that are owned by their customers, for example, repairing TV sets or washing machines, or dry-cleaning clothing for customers. Other service firms perform such services as barbering or obtaining tickets to the current hit play in town. The essential characteristic of all service firms is that they do not provide a consumable product for their customers, but a special, nonmaterial service. The amount of money spent for services is growing every year and in the 1980s is expected to reach 50 percent of all consumer expenditures.

Finance   There are also many small firms in the field of finance. Commercial banks, finance companies, mortgage companies, discount houses, savings and loans, and loan companies of various kinds are often small compared to the largest firms in their field. In only the very smallest of business firms does the proprietor normally have sufficient capital to provide for all of the financial needs of the business. That is why small business as well as big business has a great need for financial institutions to aid their operations. Smaller financial firms are more interested in small business accounts. Small firms, like large ones, not only need normal commercial banking facilities such as checking accounts; they also need loans to finance inventories, carry receivables, purchase equipment and fixtures, handle international transactions, and meet financial deadlines. Many small firms also need the facilities of security bankers to sell common and preferred stocks to build sound financial structures into their firms.

HISTORY OF SELF-EMPLOYMENT IN THE UNITED STATES

As our country has progressively changed from an agriculture-dominated society, the facts of self-employment have also changed dramatically. As recently as the turn of the century, about 80 percent of our population was self-employed, and only about 20 percent was working for other firms. In the 1980s, almost the opposite is true—20 percent is self-employed and 80 percent works for other firms.

Such facts are subject to easy misinterpretation. They do not mean that there are fewer small firms in the country, as might be suspected. The large decrease in self-employment has been due chiefly to the decline in the number of independent farmers, but this decrease has been offset, for the most part, by the increase in large firm employment. As we have previously seen, however, small firms engaged in each of the types of activities discussed have remained dominant and healthy parts of the economy and are as popular as, or more popular than, they have ever been.

Students of business should be interested in observing that this great shift in the character of the business economy from self-employment to large-firm employment has made significant changes in the total economic scene and the accompanying government philosophy. Business cycles have become far more hazardous for more people since these people are dependent upon large firm payrolls, rather than largely self-supporting farms. The burden of social security taxes has increased, and measures to combat depressions and unemployment have become more essential. Meanwhile, the economic shift has emphasized the need for competence and vision by small firm operators.

THE FEDERAL GOVERNMENT AND SMALL BUSINESS

It is abundantly clear that the federal government is dedicated to the preservation of a strong, healthy, and profitable small business society. Many legislative acts have been passed with profound policy statements to this effect. Management assistance at no charge, financial assistance in many circumstances, aid in securing government contracts,[4] and other benefits have been provided for in specific pieces of federal legislation. The Department of Commerce has pioneered much of this legislation. The Small Business Administration was created by Congress specifically to serve small firms and to assist them, particularly in the areas of management and financing. Its objective is the continued health and development of small firms throughout the nation.

Administrators of the Small Business Administration have described the SBA as "the Defense Department of the small business community." Administrators of this small but effective organization are truly dedicated to the conviction that a healthy small business community is essential to maintaining the best economic health of the nation and the freedom of its citizens. Its district offices throughout the country give continuous service to small firms seeking help.

The value of good, healthy competition is recognized in our society. Competition is deemed essential for keeping a strong free enterprise system. If we recognize that more than 50 percent of the more than 11 million firms in the United States have sales of less than $100,000 annually and employ fewer than 10 people, we can appreciate the statement that thousands of small firms act as both suppliers of materials and products to our giant firms and as distributors of products for these firms. The very large firms attract much publicity, but the many small firms in this country are essential to their operations (see Figure 1-3).

From this review of the small business scene, the reader can probably appreciate the fact that the big firm is the exception and not the rule in our business community.

SUMMARY

Small business firms are an integral part of the total business scene in the United States and in most countries of the Western world. In all major areas of business activity—manufacturing, mining, wholesaling, retailing, service and finance businesses—small firms account for a large part of the total dollar sales.

Despite any impressions to the contrary, there are more small firms per 1,000 population in the United States today than at any other time in our history.

The preservation and development of a healthy small business community is an avowed policy of our federal and state governments.

The Department of Commerce and the Small Business Administration are charged with specific activities to aid small firms. Their support ranges from management and financial assistance to help in securing government contracts.

Big business recognizes its dependence on small firms and gives more than lip service to help preserve their strength and profitability. Many suppliers of parts

---

[4]The Small Business Administration has a comprehensive pamphlet available, free of charge, entitled *How to Do Business with The Government.* Any small firm owners who are interested in securing government contracts should get this pamphlet from their nearest SBA office. See App. 3.

Small Business Week, 1981

By the President of the United States of America

A Proclamation

Two centuries ago in this country, small business owners—the merchants, the builders, the traders—rebelled against excessive taxation and government interference and helped found this Nation. Today we are working to bring about another revolution, this time against the intolerable burdens inflation, over-regulation, and over-taxation have placed upon the Nation's 12 million small businesses, which provide the livelihood for more than 100 million of our people.

To revitalize the Nation, we must stimulate small business growth and opportunity. Small business accounts for over 60 percent of our jobs, half of our business output, and at least half of the innovations that keep American industry strong. The imagination, skills, and willingness of small business men and women to take necessary risks symbolize the free enterprise foundation of the American economy and must be encouraged.

I urge all Americans who own or work in a small business to continue their resourcefulness and successes, for these efforts contribute so much to the entrepreneurial spirit which made this Nation great. It is with justifiable pride that the American small business man can point to himself as the backbone of our Nation.

Now, Therefore, I, Ronald Reagan, President of the United States of America, do hereby proclaim the week beginning May 10, 1981, as Small Business Week. I call upon every American to join me in this tribute.

In Witness Whereof, I have hereunto set my hand this 23rd day of March, in the year of our Lord nineteen hundred eighty-one, and of the Independence of the United States of America the two hundred and fifth.

Ronald Reagan

Ronald Reagan

FIGURE 1-3
Government supports small business.

and materials to large corporations are very small firms. Mass-production factories could not distribute their output without the services of thousands of small retailers. Purchasing policies of many of our largest industries specify special consideration for buying from small firms.

Small business and large business are completely intertwined in our economic society. Together they have produced the highest standard of living enjoyed by any nation in the history of the world.

Men and women who plan properly for small firm ownership and who have the right personal qualities for successful management will gain rich and varied rewards from their efforts.

QUESTIONS FOR CLASS DISCUSSION

1 Can you name a large manufacturing firm whose products are sold in more than 3,000 retail stores?
2 How many small firm suppliers of parts and materials would you suspect sell their products to the Ford Motor Company?
3 How many small businesses are there in the United States per 1,000 population? Is this more or less than we have had in the past?
4 How does the Committee for Economic Development measure a small business?
5 Do large business firms that employ more than 2,500 people represent 30 percent, 20 percent, 10 percent, or less than ½ of 1 percent of the total firms in the country?
6 How do you account for the fact that 80 percent of Americans were self-employed in 1880 but only 20 percent are self-employed today?
7 Does the United States government support small business firms? How?
8 Can you name an example of a manufacturing firm? A mining firm? A wholesaling firm? A retailing firm? A service firm? A firm in the field of finance?
9 What is meant when we say that principles of management are adaptable even though not always adoptable?
10 Can you name three service firms whose services you have used?
11 Are more small firms engaged in retailing than in manufacturing? Why do you think this is so?
12 Why would giant companies be interested in the welfare of healthy small companies?

PROJECTS FOR HOME ASSIGNMENT AND/OR CLASS DISCUSSION

1 a Prepare a list of 10 different business firms which you or your parents patronize in your hometown.
  b Explain how you would classify each of these firms as small, medium, or large according to the size measurement of the Small Business Administration.
2 Write a short essay on why you agree or disagree with the statement that a strong small business community is in the best interest of all citizens.

CONTINUING PROBLEM:
The Kollege Klothes Shop

PART 1: INTRODUCTION

As we plan our study for the semester or quarter, note that we will have available a continuing problem. Assignments will be given following each of the first 22 chapters. The continuing problem is designed to give us an opportunity to apply to an actual problem situation the business facts that we have studied in each chapter.

The problem will assume that you have been employed as a small business consultant by Mary Jones and Fernando Gomez. They are recent college graduates who plan to open a new college clothes store in College Town, U.S.A. They will ask you for reports on many phases of the business. They will want you to show them alternatives where available and then give them your recommendations on all phases of their planning. You are the consultant who is to advise Mary Jones and Fernando Gomez on each step of the total planning report. Each assignment will follow a logical sequence for any planning report.

With your instructor's approval, we will have an extensive analysis of the proposed shop at the end of each of the first 22 chapters. Each chapter's assignment will cover the material of that chapter.

Research facts necessary for some of the assignments will be provided in condensed form because students will likely not have the time to gather much basic data.

The type of analysis used can be applied to almost any kind of retail, wholesale, service, or manufacturing firm. Service firms will not use as many of the details because most do not merchandise an inventory of products. Manufacturing firms will require some digging for operating facts and special accounting records.

Your instructor may prefer that you write your continuing problem on another type of business. Perhaps you are seriously thinking about a business of your own after graduation. Analyzing that type of firm could be very beneficial. Details will unfold in following chapters.

Assignment for Part 1

Spend some time thinking about whether you wish to follow the analysis of Kollege Klothes Shop or some other type of small business. If your instructor decides to make the continuing problem a part of your regular class work, discuss your thoughts with him or her. Written assignments will begin in the next chapter.

REFERENCES FOR FURTHER READING

Baumback, Clifford M., Kenneth Lawyer, and Pearce C. Kelley, *How to Organize and Operate a Small Business,* 5th ed., Prentice-Hall, Inc., Englewood Cliffs, N.J., 1973, chap. 1.

"Checklist for Going into Business," Small Business Administration Publication, No. 71.

Steinhoff, Dan, *The World of Business,* McGraw-Hill Book Company, New York, 1979, chap. 1.

Tate, Curtis E. Jr., Leon Megginson, Charles Scott, Jr., and Lyle Trueblood, *Successful Small Business Management,* rev. ed., Business Publications, Inc., Dallas, Texas, 1978, chap. 1.

THE INDIVIDUAL SMALL FIRM: ITS ADVANTAGES, REWARDS, AND REQUIREMENTS FOR SUCCESS

I never believed that my small firm had any advantages that a giant corporation couldn't eliminate in a hurry. Knowing my true advantages has given me new confidence.

The Late Learner

Against the total small business scene we reviewed in Chapter 1, we must now turn our attention to the individual firm. What are its chances for success? What advantages does it have? What are the rewards of success? What are its requirements for success?

ADVANTAGES OF SMALL FIRMS

The fact that small firms are such an important part of our economy is not a historical accident. It is not simply the result of government programs to aid small firms or a benevolent policy by large firms. Competition in our type of society is recognized as desirable because it serves the population better. Small firms actually have advantages over large firms in many cases. All large firms were once small. They grew because they were well managed with dynamic leadership. Many of today's small firms will become giants in tomorrow's business world.

19

Some of the situations in which small firms have distinct advantages are the following:

1 *When new products or ideas are being tried*   The freedom to attempt new types of business ventures is one of our cherished rights, and when one is engaging in such a business, it is much better to start with a small firm. Growth can always come with success. The acceptability of the new product or idea may need market testing. Indeed, it is often better to check market reaction before investing too much money in a new product or idea. Management requirements may be uncertain and financial needs may be unknown in the starting period of the new firm.

2 *When the personal attention of the owner is essential to daily operations*   The owner of a fine restaurant is an example of this situation. If the owner's presence, as host or as executive, is important to the growth of the business, it will be more successful if the business is small enough for one person to supervise.

3 *Where personal services, either professional or skilled, are dominant*   Firms that offer the professional or nonprofessional services of their employees in selling their product or service to the public usually have a distinct advantage if they are small. Examples of this include beauty parlors, real estate offices,

George Rose/Los Angeles Times

FIGURE 2-1
In some businesses, such as this exclusive restaurant, the personal attention of the owner is essential.

interior-decorating firms, TV repair shops, and major heavy equipment repair firms. Medical and dental services are also usually rendered by small firms. Any possible advantages of large size in these areas are usually offset by greatly enlarged overhead, less efficiency on the job, and the loss of the personal touch of the smaller firm.

4 *When the market for the product or service is mainly local* In some types of firms, it just is not economical to attempt a scale of operation that exceeds the local market demand. The making of bricks or concrete blocks for the construction industry is an example. Transportation costs are prohibitive for moving such products. The independent real estate firm specializing in residence sales usually falls in this category of firms that do better on a smaller, local scale.

5 *When the firm deals in perishable materials or products* Small florists may join together to have their "by wire" services, but the greatest volume of business is done through local orders. Dairy products are now sold in wide markets, but local firms have distinct advantages in dealing with these perishable products. Local canneries still do much of the canning of fruits and vegetables in closely supervised small firms.

6 *When only a limited market is available or sought* One example of this is custom tailoring. Neighborhood grocers with alert managements have success- fully competed with the trend toward large supermarkets.

7 *When the industry is characterized by wide variations in demand or in styles* Examples of this include ladies' dress lines, products made by ornamen-

FIGURE 2-2
When a firm deals in perishable products or materials, the *small* firm has an advantage in serving local markets.

Randy Matusow

tal candlemakers, and custom-made chandeliers and lamp shades. These types of products do not invite large firm development in most cases. Large producers need stable markets and the ability to plan production quantities in economical lot sizes. The small, flexible firm usually can adjust to the necessary variations of specialized products more easily.

8 *When close rapport with personnel is essential*   Small firm owners usually have the advantage of being close to employees. They do not have to receive grievances through a committee or hold formal hearings on them. They know problems from daily conversations and can adjust employment to a person's abilities better because of this close association. As a result, they are usually able to maintain better morale and efficiency in the firm, which can be most important in any business.

The individual firm has benefited from having these and other advantages. In addition to the types of firms cited, small firms in such fields as construction, wholesaling, retailing, and the service industries have faced up well to their larger firm competition. Insurance and smaller finance firms have also been very successful. The profitable firms have not relied upon the inherent advantages of small firms as such, but have combined these advantages with alert and competent management to achieve their success.

REAL AND ALLEGED DISADVANTAGES OF SMALL FIRMS

It is very easy for persons who have failed in a small business to rationalize the disadvantages of being small. In many such cases, however, the failures were likely due to lack of management ability, lack of proper planning, or simply the fact that the type of firm established did not have a chance in the first place.

Small firms are often said to labor under such disadvantages as the inability to secure competent employees, the inability to finance expansion when it has been proved to be practicable, the inability to cope with monopolistic practices, tax burdens, limited vendor goodwill, lack of support by "vested interests," discriminatory practices by large shopping-center developers, lack of time for the small proprietor to handle multiple assignments, lack of research facilities, and the problems of making a new firm or product known in its market.

While it cannot be denied that there is substance to some of these alleged disadvantages (such as shopping-center developers desiring chain stores instead of small local firms for tenants), it may also be contended that many of these problems are a direct result of improper planning and operation, as will be outlined in succeeding chapters. Large firms share many of the problems that small firms have. The adage that "an ounce of prevention is worth a pound of cure" was never more aptly demonstrated than in the planning stages of a new firm. So many of the business failures that occur every year could have been avoided had the firm been properly planned. Many firms would likely not have been established (see Figure 2-3).

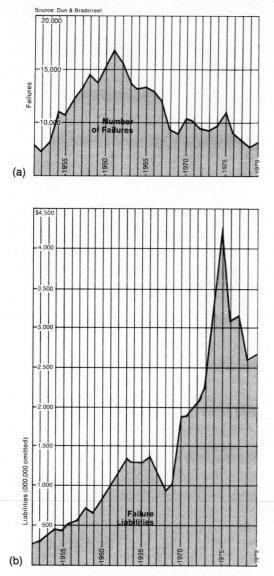

(a)

(b)

FIGURE 2-3
(a) The number of business failures has been declining steadily since 1961. *(b)* For firms that do fail, the average liabilities have been increasing. (*From Dun & Bradstreet, Inc.*)

We have cherished the right of all citizens to go into business for themselves. We have probably given more attention to preserving this right than to the matter of helping those starting new firms prepare to be successful.

Fortunately, not all Americans believe that they would be successful managers of their own firms. But a Gallup poll showed that almost two-thirds of American males over 21 perferred to own their own business. Respect for the

responsibilities of ownership and management of a business is the first requirement for success. When this respect exists, the person contemplating setting up a
new firm will recognize the need for education in management as the first step in
planning.

PREPARATION FOR SMALL FIRM OWNERSHIP

There is no better way to prepare for a successful business operation than by
learning the ingredients of good planning, having some experience in the
particular line, and knowing the essentials of good management. This truth is
aptly demonstrated by the fact that the most common causes of small firm
failures are incompetence, improper experience, and lack of management
training. It is also shown in the fact that businesses that survive the early years of
their existence then have a much better success record. In a recent study by Dun
& Bradstreet, Inc., results showed that firms in existence for less than 3 years
accounted for 34 percent of total failures, those in existence for 4 to 5
years accounted for 23 percent of the failures, those in existence for 6 to 10 years
accounted for 22 percent of the failures, and those in existence for over 10 years
represented approximately 21 percent of the failures.[1]

THE REWARDS OF SUCCESSFUL SMALL FIRM OWNERS

The rewards of success in operating one's own business are seen differently by
different people. The retired couple who wish only to maintain a small income
while they enjoy other activities in their senior years will measure rewards quite
differently from the young college graduate who opens his or her new firm with
big ideas for expansion and growth. The entire approach of this text will be
toward enabling the new small firm to grow. The discussion of rewards is
directed accordingly to such firms.

All proprietors seek the reward of *good profits*. Many small firms realize
excellent profits. Most small firm owners also find a great reward in the *satisfying nature of their work*. The ability *to be one's own boss* is an important reward to many. Additionally, the *status in the community* which comes with
being a successful firm owner ranks high on the list of rewards for most proprietors.

While these rewards are the ones that most owners seek, other owners may
gain satisfactions of a quite different nature. *Family pride, money to educate
children well, preservation of family tradition,* and an *outlet for creativeness* are
some additional benefits.

---

[1]These facts represent findings from detailed studies made by the Business Economics department of Dun & Bradstreet, Inc., New York City. This fine research firm serves business,
government, and educational institutions with many reports on operational phases of the American
business community. *(Quoted by permission.)*

Regardless of motivation, it is clear that successful ownership of one's own business can be a most satisfying and profitable experience. Furthermore, the right to start your own firm is guaranteed in our country. If this freedom is coupled with competence in planning and operation, then the individual's desire for reward can be achieved. The creation of such success stories is the objective of this book.

REQUIREMENTS FOR SUCCESSFUL SMALL FIRM MANAGEMENT

The requirements for successful small firm management do not include only the personal characteristics of the individuals involved. They also include good customer relations and an awareness of the consumerism movement; good community relations as part of a total public relations policy; good business ethics and a demonstrated social responsibility; the ability to deal with vast government regulations; and, in many cases, a willingness to operate the small firm as a wholly regulated business. These requirements for success can be summarized as follows.

1 Personal characteristics
2 Good customer relations and knowledge of consumerism
3 Business ethics and social responsibility
4 Compliance with vast government regulations
5 Willingness to operate as a completely regulated firm

As we proceed with our study of management details, the existence of these success requirements will be presumed, and not reiterated with each subject of our investigation. Therefore, brief comment on each is made here.

1 Personal Characteristics

Many studies have been made in search of the definitive list of personal characteristics that an individual should have in order to succeed in small firm ownership. No generally agreed-upon composite of characteristics has resulted, which is to be expected when one is dealing with human beings. Different characteristics appear in greater or lesser degrees in different people. Offsetting features may be more dominant in one person than in another. Still, we can attempt to make a list of those characteristics which have been found generally applicable in studies of successful small firm owners.

Especially prominent characteristics of successful managers of small firms include:

Energy
Initiative
Willingness to take risks

Ability to organize
Personality
Technical competence
Administrative ability
Good judgment
Restraint
Communication ability
Leadership qualities
Patience
Preownership experience

Experienced small firm owners will agree with any list of success characteristics such as the above. They will hurriedly point out, however, that they believe the chief characteristic for success is *willingness to work hard.* Being one's own boss means that you do not punch a clock, your hours are not 9 to 5, but instead you must do what is necessary in the total management of the firm. That usually means hard work and long hours, and, at least in the early years of the firm, hours beyond those when the firm is open for business. Experienced business owners will also point out that different types of firms will require a different combination of some of the characteristics listed above. Taking risks is a part of all firm ownership.

We can note in passing that the American philosopher William James summed up the requirements for any success in three essential components:

The idea
The act
The will to act

As we shall learn in detail through our study here, *the act* of starting a new small business involves much planning and a detailed knowledge of every phase of total management.

2 Good Customer Relations and Knowledge of Consumerism

Good customer relations (as distinguished from public relations) have always been a key to successful ownership of any firm, but today's business world has seen great new developments in the consumerism movement. Consumer groups have vociferously expressed concerns about the conduct of the business world. Consumerism goes beyond services offered. These groups speak of value, adequacy of products offered, and price policies. They are quick to speak of "rip-offs" by business firms. Much legislation was passed in the 1970s to protect consumer rights in such matters as credit arrangements, customer complaints about merchandise, financial responsibility, and related matters. A knowledge of the applicable legislation and current demands of consumers is essential to success.

3   Business Ethics and Social Responsibility

The problem of earning a profit in business goes way beyond the details of management techniques. Not the least point to consider is community expectations concerning business ethics and the social responsibility of the business world. The typical small business owner assumes that good ethics are reflected in his daily dealings. But the responsibility of the business world for all of the economic ills of the society has divided both academicians and business leaders. Entire college courses are now offered under the title of "The Social Responsibility of Business." Some critics hold the business community responsible for unemployment, crime in the streets, the ill-clothed, ill-housed, and ill-fed. Others believe that it is the responsibility of the business world to create jobs, produce products, and pay taxes to the government so that it can employ experts to cope with social problems.

It behooves even small firm owners to be aware of the issues involved, to practice honest business ethics, and to become good community citizens expressing an interest in social problems.

4   Compliance with Vast Government Regulations

New small firm owners are often not familiar with the extent to which government rules and regulations reach into almost every phase of their operations. The extensive tax structure is only one part of this problem. Frustration, expense, and government time are involved in complying with the avalanche of regulations in effect today. Chapter 29 on Small Business and the Law will expand this subject for us later.

5   Willingness to Operate as a Completely Regulated Firm

Government regulations extend even further into the operations of many types of small firms. These can be small utility companies such as local water companies, or firms like taxi companies, ambulance service firms, or towing companies. The very basics of daily operations are dictated by government agencies in such cases. Rate charges, quantity of service available, and areas to be served can all be dictated. Such regulations go well beyond the licenses or qualification certificates needed for beauty parlor operators, barbers, or truck drivers.

Rugged individualists who desire to make all their own decisions will find it necessary to compromise many of their convictions when engaging in these types of business activity. The ability to operate under strict regulation remains a requirement for success in such fields.

SUMMARY

There are many circumstances in business in which the small firm has distinct advantages over the larger firm. These include cases where new products or ideas are being tried, when personal attention of the owner is necessary for success, where personal services are dominant, when markets are mainly local, where perishable materials or products are handled, where only limited markets are sought or available, and when close rapport with employees is essential.

Many of the alleged disadvantages of small firms could be overcome with better planning. An ill-conceived business, whether large or small, has little chance of success if its planning has not been properly done. Good research in the planning stage can reveal opportunities for success. It can also indicate when a business that is contemplated should not be undertaken.

The rewards for successful small firm ownership can be significant. The personal satisfactions will vary with the individual owner. Good profits, satisfying employment, being one's own boss, community status, family pride and tradition, and an outlet for creativeness are some of them.

But these rewards are never automatic or guaranteed. Success makes many demands upon the operator of the firm. Personal characteristics and other requirements for successful ownership of small business firms have been enumerated, but sound business knowledge and willingness to work hard stand at the head of any list.

QUESTIONS FOR CLASS DISCUSSION

1 Do you agree that "competition is desirable in order to serve the population better"? Explain.
2 Do you know of a business firm where the personal attention of the owner is important to the firm's success?
3 Why do brickyards usually have a market that is essentially local?
4 Do you think that small firms can keep competent employees? How?
5 Why is it that not all Americans believe they would be successful owners and managers of their own business?
6 How would you explain that small firm failures declined in the last decade but that the average debts of those failing increased?
7 Which two rewards of success would you place first if you had your own small business?
8 Would you include preownership experience in your list of requirements for successful management?
9 What do you like about a particular small business that you patronize?
10 Do large firms share the same problems that small firms have? Explain.

PROJECTS FOR HOME ASSIGNMENT AND/OR CLASS DISCUSSION

1 Write a description of a small firm with which you are familiar where the personal appearance of the owner is considered important by its customers. Explain why this is considered important.

2 Prepare a short paper explaining your impressions of the chief disadvantages of small firms. Explain how you believe these disadvantages can be overcome.

CONTINUING PROBLEM:
The Kollege Klothes Shop

PART 2: PREPARING YOUR REPORT

Assignment for Part 2

Prepare a title page and a table of contents for your report. The title you choose should indicate that this is a study of a proposed new college clothes shop to be located in College Town, U.S.A., prepared for Jones and Gomez; underneath, give the name of the author (you). If your instructor approves, two or more students may write together. The table of contents should have a separate line for each step you will cover in your analysis. By leaving a right-side margin wide enough, you can leave room for inserting the specific page numbers of your final work where each item will be discussed. Such a column can be headed "Pages." The actual page numbers can be inserted later as you complete each section of the report.

A list of suggested subjects for the table of contents would include the following. Your instructor may wish to add others:

Present Visualization of the Firm
A Projected Income Statement
The Market Survey
Legal Form of Organization
A Budgeted Income Statement
Statement of Assets to Be Used
The Opening Day Balance Sheet
Location Analysis
Site Analysis
Merchandising and Sales Promotion Plans
Fixed and Variable Expense Analysis
The Break-Even Chart
Credit Selling Plans
Risk Analysis
Personnel Policies for the Firm

Don't let the list of subjects discourage your plans. We will go through each step carefully as we proceed through the text. You will have an adequate base of data to apply the subject matter to the new shop. Put your name, as author, under the title in the middle of the page.

REFERENCES FOR FURTHER READING

Broom, H. N., and J. G. Longenecker, *Small Business Management,* 5th ed., South-Western Publishing Co., Inc. Cincinnati, Ohio, 1979, chap. 2.

Macfarlane, William N., *Principles of Small Business,* McGraw-Hill Book Company, New York, 1977, chap. 2.

Musselman, Vernon A., and Eugene Hughes, *Introduction to Modern Business,* 8th ed., Prentice-Hall, Inc., Englewood Cliffs, N.J., 1981, chaps. 1, 2.

UNDERSTANDING THE BASIC FINANCIAL STATEMENTS FROM A MANAGEMENT VIEWPOINT

Gosh, why does a guy have to know about financial statements to be successful in business? If I sell enough merchandise, my accountant will tell me if I made a profit and make financial statements for me.

The Late Learner

This matter of understanding financial statements is so important that we will preface our entire investigation of management fundamentals by clarifying for nonaccounting students and new small firm planners the relationships between the two basic financial statements, as well as their meaning and composition. Thorough competence in managing any business demands this knowledge, which necessarily reflects the results of operations and the present financial position of the firm. Management decisions must be weighed in terms of their effect on these statements. It is not enough to wait for weeks or even months after the close of a fiscal period to have an accountant prepare the results of operation and advise the firm of its current financial position. Formal statements and tax returns may be delayed this way, but the owners need current information at all times.

The two basic financial statements are (1) the balance sheet, and (2) the income statement. In this chapter we will first review each statement and then take a closer look at an analysis of each.

THE BALANCE SHEET

The balance sheet shows the assets, liabilities, and owner's net worth in a business *as of a given date. Assets* are the things owned by the business, including both physical things and claims against others. *Liabilities* are the amounts owed to others, the creditors of the firm. *Net worth* is the owner's claim to the assets after liabilities are accounted for. Accounting has a basic equation which says *assets minus liabilities equals net worth.* In simplest terms, this means that what the business owns, less what it owes to creditors, equals its net worth. If liabilities exceed the assets, the net worth is a minus quantity. Profits made in each fiscal period add to this net worth as they are carried from the income statement to the balance sheet. See Table 3-1 for an example of a balance sheet for a very small firm. Note again that it is a *point of time* statement.

THE INCOME STATEMENT

The *income statement* shows the income received and the expenses incurred *over a period of time.* Income statements are usually issued for a year's operations, but interim statements may be made for a month, a quarter, or a half-year as well. Some firms have daily or weekly income statements. Even though formal income statements may be issued only once a year, the proprietor should know for shorter periods whether the income has exceeded the expenses and by how much.

Income received (sales) comes essentially from the sales of the basic merchandise or service which the business is formed to sell. Expenses incurred are the expired costs which have been incurred during the same period of time. The income statement for firms with an inventory to sell has three basic parts: the *income received,* the *cost of the goods sold* during the period, and the *operating expenses* incurred during the same period. The difference between sales income and cost of goods sold is known as the *gross margin.* When the operating expenses are subtracted from the gross margin, we arrive at net profit from operations.

Service firms, such as banks, insurance companies, laundries, consultants, ticket agencies, or repair services, which do not carry an inventory of merchandise for sale, will not have a cost of goods sold section on their income statement. Their statements will show total income from all sources and then deduct operating expenses, which may be classified as desired. Larger firms usually separate these expenses into administrative and selling expenses.

All accounts which record income and expenses during the fiscal period are summarized at the end of each period. The income and expense accounts are then closed and the resulting profit or loss is transferred to the owner's net worth account. This is in contrast to balance sheet accounts, which remain open in the ledger until the particular asset is disposed of, liability paid off, or change made in the ownership.

Now we should return to the example of the balance sheet statement shown in Table 3-1.

TABLE 3-1
ABC COMPANY
Balance Sheet
December 31, 1981

ASSETS

Current assets:

Cash	$1,780	
Accounts receivable	3,100	
Merchandise inventory	4,550	
Prepaid expenses	760	
Total current assets		$10,190

Fixed assets:

Store equipment	$4,200		
Less accumulated depreciation	900	$3,300	
Office equipment	$2,000		
Less accumulated depreciation	500	1,500	
Delivery truck	$3,000		
Less accumulated depreciation	1,000	2,000	
Total fixed assets			6,800
Total assets			$16,990

LIABILITIES

Current liabilities:

Accounts payable	$1,500	
Notes payable	1,000	
Contracts payable	2,000	
Total current liabilities		$4,500

Fixed liabilities:

Contracts payable	$2,000	
Long-term note payable	1,000	
Total fixed liabilities		$3,000
Total liabilities		$7,500

NET WORTH

J. Jones, proprietorship	9,490
Total liabilities plus net worth	$16,990

RELATIONSHIPS WITHIN THE BALANCE SHEET

First note that the total assets ($16,990) minus the total liabilities ($7,500) equal the owner's net worth or proprietorship ($9,490). This is the fundamental accounting equation:

$$\text{Assets} - \text{liabilities} = \text{proprietorship}$$

Every asset, liability, and net worth account is presented on the balance sheet.

Ratio Analysis[1]

Current Ratio Note that the assets are divided into *current assets* and *fixed assets*. This distinction is not necessary to make the books balance but is made for management reasons. The relationship between current assets and *current liabilities* is a prime measure of liquidity of any firm. *Liquidity* is the measure of ability to pay debts as they become due.

Current assets are those which are in the form of cash or will convert into cash within 90 days. Current liabilities are those debts which will be due within one year. The relationship between current assets and current liabilities is called the *current ratio*. Sound financing demands that this ratio be at least 2 to 1. The current ratio is found by dividing the current assets by the current liabilities:

$$\text{Current ratio} = \frac{\text{current assets}}{\text{current liabilities}} = \frac{\$10,190}{\$\ 4,500} = 2.26$$

The ABC Company, therefore, has a current ratio of 2.26 to 1 and is safely within the sound rule of a 2 to 1 current ratio.

The current assets should be analyzed to see that they do in fact qualify as assets which will convert into cash within 90 days. A merchandise turnover of three times per year, or once each 4 months, indicates that the entire inventory amount will not convert into cash within the required period. Your banker will reduce your current ratio when such circumstances exist.

Quick Ratio The *quick ratio* is also known as the acid test of liquidity. It is the relationship between only the most liquid assets (cash and accounts receivable) and the total of the current liabilities. The conservative rule in this regard is that this ratio should be at least 1 to 1. In other words, the cash plus receivables should equal or exceed the current liabilities.

$$\text{Quick ratio} = \frac{\text{cash plus receivables}}{\text{current liabilities}} = \frac{\$1,780+\$3,100}{\$4,500} = \frac{\$4,880}{\$4,500} = 1.08$$

Thus the ABC Company meets this test of liquidity because the company's quick

---

[1]Only the basic ratios are explained here. We can note that many others, such as return on assets, on net worth, and so on, are used and available.

ratio of 1.08 exceeds the minimum of the conservative rule. The quick ratio combined with the current ratio of 2.26 indicates that the present liquidity of the company is good.

Working Capital *Working capital* is the difference between the current assets and the current liabilities expressed in dollars. On the balance sheet of the ABC Company we see total current assets of $10,190 and current liabilities of $4,500. Working capital is therefore $6,690 ($10,190 − $4,500). In normal operations involving daily sales receipts, buying more merchandise, meeting payrolls and other expenses, and making payments due on current liabilities, it is the net working capital which provides the ability to meet all obligations as they become due. The measurement of adequate cash on hand, as discussed later, is a valuable supplement in determining the adequacy of working capital.

The Proprietorship Ratio The *proprietorship ratio* is the relationship between the owner's investment in the firm and the total assets being used in the business. It is computed by dividing the owner's investment by the total assets. For the ABC Company we see that the owner's investment (the equity in the assets) is $9,490. Total assets used in the business are valued at $16,990.

$$\text{Proprietorship ratio} = \frac{\text{owner's investment}}{\text{total assets}} = \frac{\$\,9,490}{\$16,990} = 56\%$$

The proprietorship ratio can be expressed as a ratio of owner investment to total assets or as a percentage of those total assets. In this case, proprietorship is 56 percent of total investment in the firm or a ratio of .56 to 1.00. This proprietorship ratio is safely above the conservative minimum of 50 percent.

There are many other ratios utilized in the analysis of business firm operations. Most small firms which maintain adequate current ratios, quick ratios, and working capital, proper inventories, and a 50 percent proprietorship ratio will maintain soundness in their financial structures.

TRADING ON EQUITY

In connection with owner investment, we should become familiar with the phrase *trading on equity*. This phrase refers to the relationship between *creditor capital* (liabilities) in the business and the *owner capital. Trading on too thin an equity* is a term used to describe owners who have too little of their own money invested compared with the creditor capital (liabilities) used to finance the business. A proprietorship ratio of 50 percent indicates that the owner or owners have invested half the value of the total assets used in the business. When this ratio falls below 50 percent, the outside creditors are supplying more of the firm's total capital needs than the owners are. This indicates, in most cases, that further credit will be more difficult to obtain either from current loans, sale of securities, or other investors. Such owners are truly trading on too thin an equity and probably need more investment capital of their own.

An example of trading on too thin an equity would be the owner of a dress shop that needs $60,000 in total assets. The owner raises $50,000 of that total with credit from merchandise suppliers, short-term loans from friends, and a 90-day bank loan. All these debts are current liabilities. The owner's investment on the opening day balance sheet is only $10,000. That balance sheet shows total assets of $60,000, current liabilities of $50,000, and proprietorship of $10,000. The resulting proprietorship ratio is 16⅔ percent ($10,000 divided by $60,000) which is far short of the recommended 50 percent. It will be most difficult to obtain further credit of any kind. The pressing debts make the business less able to weather any kind of a serious drop in profits.

The reason that creditors look to the proprietorship ratio is to see how much of the total risk is being borne by the owners of the firm. The owners' incentive to stick with the firm in less prosperous times is often influenced by the extent of their investment. When they have only a small part of the total investment, the temptation to "leave a sinking ship" is great. If that happens the creditors stand to incur serious losses.

We should also note here that *all stockholders are owners.* Both preferred and common stockholder investments count as owner capital in computing the proprietorship ratio. *Bondholders are creditors.* Their investment is listed on the balance sheet as fixed liabilities. The total face value of all bonds outstanding is counted as creditor capital in computing the proprietorship ratio. We will look at this matter more closely in Chapter 10 when we discuss financing sources for small firms.

It is recognized, of course, that there are special types of business firms in which variations from the ideal ratio rules advocated here can be justified. Public utilities are a notable example. Unless positive evidence is available to justify exceptions, however, the new firm planner will do well to abide by these conservative rules of financial soundness in making plans for the new firm.

In summary, our analysis of the ABC Company's balance sheet shows a healthy financial structure. Its current ratio, quick ratio, and proprietorship ratio all exceed the minimums dictated by sound financing principles. Its working capital seems to be adequate. Before sitting back, however, the owner should check these ratios against the available statistics for the most efficient firms in the same line of business. Sources of such data are discussed in Chapter 5.

Now we turn to an analysis of the income statement, an example of which is shown in Table 3-2.

ANALYSIS OF THE INCOME STATEMENT

Note first that the period of the ABC Company income statement shown in Table 3-2 is one year, ending December 31, 1981. As a period-of-time statement, a proper title necessitates that two dates be stated or determinable. "Year ended

TABLE 3-2
ABC COMPANY
Income Statement
January 1—December 31, 1981

Sales		$100,000
Cost of goods sold:		
Beginning inventory Jan. 1	$10,000	
Purchases during year	40,000	
Goods available for sale	$50,000	
Less ending inventory Dec. 31	10,000	
Cost of goods sold		40,000
Gross margin		$ 60,000
Operating expenses:		
Rent	$ 6,000	
Salaries to employees	17,000	
Supplies used	2,000	
Advertising and promotion	1,000	
Insurance expense	1,000	
Delivery expense	2,000	
Depreciation expense	1,700	
Bad debts	1,000	
Local and state taxes paid	1,000	
Utilities expense	300	
Miscellaneous expenses	2,000	
Total operating expenses		35,000
Net profit from operations		$ 25,000

December 31, 1981" denotes two dates and would be an acceptable title for the statement. Parenthetically, let us note here that the calendar year is not necessarily the best fiscal period (annual accounting period) for all businesses. More and more firms are now using the date of actually starting the business as the beginning of an annual fiscal period, or some other date in the year which more closely represents a complete cycle in annual operations. This is particularly applicable to firms which have a high degree of seasonal variation in their income.

The ABC Company income statement emphasizes the basic parts previously described. The firm earned $25,000 profit from operations. It had net sales of $100,000, of which $40,000 was paid for the merchandise that was sold and $60,000 was its gross margin. It paid out $35,000 in operating expenses, and thus had $25,000 profit from operations remaining in the business. The experienced student or business person will judge this a highly successful business on the basis of these facts. Not many firms operate on a markup of 60 percent of sales price. Two qualifying factors must be kept in mind, however. First, the $25,000 represents both salary and return on investment for Mr. Jones, the owner.

Second, the $25,000 profit from operations is before federal, state, and possibly local income taxes on profits have been paid. The shocking truths concerning this will be discussed later. We can be sure at this point that the proprietor with three children will not be living in great luxury if this firm is the family's sole source of income.

An attractive profit does not mean that the income statement should not have regular analysis by the proprietors. As they review their year's operation, they should ask themselves at least the following questions:

1 Is our markup high or low compared with successful firms in this type of business?

TABLE 3-3
BILL'S HOME LAUNDRY & DRY CLEANING
Income Statement*
Year Ended February 28, 1982

Income:		
From laundry operations	$125,000	
From dry cleaning	65,000	
From repairs and miscellaneous	10,000	
Total income		$200,000
Operating expenses:		
Variable expenses:		
Employee wages	$98,000	
Delivery expenses	4,000	
Operating supplies	18,000	
Repairs and maintenance	3,000	
Administrative and legal	1,000	
Advertising	1,500	
Bad debt expense	300	
Miscellaneous expenses	4,200	
Total variable expenses		$130,000
Fixed expenses:		
Rent	$ 6,000	
Utilities	8,500	
Insurance	4,000	
Taxes and licenses	2,500	
Depreciation	9,000	
Total fixed expenses		30,000
Total operating expenses		160,000
Net profit from operations		$ 40,000

* Typical income statement for a service type business which does not carry an inventory of merchandise for sale. Note that this income statement does not have a cost of goods sold section.

2 Is our consequent cost of goods sold high or low?

3 Is our inventory adequate for the sales volume which the business produced? Did we lose sales because of stockouts? Can we justify all parts of the inventory on the basis of sales of the items carried?

4 Is our total overhead in line with the most efficient firms of this type? Is our occupancy charge (rent) the proper percentage of sales? How about our other expenses?

As we shall see in Chapter 5, the availability of abundant trade statistics will give the proprietors comparative data with which to find answers to these questions. Studying their operations will usually reveal special strengths of their firm and areas which need improvement. For example, they may find that their merchandise turnover was four times per year, but the most successful firms operate with a turnover of five times per year while maintaining the same margins. They should satisfy themselves as to why other firms have this turnover and pursue the possibilities of improving their own operation. They may find that successful firms operate with a smaller loss on bad debts. If so, this should cause them to question their whole credit-account policy. Similar analysis should be made of all key items on the balance sheet and the income statement. When used in this way, the basic accounting statements become tools for management to use for decision making and not merely dreary accounts of what happened in the last fiscal period.

Income statements for *service firms* which do not carry an inventory of merchandise for sale will not have a cost of goods sold section. They will show total income from services or fees and then deduct the operating expenses to arrive at net profit from operations. See Table 3-3 for illustration.

Income statements for *manufacturing firms,* their cost of goods manufactured statements and balance sheets, are illustrated in Chapter 5. See Tables 5-2, 5-3, and 5-4.

Tables 3-4 and 3-5 summarize much of what has been discussed. They will serve as a useful guide for students having their first introduction to the preparation and use of accounting statements and their value to management. For people who are already proprietors, they will be a useful refresher.

Table 3-4 shows that there are only five different kinds of accounts used in the

TABLE 3-4
THE FIVE KINDS OF ACCOUNTS: THEIR DEFINITION AND
STATEMENT APPEARANCE

These accounts appear on the balance sheet (a point-of-time statement)	1	Assets—things owned
	2	Liabilities—amounts owed
	3	Net worth—owner's investment
These accounts appear on the income statement (a period-of-time statement)	4	Income—sales revenue
	5	Expense—expired costs

TABLE 3-5
THE FIVE KINDS OF ACCOUNTS:
HOW INCREASES AND DECREASES ARE
MADE FOR EACH

Accounts	Increases	Decreases
1 Assets	Debits	Credits
2 Liabilities	Credits	Debits
3 Net worth	Credits	Debits
4 Income	Credits	Debits
5 Expense	Debits	Credits

most sophisticated accounting systems. It defines the accounts and shows on which of the two basic statements they appear. Students should note again the difference between a *point-of-time* and a *period-of-time statement*. Table 3-5 shows how each of these accounts is increased or decreased in the operation of a double-entry bookkeeping system. Most new students are surprised to learn that there is nothing sacred in the terms *debit* and *credit*. They could as easily be called left and right, port and starboard, or gee and haw. In Chapter 27 we will study how to install a simplified journal-ledger accounting system which will adequately serve most small firms.

QUESTIONS FOR CLASS DISCUSSION

1 Where is the owner's investment plus any accumulated profits shown in the basic financial statements?
2 How can we justify showing "Accounts Receivable" as an asset on the balance sheet?
3 What is the chief difference between a balance sheet and an income statement? Explain.
4 How is the profit for a fiscal period transferred from the income statement accounts to the owner's net worth account?
5 Do the terms "debit" and "credit" mean anything different from "left" and "right"?
6 Are all accounts increased with debits?
7 What are the five different kinds of accounts?
8 What does each of the five kinds of accounts represent?
9 What is the difference between current assets and fixed assets?
10 What is the current ratio? What is the conservative rule as to a minimum limit on this ratio?
11 Is the quick ratio different from the current ratio? How?
12 When a business is said to be trading on too thin an equity, what is meant?
13 Do you agree that total assets represent the total capital employed in the business? If so, how is this capital provided?
14 What is the working capital of any business?
15 When business owners analyze their income statement, what facts and comparisons should they consider?
16 What do we mean when we say that the net worth, or proprietorship account, represents the owner's claim to the assets?

17 When a firm sells merchandise for cash, what account is credited and what account is debited?

PROJECTS FOR HOME ASSIGNMENT AND/OR CLASS DISCUSSION

1 The current ratio is often referred to as the firm's test of liquidity. Explain in a short paper how the current ratio is truly such a test and how it assures the ability to pay current bills as they become due.
2 "Trading on too thin an equity" means that the creditors have more investment in the firm than the owners.
   a Explain in a short essay how such a condition can affect the success of the business.
   b Prepare a balance sheet for a small firm which illustrates a condition of trading on too thin an equity.
3 Make up your own example of an income statement for a service business and for a retail business. Explain their basic difference.
4 See if you can obtain a balance sheet of an existing business firm and compare it with the samples in the text.

CONTINUING PROBLEM:
The Kollege Klothes Shop

PART 3: PRESENT VISUALIZATION OF THE BUSINESS IN OPERATION

From your assumed lengthy visits with Jones and Gomez, write a brief description of the Kollege Klothes Shop as they visualize it at this time. The objective is to make a record of the general picture of the firm they have in mind. Details are not needed at this time. The whole idea is to see what the general nature of the operations will be once the firm is started and as Jones and Gomez see it fulfill their expectations.

A sentence or two answering the following questions, or others you can suggest, will serve our purpose here:

Who will be its customers?
Will it be on a main street or a side street?
Will it be downtown or in a shopping center?
What size store is now planned?
What departments are desired?
What lines of merchandise will be carried?
What kinds of store hours are now visualized?
How many employees will be necessary?
What type of lighting will be in the store?
What kinds and how much store fixtures will be used?
What services will be available for customers?
Will the firm sell on credit, and if so, what kind?

Current thoughts of the new firm planners will not be binding after our analysis has proceeded, but we will have a general idea of their plans to guide our future advice to them. This is our starting point.

REFERENCES FOR FURTHER READING

"How to Read a Financial Report," new edition. Publication of Merrill Lynch, Pierce, Fenner & Smith, Inc. Available at local offices.

Niswonger, C. Rollin, and Philip E. Fess, *Accounting Principles,* 12th ed., South-Western Publishing Co., Inc. Cincinnati, Ohio, 1977, chap. 3.

"Ratio Analysis for Small Business," Small Business Administration Publication 1.12:20.

PART **TWO**

ESSENTIALS FOR PLANNING

STEPS IN PLANNING
A NEW BUSINESS:
A COMPREHENSIVE
BUSINESS PLAN

I learned the hard way that advance planning is the best illustration of the old adage that an ounce of prevention is worth a pound of cure.

The Late Learner

Chances of success for any new business are greatly increased when attention is first directed to a comprehensive business plan. A completed business plan is designed to provide a total visualization of the firm before operations are started. When financial assistance from bankers, trade creditors, or investors is necessary, their first request will be to see the total business plan. With it they can visualize the credit-worthiness of the business. In this chapter we will investigate the key parts of such a total business plan.

Because there are so many areas in total management, so many decisions to be made in proper overall planning, we must recognize at the beginning that there is no one sequence of steps in planning which is agreed upon by all authorities in the field. The most important thing in planning a new small firm is that all phases of its operations be considered in the planning stage.[1] The person

---

[1] New firm planners should pick up from their nearest SBA office the following pamphlets in the Small Marketers Aids Series: No. 150—*Business Plan for Retailers;* No. 218—*Business Plan for Small Manufacturers;* No. 221—*Business Plan for Small Construction Firms.* These pamphlets present in condensed form many of the features we shall follow in detail throughout this book.

planning a new firm should have very definite ideas about profits, financing, accounting records, merchandising plans, location, market and customers, general method of operation, policies, advertising and promotion, amount and type of expenses, break-even point, legal form of organization, depreciation policies, and inventory valuation methods, among other factors. As previously stated, there is no better application of the adage about an ounce of prevention versus a pound of cure. Mistakes in the planning stage of a new firm, or lack of proper attention to planning, can cause severe handicaps from which a new firm may never recover.

Based upon years of experience, the author subscribes to what is known as the *desired income approach* to the entire planning process. In the most basic language, this approach suggests that the planner's first question should be, "How much profit do I expect to receive from this business in return for my time and investment in it?" This approach is based upon a conviction that this question has been neglected much too often by new firm planners. No commitments, contracts, or obligations relative to a new business should be undertaken without a clear plan of profit possibilities for at least one year of operation.

FOURTEEN BASIC STEPS IN A COMPREHENSIVE BUSINESS PLAN

Using the desired income approach, there are 14 major steps in planning. They will be discussed briefly here and are followed by some additional items that may be appropriate in some cases. Full chapters are devoted to each of these steps.

Step 1 *Determine what profit you want from this business, recognizing the time you will give and the investment you will have. Then complete a projected income statement based upon your decision.*

With the profit figure clearly in mind, it is possible, using business statistics now abundantly available, to calculate the sales volume that is necessary to produce that particular profit. The planner should complete a projected income statement for a typical first year of operation, and standard statistics will help in doing this. This statement, when it achieves its final form (a budgeted income statement) in the planning process, can serve as a budget during the coming year. How to prepare a projected income statement is discussed in Chapter 5.

Step 2 *Survey the market you plan to serve to ascertain if the necessary sales volume required to produce the profit called for in step 1 is obtainable.*

The basic objective of step 2 is to find out what can reasonably be expected in sales if the business is established within the intended market area. Market surveys are very important to business success. If the market survey shows that the necessary sales volume to produce the profit called for in step 1 is not available, the planner can prevent a waste of time and money by canceling plans at this point. Good market surveys would probably have prevented many business failures for firms which never had a chance in their area of operations. The techniques for making market surveys have been vastly improved in recent years. Specific market data information is essential in coming up with a dependable or attainable sales potential. The process of making a market survey is covered in Chapter 6. Knowing its results, we will also refine our projected income statement into a budgeted income statement covering the first year of operations.

It is always good news in the second step to find that the reasonably attainable sales volume exceeds the minimum required to produce the profit desired. In the majority of market surveys the author has participated in over many years, the results have shown sales volume attainable to be in excess of that required in step 1. It must be hurriedly added, however, that about one case in three has demonstrated that the business being considered should not be established. These facts demonstrate the importance of step 2. When adequate sales and profits appear likely, we proceed to step 3.

Step 3 *Prepare a statement of assets to be used.*
A statement of assets to be used is merely a list of the assets that are essential to the operation of the business. Values in dollar amounts should be attached to each asset needed by the business. This step has the value of giving students and business people an appreciation of the workings of the business economy as they later determine how these assets are to be provided for the new firm.

For example, if the business needs delivery trucks, merchandise inventory, land and buildings, store equipment, office equipment, and cash, specific dollar amounts must be attached to each. This step requires careful thinking by the planner to be sure that all needs are thoroughly considered. This step can also involve policy decisions on such matters such as whether or not you plan to carry your own accounts receivable or even sell on credit.

If credit sales are contemplated and you plan to finance your own accounts receivable, an additional investment will be needed by the firm. This must be planned in a later step. The procedure for developing a statement of assets to be used will be further explained and illustrated in detail in Chapter 8.

Step 4 *Prepare an opening day balance sheet.*
Step 4 involves close study of the asset needs of the business as determined in step 3 and decisions on how they are to be met. Here we decide whether to rent or buy the business building; whether to buy delivery trucks and on what terms, or whether to hire a delivery service or even eliminate such service; and how we will finance the inventory from choices available. Every asset to be used, every liability to be incurred, and the resulting necessary investment by the proprietor must be clarified in this step. This will involve knowing the various types of financing available in providing each asset and how much we can safely use. Basic information provided by a balance sheet and by an income statement is necessary to do this task well. These financial statements were reviewed in Chapter 3. Details of building the opening day balance sheet will be further

discussed and illustrated in Chapter 9. Sources of financial aid are covered in Chapter 10.

Step 5 *Study the location and the specific site chosen for specific characteristics.*

Too many small firms are located in space which "just happened" to be available, without any analysis of that space as a suitable location for the specific type of firm planned.

General location and specific site can be large factors in the success or failure of many businesses. This matter merits close study by the small firm planner. Details of measuring good versus poor locations and sites will be explained in detail in Chapter 11.

Step 6 *Prepare a layout for the entire space to be used for business activity.*

Have you ever wondered why the dessert section in a cafeteria is usually first in line? Have you observed where the prescription counter is located in a drugstore? Have you noticed that some stores "seem like a jungle," without a pattern or purpose in the way merchandise is presented to customers? The reasons for each location can be found by studying good and bad principles of layout. Very positive reasons explain the first two locations. A lack of recognition of good layout principles accounts for the third situation.

Every planner should create an actual floor-plan drawing of the operation which will reflect good layout principles. The rules of layout for different kinds of small firms will be reviewed in Chapter 12.

Step 7 *Choose your legal form of organization.*

The fact that most small firms are proprietorships, as contrasted with partnerships or corporations, does not assure that proprietorship is the best legal form of organization. The author believes that many small firms should be using the other legal forms. Planners should not only study the characteristics of the three major legal forms of organization; they should also seek out the true management advantages of each. The idea that the corporate form of organization is designed only for large firms can be seriously questioned. Different circumstances in different firms may call for one legal form rather than another. These considerations will be detailed in Chapter 7.

Step 8 *Review all aspects of your merchandising plan.*

Merchandising is a broad term as it is generally used in business circles. It covers many things—plans for presenting products to customers, inventories in terms of dollar amount and lines of goods, sales promotion plans, advertising plans, pricing policy, public relations, markups, markdowns, seasonable variations in business, planned special sales, and other associated things. It will take five chapters (13 through 17) to cover these items as we progress through this book. It is through the study of these factors that many previous convictions or impressions of new business planners are seriously jarred or adjusted.

Step 9 *Analyze your estimated expenses in terms of their fixed or variable nature.*

When the budgeted income statement has been completed, it will show all operating expenses in detail. A close scrutiny of these expenses in terms of their fixed or variable nature will be of great value to the owner in making management decisions for the firm. The relation of risk to expenses should be known. This subject will be developed and illustrated in Chapter 18.

Step 10 *Determine the firm's break-even point.*

In simplest terms or in a more sophisticated formula, the old concept of a break-even chart is just as important to the small firm as to the large one. Most students know the concept in broad terms but cannot actually make a break-even chart from an income statement for a specific business. We will do that for a contemplated firm in Chapter 18.

Step 11 *If you are even considering sales on account, review the advantages and administrative decisions involved. Then establish a credit policy.*

The process of selling to customers on credit has many more implications than generally assumed. There are various types of credit plans available. Most are used by large firms. Small firms can do the same. Investment capital is necessary to carry your own receivables. Credit-card sales cost money. Open accounts risk uncollectibility. This subject, too, is a large one for small firm planners. Its many ramifications are discussed in detail in Chapter 19.

Step 12 *Review the risks to which you are subject and how you plan to cope with them.*

We all face risks in everything we do daily. Small business firms are subject to many risks every day. The more we know about the risks around us, the better we can prepare the firm to protect itself against them. Such terms as "insurable interest" and "incidence of risk" should become a part of all small firm owners' vocabularies. We will look at risks in detail in Chapter 20.

Step 13 *Establish a personnel policy at the outset.*

Small business has been accused of not being able to keep good employees. Everyone recognizes that good workers are the most valuable asset any business organization can have. Their importance may be even greater to small firms than to their large competitors. What will your policy be in this regard? How will you attract and keep good employees? Will you understand employee needs and desires? How will you establish policies regarding them? This whole matter will be covered in Chapter 21.

Step 14 *Establish an adequate system of accounting records.*

Good accounting records are essential to making decisions for any business. They are necessary for government reports, tax returns, and operations analysis. Every new firm should provide for an adequate system of accounting records in the planning stage. Details of the makeup and use of the basic financial statements were covered in Chapter 3. Establishing a basic system of records is illustrated with actual transactions in Chapters 27 and 28.

OTHER ITEMS TO CONSIDER

The preceding 14 steps in planning are deemed appropriate to almost every new small firm. Depending upon the size of the operation undertaken, other items may be considered in the planning stage. More and more small firms today have a need for minicomputers or other electronic data processing services. Chapter 25 deals with this need and how it is handled. Special financial reports such as cash flow statements can be important to any firm, large or small. Cash flow statements are explained and illustrated in Chapter 28. The average small firm can have good management control if the first 14 steps outlined are followed conscientiously. As the firm grows, investigation of these additional areas will become appropriate. For the average owner of the existing small firm and for student introduction to the subject of small firm management, we will confine our basic discussions to the 14 steps listed here.

Whether the reader's objective is academic study of small business management, preparation of a contemplated new firm, or analysis of an existing firm in line with established principles, competence in the field will be enhanced by studying each of the steps outlined in sequence or in isolation.

QUESTIONS FOR CLASS DISCUSSION

1 What is the advantage of developing a comprehensive plan before starting a new business?
2 What is the danger of starting a new firm without adequate financing?
3 Do you think it is advisable for someone planning a new firm to think about what profit it will produce before beginning operations? Why?
4 What is the objective of a market survey?
5 Are people who operate their own small business entitled to both a salary and a profit on their investment?
6 What is a statement of assets to be used?
7 What do we mean by "planning a new business"?
8 Do you agree with the steps needed for developing a comprehensive business plan as outlined in this chapter? How would you change them?
9 Could a neighborhood grocery store justify the expense of a computer? Why?
10 What is a legal form of organization?
11 Do you believe that all small business firms should sell on credit? Why?
12 What do you like about the small firms you do business with?

PROJECTS FOR HOME ASSIGNMENT AND/OR CLASS DISCUSSION

1 Explain in a short paper what the term *the desired income approach* to planning a new firm means to you.

2 Do you think it is advantageous for new firm planners to have some idea of the amount of sales that can reasonably be expected in the first year? Explain.

3 Explain how you would determine how much profit you would expect as your salary and return on your investment if you were planning a new small business.

CONTINUING PROBLEM:
The Kollege Klothes Shop

PART 4: ESSENTIALS FOR PLANNING—A COMPREHENSIVE BUSINESS PLAN

In this chapter we have reviewed 14 recommended steps in the planning of a new firm. Each is considered very important to increase the chances of success for a new firm.

As a consultant to Jones and Gomez you will likely find that clients often fail to recognize the importance of the details you recommend taking into account when you write a comprehensive plan for them. We will assume that you have encountered this problem as you advise Jones and Gomez. They have asked you for a short explanation of the importance of each step recommended.

Assignment for Part 4

Write a short paper explaining why you think each step recommended for your report to Jones and Gomez is important. How will each increase their chances for successful operation of the new firm? Because the later parts of our continuing report will follow these steps, this paper will give us a preview of where we will be proceeding in later chapters.

REFERENCES FOR FURTHER READING

"Business Plan for Small Service Firms," *Small Business Administration Marketer's Aid No. 153.*

Deitzer, Bernard A., and Karl A. Schilliff, *Contemporary Management Incidents,* Grid Publishing Co., Columbus, Ohio, 1977, Incident No. 4.

"Starting and Managing a Small Business of Your Own," *Starting and Managing Series,* vol. 1, 2d ed., Small Business Administration.

Tate, Curtis E., Jr., Leon Megginson, Charles Scott, Jr., and Lyle Trueblood, *Successful Small Business Management,* rev. ed., Business Publications, Inc., Dallas, Texas, 1978, chap. 24.

CHAPTER **5**

THE DESIRED INCOME APPROACH TO PLANNING: MAKING A PROJECTED INCOME STATEMENT

Do you really mean that when I started this business I should have made a hoped-for income statement? And based it on the profit I hoped to make? How? You must be pulling my leg.

The Late Learner

We have previously seen that those who would invest their assets in a small business should receive both a reward for their time and effort, and a return on their investment. If the planner determines that he or she desires a minimum profit of $15,000, it should be recognized what options are at hand. A position can be taken working for another firm to earn a salary, and their capital can be invested in other ways to earn a return on it. Both alternatives should be kept in mind when setting a minimum profit expectancy from the planned firm.

DESIRED PLANNING STATISTICS AND THEIR SOURCES

Once the new firm planners determine their desired income, continuing planning is made easier by the availability of abundant statistics which were not in existence when our grandparents were merchants. All potential new owners should become familiar with the statistics for the type of firm they plan. If they have had previous employment in the same kind of firm, this experience should enable them to gain valuable information about the statistics and operation of the business at first hand. But even without this experience, planners have many sources for gathering basic facts about their type of firm. Trade associations, chambers of commerce, industrial development departments, the United States Census, the United States *Statistical Abstract,* the Department of Commerce, the Small Business Administration, and great business service organizations like Dun & Bradstreet are some sources readily available. Many publications of government agencies are free of charge. Most are available in local libraries. Other agencies make only a minor charge for specific data reports.

Dun & Bradstreet regularly issues a publication that provides specific ratios and other financial data for 125 different lines of business. This publication covers firms in retailing, wholesaling, manufacturing, and construction. Comprehensive data ranging from the current ratio to the relationship of sales to fixed assets are presented. The figures are averages for hundreds of different firms in each line. Not only does this report tell new firm planners the average current ratio, for example, it also breaks the figures down into the upper quartile, the median, and the lower quartile (the best 25 percent, the overall average, and the lower 25 percent). (See Figure 5-1.)

Among the other excellent sources of data on operating statistics for all types of business firms we should note at least the following:

Annual Statements Studies, published by Robert Morris Associates, Philadelphia National Bank Building, Philadelphia, PA 19107.

Barometer of Small Business, published by the Accounting Corporation of America, 1929 First Avenue, San Diego, CA 92112.

Copies of these significant sourcebooks are probably in your school library. They should be. *Annual Statement Studies* covers manufacturing, wholesaling, retailing, service, and construction firms in each area. Both balance sheet and income statement data are included. Your commercial bank probably subscribes to this important study, which was originally planned as a bank service. *Barometer of Small Business* is a semiannual publication which concentrates on retail firms of many types. Complete income statements are presented with percentages of sales for each item instead of dollar amounts. The data are classified for firms of different sales volume. The publication even provides trends, geographical variances, and seasonal data. Complete balance sheets are presented in detail for each of the various types of firms reviewed.

A visit to the closest SBA office and the Department of Commerce should be made by all who plan to open a new firm. Small business owners can also benefit from such visits by finding data by which to compare their specific situation with the principles set forth in the available reports. Many people looking for this information will be surprised to find it available for most lines of business. They may even find a pamphlet on their particular type of business. Often it will contain additional information that can be of value in planning or checking the status of an existing firm.

With the desired income known, only three statistics are necessary to enable

Line of Business (and number of concerns reporting)	Current assets to current debt Times	Net profits on net sales Per cent	Net profits on tangible net worth Per cent	Net profits on net working capital Per cent	Net sales to tangible net worth Times	Net sales to net working capital Times	Collection period Days	Net sales to inventory Times	Fixed assets to tangible net worth Per cent	Current debt to tangible net worth Per cent	Total debt to tangible net worth Per cent	Inventory to net working capital Per cent	Current debt to inventory Per cent	Funded debts to net working capital Per cent
5641 Children's & Infants' Wear Stores (50)	4.65 2.64 1.73	3.73 1.72 0.67	16.09 7.85 3.23	16.49 9.56 4.55	6.35 4.44 3.27	8.33 5.31 4.06	* * *	7.5 5.2 3.9	5.2 17.1 27.5	30.1 56.2 95.0	95.2 147.4 287.2	57.9 111.2 154.2	42.6 60.4 95.3	15.2 37.4 93.2
5611 Clothing & Furnishings, Men's & Boys' (221)	4.49 2.75 1.96	4.39 2.35 0.85	12.70 6.68 3.02	17.50 7.70 3.23	4.43 3.11 2.17	5.02 3.64 2.65	* * *	5.7 3.9 2.9	5.3 11.1 22.5	24.5 47.3 98.2	59.6 105.6 161.5	61.4 92.0 127.2	38.8 64.1 96.7	10.9 25.5 41.4
5311 Department Stores (259)	4.47 2.89 2.06	2.92 1.55 0.52	9.28 5.42 1.61	11.81 7.05 2.05	4.69 3.13 2.37	5.98 4.15 3.05	* * *	7.1 5.6 4.3	11.7 26.0 54.2	22.4 42.1 70.6	51.9 82.0 128.1	57.6 76.9 107.5	44.1 69.8 101.9	16.3 32.2 66.2
Discount Stores (224)	2.64 1.88 1.54	2.68 1.49 0.70	15.45 9.97 5.24	21.73 13.29 6.33	8.71 6.28 4.49	11.45 7.85 5.26	* * *	7.2 5.2 3.9	14.8 28.9 51.6	52.0 83.3 135.4	74.7 120.1 197.4	103.5 146.1 195.3	54.4 72.6 93.8	12.4 32.5 64.0
Discount Stores, Leased Departments (53)	3.09 1.94 1.52	3.49 1.85 0.44	15.19 8.98 3.69	19.25 12.18 3.98	7.88 5.43 4.00	9.46 5.87 4.56	* * *	6.2 4.6 3.1	14.5 27.5 45.5	46.9 87.3 170.8	67.9 114.9 210.3	93.7 134.8 181.8	49.7 70.9 99.3	7.5 22.1 47.8
5651 Family Clothing Stores (93)	5.25 3.18 2.23	4.31 2.85 1.27	15.06 8.28 3.68	16.89 10.35 4.57	4.86 3.53 2.10	5.68 3.67 2.48	* * *	6.8 4.8 3.5	5.1 12.3 27.7	21.2 41.3 72.4	51.2 88.8 160.8	52.1 79.7 127.8	40.0 56.9 86.3	11.7 30.5 53.8

* Not computed Necessary information as to the division between cash sales was available in too few cases to obtain an average collection period usable as a broad guide.

FIGURE 5-1
Sample of Dun & Bradstreet's financial statistics for retailing. Similar information is available for wholesaling, manufacturing, and construction. *(From Dun & Bradstreet, Inc.)*

the planner to make a complete projected income statement. These three statistics are:

1 The average merchandise turnover for this type of business
2 The average markup
3 Profits as a percentage of sales

While these statistics are general financial analysis tools, they are adopted here as most effective tools for planning a new firm.

These terms may need clarification. *Merchandise turnover* is the number of times the average inventory is sold each year. If a firm carries an inventory of $15,000 and has a cost of goods sold of $60,000, the merchandise turnover is four times per year. Cost of goods sold (as remembered from our review of accounting statements in Chapter 3) is the price paid for the merchandise purchased and sold. Merchandise turnover is computed by dividing the cost of goods sold by the average inventory carried in stock. For this example, the computation is as follows:

$$\frac{\text{Cost of goods sold}}{\text{Average inventory}} = \frac{\$60,000}{\$15,000} = 4 \text{ (the merchandise turnover)}$$

Inventories carried and their adequacy and inadequacy are one of the truly dynamic subjects in management. They will be referred to many times throughout this text and discussed in detail in a later chapter.

The *average markup* is the dollar difference between the cost of goods sold and sales, expressed as a percentage of sales. In dollar amounts, the markup provides the gross margin. If sales are $100,000 and cost of goods sold is $60,000, the gross margin is $40,000. Expressed as a percentage of sales, we observe that the markup is 40 percent. It is computed by dividing gross margin by sales. In this example, the computation is as follows:

$$\frac{\text{Gross margin}}{\text{Sales}} = \frac{\$ 40,000}{\$100,000} = 40\% \text{ (markup)}$$

Profits as a percentage of sales means just that. New firm planners want to find out what percentage of the sales dollar remains in the company as profits in their line of business. Existing operators want this figure to compare their firm's average with the averages of other similar firms. The arithmetical computation is to divide average profits by the sales volume, as follows:

$$\frac{\text{Net profits}}{\text{Sales}} = \frac{\$ 15,000}{\$100,000} = 15\% \text{ (profits as a percentage of sales)}$$

This percentage can be figured on the basis of profits either before federal income taxes or after applicable income taxes have been deducted. It is important for planners to know which basis they are using.

The more searching we do for figures, the better our planning will be. Local or regional averages are generally more applicable than national averages. We may find three figures from three different sources for average merchandise turnover. We must then decide which are most applicable to our area. Without specific factors to support one or the other, it may be best to average the three for planning purposes. Similar considerations should be applied to the markup and profits as a percentage of sales figures.

BUILDING A PROJECTED INCOME STATEMENT

With only these three statistics and our desired profit, we may now proceed to construct a projected income statement for a planned retail firm. The student should follow each step and each calculation carefully.

For our illustration of this process, let us assume that the carefully gathered and adopted figures for these three items are as follows:

Profits as a percentage of sales: 12 percent
Merchandise turnover: Four times per year
Markup: 35 percent of sales
Desired profit: $15,000 (includes salary and return on investment)

From Chapter 3 it will be recalled that the key parts of an income statement are as shown in Table 5-1. Actual figures for the above situation have been inserted with each entry numbered in parentheses (1), (2), etc., so that the explanatory comments following the table may be traced.

All the figures on this projected income statement have been computed from only the four facts previously determined. The statement has been completed

TABLE 5-1
JONES HARDWARE COMPANY
Projected Income Statement
Year Beginning January 1, 1982

Sales		$125,000.00	(2)
Cost of goods sold			
Beginning inventory, Jan. 1	$ 20,312.50 (5)		
Purchases during the year	81,250.00 (7)		
Goods available for sale	$101,562.50 (6)		
Less ending inventory, Dec. 31	20,312.50 (5)		
Cost of goods sold		81,250.00	(4)
Gross margin		$43,750.00	(3)
Operating expenses		28,750.00	(8)
Net profit from operations		$15,000.00	(1)

from the bottom up and not from the top down. The numbers in parentheses indicate the order in which they were inserted. Their explanation follows:

1 The desired profit is $15,000. This is the goal desired by the planner. We therefore insert this figure first on the last line.

2 We have found that profits average 12 percent of sales, so we must find the amount of which $15,000 (profits) is 12 percent. We divide $15,000 by 12 to find 1 percent ($1,250) and multiply by 100 to find 100 percent of sales. To compute this by formula, $.12x = \$15,000$, therefore $x = \$125,000$. We can now insert $125,000, our necessary sales volume, as item (2).

3 We have determined in our search of statistics that markup averages 35 percent of sales. Accordingly, we find 35 percent of our $125,000 sales and insert this figure as our gross margin ($43,750), as item (3).

4 *Gross margin* is the difference between what we paid for the merchandise and what we sold it for. Therefore, if we subtract the gross margin ($43,750) from the sales ($125,000), it must tell us the cost of goods sold. Accordingly, we insert this figure on the projected income statement as item (4) ($81,250).

5 We have determined that the desired merchandise turnover is four times per year. This means that if the cost of goods sold is $81,250, it represents four times the average inventory which must be carried in stock to produce the sales volume we have indicated. Therefore, $81,250 divided by 4 gives us $20,312.50 as the average inventory necessary to support our sales volume. This figure is inserted on the statement for both our beginning and ending inventory as item (5). If enlarged inventories are contemplated, adjustments can be made. For present purposes, we will assume that the inventory will remain at the same level.

6 The cost of goods sold plus the inventory on hand at the end of the year must total the value of all the merchandise which has been available for sale during the year. Therefore, we add the cost of goods sold ($81,250) and the ending inventory ($20,312.50) to arrive at goods available for sale ($101,562.50), item (6).

7 If $101,562.50 of goods was available during the year but only $20,312.50 was on hand in the beginning inventory, the difference must represent the merchandise purchased during the year. Therefore, we subtract the beginning inventory of $20,312.50 from goods available of $101,562.50 to arrive at purchases of $81,250. This is item (7).

8 If gross margin is $43,750 and net profit from operations is $15,000, the difference must be the total of the operating expenses during the year. By subtracting the net profit from the gross margin, we have the total operating expenses of $28,750, item (8).

We have now completed a first-phase projected income statement. Operating expenses will have to be detailed at a later date. They will again be based upon available statistics on how much should be paid for rent, salaries, supplies, and other expenses. These amounts will all be computed as a percentage of sales. The comparable figures are easily available from the same sources we have previously noted. Most reports will express these expenses as a percentage of sales.

This projected income statement tells the planners that if they are to realize the objective of $15,000 net profit, they will have to produce a sales volume of $125,000, maintain a merchandise inventory of $20,312.50, turn that inventory over four times during the year, and maintain an average markup of 35 percent on their sales volume.

SPECIAL ASPECTS OF SERVICE FIRM PLANNING

We have previously noted that a purely service firm which does not carry an inventory of merchandise for resale to its customers will not have a cost-of-goods-sold section on its income statement (see Table 3-3). The income section of the statement will reflect the total dollars derived from sales of a service rather than from sales of a physical product. The operating expense section of the statement will include all expenses incurred, including any supplies used in the rendering of the firm's service.

Some service firms may also have sales of products—such as a TV repair shop that also sells new television sets. In such cases they should preferably separate sales income into service fees and product sales, have a special cost-of-goods-sold section for the new product sales, and, as much as possible, assign operating expenses to each phase of the operations. It is most helpful for proprietors of such firms to develop income statements in separate columns, one for retail sales and one for service operations, and then total the two across the sheet for a summary of total operations. Each phase of the business can then be closely analyzed to determine its profitability.

SPECIAL ASPECTS OF MANUFACTURING FIRM PLANNING

The same types of statistics to which we have previously referred are also abundantly available for planners of new factory operations that produce their final products from raw materials. Financial statements for factory firms, however, have distinct features that are not part of retail firm statements. Some of these are:

1 The merchandise inventory figure on the balance sheet of a factory is not one figure representing total inventory on hand. Instead, it is broken down into raw materials, goods in process, and finished goods (see Table 5-2).

This means that when one is planning a factory operation, provision must be made not only for buying the original raw materials but also for carrying the investment in goods in process (half-finished goods) and the finished goods until they are sold. That is why the total inventory investment of a small factory is usually a higher percentage of total current assets than in most other types of firms. Average statistics are available to help the new factory planner determine the required investment.

TABLE 5-2

GOMEZ AUTO BODY MANUFACTURING COMPANY

Balance Sheet

January 1, 1982

ASSETS

Current assets:		
Cash		$ 6,000
Notes receivable		4,200
Marketable securities		15,800
Inventories:		
Raw materials	$ 25,000	
Goods in process	40,000	
Finished goods	48,000	113,000
Prepaid assets		1,000
Total current assets		$140,000
Fixed assets:		
Land		$ 45,000
Plant buildings	$165,000	
Machinery and equipment	80,000	
	$245,000	
Less depreciation	105,000	140,000
Total fixed assets		185,000
Total assets		$325,000

LIABILITIES

Current liabilities:		
Accounts payable	$ 40,000	
Notes payable	20,000	
Accrued taxes payable	5,000	
Total current liabilities		$ 65,000
Fixed liabilities:		
Contracts payable		35,000
Total liabilities		$100,000

STOCKHOLDERS' EQUITY

Capital stock outstanding:		
Preferred stock	$ 80,000	
Common stock	100,000	
Retained earnings	45,000	
Total stockholders' equity		$225,000
Total liabilities and stockholders' equity		$325,000

Accounting is a bit more involved for factory operations because of the necessity of keeping track of the value of goods in process and total cost of the finished goods. This involves cost accounting procedures to add the labor expenses and overhead costs to raw materials placed in production to find the value of the unfinished products and the value of the products finished in the factory and placed in inventory for sale.

2 The income statement for a factory will show the cost of goods manufactured and sold, rather than merely a beginning inventory, plus purchases, less ending inventory, to find cost of goods sold, as is done for a retailing firm. The total cost of goods manufactured is preferably shown as a separate statement. See Tables 5-3 and 5-4 for illustrations of these statements.

This is again because the factory uses raw materials, expends labor and overhead on them, has products in all stages of manufacture in its inventories at a given time, and must calculate the total cost of its completed products.

Some factories produce products only to order, rather than producing for inventory stock on hand. This enables them to minimize the investment in materials and assures that all goods finished are sold as soon as they are ready for delivery.

The examples of a balance sheet, an income statement, and a statement of cost of goods manufactured for a small factory shown in Tables 5-2, 5-3, and 5-4 illustrate the preceding comments.

In our desired income approach to planning, we can now turn to the market survey (step 2 in Chapter 4) to find out if the necessary sales can reasonably be achieved in the market we plan to serve. It is useless to further refine our financial planning unless that volume of sales can be achieved. When we know that the results of our market survey are favorable, we will then determine what assets are required for the business and how they will be provided.

TABLE 5-3
THE KELLY MANUFACTURING COMPANY
Income Statement
For Year Ended December 31, 1981

Sales		$2,150,000
Less cost of goods manufactured and sold		1,450,000
Gross margin on sales		$ 700,000
Operating expenses:		
Marketing Expenses		
(listed in detail)	$350,000	
Administrative expenses		
(listed in detail)	175,000	
Total operating expenses		525,000
Profit from operations before taxes		$ 175,000

TABLE 5-4
SMUCKER MANUFACTURING COMPANY
Statement of Cost of Goods Manufactured
Year Ended December 31, 1981

Direct materials:		
Raw materials inventory January 1	$100,000	
Plus purchases during year	65,000	
Materials available during year	$165,000	
Less inventory December 31	40,000	
		$125,000
Direct materials used during year		
		265,000
Direct labor expenses for year		
Factory overhead		
(All factory overhead expenses would be listed in detail: indirect labor; power, heat, and light; salaries; factory supplies; depreciation; repairs and maintenance; patent expenses and insurance; and so on.)		80,000
Total manufacturing costs		$470,000
Add work in process January 1		45,000
		515,000
Less work in process December 31		65,000
Cost of goods manufactured during the year		$450,000

QUESTIONS FOR CLASS DISCUSSION

1 How much would you plan on as your profits before taxes and as a return on your investment if you started a new small firm today?

2 What does "the desired income approach to planning" mean to you? Do you agree with it? Why?

3 Where can people who plan new firms find some statistics to guide their planning?

4 Where would you look for industry statistics if you were planning a new hardware store?

5 What are the key items of statistics needed to make a projected income statement?

6 Why would it be desirable to have key statistics, like the current ratio, broken down into the upper quartile, median, and lower quartile? In which quartile would you want your firm to be?

7 What is meant by the merchandise turnover? How is it computed?

8 What is average markup? Can it be expressed both in dollars and as a percentage of sales? Give examples.

9 Why is it important to know whether profits as a percentage of sales are computed on profits before or after income taxes?

10 If we know goods available for sale and the beginning inventory, how do we find purchases?

11 If we know cost of goods sold and merchandise turnover, how do we find the average inventory?

PROJECTS FOR HOME ASSIGNMENT AND/OR CLASS DISCUSSION

1 Explain what is meant by saying that "today's students have one great advantage over their grandparents in planning new business firms."
2 How can today's planners effectively use industry statistics in planning? How do you account for the fact that different sources of statistics vary in their averages?
3 Write a brief explanation of the meaning and importance of merchandise turnover.

CONTINUING PROBLEM:
The Kollege Klothes Shop

PART 5: THE PROJECTED INCOME STATEMENT

We are now ready for the first step in planning operating statistics for our report. We have found that in addition to our own setting of a desired profit, only three figures must be gathered from industry statistics. These are the merchandise turnover, profits as a percentage of sales, and the average markup (gross margin). A thorough review of the various sets of industry statistics would be involved in an actual situation. We have done that job for you.

Condensed Research Figures

We have reviewed various sets of industry statistics, including those of Dun & Bradstreet, Robert Morris Associates, National Cash Register, Bank of America, the Barometer of Small Business, and the Small Business Administration. In addition, we have talked with trade association people and business owners of other clothes shops like the one we plan. National, regional, and local figures have been studied and compared. We have found that some modest variations exist between the sources of data. After reviewing all our work, we have decided to use the following optimistic figures as best representing goals for our own area:

Profits should average 10 percent of sales.
Gross margin (average markup) should be 40 percent of sales.
Merchandise turnover should be 6 times per year.

In addition, Jones and Gomez have advised that they will expect a net profit from operations of $20,000 to cover their salaries and a return on their investment.

Assignment for Part 5

Construct a projected income statement for the Kollege Klothes Shop based on the above figures.

Your instructor will have a projected income statement available based on the above data.

REFERENCES FOR FURTHER READING

Fox, Edward J., and Edward W. Wheatley, *Modern Marketing,* Scott, Foresman and Co., Glenview, Illinois, 1978, chap. 3.

"Keep Pointed Toward Profit," Small Business Administration Pamphlet No. MA206.

Niswonger, C. Rollin, and Philip E. Fess, *Accounting Principles,* 12th ed., South-Western Publishing Co., Inc., Cincinnati, 1977, chap. 5.

SURVEYING THE MARKET TO BE SERVED: FINDING ITS LIMITS, ITS NATURE, AND ITS SALES POTENTIAL

If I had known more about studying my market when I first started my business, I would not have had to move twice and suffer substantial losses before success came.

The Late Learner

It often comes as a severe shock to new small firm planners when they are told they should study their market carefully before investing. Why? Such surveys will show the planner much about where customers will come from, and the nature of the people in that market, so that he or she can determine whether they will be prospective customers for the proposed firm. Most important, this kind of survey will give the planner some idea of a reasonably attainable sales potential if a good merchandising job is done by the firm.

When a new firm is started without a fairly accurate idea of the sales potential, poor planning is in evidence. Such neglect may easily place the future of the firm in jeopardy from the beginning. With luck, the firm may succeed anyhow, but it is much better to first study the market thoroughly and then to build the firm to fit that market.

Few aspects of total business management have improved as much in recent years as accuracy in making market surveys. Planners may employ an outside firm to make the survey of their suggested market. Advertising firms and market research firms often specialize in such surveys. The abundance of data available for use in these surveys is amazing. Some sources are listed later in this chapter. The cost of having market surveys made for a newly planned firm will vary from city to city and with degree of detail requested. Costs of $500 to $2,000 are common for small firms.

If new firm planners themselves cannot undertake the survey, any costs they pay for a good market survey may be the best investment they can make. If the survey shows that the desired or required sales potential does not exist in the market, their expenditures for the survey will protect them from losing their contemplated investment in a firm that cannot produce profitable results. If it should demonstrate that potential sales volume exceeds that required to produce desired minimum profits, they can rearrange their planning to support this larger volume and larger profits.

THE OBJECTIVE OF A MARKET SURVEY

Stated most simply, the objective of a market survey is to determine a reasonably attainable sales volume in a specific market area for a specific type of business. This means finding out how many potential consumers of the planned merchandise or service there are in this market and how many of them can reasonably be expected to become customers of the firm under consideration.

The thoroughness of a market survey will vary under different conditions. The survey is essential for stores that plan to develop much of their own customer traffic. If sales are to depend on the firm's merchandising policies, sales promotion efforts, special services, or uniqueness, a particularly thorough market survey should be made in advance. Firms that plan to rely on the established customer flow already generated by other businesses in the area may follow less thorough procedures. The latter types of firms have often been described as "parasite stores," meaning that their location has been dictated by the existing firms in the area that have attracted a substantial traffic flow and which the new firm will tap for its own sales. Examples of small firms in this category are a restaurant in a skyscraper lobby, a medium-priced dress shop next to a large department store, an office-building tobacco shop, or a drugstore in an airline terminal. In these cases, the amount and nature of the traffic and its sales potential are pretty well established. Such firms may still, however, exert various types of sales promotion activities to increase total income within that traffic.

Our chief concern here is with the types of firms that must rely heavily on a market survey to help them build much of their customer traffic.

WHAT IS A MARKET?

The market, or trading area for a particular firm, is the area which it seeks to serve with its products or services. From the buyer's point of view, it is the area within which the buyer knows he or she can find desired goods and services at desired prices. The definition of a market, or trading area, from the buyer's and the seller's view may not be the same. Sellers may desire to expand their markets beyond the limits that are normally recognized by buyers. Experience will tell merchants the proper limits of their trading areas if they have the means of measuring the sources of sales. Market areas may change with the development of new shopping centers in adjacent areas. At any given time, a market has its limits set by the area within which the firm can economically sell its goods or services.

PROCEDURE FOR MAKING A MARKET SURVEY

We know that the objective of the market survey is to determine a reasonable sales forecast. How is this accomplished? The procedure will vary from factory to wholesaler to retailer. In all cases, however, it will seek to determine the number of customers in the market area who may become customers for the planned business. For retailing, the steps should include the following:

1 Determine the limits of the market or trading area.
2 Study the population within this area to determine its potential sales characteristics.
3 Determine the purchasing power of the area.
4 Determine the present sales volume of the type of goods or services you propose to offer.
5 Estimate what proportion of the total sales volume you can reasonably obtain.

Each of these steps involves special considerations which deserve discussion here.

1 **Determining Limits of the Marketing Area** Firms in downtown locations, especially those in the central business districts of large cities, tend to draw customers from a wider market area than those in suburban or small-city locations. The decline of public transportation systems in most cities in past years was accompanied, in many areas, by an increase in the number of freeways and express highways, so that potential customers still go downtown despite increased suburban and small-city shopping centers. But partly because of decreasing public transportation and today's energy crisis, the number of suburban shopping centers has continued to increase. The conclusion remains that for small firms the market limits in urban locations are generally the same as for larger firms.

Interestingly, even a large department store reports that it measures its market area in terms of ease of access. This access is measured in 5-minute, 10-minute, 15- and 20-minute drives from its location in the central business district. Whenever travel obstacles, such as bridges, narrow streets, or congested areas, are encountered, the area beyond is considered less significant as part of the market area to be served. Cities bordering on a river, such as Memphis, find that their market area is limited by that factor. Railroad yards, cemeteries, and other traffic obstacles can have similar effects on a given market area.

In suburban and small-city locations, the market area is determined more by neighboring population and its characteristics, the nature of other stores in the area, and parking facilities. Ease of access and location, size, and quality characteristics of the firm are also important. Although many shoppers visit various shopping centers, they generally tend to patronize the nearest center if it is otherwise satisfactory for their needs.

A popular method of measuring market areas for small firms in suburban and small-city areas is, therefore, to draw a map of their area and plot the location of competitors. By measuring the distance in each direction from closest competitors, small firm proprietors may establish an area in which, other things being equal, they should be thought of first by most shoppers. This assumes, of course, that the firm's existence is well known.

Adequacy of market area for a new small firm can be measured by knowing approximately how many people are necessary to support an average firm in this line of business. A composite of some of the best market research in this area shows, for example, that 600 people are needed to support one grocery store. See Table 11-1 for population requirements estimated to support one store in several other types of business. If a town of 10,000 population has 10 grocery stores, or an average of 1 grocery for every 1,000 people, the figures would suggest that the local population could support another grocery. Grocery retailers normally serve only their immediate neighborhoods and the limits of their market area are almost determined by that neighborhood.

The factor of economical limits to a market area is most applicable when such elements as free delivery expense are involved. It just does not pay to deliver to remote areas when the time and expense required are prohibitive. Today the trend is to have a special delivery charge if the service is offered.

Recognition of primary areas (where the firm has distinct advantages) as opposed to secondary areas (where some trade is still possible) has less significance for the typical small firm than for larger ones.

2   Studying the Population within the Market Area   What does the market researcher look for in studying population to make a market survey? Its *size* is important—but size does not guarantee that the population has sufficient numbers of the type of customers sought. The *trend* of the total population is important. Growing populations are usually better markets than stable or declining populations. For many market surveys, the population should be translated into *number of households* in order to make a more meaningful survey. The *part-time* nature of a population can be very significant, especially in resort towns.

After the size of the population is determined, a study of its characteristics may be even more important to the new firm planner.

The first classification of vital statistics relative to the population would include determining its composition by sex, age, income, occupation, marital status, average family size, race, religion, and average educational level. These characteristics vary sharply from city to city. St. Petersburg, Florida, is not a likely market for many baby-clothes stores. College towns are usually good markets for men's clothing. Bookstores do better when average education is high. A market survey for a particular type of business looks for those characteristics which make demand for its products or services.

Behavioral characteristics of the population are also very important. Do people buy the subject products weekly, monthly, on impulse or after shopping around, in certain seasons or regularly? Is the usual objective in buying these products their obvious usefulness or their ability to satisfy psychological desires, or do they have special uses of significant quantity? Who makes the purchasing decision? Who makes the purchase? Who uses the product? Are the people brand-conscious or price-conscious? Is the population responsive to good promotion and advertising?

It should be obvious that the more planners know about the population and its characteristics, the better sales forecast they can make.

3   Determining Total Purchasing Power of the Market Area   The next step in a thorough market survey is to determine the total purchasing power of the market area. The average income, found by studying population characteristics, is most helpful here. Occupations carry certain income ranges and can assist in determining total purchasing power. Other sources of key data are listed later in this chapter.

4   Determining Present Sales Volume in the Line of Business   Students may be amazed to find that they can obtain statistics for the present sales volume for established lines of business. The market surveyor not only wants to know the total sales in his line, but he also wants to estimate how the present sales volume is divided among the local firms engaged in this line. Average consumer expenditures in any given line are available. See the sources listed later in this chapter.

5   Determining What Proportion of Sales Volume You Can Obtain   It should be recognized in approaching this final objective of the survey that one new firm generally has little effect either on the total purchasing power in a market area or on the distribution of consumer expenditures. Until the new firm becomes better established, it must rely upon capturing a portion of the existing sales volume in that market area. Its initial merchandising and promotional activities will be directed toward that objective. Concentrated attention, however, may be given to what additional demand may be created by promotion. This is especially important for new products.

This initial sales forecast will be governed by whether or not the market area is saturated with similar stores or has fewer than the normal number of competitors. Substantial information about this factor will have been gathered in step 4 above.

Barring special circumstances, a market survey will determine whether the new firm can obtain a proportionate share of the total sales in its field. This means that if five competitors are now dividing $500,000 of sales in a specific market, entrance of the new firm should make it six firms dividing $500,000 of sales. Anticipated growth in population can be reflected in the forecast. Merchandising policies should be directed to the set objective. Promotion activities of all types should be consistent with this objective. The new small firm has in its favor its closeness to customers within a certain area, potential customers, discontent with existing firms, the promotion value of its opening, and the accompanying opportunity to make permanent customers of the first visitors; it can also have a set of services that have been planned to meet the competition. New small firms may have other advantages, too, such as established contacts or contracts for substantial sales, exclusive distributorships for highly desired merchandise, well-known persons employed there who bring in customers, handier parking facilities, or price lines or lines of merchandise not offered by the competition. All these factors should be taken into account as the final sales forecast is determined.

This forecast of potential sales can then be used as the foundation of a budgeted income statement for the coming year. It is this statement that provides the basis for all budgeting and policy making.

It must be emphasized here that many newly planned small firms have neglected to use good market surveys. This is probably due to lack of familiarity with the easily obtainable proper sources of market data and/or lack of knowledge of how to use analytical procedures. For these reasons, the next section of this chapter is devoted to sources of data for making market surveys.

"PEOPLE SURVEYS" FOR COLLECTING MARKET INFORMATION

One effective method for gathering market information is the use of "people surveys," which are made by surveying the population who live in a designated market area. Such surveys can rarely attempt to reach all persons in the area—instead the market researchers select a representative group of persons to be contacted. Even the highly important national television ratings, for example, involve the use of only about 1,200 homes. The selected group becomes known as *the sample*. Care in choosing a true cross-section of people represented in the sample will greatly affect its accuracy and reliability.

Small firm planners may use three different types of people interviews: These are:

1 Telephone surveys
2 Mail surveys
3 Personal interviews

The techniques in formulating questions for each of these types of interviews vary. Specific questions that will provide meaningful answers which can then be analyzed should be built into each type of interview questionnaire. Each type of interview has characteristics that can be summarized as follows:

1   Telephone surveys   This type of interview offers the advantage of economy and speed in the collection of desired data. To be effective, telephone surveys demand short, clear, and easily understood questions. A sound questionnaire, a truly representative sample group, and courteous telephone interviewers are the only requirements for gathering the key data which is then analyzed.

2   Mail surveys   Using the mail to gather basic data is more expensive than telephone interviews but still much less expensive than personal interviews, especially when a large market area is being studied. The rate of return is the key to whether or not it is successful. Today a 40 percent return on such mail surveys is considered excellent. Experience has shown that the shorter the interview sheet, the higher the rate of return.

3   Personal interviews   Personal interviews require much more time than other types and, accordingly, are the most expensive kind of survey to conduct. But when a broad section of opinion is being sought they are usually considered the most reliable. They enable the interviewer to interpret questions, to explore the respondents' opinions, and to identify areas of information that although not anticipated may be valuable in the final analysis of data collected.

OTHER BASIC SOURCES OF DATA FOR MAKING MARKET SURVEYS

1   Maps   Maps showing major trading areas of counties and states are available from chambers of commerce, industrial development boards, trade development commissions, and city newspaper offices. Such maps indicate where the major business of the subject area is being done and thus reflect buying habits of the population.

2   Road Maps   A study of the road network of any area gives information on ease of access to a particular site. We have seen that access is an important consideration in determining area limits.

3   Census Tracts   Population density and distribution are given in easily available census tracts. Almost every county government has such reports. They usually show the number of people living in specific parts of the county. Often-used breakdowns of the area are by precincts, by minor political subdivisions such as water districts, or even by 10-block areas. The exact number of people living in each section is given. Some counties have reports which show the population 10 years ago, 5 years ago, and currently. These reports can indicate the population trend.

4   The United States Census   Most students have never seen a copy of the United States census report, which is made every 10 years with some intermittent supplements. A visit to the nearby library can be an enlightening experience. Much of the desired information about population breakdown statistics will be found in the census reports. Items we have discovered to be important— age, sex, race, religion, educational level, native- versus foreign-born, occupation, and so on—are abundantly available in the census. When only a portion of a town is involved in a market survey, the figures may require different interpretation.

5   Sales Management Magazine   This highly significant publication is considered indispensable by professional market research people. Once each year it publishes its "survey of buying power" issue, which gives the buying power figures for every county in the country and for every city over 10,000 in population. Because the United States census is completely taken only once in 10 years, this annual magazine report is particularly valuable for the years between census dates. It contains information on total population, households, breakdown of retail sales into divisions for different kinds of business firms, and total purchasing dollars represented in each city and county. The households are even divided into income levels. (See Figures 6-1 and 6-2 for sample data.)

6   United States Census of Business   This gigantic study includes information on total volume of business done in a particular line. Numbers of firms in each line of business are reported for towns as small as 2,500 population. Larger city reports are more detailed. Your own state census of business is also very valuable in this regard.

7   Trade Association Reports   Most trade associations issue regular reports on total sales volume divided into specific areas in their line of business. These reports often contain operating data that can assist the new firm planner.

8   Chambers of Commerce or Their Business Development Departments   Major cities have these organizations, which have the important job of encouraging the development of new business firms in their communities. They will gladly supply all types of information regarding population studies, income characteristics of the community, trends, payrolls, industrial development, and so on. Such information is usually free for the asking.

9   Bureaus of Business and Economic Research at Universities   These organizations are usually fortified with many studies about local markets. Published reports are available to the public.

10   Market Research and Advertising Firms   Many of these firms offer their professional services in making complete market surveys. They also, however,

TEXAS

SM ESTIMATES

COUNTIES CITIES	Met. Area Code	POPULATION 12/31/72 Total (thousands)	% of U.S.A.	House-holds (thousands)	$$ Net Dollars (000)	EBI 1972 Median Hstd. Cash Income	% Hstds. By Cash Income Groups: (A) $0-2,999; (B) $3,000-4,999; (C) $5,000-7,999; (D) $8,000-9,999; (E) $10,000-14,999; (F) $15,000 and Over A	B	C	D	E	F	RETAIL SALES—1972 Total Retail Sales ($000)	% of U.S.A.	Food ($000)	General Mdse. ($000)	Furn.-House. Appl. ($000)	Auto-motive ($000)	Drug ($000)	Buying Power Index
Anderson		29.1	.0139	10.1	69,305	4,397	38.9	14.5	16.2	10.2	13.8	6.4	57,680	.0130	12,986	6,924	1,794	14,227	3,313	.0111
Andrews		9.3	.0044	3.0	31,022	9,080	16.9	8.0	17.0	15.0	29.9	13.2	18,786	.0042	4,781	1,360	611	5,991	557	.0041
Angelina		51.6	.0246	16.7	139,311	6,310	26.0	14.9	20.6	13.0	16.3	9.2	101,426	.0229	27,702	9,261	5,723	21,442	3,461	.0206
Aransas		10.0	.0048	3.5	32,538	6,748	20.3	15.8	22.5	10.9	18.5	12.0	17,495	.0039	6,267	298	508	1,725	209	.0042
Archer		5.5	.0026	1.9	18,150	7,651	20.3	10.6	22.0	15.0	20.7	11.4	12,310	.0028	1,986	231	177	3,921	330	.0025
Armstrong		2.2	.0011	.8	7,706	6,821	20.9	13.2	26.4	11.4	15.2	12.9	4,419	.0010	386	633		1,054	185	.0010
Atascosa		19.1	.0091	5.6	39,461	4,603	35.8	17.4	17.6	9.0	13.1	7.1	27,018	.0061	6,534	1,379	167	6,448	932	.0062
Austin		14.4	.0069	5.3	39,444	4,764	35.3	16.4	18.3	8.8	13.2	8.0	28,735	.0065	6,909	1,869	1,134	5,467	946	.0058
Bailey		8.3	.0040	2.6	26,161	6,797	20.1	15.5	25.8	11.4	12.3	14.9	20,060	.0045	3,333	1,681	554	4,761	330	.0038
Bandera		4.9	.0023	1.9	12,689	4,369	37.0	19.2	18.4	7.7	10.4	7.3	5,290	.0012	1,630	312	161	583	267	.0016
Bastrop		18.5	.0088	6.4	48,756	5,183	30.4	18.2	20.9	9.1	13.4	8.0	26,640	.0060	7,092	1,553	1,094	7,540	952	.0067
Baylor		5.0	.0024	2.0	16,172	5,828	25.1	18.3	24.3	10.6	13.4	8.3	13,241	.0030	3,763	381	224	3,894	347	.0024
Bee		24.1	.0115	7.1	60,568	5,667	29.3	16.0	19.6	10.2	14.8	10.1	40,188	.0091	9,280	3,950	2,098	7,996	1,253	.0089
1 Bell	127	135.2	.0646	40.8	412,779	6,716	18.3	14.5	28.7	12.2	15.7	10.6	281,942	.0635	52,240	40,224	14,694	73,014	4,801	.0581
▲Killeen		39.5	.0189	13.8	122,679	6,783	12.6	15.9	33.8	12.7	15.0	10.0	96,403	.0217	13,525	18,995	8,436	24,838	1,126	.0180
▲Temple		37.9	.0181	13.2	128,347	7,032	19.6	13.8	24.8	12.4	17.3	12.1	133,281	.0300	27,408	19,469	5,995	33,445	2,893	.0207
2 Bexar	238	877.2	.4188	257.4	2,785,664	7,603	16.6	13.4	23.0	13.4	19.0	14.6	1,567,935	.3534	293,491	344,492	71,508	358,389	41,444	.3657
▲San Antonio		677.7	.3236	206.5	2,015,381	7,414	17.2	13.8	23.5	13.9	19.3	12.3	1,442,248	.3251	257,117	320,168	64,207	351,590	38,346	.2896
Blanco		3.9	.0019	1.5	12,940	4,772	37.6	13.8	18.1	8.3	13.2	11.0	6,458	.0015	1,106	362	212	504	230	.0016
Borden		.9	.0004	.3	2,595	5,875	30.6	17.0	10.0	19.7	11.7	11.0	28	.0000					15	.0002
Bosque		11.0	.0053	4.5	32,917	5,020	31.3	18.5	22.1	9.7	11.8	6.6	13,948	.0031	3,453	628	221	2,303	708	.0041

1 Military sales of $44,724,000 are not included in the totals above.

2 Military sales of $112,195,000 are not included in the totals above.

FIGURE 6-1

Sample of the detailed information available for making market surveys. *Sales Management* magazine has such data available for all counties and major cities in the United States. *(Reproduced with permission of Sales Management Survey of Buying Power. Further reproduction is forbidden.)*

TEXAS

POPULATION—12/31/72

METRO. AREA

County	Total (thousands)	% of U.S.A.	% White	% Male	0-5 Yrs.	6-11 Yrs.	12-17 Yrs.	18-24 Yrs.	25-34 Yrs.	35-49 Yrs.	50-64 Yrs.	65 & Over	House-holds (thousands)	1	2	3	4	5	6 & Over
					% Population by Age Groups									% of Total Households — Number of Persons Per Household					
ABILENE	125.3	.0598	94.3	48.5	9.7	10.4	11.6	14.1	12.7	15.9	14.4	11.2	41.5	18.2	33.4	16.9	15.7	8.7	7.1
Callahan	7.4	.0035	99.9	48.2	6.5	8.1	11.6	10.1	8.2	15.8	18.2	21.5	2.8	22.3	38.8	12.9	12.1	7.5	6.4
Jones	15.9	.0076	93.7	47.8	8.2	9.8	10.9	10.3	8.7	14.8	19.1	18.2	5.9	21.9	37.4	14.5	12.5	7.4	6.3
Taylor	102.0	.0487	93.9	48.6	10.1	10.6	11.7	15.0	13.7	16.1	13.4	9.4	32.8	17.2	32.1	17.7	16.6	9.1	7.3
AMARILLO	145.1	.0693	94.7	48.5	10.3	11.0	12.2	13.5	13.2	17.7	14.0	8.1	49.2	17.6	30.4	17.9	17.7	9.3	7.1
Potter	85.5	.0408	91.5	47.9	10.8	10.7	11.6	12.4	12.4	16.6	15.3	10.2	30.6	22.3	31.6	16.4	14.3	8.2	7.2
Randall	59.6	.0285	99.3	49.3	9.5	11.5	13.0	15.1	14.3	19.5	12.1	5.0	18.6	10.1	28.1	20.5	23.3	11.2	6.8
AUSTIN	366.8	.1752	88.4	49.5	10.6	10.3	10.6	17.9	16.5	15.2	11.7	7.2	114.5	17.7	31.7	17.8	16.6	8.2	8.0
Hays	30.7	.0147	94.8	49.6	10.3	9.3	9.8	26.4	13.7	12.2	10.3	8.0	8.2	15.2	32.4	16.6	16.2	8.0	11.6
Travis	336.1	.1605	87.9	49.6	10.6	10.3	10.7	17.1	16.7	15.6	11.8	7.2	106.3	17.8	31.8	17.9	16.6	8.2	7.7
BEAUMONT-PORT ARTHUR-ORANGE	352.0	.1681	78.9	48.7	10.0	11.3	13.0	12.6	12.0	17.5	15.1	8.5	112.9	15.7	29.4	18.1	17.0	10.0	9.8
Hardin	30.2	.0144	84.8	48.8	10.8	11.7	13.3	11.3	12.1	16.7	14.3	9.8	9.6	14.6	29.3	17.3	18.5	10.1	10.2
Jefferson	248.8	.1188	74.7	48.4	9.5	10.9	12.8	12.9	11.6	17.6	15.7	9.0	80.9	16.8	30.0	18.0	16.2	9.4	9.6
Orange	73.0	.0349	90.5	49.4	11.0	12.6	13.7	11.9	13.3	18.1	13.2	6.2	22.4	12.4	26.6	18.8	19.5	12.0	10.7

FIGURE 6-2

Another sample of detailed information available for making market surveys. *(Reproduced with permission of Sales Management Survey of Buying Power. Further reproduction is forbidden.)*

have reports covering special market areas, which in many instances may be procured.

READJUSTING THE PROJECTED INCOME STATEMENT TO REFLECT RESULTS OF THE MARKET SURVEY

It will be recalled that in Chapter 5 we constructed a projected income statement based upon average firm statistics and the desired profit. Our chief objective there was to find what volume of sales was necessary to produce the desired profit. In that process we found that $125,000 of sales was required if the small firm planner had the average merchandise turnover, average markup, and profits as a percentage of sales, in order to achieve the desired profit of $15,000.

If our market survey now shows that we can reasonably expect a sales volume of $200,000, for example, we can refine that projected income statement to reflect this sales volume; thus, we can convert that statement into a budgeted income statement for the first year of operation. This can be done by applying the same standard statistics to the newly determined expected sales volume. In Chapter 5 we found those statistics to show profits as 12 percent of sales, merchandise turnover four times per year, and markups as 35 percent of sales. With the increased sales volume, we would naturally expect the profits to exceed the $15,000 previously planned for. As we apply these figures against the new sales volume, the profit becomes $24,000 (12 percent of $200,000), gross margin becomes $70,000 (35 percent of $200,000), cost of goods sold becomes $130,000 ($200,000 less $70,000), and average inventory increases to $32,500 ($130,000 divided by turnover of four times per year). Operating expenses will increase from the $28,750 for a volume of $125,000 to $46,000, the difference between a gross margin of $70,000 and a net profit of $24,000. Individual expenses will increase at the same percentages of the increased sales volume.

To clarify this process, we can compare the projected income statement from Chapter 5 with the refined budgeted income statement, which now reflects the results of the market survey. This comparison is shown in adjacent columns in Table 6-1.

The right column, based on a reasonable sales forecast of $200,000, becomes the basis of all budgeting for the new firm. It is now appropriate to detail each operating expense in dollar amounts, based on industry statistics showing what percentage of sales should be spent on each operating expense. Reference to our basic sources of statistics, cited in Chapter 5, may be necessary. These will tell us the percentage of sales that should be spent on rent, employee salaries, average owner salaries, bad-debts expense, depreciation, advertising, and miscellaneous expenses. Precise expense accounts will, of course, vary with the particular type of business being planned. We know now from our budgeted income statement that a total of $46,000 is appropriate for total operating expenses. We must divide this total into the individual expense accounts that make up this total.

TABLE 6-1
JONES HARDWARE COMPANY
Comparison of Projected and Budgeted
Income Statements Which Reflects Market Survey

	Projected statement based on income needs to make desired profit	Budgeted statement based on sales volume as per market survey
Sales		
Cost of goods sold:	$125,000.00	$200,000.00
Beginning inventory, Jan. 1	20,312.50	32,500.00
Plus purchases during year	81,250.00	130,000.00
Goods available for sale	$101,562.50	$162,500.00
Less ending inventory, Dec. 31	20,312.50	32,500.00
Cost of goods sold	$ 81,250.00	$130,000.00
Gross margin	$ 43,750.00	$ 70,000.00
Operating expenses (total)	28,750.00	46,000.00
Net profit from operations	$ 15,000.00	$ 24,000.00

DETAILING THE OPERATING EXPENSES

Our budgeted income statement was based on an average markup of 35 percent, which provided the gross margin of $70,000. Our net profit from operations was 12 percent of sales, or $24,000. The difference between these two amounts, $46,000, is listed on the statement as operating expenses. This means that 23 percent of sales (this $46,000) must cover all our operating expenses if we are to arrive at the profits of $24,000 as planned.

The same statistical sources used in Chapter 5 will provide typical break-downs of operating expenses for our type of business. Modest variations will be found, depending upon the precise type or size of the store under consideration.

A typical set of operating expenses, expressed as a percentage of sales, for an average hardware store can be as follows:

Rent, 4 percent
Employee salaries, 8 percent
Advertising, 1 percent
Bad debts, 1 percent
Delivery expense, 2 percent
Depreciation, 1 percent
Supplies, 1 percent
Miscellaneous expenses, 5 percent

These expenses total 23 percent of sales, as per our budgeted income statement. This is not the normal case. All new planners must study their expense structures to ascertain the appropriateness of the individual expenses to their particular firms. Perhaps in our case delivery service is not contemplated.

Perhaps the owner plans a greater expense for employee salaries. The important thing in planning in this case is that the total operating expenses not exceed 23 percent of sales if the firm is to stay on schedule, as per the budgeted income statement.

If we assume that the above percentages are acceptable to our planning for the Jones Hardware Company, we then convert the percentages into dollar amounts. These would be as follows:

Rent, $8,000
Employee salaries, $16,000
Advertising, $2,000
Bad debts, $2,000
Delivery expense, $4,000
Depreciation, $2,000
Supplies, $2,000
Miscellaneous expenses, $10,000

Since the generous amount left for miscellaneous expenses may seem excessive to the uninitiated, we should emphasize here that there are always unanticipated expenses in any business. It is usually wise to abide by the suggestions of standard statistics in this regard.

We have now examined every detail in planning income, margins, inventories, and expenses for the new firm. The complete budgeted income statement

TABLE 6-2
JONES HARDWARE COMPANY
Budgeted Income Statement
First Year of Operations

Net sales		$200,000
Cost of goods sold:		
Beginning inventory, January 1	$ 32,500	
Purchases	130,000	
Goods available for sale	$162,500	
Ending inventory, December 31	32,500	
Cost of goods sold		130,000
Gross margin		$ 70,000
Operating expenses:		
Rent	$ 8,000	
Employee salaries	16,000	
Advertising	2,000	
Bad-debts expense	2,000	
Delivery expense	4,000	
Depreciation	2,000	
Supplies	2,000	
Miscellaneous expenses	10,000	
Total operating expenses		46,000
Net profit from operations		$ 24,000

can now serve as a schedule against which to check operations each month or at other periods. Conformance to that schedule will ensure that the planned results will become fact. That finalized budgeted income statement will be as shown in Table 6-2.

As we take a look back at what we have accomplished in our planning to this point, we will recall that we planned to have a profit expectancy of $15,000 on our projected income statement to cover the owner's time and return on the investment. Because our market survey showed a higher than minimum sales volume attainable, we now have a planned profit of $24,000 on our budgeted income statement. It is always good news in planning to find that we can achieve more than planned minimums of sales and profits.

But even in our continuing study for Mr. Jones we should not assume that he will become rich overnight. That $24,000 net profit from operations represents profits before federal income taxes are applied. If he has incorporated the business, his federal income taxes will be less at most levels of profits. If he is operating as a proprietorship, his federal income taxes will be higher at most levels of profits. Possible surtaxes may be in effect in the first year of operation as well. The matter of legal forms of organization and applicable income taxes will be further explored in Chapter 7.

We can be satisfied with our planning since we have found that our desired profit is more than attainable. Our sales volume seems reachable with good merchandising. With good management we should achieve our objectives.

Our attention can now turn to the next step in planning—providing a financial structure for the firm. This will be covered in Chapters 7, 8, and 9.

QUESTIONS FOR CLASS DISCUSSION

1 What is a market survey? What is its objective?
2 What kinds of firms should make especially thorough market surveys? Why?
3 What is a parasite firm?
4 How can inaccessibility limit a market area? Give examples.
5 Why is a study of population characteristics important in making a good market survey?
6 Do you agree that the urban small firm gets business from a wider area than its neighborhood residents? Explain.
7 How can new firm planners find the total purchases in their counties for a particular line of goods?
8 Compare telephone surveys, mail surveys, and personal interviews for cost, coverage, and effectiveness.
9 What services does *Sales Management* magazine provide for new firm planners and for established retail firms?
10 Do you think a professional market survey is worth $1,000? What advantages would such a report have, even if it shows that the planned firm should not be established?
11 Do you feel competent to make a market survey now?
12 How would you compare the projected income statement prepared in Chapter 5 with the budgeted income statement which is prepared after the results of the market survey are known?

PROJECTS FOR HOME ASSIGNMENT AND/OR CLASS DISCUSSION

1 Explain how you would proceed if you planned to make your own market survey for a new independent grocery in your hometown.
2 Prepare sample questions you would include in a telephone survey, a mailing survey, and a personal interview. Explain how they would differ.
3 See if you or your instructor can obtain a census tract and/or a trading area map of the local town or district. Study it and determine the key items revealed on each.

CONTINUING PROBLEM:
The Kollege Klothes Shop

PART 6: MEASURING SALES POTENTIAL

Our next step is to measure the sales potential for our clothes shop in the specific market we plan to serve. This involes a detailed survey of the area and the people we plan to have as customers for the shop. Again, this research involves much study and collection of data about that market. We could hire marketing experts to do the job, but with conscientious application of the techniques studied in this chapter, we should be able to do the job ourselves. Again, we have done that work for you. Following is a summary of our data sources, information gathered, and a sales estimate based upon that data after studying it closely.

Condensed Research Figures

We studied all the information we could find. We reviewed census tracts, aerial views, maps of trading areas, the United States Census, *Sales Management's* special annual issue on buying power, the *Census of Business,* both national and state, data from the Retail Clothiers Association, and reports from state and local chambers of commerce. We clearly defined our market area and found we could expect business from outside the immediate area as well as from local residents. We found a seasonal factor in the college population of our town because college students are fewer during the summer and vacation periods than during the regular school year. We studied the buying habits of the population, we conducted surveys of all three types in the community, and learned product preferences in our line of merchandise. We found that the average college student spends $300 to $400 per school year for new clothing. Jeans proved a most popular product.

We found that the community we plan to serve has a population of 85,000. Average income of the 1,000 families plus college students is above the national average. There are now four independent clothes shops, plus one large and one small department store which also sell college clothes in our market. Sales of college clothes average $1,500,000 in the market with an almost even division of this total among the six competitors.

Because of the special advantages of the location on which we have a nonbinding option, Jones and Gomez feel assured that they could develop at least 15 percent more than the average sales total. If the present $1,500,000 of sales was divided by seven firms (we would become the seventh), the average would be approximately $214,000 each. We concluded that because of our location, special lines, excellent parking, and personnel plans to hire college students, we could have a sales potential of $250,000. It is always good news to find that the market holds a better than minimum sales potential. If it is less than required on the projected income statement, other decisions will have to be made about continuing plans for the firm.

Assignment for Part 6

Using the sales figure derived from the market survey, prepare a budgeted income statement for the new firm. This time we will start with the sales figure and then apply the same percentages we used for the projected income statement before. We will, accordingly, expect a higher profit, more expense allowances, and a larger inventory to be necessary. These are all results of the fact that our sales volume expected now exceeds that which we found necessary to support our planned profit on the projected income statement.

We must detail the operating expenses now, since this statement will become the guide for all future decisions. Use the following percentages of sales, which we have gathered from industry statistics, for detailed expenses:

Rent, 5 percent
Supplies, 2 percent
Employee salaries, 10 percent
Utilities, 2 percent
Depreciation, 1 percent
Repairs and maintenance, 1 percent
Advertising, 3 percent
Delivery expense, 2 percent
Insurance and taxes, 1 percent
Miscellaneous expenses, 3 percent

Your instructor will have a completed budgeted income statement based on these data.

REFERENCES FOR FURTHER READING

Lasser, J. K., *How to Run a Small Business,* 4th ed., McGraw-Hill Book Company, New York, 1974, chap. 3.

Macfarlane, William N., *Principles of Small Business,* McGraw-Hill Book Company, New York, 1977, chap. 17.

"Marketing Planning Guidelines," Small Business Administration Pamphlet No. MA194.

PART THREE

FINANCING THE NEW FIRM

CHOOSING A LEGAL
FORM OF ORGANIZATION

What is all this stuff about legal forms of organization? All corporations are big business. When I look at a business I can't tell if it is a proprietorship, a partnership, or a corporation.

The Late Learner

New firm planners should do some serious thinking about the legal form chosen for their new endeavor. This means determining what will be *the status of the business in the eyes of the law.* Very important consequences are at stake.

More than 99 percent of the more than 11 million firms in the United States are organized legally as (1) single proprietorships, (2) partnerships, or (3) corporations. It is our intention here to evaluate the characteristics, advantages, and disadvantages of these legal forms. Other legal forms, such as joint ventures or investment trusts, are rarely used and need not be considered pertinent to our purposes here.

When confronted with the choice of a single proprietorship, a partnership, or a corporation, many students and small firm planners and operators mistakenly believe that the corporation is intended only for very large firms. All three of these legal forms are available to small firms. Factors other than size affect the choice in a particular case. In all cases, all three forms should be looked at carefully. Some of the factors which will affect the decision include plans for expansion, product or service being sold, needs for raising capital now and in subsequent years, liability characteristics of the planned firm, the proprietor's available investment funds, need for continued life of the firm, alternatives for bringing desired people into the firm, and legal requirements of the particular locality.

We can note that of the total number of business firms in the United States, approximately 70 percent are proprietorships which do about one-third of the total sales volume; approximately 15 percent are partnerships doing about 15 percent of total sales volume; and approximately 15 percent are corporations doing more than 50 percent of the total sales volume in the country. Statistics such as these encourage the erroneous belief that proprietorship is the almost exclusive choice of legal form for small firms. The data do not reveal to the casual observer the reasons why the larger firms have chosen the corporate form. Business prudence should include an understanding of the options.

THE SINGLE PROPRIETORSHIP

By definition, a single proprietorship is a business owned and operated by one person. The owner and the business are synonymous in the eyes of the law. All assets in the firm are owned by the proprietor, subject only to the liabilities incurred in its establishment and operation. The proprietor is solely responsible for its debts, incurs any losses, assumes all its risks, provides all its capital, and provides its total management. The only requirement for its establishment is that the owner obtain any licenses required by the city, county, or state, and start operations.

The simplicity in establishing this legal form of operation has probably accounted for its popularity. The choice, however, may represent an oversight of other factors which would indicate another legal form.

Advantages of the Single Proprietorship

The literature on business asserts that the proprietorship form has several advantages, such as:

1 Simplicity of organization
2 Owner's freedom to make all decisions
3 Owner's enjoyment of all profits
4 Minimum legal restrictions
5 Ease of discontinuance
6 Tax advantages

These *alleged* advantages should be carefully reviewed to distinguish between mere characteristics of this form and true management advantages.

1   Simplicity of Organization   If the new firm owners choose a legal form of organization only because of its simplicity, they are probably demonstrating that they lack overall business competence and a thorough knowledge of legal forms, and that they are the type of owners who always look for the easiest way to make decisions. Simplicity of organization is truly a characteristic of the proprietorship, but no inherent management advantages are to be noted because of this simplicity.

2 and 3   Owner's Freedom to Make All Decisions and Enjoy All Profits   To allege that one advantage of the proprietorship is that the owner is free to make all the decisions and to receive all the profits completely ignores the facts of a closed corporation (explained later in this chapter). If these same business people have their businesses incorporated for 100 shares of common stock and are required by their states to have three stockholders, they can each give 1 share to their spouses, 1 share to a son or daughter, and retain 98 shares in their name. Who then makes all the decisions? Who then receives all the profits? Surely the owner has the same authority as if the firm were a proprietorship. So again, these alleged advantages become merely nonexclusive characteristics of a proprietorship

4   Minimum Legal Restrictions   This factor, which means that there are fewer reports to be filed with government agencies, no capital stock taxes to be paid, and no charter restrictions on operations, can be an advantage from the standpoint of time and expenses involved. Whether or not this advantage would dominate in the final selection remains to be seen after the total business picture has been reviewed.

5   Ease of discontinuance   This is a true characteristic of the proprietorship. To discontinue a proprietorship means essentially closing the front door. When we recognize, however, that sound business firms are not organized with the thought of discontinuing them, we must question whether this is truly an advantage of this particular form. Our concern is not the establishment of casual Mom and Pop type of firms but solid business firms which may start small but have the potential for growth, good profits, and a good future for the owner. These objectives should be kept in mind as we choose our legal form of organization.

6   Tax Advantages   Alleging tax advantages as a bonus of the proprietorship form of legal organization defies the fact that as taxable income increases, the rate on individual income is higher than on corporate taxable income or total taxes on the divided income of a partnership. Total federal income taxes are a prime consideration in the choice of any legal form. The government wants business people to practice tax avoidance rather than tax evasion, and the choice of an appropriate legal form may be of assistance in this regard. Examples of various taxable income levels and the applicable federal income taxes for the different legal forms of organization are presented in a later section of this chapter.

Disadvantages of the Single Proprietorship

The literature describes the various disadvantages of the proprietorship as follows:

1 Owner's possible lack of ability and experience
2 Limited opportunity for employees
3 Difficulty in raising capital
4 Limited life of the firm
5 Unlimited liability of proprietor

A brief evaluation of these disadvantages follows:

1   The Owner's Lack of Ability and Experience   The owner may truly lack these qualifications. It is to guard against this possibility that preownership experience is recommended for those planning to own their own firms. Sound college courses in management are available to college students. Participation in management consulting courses can be tremendously helpful. Those without formal study in management can learn much from working for other firms in the same line of business. Testing one's own competence by studying good business texts should be a prelude to investing in and opening a new firm. Only when owners feel that they know a great deal about the particular firm they propose should they proceed. It should be pointed out, however, that this flaw in the owner's capability does not apply in only one legal form of organization. Lack of ability and experience can ruin a partnership or a corporation just as easily as it can a proprietorship.

2   Limited Opportunity for Employees   This point has been overdone as a disadvantage of the proprietorship. Aggressive, capable employees may indeed desire rewards faster than the firm can provide them. You can promote some people only so far, though, and the best thing you can do for them sometimes is to promote them out the front door. But let us realize that if the same firm is a partnership or a small firm corporation, the employees' environment, potential rewards, and promotions are the same. Small firms generally face the problem of keeping good employees, but large firms face this problem as well. Also, it is probably a refreshing thought in this regard to realize that small firms have not fully utilized profit sharing, bonuses, or a share in the ownership of the firm in order to keep key people on the payroll. Possibilities of stock ownership in a corporation add to these benefits. Good employees are a firm's most valuable asset. The problem of obtaining and keeping them is not solved merely through the choice of a legal form. Personnel policies are discussed in Chapter 21.

3   Difficulty in Raising Capital   This can be a problem. On the average, two people have more capital than one. It follows that, on the average, two people would have more to invest in providing the capital needs of a new small business. Not all firms have this problem, however. If it does exist and the planner does not wish to share ownership of the firm, this would restrict the alternatives in raising adequate capital. When the planner has seriously faced the problem of building a sound financial structure for the firm, as we will do in Chapters 8 and 9, its investment needs can be compared with available funds, and a decision can be made. If the assets are adequate, the planner will have no disadvantage due merely to the difficulty in raising capital.

4 Limited Life of the Firm Discussions of this feature of legal forms are usually restricted to the partnership form of organization, but it also applies to proprietorships. What is involved is the matter of legal discontinuance of the firm. Untimely, unanticipated, or unplanned removal of the proprietor from operation of the business may have ramifications for creditors of the firm. Restrictions on credit granted may be founded in this matter of limited life. An owner's record for stability, honesty, and capability can largely overcome this practical problem, when these are unknown, as in the case of a new firm, the possibility of a firm's limited life may be a disadvantage.

5 Unlimited Liability By far the greatest disadvantage of the proprietorship is its inescapable feature of *unlimited liability*. This disadvantage is one that applies directly to the owners. It means that, even though they believe that they have invested only part of their total capital in the business, they are liable to the full extent of their total assets for the liabilities of the firm. A damaging lawsuit lost, a judgment for injuries suffered by a customer on the premises, or a serious accident involving injuries to outside persons are some of the things that can create liabilities far beyond anything anticipated when the firm was planned. It is this feature of the proprietorship that causes many owners, when aware of unlimited liability, to put their homes in their spouses' names in order to keep the home from being available to pay such claims. The present divorce rate in our country makes this a doubtful procedure in many cases. The owner's savings accounts, investments, and any other assets are liable in such suits. As we noted earlier when discussing the proprietorship legal form, the owner and the business are synonymous, and all assets, not just those the owner thinks are invested in the firm, are liable to pay its debts. Insurance protection can be provided, of course. This matter will be discussed in Chapter 20.

THE PARTNERSHIP

A partnership is usually defined as an association of two or more persons to carry on as co-owners of a business for profit. Partnerships are based upon a partnership agreement, also known as the articles of co-partnership. The partnership agreement should always be reduced to writing, even though this is not a legal requirement. It should cover all areas of possible disagreement among the partners. It should define the authority and the rights and duties of each partner, and the limits to such authority. It should include an agreement on how profits and losses are to be divided; their treatment need not be the same. In the absence of an agreement to the contrary, profits and losses are divided equally among all partners. Partners may make special arrangements to pay members of the firm for services rendered, interest on capital investment, time spent, or advance drawings before the balance of profits is to be divided in an agreed ratio.

Many successful partnership firms have been dissolved because of serious disagreements between original partners that were not anticipated in the partnership agreement. Thoroughness in this matter cannot be overemphasized.

Advantages of the Partnership

The following advantages of the partnership form of organization are usually cited in business books.

1 Ease of organization
2 Combined talents, judgment, and skills
3 Larger capital available to the firm
4 Maximization of personal interest in the firm
5 Definite legal status of the firm
6 Tax advantages

With the benefit of our previous discussion of the proprietorship, we can quickly evaluate these alleged advantages. Ease of organization should not be a management consideration in starting a new firm. Greater financial potential is true only in average terms; personal interest of partners should be no greater than if each had stock in a corporate form of organization; and definite legal status can be important to creditors. In most income brackets, a group of partners would pay less total income tax than the owner(s) would under either of the other chief legal forms. This is because they divide the profits and each pays individual rates on his or her share.

As compared with the proprietorship, then, advantages of potential substance seem to be greater capital available, generally less income tax on the same net profits, and a positive legal status. Compared with the corporation, only the tax consideration would remain as a potential advantage.

Disadvantages of the Partnership

The partnership has some very real disadvantages, which can be serious to well-meaning people who start their firms in good faith. Four disadvantages merit brief discussion:

1 Unlimited liability
2 Limited life
3 Divided authority
4 Danger of disagreement

1 Unlimited Liability   Just as this condition applied to the proprietorship, it is even more serious in the partnership. Not only is a partner liable for debts he or she contracts for the firm, but a partner is also responsible to the full extent of his or her resources for debts contracted by the other partners.

2 Limited Life   Any change whatsoever in the list of general partners automatically ends the life of the existing partnership, and a new legal entity must be created by the remaining partners. Admission of a new partner, death of an existing partner, and withdrawal of any general partner are cases in point. Restatement of all assets and readmission of all liabilities and individual capital accounts are part of the process. This is also known as *mandatory dissolution.*

3 Divided Authority   It is one thing for a good factory manager and a good sales person to combine their talents in a partnership. Each can have clearly defined areas of operation. Other areas, however, such as policy for the total firm, financing plans, personnel management, and ideas on expansion, can create divided authority and delay decisions for the firm. Some activities always seem to provide possibilities for conflicting authority.

4 Danger of Disagreement   The ever-present possibility of a disagreement between the partners can be extremely serious. Even though a very thorough partnership agreement is written, clauses are subject to various interpretations, some partners may willfully exceed clearly defined authority, and discontent can develop between the partners. Only honest and capable people having great mutual respect should engage in partnerships.

Types of Partners

Partnerships are usually either *general partnerships* or *limited partnerships.* A general partnership is one in which each partner carries the unlimited liability for the firm's debts. A limited partnership is one in which some partners may have their liability limited to the extent of their investment. A firm must have at least one general partner who carries the unlimited liability obligation. Withdrawal of a limited partner does not dissolve the partnership as withdrawal of a general partner will do. Limited partnership agreements must usually be filed with a government official. Without notice as to the acceptance of a limited partner, all partners are considered to be general.

There are many other special types of partners which new firm planners may wish to investigate. *Secret partners* are those who plan an active role in the business but are not identified to the public as partners. *Silent partners* are those who are not active in operations but share in the profits. *Dormant partners* are those not active and not known to the public. *Nominal partners* are really not partners at all but allow the public to think they are by their actions and words.

Special circumstances may make it necessary to choose these types of partners, but their use is not normally recommended. The limited partnership, on the other hand, enables many new firm planners to obtain capital which might otherwise not have been available. In most of the cases which we have reviewed, the corporate form of organization would have served everyone's purpose in a superior manner.

THE CORPORATION

Just as the problems of size and need for acquiring more capital motivated the creation of the partnership rather than the proprietorship, they also motivated the next step to the modern corporation as a legal form of organization. The second step was also made necessary by the problems of unlimited liability and limited life that characterized the partnership. The need of a developing industrial world was for a legal form of organization that would provide limited liability for owners and perpetual life for the business firm. Accordingly, in 1819 in the famous Dartmouth College case, Justice John Marshall gave the first legal recognition to a new type of business organization, which was to become known as the corporation. He defined it as "an artificial being, invisible, intangible, and existing only in contemplation of law." Its ownership would be divided into shares of stock.

Though the corporate form of organization originated in this way, it was never meant to be used only by giant firms. Its advantages and disadvantages have always been equally available to small firms as well.

How to Organize a Corporation

Those desiring to form a private corporation must file an application with their State Corporation Commissioner (or other appropriate official) and include a statement of the proposed bylaws (rules of operation) of the proposed corporation. The application must specify the types and amount of stock to be authorized for sale by the corporation. A small fee is charged for charter issuance. The charter is not necessarily issued in the state of chief operations. States compete for such business by offering lower capital stock taxes and other incentives. The recent trend is toward more strict and more uniform charter requirements. A *foreign corporation* is one chartered in a state other than its state of major business. An *alien corporation* is one chartered in a foreign county. In the past all states required that a new corporation should have at least three stockholders, but in recent years many states have required only one stockholder. Although the applicants for a new charter may complete the entire process themselves, states often recommend that they would be wise to employ an attorney. A friendly attorney will usually handle the charter procurement for a small firm for a fee of from $250 to $500, including a minor fee charged by the state.

Types of Corporation Stock

Most small firms have only one issue of stock. This is *common stock,* which is often given a par value of $100 per share. Any dollar amount may be designated as par value or common stock may have no par value. The market price of common stock will reflect the earnings of the firm. As business firms grow, they may issue *preferred stock.* Preferred stock is so called because it normally gives up the right to vote in exchange for a priority of dividends. Preferred stock also carries priority in case of dissolution. Stated preferred stock dividends—such as 8 percent preferred—must receive its dividends before any dividends may be declared on the common stock. *Cumulative preferred* means that the preferred stock must receive its dividends for any years in which no dividends were paid before the common may receive dividends. *Participating preferred* means that the preferred must share in any further dividends after the common has received a specified maximum dividend. Preferred stock's priority in case of dissolution is of little satisfaction in most instances since firms go broke because they can't pay their creditors; hence, liquidation usually leaves little for the stockholders.

Advantages of the Corporation

After discussing the operation of the other forms of organization, we can find little to argue with in the claimed advantages of the corporation. These are:

1 Limited liability to stockholders
2 Perpetual life
3 Ease of transferring ownership
4 Ease of expansion
5 Applicability to all sizes of firms

1 Limited Liability to Stockholders Rather than risk their entire assets to the debts of the business, the new firm owners or investors in stock buy shares at a given price, and this investment is the total liability to which they can be subjected. Only those assets which a small firm planner turns over to the firm in exchange for shares become corporate property. Total corporate liability is the assets listed on its balance sheet. No longer need the owners of a small corporation fear the unexpected judgment against them as a threat to their other assets.

2 Perpetual Life If all the stockholders of a given corporation died on the same day, the business would go on as a legal entity. Shares would pass to the heirs of the original owners of the stock and they would inherit a going concern.

3 Ease of Transferring Ownership Any stockholders can sell their shares when they want to. Formal transfer of stock certificate titles is normally handled by a fiduciary agent, usually a bank, that will issue a new certificate in the name of the new owner of the shares. Operations of the company are not affected by this transfer.

4   Ease of Expansion of the Company   Although additional stock sale is not the only way to raise capital for expansion, it is usually the easiest way.. Many corporations, large and small, will receive permission from their state officials to sell more stock than originally planned for sale. The balance is held as "authorized but not issued" stock. It should appear on the balance sheet in the net worth section for informational purposes. If all authorized stock has been sold, a corporation may request permission to sell additional stock when an expansion is contemplated.

5   Applicability to Both Large and Small Firms   A true advantage of the corporate legal form is its versatility. In many states a corporation may be formed for as little as $500 of stock. Large corporations issue millions of dollars worth of stock. Regulations and charter requirements are the same for both.

Other advantages often claimed for the corporation, such as permitting employee profit sharing and encouraging efficiency in management, must be termed as possible but not exclusive characteristics. Profit sharing is possible other than through stock in any legal form of organization. Efficiency in management is not guaranteed to any firm because of its legal form. This is the responsibility of management in all cases.

Disadvantages of the Corporation

The chief disadvantages are:

1 Government regulation
2 Expense of organization
3 Capital stock tax

1   Government Regulation   All good things demand some sacrifice. In the case of the corporation, the chief sacrifice is the necessary acceptance of government regulation. This begins with the necessity of obtaining a charter from the home state of the corporation. This need not be the state in which operations are founded. For small firms operating in only one state, it is recommended that the charter be obtained in that state. The activities of the corporation will be restricted to those specified in the charter. For instance, a small firm authorized to engage in the men's clothing business cannot open a grocery store unless the terms of the charter are broad enough and/or so specify. The sometimes cited disadvantage of impersonal management of a corporation need not apply to small firms using the advantages of the corporate form of legal organization.

2   Expense of Organization   There is an expense in organizing a corporation. Although some states maintain that an attorney is not needed, the use of an attorney is recommended when applying for a charter. Total expenses for this process range from as low as $250 to $500 in most cases. Requirements for the charter include specifying the business activity in which the firm will engage, types of stock it desires to issue, and quantities of each to be authorized.

3   Capital Stock Tax   The state in which the firm is incorporated will levy an annual capital stock tax of a few cents per share on outstanding shares.

MAKING A DECISION ON LEGAL FORMS FOR THE NEW FIRM

How, then, will the new planners decide upon their legal form of organization? As previously mentioned, they will consider the importance of unlimited liability, the protections available through public liability insurance, their expansion plans, the nature of the product, dangers inherent in the service or product, and the relative incidence of risks in normal operations which might provoke lawsuits and judgments against them. Through the potential of pre-ferred stock, a corporation can attract investors who prefer dividends to increased market price. Preferred stock does not normally carry voting power, and the planner is able to keep control of the company by retaining 51 percent of the voting common stock. It is the author's view that far too many small firms have neglected the use of the corporate form. Its protections and potentials should be carefully considered by any new firms which plan to grow large and profitable.

FEDERAL INCOME TAXES AND LEGAL FORMS OF ORGANIZATION

Students today have heard that tax considerations are an important part of most business transactions. The choice of a legal form of organization can be one of those decisions with significant tax consequences. Existing small firm owners and prospective owners of new small firms should always take time to review the tax laws currently in effect as they apply to their business. College students will develop additional business prowess with such study.

There is no one form of legal organization that can claim the best advantages in all instances or at all levels of net taxable income. In fact, one of the results of our newest tax laws was to minimize tax differences among those alternatives. The income tax on a business firm is affected by the amount and distribution of net taxable income. All the legal forms of organization we have studied have progressive rates of income tax—meaning higher tax rates apply as the income reaches higher dollar levels.

Because state and local taxes vary so widely around the country, we can concentrate here only on the new *federal* income tax laws, parts of which went into effect on October 1, 1981. The effective date for other portions was January 1, 1982. Highlights of this tax act of 1981 as they affect small firms are as follows:

TABLE 7-1 OUR NEWEST PROGRESSIVE FEDERAL INCOME TAXES

Tax Rates On Proprietorships, Partnerships and Corporations For Current Years and Future Year Reductions

Taxable Income	Proprietorships (Joint Returns) New Law				Partnerships
	1981	1982	1983	1984	
	%	%	%	%	Tax rates stay
0 to $3,400	0	0	0	0	the same but
$3,400 to $5,500	14	12	11	11	each partner
$5,500 to $7,600	16	14	13	12	pays tax only
$7,600 to $11,900	18	16	15	14	on his or her
$11,900 to $16,000	21	19	17	16	share of firm's
$16,000 to $20,200	24	22	19	18	profit and loss
$20,200 to $24,600	28	25	23	22	sharing ratio
$24,600 to $29,900	32	29	26	25	
$29,900 to $35,200	37	33	30	28	
$35,200 to $45,800	43	39	35	33	
$45,800 to $60,000	49	44	40	38	
$60,000 to $85,600	54	49	44	42	
$85,600 to $109,400	59	50	48	45	
$109,400 to $162,400	64	50	50	49	
$162,400 to $215,400	68	50	50	50	
$215,400 and over	70	50	50	50	

Corporations	1981	1982	1983 and after
	17%	16%	15%
$0-25,000			
$25-50,000	20	19	18
$50-75,000	30	30	30
$75-100,000	40	40	40
over 100,000	46	46	46

The corporation can also be taxed on an unreasonable accumulation of earnings.

Source: Economic Recovery Tax Act of 1981.

The Economic Recovery Tax Act of 1981

This current set of tax laws was enacted under President Reagan's leadership with the help of conservative Democrats who assisted the President's Republican colleagues. It was finally passed by Congress and signed by the President in August 1981. It provides the largest reduction in income taxes the country has ever known. It reflects an ever growing clamor from the small business area and others for tax relief and less regulation. Such demands were the outstanding recommendations which came out of the White House Conference on Small Business held in January 1980. Tax relief was a large issue in the presidential election of 1980. In addition to lower federal income taxes, the new act also contains eased depreciation allowances, lower estate taxes, lower rates on investment income, lower capital gains taxes, and inventory valuation method changes—all of which are designed to assist business firms to retain earnings for firm expansion and working capital demands.

By far the most important feature of our new tax laws is the lowering of taxes on individuals. Because more than 80 percent of all small firms in the country still operate as proprietorships which pay these individual rates, it is clear that small business is one of the chief beneficiaries of the reduced rates.

The income tax brackets and tax rates for individuals under the current law in 1982 vary from zero tax on the first $3,400 of net taxable income to 12 percent on net income between $3,400 and $5,500 to 50 percent on net taxable income exceeding $85,600. The rates in effect until recently varied from zero tax on the first $2,300 of net taxable income to as high as 70 percent on income over $100,000. See Table 7-1 for a condensed summary of present rates and planned future reductions for all the major forms of legal organization.

Corporations, too, have various income tax brackets. The only changes made for corporations in the current tax act provide for lowering the tax on the first $25,000 and the second $25,000 of net taxable income. Corporations paid the following rates in 1982:

16% on the first $25,000 of net taxable profits
19% on the second $25,000
30% on the third $25,000
40% on the fourth $25,000
46% on all net taxable income over $100,000

TABLE 7-2. SAMPLES OF TOTAL FEDERAL INCOME TAXES FOR 1982 ON IDENTICAL NET TAXABLE INCOME BY DIFFERENT LEGAL FORMS OF ORGANIZATION

Net taxable income	Tax on Proprietorships (joint return)	Tax on two equal partners (joint returns)	Tax on corporation (owner salaries may or may not be deducted)
$20,200	$2,937	$1,892	$3,232
$35,200	$7,323	$4,730	$5,938
$60,000	$17,705	$11,214	$11,750

Because most small firms have net profits of less than $100,000 per year, it is clear that small firms will benefit most from these new rates. See Table 7-1 for further corporation tax reductions planned.

Table 7-2 illustrates net federal income taxes for different legal forms of organization in three net taxable income brackets.

Students should clearly understand that we are talking about tax rates on *net taxable income* and what that term means. Net taxable income is the remaining income after all legitimate deductions have been taken. Charitable, educational and dependent deductions, for examples, are subtracted from gross income to arrive at net taxable income.

Students should also be reminded of one very important difference between legal forms of organization in computing the taxable income of the firm. In proprietorships and partnerships any withdrawals of cash by the owners are considered as withdrawals of capital for tax purposes, even though the owners may consider them as regular salaries for themselves. If they have charged such "salaries" to an expense account, their income tax covers the remaining profit on the firm's income statement plus the withdrawals they have made. Proprietorship and partnership firms are not taxable units in themselves but their income is paid at individual rates by the owners. The owners and the firm are one unit at law.

This is quite different from the corporation. As we have seen, the corporation is an artificial being (person) at law. It is, therefore, recognized as a separate unit for tax purposes. Small firm owners who operate as corporations can charge reasonable salaries to the business and these become operating expenses of the firm. Such salaries are accordingly deducted before arriving at net taxable income for the corporation. It is the remaining corporate net income that is taxed to the corporation at the rates we have just reviewed. The owner(s) file separate individual tax returns on salaries withdrawn.

It is this situation that gives rise to the much quoted and often misunderstood "double taxation" that is attributed to the corporation. The owners pay personal income taxes on their salaries, which are a deductible expense to the corporation. They also pay individual tax rates on any dividends declared on their shares of stock in the corporation which they own. Dividends paid by a corporation are not a deductible expense to the corporation but are considered a distribution of accumulated earnings.

SUBCHAPTER S CORPORATIONS

In an early attempt to aid small business, Congress created Subchapter S corporations in 1958. They were designed to give small firms the operating advantages of the corporate form of organization without incurring double taxation. Shareholders can divide the corporate net taxable income in their own profit and loss sharing ratio and pay only individual tax rates by each shareholder. No corporation taxes are thus incurred. Originally, the law specified that such corporations could not have more than 10 stockholders, all must be U.S. citizens or resident aliens, receive at least 20 percent of their income from operations in the United States, and not more than 20 percent of their income from investments. Over the years requirements have gradually changed.

The new tax act increases the number of shareholders to a possible 25 and provides that a "qualified Subchapter S Trust" may hold stock in the corporation if its sole income beneficiary is a disabled citizen or resident alien. Such trusts must distribute all income currently and terminate at the death of the beneficiary. At least 90 percent of the assets of such trusts must be stock in one Subchapter S Corporation. The new rules became effective January 1, 1982.

1244 CORPORATIONS

Congress has also endeavored to aid small business firms to obtain adequate financing by providing some tax relief for those who incur losses from small firm investment. While it is never desirable to invest in a new firm with tax consequences of losses foremost in mind, this recent feature of the law does provide some relief in such cases. It provides for creation of "1244 corporations." When so specified, any losses incurred by investors may be charged against individual income tax on the loser's federal income tax return, rather than the usually lower capital gain loss rates. Such losses are limited to $500,000, as the law was designed to encourage investment only in small firms.

SUMMARY

We have taken a serious look at the makeup and legal aspects of the three major forms of legal organization for business firms. Alleged advantages versus true management advantages of each have been demonstrated. Characteristics versus advantages have been pointed out. We have found that no one legal form has claim to superiority in all cases. Yet it is important for every existing small firm owner and those planning new firms to review seriously the status under the law of the alternative forms they have available.

We have reviewed the encouraging news of the 1981 tax act for small firm owners and others filing only individual federal income returns. Its tax reductions are the largest ever in American business history. The current tax status and future tax reductions planned for all legal forms of organization have been detailed. Particular attention has been directed to the benefits to small firms by making possible more capital retention for firm needs. Hopefully the importance of care in choosing a legal form by studying the details of each has been established.

QUESTIONS FOR CLASS DISCUSSION

1 Why would a small business proprietor ever consent to being a general partner and allow a partner to be a limited partner?
2 Evaluate "ease of discontinuance" as an advantage of the proprietorship form of legal organization.
3 Is the owner of a small corporation as "free to make all the decisions" as a single proprietor? Explain.
4 What are the legal requirements for starting a business as a proprietorship?
5 Is "limited opportunity for employees" an exclusive problem for small firms? How does this problem affect large firms?
6 What does "limited liability" really mean to holders of corporation stock?
7 Can lack of ability and experience in small firm owners be corrected solely by their adopting another legal form of organization for the business?
8 What is a partnership agreement? What should it include?
9 At what level of net taxable income does an American citizen reach the 40 percent federal income tax level? 50 percent? 60 percent?
10 What are the federal income tax rates on corporations?
11 What factors in a business would suggest to you that limited liability should be in effect?
12 How could expansion plans affect the choice of a legal form of organization?
13 How much federal income tax do you think should be paid by a proprietorship which earns $23,500 before taxes? How much does it pay currently?
14 What were the most recent changes in the federal income tax laws for corporations?

PROJECTS FOR HOME ASSIGNMENT AND/OR CLASS DISCUSSION

1 Write a short paper explaining why the author believes that more small firms should be incorporated. Do you agree?
2 Demonstrate in writing your understanding of what the term "unlimited liability" means to owners of small firms.
3 Why was the Subchapter S corporation heralded so much as a great thing for small firms?
4 Compute the federal income tax on a small corporation which made $75,000 net profit last year. Compare your answer with the tax paid on the same profit by a single proprietor.
5 See if you can obtain an actual partnership agreement or a corporate charter. Ask your instructor to review its provisions with the class.

CONTINUING PROBLEM:
The Kollege Klothes Shop

PART 7: CHOOSING A LEGAL FORM OF ORGANIZATION

Before we get into any further details of the planning for our new store, we should take a serious look at what type of legal form of organization we will use. This demands that we take a serious look again at the advantages and disadvantages we have studied of the basic types of legal forms. Do we plan to have a proprietorship, a partnership, or a corporation? Maybe we should become a Subchapter S corporation, because these were particularly created to serve small firms.

It is clear that if Mary Jones and Fernando Gomez are to become equal "partners" they will not have a proprietorship, which is a one-person legal form. But if they mean to become equal "owners" that doesn't necessarily mean they should be a partnership. They could have an arrangement where one is the proprietor and the other is a full-time employee. Or they could incorporate and be equal stockholders. As we make our recommendation we should demonstrate our familiarity with all of the legal forms.

Assignment for Part 7

Write up your recommendation to Jones and Gomez for a legal form for the new firm. Show the main reasons for your recommendation and why you believe it is superior to the choice of other forms of legal organization for this particular business. Check the facts in this chapter. Take a particularly close look at the income tax facts.

REFERENCES FOR FURTHER READING

Corley, Robert N., Robert Black, and O. Lee Reed, *The Legal Environment of Business,* 5th ed., McGraw-Hill Book Company, New York, 1981, chap. 10.

Lasser, J. K., *How to Run a Small Business,* 4th ed., McGraw-Hill Book Company, 1974, chap. 6.

Musselman, Vernon A., and Eugene Hughes, *Introduction to Modern Business,* 8th ed., Prentice-Hall, Inc., Englewood Cliffs, N.J., 1981, chap. 3.

CHAPTER 8

STATEMENT OF ASSETS
TO BE USED

I had no idea how many more assets would be needed to operate this business when I started. Almost all the profits went to buy new assets the first few years. Next time I will know better.

The Late Learner

Every new firm needs various kinds of assets with which to begin operations. Cash assets are needed for working capital; cash funds are needed to invest in accounts receivable; inventories are a large asset which must be purchased. Buildings and land are expensive assets which must be acquired by purchase or rented. Supplies are assets which must be purchased. Prepaid insurance policies must be provided and premiums paid. Store fixtures and equipment, and office furniture and fixtures are other assets which must be provided for the firm. Perhaps delivery trucks need to be purchased.

One of the commonest causes of financial difficulty for a new firm is the owners' failure to look seriously at the total asset requirements of the firm in the planning stage. Many new firms open their doors literally "on a wing and a prayer," only to find that they have not anticipated or provided all the assets needed to start operations properly. This results in the acquisition of needed assets through expensive and dangerous financing or the appropriation of anticipated profits in advance to buy the assets that should have been provided from initial investment capital.

To avoid these dangers, the planner should analyze his or her firm by listing every asset the business will need. The result will be a *statement of assets to be used*. This statement can be compared to the left side (asset side) of a balance sheet.

PROCEDURE FOR DEVELOPING ASSET REQUIREMENTS

When preparing a list of all types of assets you need not take into consideration their cost or how they will be provided. Assume that cost is not a problem at this point. In a later planning step (scc Chapter 9), we will decide how to provide these assets or the services they render. In that process, we can learn much about how the business economy really works as it supplies credit, financial loans, or services under various circumstances.

The important thing at this point is that we list every asset of every kind which the business will need. The new student will recall that assets were defined in Chapter 3 as "things owned." They can be in the form of cash, claims against others, inventories, supplies, buildings, fixtures and equipment, delivery trucks, and prepaid insurance policies. All require investment capital; all are basic assets the new firm will need.

Continuing our example of a newly planned firm from Chapter 6, we have produced a budgeted income statement to serve as a guide to operations for the first year. We must now develop a statement of assets to be used to list all the things (assets) which will be needed to operate the firm at the level indicated on the budgeted income statement.

As we have contemplated the firm's asset needs, let us assume that we have found the following to be essential:

Cash
Funds to carry accounts receivable
Merchandise inventory (the amount here is provided from our budgeted income statement)
Prepaid supplies
Prepaid insurance
Land and buildings
Store fixtures
Office furniture and fixtures
Delivery truck(s)

This listing of assets can be entitled a "Statement of Assets to be Used."

We can now turn our attention to finding a dollar value to attach to each asset and/or to determining how much cash we should have on hand when all noncash assets have been provided. We can find out how much cash will be needed to cover our planned investment in accounts receivable. Market prices can be used to give dollar amounts to our noncash assets. Details for the cash calculations and conservative rules relating to them are as follows:

Cash Requirement for Merchandising Firms: Cash on Hand   How much cash should the firm have on hand? The suggested conservative rule is: *Cash should equal the out-of-pocket operating expenses for the period of one turnover of the merchandise inventory.* This will seem extremely conservative for some types of firms. Unless positive reasons for relaxing the general rule are identified, however, good management demands adherence to it.

How would we find this amount for our planned firm? First we go back to our budgeted income statement (see Chapter 6) and find that total operating expenses for the first year are planned at $46,000. This figure must be divided into out-of-pocket and noncash expenditures. The out-of-pocket expenses are those which are paid in cash by the firm in the form of checks written or petty cash expenditures. Noncash expenditures are those which are recorded in the expenses but do not result in the firm's actually giving up cash. Examples of this are depreciation expenses on buildings, store equipment, or office furniture and fixtures.

If $10,000 of the total year expenses of $46,000 represents noncash expenditures, the balance of $36,000 is the total of out-of-pocket expenses for the first year. This amount represents $3,000 per month ($36,000 divided by 12). Our merchandise turnover is 4 times per year, or once every 3 months. We must therefore provide 3 months of out-of-pocket expenses as our cash requirement under our rule. Three times $3,000 is $9,000, which is our cash requirement for opening day.

The calculation of the cash requirement may be more easily understood this way. Merely divide the annual out-of-pocket expenses by the merchandise turnover. Thus, in our example here, the annual out-of-pocket expenses are $36,000. Divide this total by the merchandise turnover of 4 and we get the same $9,000 answer.

If the merchandise inventory turnover were 6 times per year, the cash requirement would be $6,000 ($36,000 divided by 6). If the turnover were once every 45 days (one-eighth of a 360-day business year), the cash requirement would be $4,500 ($36,000 divided by 8). These figures demonstrate the variable nature of the cash requirement and how our rule allows for this variance. The higher the inventory turnover, the lower is the requirement for cash on hand.

Cash Requirement for Service Firms   Our conservative rule for cash requirements thus far applies only to merchandising firms that have an inventory and a merchandise turnover on which the cash requirement rule is based. But service firms do not normally carry an inventory of merchandise. A separate rule for minimum cash available is required for service firms. The conservative cash rule for service firms is: *Sufficient cash to pay out-of-pocket expenses for three months.* This rule is practiced by many service firms with full recognition that the particular circumstances of some types of firms may justify variations from the three months' basis.

Funds to Carry Accounts Receivable New firms that decide to sell on credit to approved customers and plan to carry the accounts receivable on their books cannot neglect the fact that they will have money invested in those accounts receivable. They may, of course, decide to sell on established credit cards only. In this way the credit-card company advances the account balances to them, usually monthly, less its charge for the service. Various credit-card companies have arrangements that cost the firm from 3 to 10 percent of the amount of the sales for their service to the business firm. Such charges represent a true sales discount to the firm and must be accounted for in pricing policy. If the firm has many customers who prefer to use credit cards, this may be the most desirable method of operation. If the new firm has limited capital resources, this fact may encourage a decision to make credit sales on credit cards only. In exchange for the credit-card company's charges, the firm is protected against loss on bad debts and the expenses of administering its own credit policy. It should be noted, however, that a well-managed credit policy usually has bad-debt losses which are less than the average credit-card company charges. Another alternative available to new firms is to sell for cash only. This policy defies the basic truism that firms selling on credit will sell more merchandise to the same customers if credit is available.

If the firm is able to carry its own accounts receivable, it can usually make the credit operation pay its own way when it charges for the credit privilege, such as in installment sales contracts or interest on monthly balances. Small firms have not exercised these possibilities nearly as much as the larger firms with various credit plans available for their customers. Details of credit policies are discussed in Chapter 19.

Financial difficulties may be encountered by the small firm which decides to carry its own receivables and is not financially prepared to tie up much of its working capital in such an asset. The proprietor who believes that all credit accounts are paid in full on the first of the following month is due for a great surprise when he gets into operation. The question therefore arises, "How much investment capital should be provided to carry accounts receivable?"

The conservatilve rule suggested here for firms planning to carry their own receivables is: *Sufficient working capital to carry 1½ to 2 times the credit sales in the maximum credit period.* Applying this rule to our planned firm, we must first determine what percentage of the planned annual sales of $200,000 will be on credit. If experience and/or available statistics show that about 30 percent of the sales are on credit, we will use $60,000. This means that credit sales average $5,000 per month. If the maximum credit period is 30 days, we should plan on 1½ to 2 times the monthly credit sales to be invested in accounts receivable by the end of the first year of operation. This means $7,500 to $10,000. The variation will be determined by the strictness of the credit-granting policy and the follow-up policies adopted on collections.

We can see from the foregoing comments why small firms decide to absorb the credit-card company charges or to discount their sales contracts with finance companies. It is sad indeed to observe a company which has a good current ratio but is, nevertheless, unable to pay its current bills because too much cash is tied up in delinquent accounts receivable or slow-moving inventory that has not been converted into cash according to a planned schedule.

Merchandise Inventory   In our calculations for the budgeted income statement, we found that an inventory of $32,500 was necessary to support our contemplated sales. We must accept this figure for our statement of assets to be used.

Prepaid Supplies and Insurance   After studying the need for supplies of various kinds and learning the costs for the insurance policies we must have, we total the costs of these items. This figure becomes the dollar amount for our statement of assets to be used. We can use $1,000 for our illustration.

Land and Building   Even though we do not consider buying the land and building to be used by our firm, it is good business experience to find out what they would cost if that were our plan. Landlords are not philanthropists and we would not desire that they be so. There are distinct advantages to renting as opposed to buying, and there are also advantages to owning your own building. These considerations will be discussed later. At this time, we should get a cost estimate for the type of land and building we plan for our operation. Such an expenditure, when undertaken, is usually the largest single investment for the typical small firm.

If land available in your desired area is priced at $400 per front foot for a 50-foot lot, its cost would be $20,000. If the building you desire calls for 2,000 square feet and construction costs are $10 per square foot, its costs would be $20,000. Such investments can be financed after a good down payment. The mistake often made, however, is believing that the mortgage payments are an operating expense and not the provision of investment capital. Such payments are not operating expenses on the income statement but must be paid out of the net profits from operation. Similar consideration must be given to providing all the fixed assets for the firm. When these are purchased on credit contracts, the payments are not operating expenses but must also come out of the net profits or new investment capital. Many a potentially successful small firm has been forced to close its doors because of this mistake in financial planning.

For our purposes here, we insert $40,000 on our statement of assets to be used as the value of land and buildings. A final decision on the matter of renting or building will be made when we make our transition to an opening day balance sheet (see Chapter 9).

Store Fixtures, Office Furniture and Fixtures   The important thing here is that we clearly understand our needs for these items. We can obtain prices from several suppliers and insert the appropriate one in our statement of assets. We will use $7,000 for our illustration—$5,000 for store fixtures and $2,000 for office furniture and fixtures.

TABLE 8-1 STATEMENT OF ASSETS TO BE USED

Cash	$ 9,000
Funds to finance accounts receivable	7,500
Merchandise inventory	32,500
Prepaid expenses (supplies and insurance)	1,000
Land and buildings	40,000
Store fixtures	5,000
Office furniture and fixtures	2,000
Delivery truck	3,500
Total assets required	$100,500

Delivery Truck For purposes of this statement of assets, we assume that we will purchase a delivery truck. We do not have to make the decision now about whether we will use other methods of making deliveries. Accordingly, we insert $3,500 as the cost of the truck.

When we have obtained dollar amounts for all these items, we can refine our statement, as shown in Table 8-1.

New firm planners who have approximately $20,000 to invest may easily get discouraged when they see that the firm will use more than $100,000 of assets. They should not. It is good to realize that the firm will actually use this dollar amount of assets if things go as planned. It is good to appreciate how business institutions are interwoven, what credit means to the total business economy, and what alternatives there are in providing these assets for the firm. We will demonstrate that the firm can be started with the $20,000 and provide a capital structure which is sound when we proceed to an opening day balance sheet.

To relieve any early discouragement, we can point out several very obvious factors. First, the amount we provided for investment in accounts receivable does not have to be available on opening day. The whole consideration here was to warn the new planners that they will have capital invested in these accounts during the first year. Second, new planners may quickly determine that they will rent store space rather than build, and thus eliminate a $40,000 investment. Third, we must consider credit available in providing the other assets. Good management should always take advantage of available free credit. We will look again at all these items in Chapter 19.

QUESTIONS FOR CLASS DISCUSSION

1 Do you agree that a "statement of assets to be used" should be made by all new firm planners? Why?
2 Why should prepaid assets like insurance and supplies be included in a statement of assets to be used?

3 If a person invests in a delivery truck for a business as part of the total investment, is that truck an asset of the firm?

4 Is it possible to determine accurately in advance all the assets a business will need when it starts operations? Explain.

5 What is the conservative rule for determining how much cash a firm should have on hand? Explain the rule with an example.

6 Why is it necessary to consider whether or not sales will be made on account when evaluating total asset needs?

7 If credit sales are to be made, how much investment to carry the accounts receivable should be planned?

8 What are the pros and cons of making credit sales only on the basis of credit cards held by customers?

9 Should small business owners know the costs of the land and building even though they plan to rent? Why?

10 Can someone with only $20,000 to invest establish and control a business that requires $97,000 of assets? What are some of the alternatives?

11 What are the pros and cons of doing business with family members who help finance your new firm?

12 "Good management takes advantage of any free credit available." Do you agree? Why?

PROJECTS FOR HOME ASSIGNMENT AND/OR CLASS DISCUSSION

1 a How would you define a statement of assets to be used?
  b Prepare all account titles you would expect to find on a statement of assets to be used for a drugstore when the owner will own the building, will give credit to customers which will be carried on the firm's books, will own its own truck for delivery service, and will have regular purchases of inventory products on credit.

2 How does the cash requirement for service firms vary from that of a product retailer? Explain with an example of each.

3 Do you agree that firms which plan to carry their own accounts receivable should plan investment capital to do so? Explain how this can become important.

CONTINUING PROBLEM:
The Kollege Klothes Shop

PART 8: THE STATEMENT OF ASSETS TO BE USED

Knowing now that the potential sales volume determined justifies continuing our planning, we can proceed to the building of a financial structure for the business. The basic step here is to produce a statement of assets to be used. This statement is really the left side of a balance sheet. It lists all of the current and fixed assets necessary to put the firm into full operation on opening day.

In preparing this statement we assume in the first stage that money is no problem. This is good experience because it shows us what the total investment of economic assets used in the business will be. For example, in our first stage statement we will assume that the land and buildings required will be purchase outright. We may later decide to rent instead of buying the building. That will depend on the investment funds that we will have available. We can also assume on our first stage statement that Jones and Gomez now plan to carry their own accounts receivable on the firm's books.

Assignment for Part 8

Prepare a statement of assets to be used for the new firm. Required assets are cash, funds to invest in accounts receivable, merchandise inventory, prepaid assets (insurance and supplies), building, store fixtures, office fixtures, and a delivery truck.

Use the rules given in Chapter 8 to compute cash, and funds to invest in accounts receivable. Assume that $1,000 will cover prepaid assets. Other asset values will normally be gathered in the marketplace but we can assume $60,000 for the building, $20,000 for store fixtures, $9,000 for office fixtures, and $6,000 for a delivery truck. Merchandise inventory value comes from the budgeted income statement.

In computing cash on hand using the conservative rule, assume that all operating expenses on the budgeted income statement are out-of-pocket expenses except the $2,500 of depreciation expense. This means annual out-of-pocket expenses of $72,500. Use the same merchandise turnover we used in preparing the budgeted income statement to make our cash calculation. Then assume that your clients plan to have no more than $50,000 of credit sales for the year which they now plan to carry on their books. These sales are assumed at this time to be spread evenly throughout the 12 months of the year. All other sales will be for cash or credit cards.

The asset total you develop will represent the total capital to be invested in the firm. In our next assignment we will decide how to provide those assets with trade credit and the investment of the owners.

Your instructor will have available a statement of assets to be used based on the above data.

REFERENCES FOR FURTHER READING

"Business Plan for Small Construction Firms," Small Business Administration Pamphlet No. MA221.

"Keep Pointed Toward Profit," Small Business Administration Pamphlet No. MA206.

"Management Checklist for a Family Business," Small Business Administration Pamphlet No. MA225.

Steinhoff, Dan, *The World of Business,* McGraw-Hill Book Company, New York, 1979, chap. 30.

DEVELOPING AN OPENING DAY BALANCE SHEET

An opening day balance sheet? I didn't know what a balance sheet was when I started this business. It scares me now to think that I ever started without it. Profits would have been better and come much sooner if I had known more about planning.

The Late Learner

We have seen from the previous chapter and from our study of the assets that will be needed to operate the planned business that a total of $100,500 would be required to finance all these assets, if they were paid for outright by the proprietor. People with abundant personal capital might be satisfied just to go ahead and buy all these things and get started. Such people often decide not even to finance the land and building, which we know to be necessary. A person with a modest amount of personal assets to invest might go to the opposite extreme and use every possible assistance in the form of credit. There are options. Some of them are:

1 Invest $100,500 and buy all the assets outright. The business would then start without liabilities of any kind.

2 Finance construction of the building and purchase of the land and plan to make the mortgage payments out of profits or other capital to be obtained later.

3 Decide to rent a store space instead of investing $40,000 in order to own your own building.

4 Decide to sell on credit only to customers who have approved credit ca

5 Purchase the inventory with a minimum down payment and pay the balan as the merchandise is sold.

6 Finance the acquisition of store fixtures, office furniture and fixtures, and the delivery truck on available 24-month contracts which are obtainable after 25 percent down payment has been made. Perhaps leasing is available on these items.

7 Decide to open the doors with less than the required cash on hand; give credit on open account, even though proper capital is not on hand; carry the receivables on the books in the hope that all will be collected on the first of each month; provide fewer than the desired amount of store fixtures in the hope that the future profits will provide money to buy more later; leave the delivery service to a hit-or-miss arrangement with deliveries being made in the proprietor's personal car whenever a family member can be left in charge of the store.

Option 7 is included only because it demonstrates the errors made altogether too often by new firms. Adopting this plan defies all the planning we have been talking about and makes the firm immediately susceptible to the risk of failure. Such action is not even a calculated risk. It is foolhardy action which constitutes an invitation to failure.

Each of the other alternatives bears investigation. Final choices must be governed by such considerations as the following:

1 We anticipate $24,000 net profit before federal income taxes. (We originally planned on $15,000, but our market survey showed a sales volume which should produce $24,000 profit.)

2 Unless other investment capital is known to be available (including a possible loan from Grandma or Uncle John), we cannot let the payment of the liabilities incurred in the provision of the assets cut into our planned profits to the point that the proprietor's family expenses are impaired.

3 We cannot minimize the cash and inventory needs which have been carefully calculated in our planning.

4 It is good business to use any credit that is available without charge.

5 Excessive interest charges should be avoided whenever possible. The fact that interest expense is a deductible income tax item is little solace if profits disappear and there is nothing left on which to pay any tax.

PROCEDURE FOR DEVELOPING A BALANCE SHEET

The development of an opening day balance sheet necessitates making decisions on how each of the assets or services is to be provided. The decisions will vary with the individual owner. As hypothetical proprietors, we have the following facts or constraints to assist us in making these decisions:

1 We have about $20,000 to invest.

2 We will rent an excellent building located at the desirable site previously

en. This will eliminate the large investment required to purchase the
ding. The landlord will now have funds invested in the building. Our planner
ill now show rent expense on the income statement, rather than a building on
the balance sheet.

3 Uncle John has indicated a willingness to lend us up to $15,000 on a 5-year
note with only the interest to be paid for the 5 years until the principal of the
note becomes due. This is called a balloon note.

4 A wholesaler in our line has offered the usual terms in this type of business
if they can sell us most of the inventory. These terms are 50 percent down and 50
percent in 30 days with no interest charge.

5 We have found a delivery truck, slightly used, which we can purchase for
$2,000 with an $800 down payment and monthly payments of $100 plus interest
for 1 year.

6 We must have the new store equipment, but we find slightly used desks,
files, and office machines which are available for $1,000 cash and which will meet
the needs for office furniture and fixtures.

7 The store equipment (showcases, shelving, window displays, cash registers)
can all be bought from one firm with 50 percent down and 50 percent due in 1
year.

8 We have decided to push credit-card sales and reduce the open accounts
receivable we carry on our books. We expect this to reduce the amount we will
need for our investment in these accounts. We will accordingly keep $6,250 in
our savings account (rather than the $7,500 previously calculated), where it will
earn interest until it is needed to maintain current debt payment. We will list this
on our opening day balance sheet as "other bank accounts." If this $6,250 were
in the form of government bonds or other readily salable securities, we could list
it as "marketable securities."

Against this background of soundly gathered information, the proprietors are
now in a position to make a first draft of an opening day balance sheet and test it
for financial soundness. With explanatory comments, it would look like Table
9-1.

PUTTING THE OPENING DAY BALANCE SHEET TOGETHER

Remember that our opening day balance sheet must provide for each of the
assets found to be necessary for proper planning, as shown in our statement of
assets to be used developed in Chapter 8. Our basic decisions or constraints
given in the preceding list tell us how each of those assets will be provided. The
balance sheet lists all assets at full purchase price. Amounts owed on any of them
are shown as liabilities. Notice each of the following steps in Table 9-1.

We cannot compromise with proper cash on hand, so we can first insert
$9,000 cash on hand as a current asset. Next we list the $6,250 as other bank
accounts, which represents the funds we will hold to finance our accounts
receivable. (Remember, we reduced this amount from the $7,500 listed in the

TABLE 9-1 P. M. JONES COMPANY
Opening Day Balance Sheet
November 1, 1981

ASSETS

Current assets:

Cash on hand (as per calculation in statement of assets to be used)	$ 9,000	
Other bank accounts	6,250*	
Merchandise inventory	32,500	
Prepaid expenses (supplies, insurance, etc.)	1,000	
Total current assets		$48,750

Fixed assets:

Store fixtures (half cash, half credit)	$5,000	
Office furniture and fixtures (paid for in cash)	1,000	
Delivery truck ($800 cash, $1,200 credit)	2,000	
Total fixed assets		$ 8,000

ᵗˡ assets	$56,750

* ...nti needed to finance accounts receivable.

† As... Liabilities, $34,950 = Net worth, $21,800

LIABILITIES

Current liabilities:

Accounts payable (due to wholesalers for balance of beginning inventory)	$16,250	
Contract payable (one-year note on store equipment)	2,500	
Notes payable (delivery truck)	1,200	
Total current liabilities		$19,950

Fixed liabilities:

Notes payable (five-year loan from Uncle John)	$15,000	
Total fixed liabilities		15,000
Total liabilities		$34,950

NET WORTH

P.M. Jones, proprietorship	21,800†

Total liabilities plus net worth	$56,750

nt of assets to be used via a basic policy decision in our constraints in the
ing section.)

next we list the full value of the inventory purchased, $32,500, as merchan-
se inventory. But we are not paying for the entire purchase now, so we list 50
percent of this amount as a current liability—accounts payable, $16,250. Then
we can list as prepaid expenses the full value of those items (supplies and
insurance—$1,000), which we pay for in full before opening day.

In the fixed asset section we can then list the full purchase price of the store
fixtures ($5,000), the office furniture and fixtures ($1,000), and the delivery
truck ($2,000). But we received some help in providing these by incurring some
liabilities to cover the balance of their purchase prices. Therefore, we must list
the $2,500 contract payable on the store fixtures as a current liability and the
$1,200 still owed on the delivery truck as notes payable. We were also provided
with $15,000 cash by Uncle John. This is not due, except for interest, for five
years, so we list that note payable as a fixed liability.

If we now total our current and fixed assets, we find that we have total assets
of $56,750. Our total current and fixed liabilities are $34,950. Following our basic
accounting equation that assets minus liabilities equals proprietorship, we
subtract the liabilities of $34,950 from the assets of $56,750 and find that Jones's
necessary investment is $21,800. This becomes the "net worth" or total
investment of the owner. We then insert the proprietorship account in our
balance sheet for this amount and we have a completed opening day balance
sheet on Table 9-1.

As our fledgling proprietors review this first draft of a proposed opening day
balance sheet, the ratio analysis that we studied in Chapter 3 should be applied.
We will find that we have proposed a current ratio in excess of 2 to 1 (current
assets, $48,750, divided by current liabilities, $19,950), which is good. The quick
ratio proposed is substantially less than the desired 1 to 1 (cash plus receivables,
$15,250, divided by current liabilities, $19,950). The reason seems to be our
decision about reducing the capital necessary to finance the receivables. The
proprietorship ratio is less than 50 percent (proprietorship, $21,800, divided by
total assets, $56,750). The 50 percent minimum would require an investment of
$28,375 by Jones.

If we are to strictly apply the rules we have learned about financial soundness
d ratio analysis, we would go back to the drawing board and make adjust-
n s to bring the deficient ratios into line. Possibilities that appear are:

o not buy the delivery truck, thereby eliminating a $2,000 truck on the
asse
It wo e and a $1,200 liability. This would add the $800 down payment to cash.
operat also necessitate adding the cost of a hired delivery service to the
2 R xpenses on the income statement.
thus mak that the contract on the store fixtures be lengthened to 2 years,
hence) ra lf the balance due a fixed liability (amounts due more than 1 year
3 Ask an a current liability, all of which must be paid in 1 year.
him 5 perce hn to become a partner, silent or active, as he desires. Offer
rofits as an inducement. His note payable of $15,000 would

ve made her a full-fledged partner.
she bought some of our capital stock.

CONTINUING PROBLEM:
The Kollege Klothes Shop

PART 9: DEVELOPING AN OPENING DAY BALANCE SHEET

When we submitted our statement of assets to be used to our clients, they were quite amazed. It calls for total capital of $139,333. Jones and Gomez were discouraged because they plan to have available less than $40,000 for their owners' investment. But you soothe their concern by showing them how the assets will be provided within their investment expectations.

You give them the following constraints (or decisions) as a basis for converting the statement of assets to be used into an opening day balance sheet.

1 Rent a building, don't pay $60,000 to buy one. This means that we will have *rent expense* on the income statement rather than an asset *building* on the balance sheet. (We anticipated this decision as we prepared our budgeted income statement.)

2 Buy the inventory by paying $10,000 down payment and receiving trade credit for $15,000. Thus we will show an inventory on the balance sheet of $25,000 and an account payable of $15,000.

3 Decide to sell merchandise for cash and credit cards only. This will eliminate our investment of funds to carry accounts receivable.

4 Buy used but beautiful store fixtures for $15,000 with no down payment, then repay $5,000 the first year, and $5,000 the second and third years.

5 Pay cash for the office fixtures, and for prepaid assets.

6 Buy the delivery truck with 50 percent down and 50 percent over a 24-month contract. This will mean $3,000 cash down payment and monthly payments of $125 for two years.

Assignment for Part 9

Prepare a first draft of an opening day balance sheet by applying the above decisions to the statement of assets to be used. In the net worth section, we can use the wording "owners' investment" at this time.

What would the current and proprietorship ratios on your first draft of the opening balance sheet? Would you recommend proceeding with this plan, or would you make further changes in the decisions?

Your instructor will have an opening day balance sheet based on the above decisions, purposely designed to provide a lively discussion of its good and weak points.

REFERENCES FOR FURTHER READING

Niswonger, C. Rollin, and Philip E. Fess, *Accounting Principles,* 12th ed., South-Western Publishing Company, Inc., Cincinnati, Ohio, 1979, chap. 5.

Tate, Curtis E., Jr., Leon Megginson, Charles Scott, Jr., and Lyle Trueblood, *Successful Small Business Management,* rev. ed., Business Publications, Inc., Dallas, Texas, 1978, chap. 19.

"The Small Businessman and Sources of Loans," U.S. Dept. of Commerce Publication.

represents one of the larger investments in a typical small firm. If a $20,000 inventory can be purchased for $10,000 down payment and the balance in 30 days, the wholesaler has virtually provided $10,000 of required capital to open the business. The owner then has an opportunity to sell that inventory at a profit and thus have the funds to pay off the original balance. As a record for successful operation is established, even more attractive terms may be offered on subsequent purchases. A grocer may have several such suppliers. Others firms may have only one or two major suppliers. The inducement of a sales discount for prompt payment of invoices should always tempt the owner to pay within the maximum discount period.

Loans or Credit from Equipment Sellers This type of financial aid is often considered another form of trade credit. It does, however, have distinct characteristics. The new firm may need counters, shelves, display cases, delivery trucks, and other equipment such as air conditioning, refrigeration units, and food counters. These, too, represent a large investment for the new small firm and are so recognized by the major suppliers of such items. These purchases usually are not made on a regular basis but represent a large part of the capital needed to get started. The suppliers usually offer good credit terms, with a modest down payment and a contract for the balance spread over 1, 2, or 3 years.

When financing charges are reasonable, this type of credit can be most helpful to the planner. The caution is in its overuse—remembering, again, that the payments must be paid out of profits anticipated. Also, any payments of this type are for the provision of capital and are not operating expenses. Too much of this type of financing can distort the current and quick ratios and upset the firm's financial liquidity. There are many cases on record where the monthly payments on such fixed assets exceed the profits earned from sales in the month.

Mortgage Loans If the new firm planners own a commercial building, they can usually secure a mortgage on it with payments over as many as 30 years. It may be the building in which the new firm will operate. In that case, the planners will be making mortgage payments instead of rental payments to a landlord. They may wish to risk a mortgage on their homes. Even second mortgages are sometimes used, although this is not recommended. Mortgage loans are typically made by savings and loan associations, mutual banks, and mortgage banking institutions. When profits are uncertain, caution is advised in committing any assets to mortgage claims. As a clear profit pattern becomes more established, the use of mortgage credit becomes less risky.

Commercial Bank Loans Historically, a line of credit at a commercial bank was designed to enable a merchant to purchase an inventory of merchandise. When the merchandise was sold at a profit, the bank was paid its loan. This situation is still followed by many banks. The use of bank credit is still the best way to establish credit with a commercial bank. Since the relaxation of bank

Sybil Shelton/Monkmeyer

FIGURE 10-1
New firm planners should investigate all phases of the contemplated firm with experienced business people, bankers, or consultants.

restrictions in recent years, however, many other types of loans and financing are now available to qualified applicants. In fact, we have banks now which advertise, "If you are planning to go into business, come see us." The cold, hard facts of economic reality will be faced in such a visit, but the prospective firm owner with an otherwise sound financing plan, a reputation for integrity, and a business deemed likely to succeed may still establish some bank credit in the planning stage. Long-term loans are generally less available than short-term loans. Short-term loans are usually considered those for not more than 1 year. If adequate collateral is available, longer term loans may be obtained. Getting influential or wealthy friends to cosign notes also may be helpful.

The policies of the local bank should always be checked in the planning stage. Many small firm owners with experience have long described banks as "a place where you can borrow money when you prove that you don't need it." Some banks are trying to remove that image today. In keeping with our previously noted axiom that rewards must be commensurate with cost and risk, however, interest rates charged by banks to small firms are often significantly higher than the rates charged to large firms.

Small Business Administration Loans Even if a commercial bank turns down an application for credit from a new small firm, the firm may still file an application to the Small Business Administration for the same loan if it is deemed to have merit. Under such an arrangement, the SBA agrees to underwrite a large percentage of the loan and thousands of such loans are in existence today.

The SBA was originally set up by Congress for the specific purpose of aiding small firms in financing and management problems. Both the Department of Commerce and the Small Business Administration have done much in this area. The losses incurred on such loans as reported by SBA officials are surprisingly small. Chapters of SCORE (Service Corps of Retired Executives) are utilized by the SBA to render management assistance to small firms that request it. Recently the SBA added a program under which senior business administration students in colleges and universities throughout the country are brought in to help firms that have requested management assistance. Innumerable publications have been made available to aid small firms.

All these developments represent a very positive commitment by the government to assist small firms wherever possible. This is done in a belief that successful small firms are essential to maintaining a healthy and prosperous economy for the country.

New business planners who are pressed for capital will do well to check with their nearest office of the Small Business Administration or the Department of Commerce. They may find themselves eligible for loans, and they may also gather other valuable assistance.

Small Business Investment Company Loans   Congress has also provided the Small Business Investment Company Act, which is designed to encourage the creation of privately owned companies whose sole purpose is to make long-term loans or even equity loans to small business firms. These are popularly known as SBIC companies. They are licensed by the Small Business Administration and are subject to regulation by that body. These companies must have a minimum capital of $300,000, of which at least $150,000 is from private funds. The SBA will then supply one-half the total capital up to a maximum of $400,000, for which they take an ownership position in the SBIC. In addition, the SBIC may borrow additional amounts from the SBA for the purpose of making additional long-term loans, or equity loans, to small business firms.

Many of these companies have been formed in most of the states. They eagerly seek small firms with good potential as clients. Many have had an excellent record in their operations, which reflects success by the small firms to which they have rendered financial aid.

State and Regional Business Development Companies   Those who believe in the private enterprise system have been pleased to see the development of strictly private business development companies in many parts of the country. Many states, as well as local communities, have sponsored such companies to develop sound business organizations in their economy. But their capital is provided entirely by private sources. Banks, large manufacturing firms, utility companies, and transportation firms have been large contributors to their financing. Many of these companies emphasize the number of new jobs that will be created by the suggested new firms. They are interested in attracting new firms and new types of firms to their area. They have taken pride in their success in granting loans to companies that were turned down by banks. In many cases they even build plants and sell them to the new firms, or assist in providing attractive leases. They make outright loans on a longer term basis or even buy stock in the new venture. Many a discouraged new firm planner has found success by asking the chamber of commerce or by writing to the state business development office for information as to the existence of such a firm in the community.

Taking in Partners   Despite all the cautions previously discussed, raising capital often necessitates taking one or more partners into the business. If no more than one manager is needed, the new partners may not be employed in the firm but may hold full partner status as a result of their investment in the firm. The partnership agreement (discussed in Chapter 7) is important here. Inducements can be offered to such a finance partner, but the duties, responsibilities, and authority of each partner must be clearly understood. At this point we are looking at the partnership only from the standpoint of providing a source of investment funds.

Selling Capital Stock   Aside from the technical, legal, and operational advantages of the corporate form of legal organization, its advantages as a

FIGURE 10-2
Small businesses may issue creditor securities as stocks or bonds or promissory notes.

device for raising capital are extremely significant. Many small firm owners seem to believe that the corporate form was designed only for the very large business firms. This is false. It is true that this legal form has not been as widely used as it might, but this has probably been because of a lack of knowledge of its advantages. Chapter 7 explains details of the corporation.

Let us consider the new firm planner who needs $100,000 in ownership capital but has only $30,000 to invest. Would it not be desirable to go to a local investment banker as a corporation and request the sale of $50,000 of 12 percent preferred stock and $50,000 of common stock? The planner takes title to $30,000 of the voting common stock. The charter provides authorization to sell $100,000 of each type of stock. The planner can hold the unsold stock in the firm for possible future financing for expansion. The preferred stock is given a priority of dividends in exchange for its voting privilege. Only the common stock has voting power. The planner still owns a majority of the common stock outstanding and has no problem of control. The investment banker sells the stock to customers who are probably unknown. A detailed study of the plans of the firm is contained in a prospectus, which the banker will prepare. The firm planner does not have to pursue relatives to plead with friends for financial "favors," does not have to take in undesired partners to raise capital, has assured a financial plan for expansion, and has all the protections of the corporate form of organization. The investment banker will charge for this service. The charge will be higher if the banker guarantees the sale of the full amount, and less if the stock is sold on a "best efforts" basis. The banker's fee is chargeable to organization expense and can be amortized over the succeeding 5 to 10 years.

This procedure is followed by the best informed new firm planners who desire growth. It should be investigated for appropriateness by many more. Details for forming a corporation are covered in Chapter 7.

Miscellaneous Sources of Funds Most of the other miscellaneous sources of funds are more available to going concerns than to persons who need financial aid for a newly planned business. If the new firm has equipment paid for through investment by the owner, if it has an inventory of merchandise which is free and clear, or if it has some accounts receivable from other sources which are being invested in the firm, loans against these can usually be obtained. *Commercial finance companies* are available in every town and most make loans against this type of collateral. Similar companies will make credit available in "floor planning" arrangements to make merchandise available. Others will purchase installment-loan contracts from the small firm owner. *Insurance companies* often engage in long-term loans to substantial small business firms. These are usually secured by mortgages on real estate. *Personal finance companies* will make personal loans to small firm owners with precise repayment schedules. When *factors* or *sales agents* (firms that handle all of a small business's sales or receivables) are used to handle the bulk of the firm's business, working capital is often advanced to the firm by such factors or sales agents. The textile industry is the most prominent example of this type of business activity.

QUESTIONS FOR CLASS DISCUSSION

1 Why do preferred stockholders have a priority of dividends?
2 What is meant by selling stock on a "best efforts" basis?
3 Why is it important for new firm planners to have some capital of their own to invest?
4 Do you think it is advisable to borrow from relatives and friends to raise capital to start a business?
5 How can loans from relatives and friends be made more businesslike?
6 What are the pros and cons of having partners in your business?
7 Are stockholders creditors or owners? Explain.
8 Are there possible dangers in borrowing too much, even if funds may be available? Explain.
9 What is a Small Business Investment Company?
10 What is trade credit? Is it usually more expensive than bank loans?
11 Can trade credit be used in planning a new firm? How?
12 What other miscellaneous sources of funds may be used by small business firms?
13 Why do established firms have less trouble in getting outside financial assistance than newly planned firms?
14 How do equipment suppliers help provide financing for a new firm?
15 Does our government assist small firms in obtaining financing? How?
16 Do you believe that private business development companies to assist new small firms should be expanded?

PROJECTS FOR HOME ASSIGNMENT AND/OR CLASS DISCUSSION

1 Explain how you would distinguish between short-term, intermediate, and long-term capital if you were raising $100,000 to finance a new clothing store. Would you assure that the firm had a 50 percent proprietorship ratio? How?
2 Explain how the investment of others can contribute to the proprietorship ratio of the firm rather than increasing the borrowed capital.
3 Can you explain the most popular forms of trade credit that would be used by a men's clothing store? Do you recommend its use?

CONTINUING PROBLEM:
The Kollege Klothes Shop

PART 10: SOURCES OF FINANCING

It is good for our new firm planners to know the various types of financing that may be used in their new firm. Our opening day balance sheet has used some of them. Our immediate task, however, is now to clarify the details of the net worth section of that balance sheet. Our clients decided way back in Chapter 7 that they desired to incorporate their business, after studying our report on the advantages and disadvantages of the three major legal forms. But this decision leaves alternatives to the new firm owners. Do they wish to sell only common stock which carries the voting power in controlling the corporation? Or would they prefer to sell some preferred stock and some common stock? It is important that they keep ownership of 50 percent plus one share of any common stock issued.

We have seen in Chapter 9 that they need to provide $35,083 of owner capital of all kinds. After we discuss the options with Jones and Gomez, they decide to support your recommendation that they make their firm a regular corporation, and that they sell $25,000 of preferred stock to outside investors and buy for themselves $25,000 of common stock. By thus raising $50,000 they would have almost $15,000 of additional capital for the firm. This could be used to retire some of the current and fixed liabilities they have contemplated on that opening day balance sheet. By selling preferred stock they must guarantee its holders that they will receive a dividend before any could be paid to the holders of common stock.

Assignment for Part 10

1 Reconstruct only the net worth section of the opening day balance sheet on the basis of the sale of $25,000 of preferred stock to outsiders and issuing to themselves equal parts of $25,000 of common stock.

2 How would the net worth section look if they sold no stock and equally provided the $35,083 in common stock required to get into proper operation?

REFERENCES FOR FURTHER READING

"A Venture Capital Primer for Small Business," Small Business Administration Pamphlet No. MA235.

Broom, H. N., and J. G. Longenecker, *Small Business Management,* 5th ed., South-Western Publishing Company, Inc., Cincinnati, Ohio, 1973, chap. 8.

Steinhoff, Dan, *The World of Business,* McGraw-Hill Book Company, New York, 1979, chap. 17.

LOCATION, LAYOUT, AND MERCHANDISING

CHAPTER 11

LOCATION OF THE FIRM

You guys talk so much about location but what can I do about it? I signed a 10-year lease at too much money and I am stuck here for the remaining 8 years of that lease. I thought it was a good location when I moved here.

The Late Learner

People in the field of real estate loudly proclaim that there are three factors that determine the value of property—either as an investment or for profitable business operations. Those three factors are:

1 Location
2 Location, and
3 Location

Business experience seems to indicate that real estate people know more about choosing proper locations for small firms than many of the small firm owners who learn only belatedly what constitutes a good versus a less desirable location. Location merits some advance planning by those who would establish a new small firm. There are important guidelines, and we will review some of them here. Location is important for retailing, wholesaling, manufacturing, and service firms alike.

Small firm owners should distinguish between general location factors and site factors. In this sense, *location* means the region, the state, the county, or the city which represents the general market area for the planned firm. The *site* factors are the particular street, the corner, and the building within the location area. The advantages of a good location can be minimized by a poor site.

In the early 1970s the three fastest-growing geographical areas in the United States were California, Texas, and Florida. Now Arizona has joined this group. This means that expanded markets are developing in these areas. In isolation, the growing markets suggest that these states would be good areas in which to establish new firms. It would be foolhardy, however, to think that there are not many other areas of the country where location of a new firm would be desirable. Moreover, not all types of firms are needed in all growing areas. We must investigate even general location factors more closely.

Small business failures often reflect complete neglect of a consideration of specific location factors. Too many small firms are established in locations because a store space happened to be available for rent. Most students can probably recall a section of their hometowns which became known as the cemetery for small firms. New ones come and go every year. Business firms which otherwise would have been quite successful suffer from the start when not properly located. Some new proprietors have as the predominant factor in their choice of location such things as a desire to live in their hometown, to be close to friends or relatives, to locate in a climate they prefer, to be close to a particular religious group, or to be near a particular ethnic group. Others attach a certain social atmosphere to their location. In themselves, these factors may not be bad for choosing a location, but it is important that within these considerations, the proper location and proper site be chosen. Never should a particular store space be selected merely because it is available, without subjecting it to some specific tests of suitability. Being well known in one's hometown can be a great advantage if other considerations are in line. Knowing the population of the hometown, its atmosphere, the mode of living of its residents, its general business climate, and also being known to bankers in the hometown can all be advantageous for new proprietors if they choose a location consistent with the considerations we will discuss below.

If planners are not restricted by a desire to locate in a particular town or region but are looking for a location anywhere in the country, they can apply all of the following general considerations.

LOCATION FACTORS FOR RETAILING

Industry   Study the industry of the area under consideration. Payrolls create buying power for your potential customers, and unless their permanence and growth seem probable, making a big investment is probably unwise.

The ideal location is a community with substantial permanent industry, an upward trend in community payrolls, diversification of its industries, stability of its industries, and a minimum of seasonality in the total activity. Seasonal business firms *can* be very successful. The important thing is to know the facts about the seasonal variations.

Population   Study the nature of the population in the area. Many students seem surprised to learn that there are some areas of our country where the population has actually decreased in recent years. Declining, stationary, or small populations do not bode well for new firms for the area. Growing and wealthy populations desiring the goods or services you propose to offer in an expanding population area represent ideal situations. The mode of living of the community under consideration must be studied. The author recalls the proprietor of a small hardware store on the ground floor of a 20-story apartment building complaining about his lack of sales of garden hoses. When asked if apartment dwellers buy many garden hoses, he realized that the mode of living of most of his customers did not require many units of such a product. Gift shops and bookstores require a somewhat affluent population with at least average income to be successful.

Study your potential market area in terms of the needs and desires of the people you want to serve. Are they home owners? Are they renters? Do they live in apartments? Are the rents high, low, or medium? Condominium owners may have a different mode of living from apartment renters. Another factor in the mode of living in a particular area is the general character of the population. Is it composed mostly of older people, a dominant religious group? Are the people native-born, mostly foreign-born, or a truly mixed group?

Competition   Know your competition in advance. Our free enterprise system is based upon competition. Our business history has proved that customers are best served when healthy competition prevails. Competition should not be feared. It should be known and coped with.

The two time-honored justifications for opening a new firm in an existing line of business are (1) *an expanded market,* and (2) *presence of inefficient firms.* Expanded markets are almost always the result of expanding populations. The trend of our population to the cities in recent years has provided the basis for many new firms. Much of this population growth, of course, has been in the suburbs of the larger cities. The attendant growth of sales and new firms in the suburbs has been one of the outstanding characteristics of our recent business history.

As mentioned earlier, new planners can learn a great deal about a particular area relative to its population growth and existing competition. Chambers of commerce, trade development associations, county industrial planning boards, and similar organizations can provide details about many areas. Cities are divided into voting precincts or other smaller areas for various purposes. The population of each is usually recorded annually and is available at least by census years.

When the population of an area is compared with the number of competing firms in that area, a first conclusion can be made as to whether or not the area needs another firm in this field. For example, if it takes 700 people to maintain a modern grocery store and the area now has a grocery store for every 500 people, the conclusion, on this basis, must be that this is not a good place to establish another store. The total market has not expanded. If there is only one grocery store for 1,200 people, the evidence suggests this is a good location. Table 11-1 shows the size of population necessary to support various types of retail stores.

But even if the population doesn't justify another firm, planners can still consider the presence of inefficient firms. Customer reaction to existing stores, the nature of stocks carried, services available, and the type of management reflected by competitors may present a situation in which a new, efficient firm would be successful despite the number of competitors now attempting to serve the same population.

Competitors should be studied in terms of their numbers, their management, how many of them are chain stores, the attractiveness of their stores, and the completeness and nature of their stocks of merchandise. If it is found that customers are dissatisfied with service, lines of merchandise, price ranges, attractiveness of stores, or anything else, a basis may be found for successfully competing in that area.

Facilities   Consider the city or town facilities. Is public transportation important to your plans, and if so, is it available with good service? Are there special problems in obtaining merchandise supplies through normal channels of distribution? Does the area have good banking facilities? Are civic associations, schools, churches, and professional services conducive to good community life and healthy business conditions? Is the local government attitude toward

TABLE 11-1   POPULATION REQUIREMENTS FOR VARIOUS TYPES OF RETAIL STORES*

Camera and photography supplies	40,000
Drugs	2,500
Dry goods	25,000
Florist shops	7,500
Grocery stores	700
Hardware stores	5,000
Hobby shops and toy stores	25,000
Household appliances	8,500
Jewelry stores	7,500
Men's and boys' clothing	7,500
Restaurants and lunch counters	1,000
Shoe stores	6,000
Sporting goods	12,000
Stationery stores	25,000
Women's clothing	5,000

* *Source:* Independent study made by a group of advanced business administration students at the University of Miami. Starting from established studies, their procedure was to use data from the United States census, census of business, trade reports, and local market surveys in order to update figures for this table. Their results do not vary widely from other established studies. They emphasized in their conclusions that varying localities and conditions need study before adopting these averages.

business encouraging or restrictive? If labor supply is important to your business, is an adequate supply available?

SITE FACTORS FOR RETAILING

Having decided upon a favorable city or even a part of a city after considering the preceding factors, the planner can turn his or her attention to the specific site to be chosen within the generally desired location. Some of the site factors and their implications follow:

Parking   Does the particular site provide easy parking, access, and other comforts for customers? Grandma and Grandpa never worried about this factor with their general store. Hitching posts provided a place to tie the horses and were usually provided by the local government. Fields surrounded many stores and were free parking areas. Perhaps the most significant change in downtown retailing management in recent years has been the expense and importance of providing parking space for customers. Parking and heavy traffic in urban areas have contributed greatly to the growth of suburban shopping centers. As recently as 15 years ago, many downtown merchants still resisted the idea of paying for their customers' parking or of providing it free or at low cost. Today parking is a fundamental part of every "save the downtown" or "bring the customers back downtown" or "revitalize the main downtown" program. An

FIGURE 11-1
Even large free parking lots around shopping centers can sometimes be inadequate for peak periods.

Van Bucher/Photo Researchers, Inc.

hour's free parking is now available in almost all department-store lots when a purchase is made. Small firms must rely upon availability of low-cost parking or follow the same policy.

Surrounding Firms   What types of firms surround the site? It must be recognized that some types of business firms attract customers of one type and others attract other types. Good site choosing must consider this factor. What kinds of business firms surround the site you have under consideration? Sites close to department stores are generally considered good for most types of retail stores. The general appeal of the department store to all types of customers makes this so.

Market research has provided some conclusions in this regard. For example, studies have shown that men's stores should not be located next to gas stations, beauty shops, or women's apparel shops. Such neighbors just do not normally attract customers who are looking for men's clothing when visiting these shops. Those who might disagree have not provided substantial evidence to support their views. Like electricity, it is more important that we know how to use research than to understand its foundation. The innovation of clothing stores which sell both men's and women's apparel has not made sufficiently significant inroads on the principle to warrant its revocation.

Traffic Density   What kind of traffic is there at this site, and is it adequate? Modern site analysis distinguishes between automobile and pedestrian traffic. If only automobile traffic were considered, most businesses would be located on expressways or main highways. Pedestrian traffic of potential customers is the key item here. Heavy automobile traffic adjacent to a suburban shopping center can be very important, but the number of people who convert into pedestrian traffic is of even greater concern.

In urban sites, passing cars become less important. Getting these cars parked and bringing customers to the street and the store is the crucial consideration.

People traffic alone is not the most significant item in pedestrian traffic, however. Are they the type of people who are shopping for your type of merchandise? Why are they on this street at this time? Significantly, a large drug chain has staff people interview passersby on a site it is considering. With clip boards and questions they observe, interview, and study the traffic. They ask about and record age bracket, sex, employment, income range, objective of the trip past this site, shopping habits, interest in this type of store, and so on. The conclusion of their research is that the site with the heaviest count of potential customers per half-hour between one and five o'clock in the afternoon and on Saturday evenings is the preferred site for the company's stores. They have found by experience that stores doing well in these hours are most successful.

The "Going-Home" Side of the Street   Marketing research has produced the principle that the going-home side of the street is usually to be preferred to the going-to-work side of the street. This may be only a reflection of people's buying habits, but it has proved true in cases studied by advanced students. Those interested in the psychology of human conduct can form their own reasons for this principle of site choosing.

The Sunny Side of the Street   Market studies have also established that the sunny side of the street is less preferable for retail operations than the shady side. Our own research has found rents higher on the shady side in high-priced shopping areas. Perhaps in northern Alaska the reverse might be true because the sunshine is less frequent and may even be sought by shoppers. Merchants recognize the sunny-side-of-the-street principle by the installation of expensive awnings to combat the sun and to make customers more comfortable.

Preferred Site

We must not leave this discussion with the implication that all types of retailers must be in prime, high-rent locations. Lower rents also have attractions, but these may be offset by the need for higher advertising and promotional budgets to attract customers to the lower-rent area. Some types of firms need such areas for best results. Firms that sell by mail or through traveling salesmen are obviously exempt from the considerations just discussed. Firms selling shopping merchandise should normally be close to their competitors, as we shall discuss in a later chapter. Firms concentrating on specialty goods emphasize comfort for their customers above all (see Table 11-2).

Site studies that have been made over many years, by both government agencies and private market research groups, have generally agreed that the preferred site can be associated with characteristics of the business in question. For instance, firms should generally seek low-rent locations if they have a high gross margin and low merchandise turnover, need much space for interior displays, sell merchandise which is low in value compared with bulk, sell what are considered shopping goods by most people in the area, have an established customer demand, resort to much advertising and promotion effort, or have a high overhead expense. High-rent locations are more appropriate for firms that feature window displays, have a high rate of turnover, have low gross margins, appeal to transient trade, feature price appeal and convenience merchandise, sell merchandise of high value compared with bulk, have low overhead, and do little advertising.

It is unlikely that the individual firm would meet all the characteristics suggesting either a high-rent or low-rent location. The decision is usually reached in the planning stage by determining which type of location is suggested by the preponderance of characteristics represented. If the firm's characteristics imply a low-rent location on a majority of the measures, prudence recommends that such a location be given serious consideration. The many exceptions to such rules only prove the rule. Local circumstances usually account for the exceptions. A study of such a list may aid policy making in merchandising.

TABLE 11-2   FIRM CHARACTERISTICS THAT SUGGEST HIGH- OR LOW-RENT
LOCATIONS AND FIRMS THAT USUALLY ARE IN EACH CATEGORY

Characteristics that suggest high-rent locations	Illustrative firms
Window displays featured	Department stores
High rate of turnover	Style clothing shops
Low gross margin	Urban drugstores, banks
Appeal to transient trade ✓	Men's shops, drugstores
Feature price appeal and convenience merchandise	Discount stores
Sells merchandise of high value ✓ compared to bulk	Fine jewelry stores
Low overhead	Liquor stores
Does little advertising	Independent hardware stores

Characteristics that suggest low-rent locations	Illustrative firms
High gross margin	Furniture stores
Low merchandise turnover	Plumbing supplies
Need much space for interior displays	Automobile agency
Merchandise is low in value compared to bulk	Grain and feed stores
Merchandise is essentially shopping goods	Carpet stores, TV stores
Has an established clientele	Neighborhood drugstore
Does much advertising and promotion	Florist, grocery chains
Has a high overhead expense	Specialty food franchise, super service station

LOCATION FACTORS FOR MANUFACTURING

Factory locations are usually restricted to specified industrial areas of any city.
Recent trends show an increase in county regulations in this regard. As a first
consideration, the new factory planner must check the zoning laws in his or her
area. Some industrial zones allow some types of factories and not others.

Once the available industrial zones are determined, attention is turned to the
adequacy of shipping facilities, adequacy of the types of buildings available for
lease or rent, and distances from factory to market and attendant shipping costs.

For manufacturers, the questions of nearness to raw materials or markets, the
availability of cheap fuel, power and water, skilled labor of a special type, and
financing facilities take precedence over any other considerations involving
location.

The factory which can be located in the central part of its total market area

FIGURE 11-2
Small factories can also be attractive.

usually has an ideal location. This holds true for most manufacturers of consumer and industrial goods. Nearness to market usually takes precedence over nearness to raw materials. Two notable exceptions are to be observed.

When the manufacturing process involves (1) much waste in the processing of the product, or (2) dealing with perishable raw materials, then the factory should be located close to its raw materials. An obvious example of the first situation is a sawmill which makes finished lumber from giant logs. Shipping the logs to a mill near the final market would be wasteful and expensive. An example of the second situation is the processing of fresh fruit. Peach- and strawberry-canning factories must be near the orchards where the fruit is harvested. Excessive spoilage and/or expense would result from long-distance hauling.

The speed of modern transportation systems has expanded many markets in ways not thought possible only a few short years ago. Planeloads of fresh tulips and other flowers are flown from Holland to many cities around the world. Fresh fruit from Australia is available in New York City as well as other markets without the benefit of freezing facilities. These instances, however, are the exception and not the rule. When considering utility versus uniqueness in consumer products, it is good to know that many people desire and can afford the products of uniqueness. The final test of any business economy, however, is the total goods and services that can be economically produced for its citizens. The average standard of living of any nation still depends on products of utility and their economical production. This truth is not intended to discourage innovations in manufacturing, distribution, and selling. It merely indicates that the greatest share of our total production is done with the objective of economical production as a first consideration. The rules of experience still prevail.

LOCATION FACTORS FOR WHOLESALING

Wholesalers also are restricted by zoning laws in most cities. The objective is to be located as close to most customers as possible in a building that is suited to the type of operation planned. Good transportation facilities by rail or truck are essential for efficient reception of inventories. Local wholesalers make most deliveries by truck. When customers regularly visit the wholesaler, rather than phone in their orders, it is important that the customer area be attractive and efficient. This is not the normal situation though. Most customers telephone their orders and desire speedy delivery. Emphasis should accordingly be placed on a location which makes this possible.

LOCATION FACTORS FOR SERVICE FIRMS

Locations for service firms are almost as varied as the types of firms involved. The beauty shop, the shoe repair shop, the TV repair shop do not need high-rent locations. They have become largely residential-area types of businesses. Closeness to a shopping center is usually considered ideal. Yet there are differences, even among these service shops. Beauty shops must be attractive. Shoe-repair shops have a character all their own, which is not necessarily attractiveness. Shopping-center promoters do not encourage this type of shop, and they are usually found in an adjacent lower-rent area. TV repair shops are seldom seen by the customers. Their chief location problem is an area suitable for doing their work. By advertising, they compensate for avoiding the high-rent districts.

Travel agencies depend upon drop-in traffic and therefore require locations on busy streets. Firms selling theater tickets may do all their business by phone or from an upstairs office.

The most important location factor for all service firms is to know the type of customer to whom they plan to appeal. With this knowledge, they should choose a location and site which best fit that customer group.

QUESTIONS FOR CLASS DISCUSSION

1 Would you recommend a hay, grain, and feed store for the main street in your hometown? Why?
2 Where are the auto dealerships located in your town? Is this the high-rent area?
3 What is the difference between a good location and a good site?
4 In seeking a good general location, why should the nature of the industries in the community be studied?
5 What should be your attitude toward competition when seeking a good location for your business?

6 What are the two most important justifications for establishing a new firm in an existing line of business?

7 Where can information be found about a community's population growth, its industry, and its community facilities?

8 Why should the planner of a new small firm consider the nature of the other stores that surround the site being considered?

9 How should the traffic at a specific site be analyzed?

10 When should a factory be close to its source of raw materials rather than its markets?

11 Why is it important to know the buying habits of potential customers when choosing a site?

12 Should a dry-cleaning business be located in a high-rent district? Why?

PROJECTS FOR HOME ASSIGNMENT AND/OR CLASS DISCUSSION

1 In a brief essay explain your understanding of how a more affluent society has reduced the number of people needed to support a sporting goods store.

2 How would you cope with the parking problem for your business in an urban location?

3 How would you value the location of a store you like?

CONTINUING PROBLEM:
The Kollege Klothes Shop

PART 11: CHOOSING THE PROPER LOCATION AND SITE

Now that we have arranged the financing for the new firm, we must turn our attention to the matter of evaluating the general location and specific site that our clients, Jones and Gomez, have chosen.

We must assume that research has been gathered. We have found that the rent is a bit higher than recommended by industry statistics. Justification for this fact is that a corner location on the main trading street near the campus has been chosen. Rear-lot parking is abundantly available. Wide swinging doors are installed in the main entrance. A side-door entrance is used for receiving new shipments of merchandise to be stored and processed in the rear of the building, as well as for use as an additional customer entrance.

In view of the fact that our clients have restricted our consulting work to evaluating this particular site, the best we can do for them is to make an evaluation on the basis of the factors we have studied which suggest a high-rent or a low-rent location.

Assignment for Part 11

Prepare a list of all the firm characteristics given in this chapter that suggest a high-rent location and a list of all the firm characteristics that suggest a low-rent location. Then look at each characteristic and see if it applies to our new firm. Place an X opposite the characteristics suggesting high rent which apply to our firm. Then place an X opposite the characteristics that suggest low rent. Our objective is to find which list has the highest applicability to our firm. How many X's do you find suggesting high rent? How many suggest low rent? For this purpose we can assume that a markup of over 35 percent is considered high; a merchandise turnover of over 5 times per year is considered high; low overhead would be operating expenses of less than 30 percent of sales.

REFERENCES FOR FURTHER READING

"Locating or Relocating Your Business," Small Business Administration Pamphlet No. MA201.
"Store Location: 'Little Things' Mean a Lot," Small Business Administration Pamphlet No. SMA168.
"Using a Traffic Study to Select a Retail Site," Small Business Administration Pamphlet No. SMA152.

CHAPTER

LAYOUT

It's funny we never thought of some of those things you say about layout before. Our sales have increased since we tried some of your suggestions.

The Late Learner

The physical arrangement of the business area of a firm is known as its layout. Layouts can be good or bad and can have important effects on sales and profits. Proven established principles can be applied although guiding principles of layout will vary with the type of business. These principles or guidelines are different for retailers and for wholesalers, for manufacturers and for service firms. In all types of firms, however, the objective is maximum efficiency, maximum sales, and hence maximum profits. Key considerations in good layout are best discussed in terms of the general type of firm involved.

LAYOUT FOR THE RETAIL FIRM

Layout for retailers has been defined as "a selling machine." This definition encompasses much of what experienced business owners include in their applications of good layout. Good layout does a great deal to maximize sales and is a vital part of the selling objective. Its basic objective is to do just that—maximize sales. How is this accomplished? The answer lies in observing

Rene Burri/Magnum

FIGURE 12-1
Dessert sales are higher in a cafeteria when they are the first item in the line.

and applying generally accepted rules of layout. Some of them are outlined and discussed briefly below.

GUIDELINES TO GOOD LAYOUT FOR RETAILERS

1   Customer Buying Habits   Know the buying habits of your customers. We have already noted the location of the dessert counter in a cafeteria and the prescription counter in a drugstore. These locations represent applications of knowing customers' buying habits. The hungry patrons of a cafeteria are awed by attractive displays of desserts as they enter the food line. They happily pick one quickly before even knowing what their main course will be. If they had first chosen their vegetables, main dish, and salad, they would likely have been much more reluctant to pick up that luscious dessert. Studies have shown a large decrease in dessert sales when that counter is at the end of the line rather than at its beginning.

Customers who enter a drugstore with prescriptions from their doctors in hand are not concerned with convenience in finding the prescription counter as much as they are with getting the medicine. The purchase will not be lost because they do not find the druggist immediately. If they have been in this particular store before, they know that prescriptions are filled at the back of the store. As they pass along attractive counters of merchandise en route to the prescription counter, they see many other kinds of products and effective displays. That is the key to layout. In making that trip through the store,

FIGURE 12-2
Good layout places the prescription counter at the rear of the drugstore.

customers are likely to make many impulse purchases—those which the customers never anticipated when they entered the store. Each such purchase is a credit to the application of this layout principle.

2 Merchandise Display   Display merchandise attractively. The day when all merchandise in a store was kept in closed drawers, locked showcases, stocked on shelves behind the counter, or generally out of sight is long past. Customers want to find attractive displays of most items they desire to purchase. They want to be able to make ready comparisons: comparisons of price ranges, styles, designs, or alternative products. This is all part of providing customer satisfaction. Open displays are important.

3 Customer Service   Provide good services for customers. They can include pleasant surroundings and courteous personnel in charge of opening credit accounts, competent and agreeable sales people, clean rest rooms, and convenient passageways and stairs.

4 Physical Surroundings   Make maximum use of light, ventilation, and heat. This layout guide serves the comfort of customers and employees as well. Customer comfort aids merchandise selection. The public image of a firm can be a reflection of how well this layout principle is observed.

5 Organization of Merchandise   Display associated lines of merchandise close together. That is, products which most people tend to purchase at one time should be located in close proximity on shelves, in showcases, or on counters. Toothpaste and shaving cream are the classic examples. Shirts, blouses, and skirts are usually displayed adjacently. Customers' convenience is violated when they must travel around the store to find items they consider to be in the same group. There can be no final or all-inclusive answer on this matter because different customers associate different products in groups. Knowing your customers is a great help in this regard.

6 Visual Spaciousness To whatever extent possible, provide a maximum view of the entire store for customers, employees, and managers. Customers prefer seeing other departments when shopping in one. An impression of spaciousness leads to a better image. Managers can do a better job of handling problems such as relieving crowded departments by reassigning sales persons and detecting emergencies. Employees have better morale when they are in closer contact with, or in view of, other employees and customers.

7 Separation of Activities Separate selling from nonselling activities. Generally, this means that such activities as the wrapping and accounting departments, credit offices, repair services, cashiers, public telephones, and customer-service counters should be located near the rear of the store. The front of any store is considered prime selling space.

8 Customer Image Store fixtures should reflect the desired customer image. If the appeal is mainly to men, the fixtures should reflect the "he-man," atmosphere. For women, a more refined image with a feminine touch is, perhaps, appropriate. Colors and decorations are important here. This feature of layout may be observed in sports shops and beauty shops. When customers are equally divided between men and women, general attractiveness is foremost.

9 Utilization of Space Know the value of your space and place merchandise accordingly. The average small retail store is 30 to 50 feet wide and from 50 to 100 feet deep. It has several departments or displays several lines of merchandise for its customers. How should those departments be arranged? Three governing principles apply:

a Most new shoppers turn to the right when entering a store.
b Space in the front of the store will have more customer traffic than rear sections. Front space is, accordingly, more valuable for sales.
c The type of merchandise offered must be considered. Convenience goods, shopping goods, and specialty goods demand different answers because buying habits vary with goods desired (see Chapter 15). It follows that allocation of space among departments should reflect these facts.

In terms of traffic and potential sales, the average floor space can be divided into specific areas. Dividing the total space into nine major sections, as in the floor plans shown in Figures 12-3 and 12-4, we can attach priorities of value for first, second, third, etc., choices.

It will be noted that of the nine areas, two are tied for second choice, two for third choice, and two for sixth choice. Only areas (1), (4), and (5) seem to be clear choices.

Whether the individual planner adopts this valuation in total or not, the important thing is to realize the general relationship of the different areas. There is no definite rule for assigning specific departments or merchandise to these areas. Some guidelines are available. They include the following:

1 Impulse merchandise, convenience goods, and high markup merchandise should be located in the front areas.

2 Shopping merchandise (demand goods) should be located at the rear or upstairs in the multistoried store.

3 Nonselling departments and service departments should be in the rear.

4 It usually does not pay to move a successful department to a less valuable space in order to give a losing department a more valuable space.

5 Wide aisles for customer comfort are recommended, but creation of an occasional "obstacle course" by placing sale merchandise or other special items in an aisle may be good merchandising.

Sixth	Fifth	Sixth
Fourth	Third	Second
Third	Second	First
Windows	Door	Windows

FIGURE 12-3
Space values in a typical retail store.

Office	Beauty Salon	Rest Rooms
Credit Department	Rugs	Will–call
Public Telephones	Drapes	Layaways
Yard Goods	Swim Wear	Men's Shop
Knitting Supplies	Resort Wear	Suits
Major Appliances	Children's Wear	Shoes
China	Lingerie	Shirts
Cutlery	Shoes	Sports
Fine Jewelry		Ties
Better Dresses	Sweaters	Toiletries
Teen's Dresses	Hosiery	Cosmetics
Budget Dresses	Ladies' Bags	Jewelry
		Watches
Windows	Door	Windows

FIGURE 12-4
Possible department locations for a small department store showing space values and types of consumer goods sold.

6 Make good use of available window space by placing attractive displays in them as well as on the selling floor.

Layout, Merchandise Displays, and Shoplifting

We have seen that a vital part of good layout is to have merchandise readily available for customers to view and compare. Many marketing tests have established that sales of particular items are much larger when the item is on an open table or open rack. At the same time, all merchants are confronted with the ever-increasing problem of shoplifting, which has reached tremendous proportions throughout the country in recent years.

There are two aspects of the shoplifting problem: stealing by employees and stealing by visitors in the store. Many millions of dollars are lost by American businesses every year by each type of stealing. The problem of employee stealing demands closer control of employee activities on the premises. It is unfortunate that the necessary measures should be imposed on the honest as well as the

Sensormatic Electronics, Inc.

FIGURE 12-5
Shoplifting is a serious problem today for all small firms too.

dishonest employees, but common sense dictates, however, that these procedures should be viewed in the same light as the commonsense procedures against
airplane hijacking. Application of precautions to all is a necessary evil to protect
the innocent. If personal inconvenience for the innocent can eliminate or reduce
the crime, the result must be to the benefit of all. Fidelity bonds may be
purchased which ensure the firm against employee thefts.

Stealing by outsiders in the store is a different matter. Even the laws of some
states make it very difficult to arrest shoplifters on the premises. Public images
sometimes suffer, even when obviously guilty persons are prosecuted. Large
expenses are incurred in maintaining security staffs within stores. Yet the crime
goes on in untold millions. Large and small firms suffer in the same manner.

Firms which acquire a reputation for prosecuting all shoplifting cases will find
that the problem is reduced. Law enforcement officials recommend prosecuting
as a strong deterrent to shoplifting.

Training sales people to be alert to the problem is also helpful. When people
in a store are immediately welcomed with a "May I help you?" shoplifting is
discouraged.

Various devices have been introduced to cope with this problem. One is the
placing of metallic tags inside clothing items. These tags turn on alarm systems at
all exits unless removed by the sales person when the item is paid for or the
charge slip is signed at the cash register. Other alarm systems can be provided
which buzz upon disconnection of attaching cords when items are removed from

open counters. The cords allow ample space and distance for complete inspection of the merchandise, but only the sales person is to remove them with the alarm system deactivated.

One significant conclusion has been forced upon retail firms. Limits must be placed upon the customer access to some types of merchandise. Items of small bulk and relatively large value must be kept in transparent showcases or glass-doored shelves, which may be necessarily protected by lock and key. Such items as wristwatches, expensive costume jewelry, diamonds, costly cutlery, and even expensive gowns may fall in this category. Some department stores and ladies' ready-to-wear shops have even found it necessary to protect expensive sweaters or dishware in this manner. It is important that the new firm owner be aware of this problem and be prepared to cope with it, at least to keep it to a minimum. It is a sad commentary on our society that we must accept the reality of this serious problem. It is only to be hoped that improved morality may eliminate the problem or reduce it to a minimum. It is the honest consumers who pay the final bill for this outrageous situation.

LAYOUT FOR THE WHOLESALER

Layout considerations for a wholesaling firm are dominated by the objective of filling orders with speed and economy. This goal also emphasizes the speed and economy with which inventories are stacked in the warehouse. Emphasis must be placed on the labor costs expended in the process of storing the inventories and in filling the orders received. More than 60 percent of total operating costs of the average wholesaler consists of labor costs, and the ability to compete depends on efficiency in controlling labor costs.

Methods that can be of assistance to wholesalers include:

1 Keeping most often demanded merchandise easily accessible
2 Using conveyors, material-handling equipment, and overhead cranes wherever feasible
3 Using the principle of gravity when possible

These methods help speed order filling and inventory stocking.

Wholesalers handle many different lines of merchandise. Hence, no one rule for inventory arrangement can be suggested. Common to all wholesalers, however, is the necessity of knowing the most frequently ordered items so that application of the above suggestions may be possible.

LAYOUT FOR THE FACTORY

Factories that produce only one product, or one product at a time, have the advantage of being able to use a *continuous-production layout*—usually called a *product layout*. All operations follow the same path through the manufacturing process. Materials are received where needed in the assembly or manufacturing process, all machines are placed at the point where needed without unnecessary moving of materials or products in process, and all product comes from the assembly line at one point.

The ideal product layout calls for having raw materials delivered at the factory door nearest to where the materials go into the assembly or manufacturing line, having a continuous conveyor belt move the product in process frcm one station to another nearby, having any required subassemblies delivered close to the point of need, and having all finished products arrive on the same conveyor belt, even packaged and ready for delivery or storage.

The obvious goal of all factory layout is to minimize the unproductive movement of products and materials. Possibilities for doing this are much greater in continuous-production, or product, layouts.

Factories that produce different kinds of products, or even produce products to individual orders, cannot use this arrangement for their machines and operations because the routes through the manufacturing process are different for each product manufactured. They use a *process layout*—also known as *intermittent manufacturing layout.*

Foundries and job-order printing firms are examples of factories that produce many different products, each of which may require a special sequence of machines or other operations in the process of being completed. Each product usually follows a different path through the manufacturing process. The big problem in layout here is to minimize the movement of work in process which does not add value to the final product. Having people move half-finished products in wheelbarrows from one machine to another some distance away adds nothing to the value of the finished product. Yet, much movement is often necessary to complete the orders. Another problem is that some machines may be kept busy all the time, and others are in use only part of the time. Efficient layout therefore means having the most frequently used machines in proper quantity handy for all orders.

Because of the differences in product and process layouts, costs for process layout manufacturing are usually higher than for most product layout manufacturing.

With the guiding rule of keeping unproductive movement of materials and work in process to a minimum, ncw firm planners should first study their production lines to see how closely they can keep them to the ideal. Keeping the production-control and production-planning personnel in close proximity to the factory production line can contribute to this overall objective.

LAYOUT FOR THE SERVICE FIRM

Service firms are so varied that little can be said of common factors shared. A barber or beautician needs an attractive shop with enough chairs to handle customers in good time, space for all the equipment used for hair treatment, an attractive space for waiting customers, and a receptionist. Many of these shops also maintain a stock of products for sale. Repair shops for major appliances are seldom seen by their customers. Customers phone the TV repair shop or the washing-machine repair shop. The person doing the repairs visits the home, does the work, and is paid. The only need is for an efficient workshop at his or her headquarters. A travel agency, if catering to transient trade, needs a well-located office with adequate counters, phone service, and comfortable places for customers to wait or to be interviewed. A firm selling only theater tickets may operate from a home telephone or a hired desk in a business office. Others may maintain offices on a popular street, if they are catering to drop-in traffic. A cleaning establishment needs to have its equipment arranged like a product-line factory and room to receive its customers and return finished dry cleaning. Laundries generally follow the product line in processing their services. Most of their customers may be served via delivery trucks, but counters are also usually provided to receive customers and make deliveries.

The one common factor shared by all service firms is the importance of keeping their facilities consistent with the volume and type of service they are rendering.

QUESTIONS FOR CLASS DISCUSSION

1 What action would you take against employees guilty of stealing merchandise from your business?
2 Compare a product layout (continuous production) with a process layout (intermittent layout).
3 Why is the prescription counter in a drugstore usually found at the rear of the store?
4 Can you think of any practical reasons why grocery stores place the frozen goods close to the checkout stations?
5 How do displays of merchandise become important in layout?
6 Would you advocate open counter displays of wristwatches? If not, why not?
7 What do we mean by the relative value of space within a retail store?
8 Why shouldn't the nonselling activities be in the front of the store?
9 What are impulse goods? Where should they be located in a retail store?
10 Do you believe that window displays are an important part of total layout?
11 How would you combat the problem of shoplifting in your store?
12 What is the prime objective in layout for a wholesaler?
13 What is the difference between a product layout and a process layout?
14 "Factory layout seeks to minimize the unproductive movement of goods in process." What does this statement mean to you?

PROJECTS FOR HOME ASSIGNMENT AND/OR CLASS DISCUSSION

1 How have shoplifting and dishonest employees affected the problems of layout and employee policies? Do you have opinions on these subjects?
2 Explain what the statement "layout can be called a selling machine" means to you.
3 Do you agree that different parts of the same store have different "space values"? Do you agree with the space values attached to the floor plans in this chapter? Why or why not?

CONTINUING PROBLEM:
The Kollege Klothes Shop

PART 12: LAYOUT

Jones and Gomez have requested that you prepare for them a brief report on the principles of layout which they should be familiar with as they proceed with their planning. They would also like to see a simple floor plan sketch of where you would place departments, products, and dressing rooms on the 50-ft by 70-ft selling space in the front of the store building. The rear 50-ft by 30-ft space they have asked us to reserve for storage space, order filling, and so on.

Assignment for Part 12

Name and give a brief explanation of some of the general layout principles you have studied for use by your clients. Then make a tentative floor-plan sketch showing where you suggest placing some of the products normally sold in a college clothes and accessories store. Even though product lines are not all certain as yet, your clients wish to rely on your experience as college students. They do request that you include suggested locations for an office where hiring, credit applications from customers, and sales people conferences will be held. One lavatory in the warehouse is planned. Include the warehouse space on your sketch.

REFERENCES FOR FURTHER READING

Macfarlane, William N., *Principles of Small Business,* McGraw-Hill Book Company, New York, 1977, chap. 7.
"Signs and Your Business," Small Business Administration Pamphlet No. 161.
"Stock Control for Small Stores," Small Business Administration Pamphlet No. 123.

CHAPTER **13**

ADVERTISING AND PROMOTION

I was always afraid of advertising. I tried it once, and the increased sales didn't pay the cost of the advertising. Maybe I used the wrong kind. But how can I know which kind to use? How can I tell if it pays?

The Late Learner

"Running a business without advertising is like winking at a pretty girl in the dark—you know what you're doing, but she doesn't."[1] The president of one of the largest advertising companies in New York concluded a formal address on the billions of dollars spent on advertising each year in the United States by saying, "We know that half of these billions were wasted. The only trouble is we don't know which half."

These two statements point out the importance of advertising and the size of the advertising bill in this country every year, and should caution all business people to make their advertising effective. This warning is even more true for small firms that normally cannot absorb wasteful expenditures as well as larger firms.

[1]Copyright, General Features Corporation. Reprinted with permission.

154

THE NATURE OF DEMAND

The total demand for the goods or services offered by any small firm can be divided into (1) established demand and (2) promoted, or created, demand.

Established demand is that volume of sales which comes without conscious outside promotion by the firm. It assumes that the firm is established with some degree of attractiveness and relies basically on that fact to bring customers to the firm to buy products or services. Reliance is also placed on the fact that people see the store and think of it, perhaps, when products or services are considered. It is recognized that pedestrian traffic is already in the area and that some of the people will stop en route to other places. Distance from competitors will usually assist in bringing in established demand for most types of merchandise.

Promoted demand, by contrast, is the volume of sales which results from the firm's engaging in all types of activities to draw people to the firm. Promoted-demand customers, if pleased, can become established customers.

It is not true that small firms cannot operate profitably when they rely solely on established demand. However, those firms which supplement this established demand with promoted demand show much better sales volume and profits. Too many small firms restrict their operations by ignoring the possibilities of creating more sales. Case studies often show that the reasons are a *lack of working capital* to pay expenses of promotion, a *belief that their market is inelastic,* or a *lack of knowledge of how to design a sales promotion program.*

All the activities that go into the development of sales can be grouped under the title *sales promotion.* Sales promotion can use either *direct* or *indirect* methods. There are no guarantees that any one method will show a precise dollar return in sales, but the effectiveness of each can usually be measured with some degree of accuracy. Every small firm owner should think about using some of the following types of sales promotion:

Direct promotion methods	Indirect promotion methods
1 Advertising	1 Public relations
2 Publicity	2 Customer relations
3 Displays	3 Customer services
4 Special event sales	4 Product styling and
5 Manufacturers' aids	packaging
6 Personal selling	

Each of these promotional methods may be important in the individual case, and surely all of them are valuable ways of trying to expand business sales in the short or long run.

DIRECT SALES PROMOTION

Advertising

It must be recognized that advertising is essential to almost every business. Large-scale advertising has made possible the benefits of mass production by

FIGURE 13-1
Attractive store fronts will lure customers. Unattractive fronts will discourage walk-in traffic.

creating a demand for the increased flow of products and services that mass production has made possible. Unit costs have been reduced in most cases because the economies of large-scale production have more than offset the cost of advertising.

Advertising can be defined as commercial messages to the public, designed to inform potential and established customers and to encourage sales for the advertiser. Advertising can be either *institutional* (designed to sell the firm name) or *direct action* (designed to sell the firm's product or services). An advertisement saying, "Our employees subscribed to the United Fund 100 percent" is an example of institutional advertising. "Raincoats are on sale today at $10.95!" is an example of direct-action advertising. Most small firm advertising is of the direct-action type. Service firms may stress the services available from the firm, but this is still direct action to sell that service.

Types of Advertising Media

Among the media generally used in advertising are:

1 Television
2 Radio
3 Newspapers
4 Magazines
5 Outdoor billboards

6 Specialty advertising (distribution of such items as matchpads, pencils, calendars, blotters, gummed labels, telephone pads, shopping bags)

7 Public transportation

8 Yellow pages

9 Direct mail

10 Other media (catalogs, samples, handout leaflets, etc.)

Small firms have a special problem in choosing the medium or type of advertising that is best for them. Big city *television* is not appropriate for most. Large city *newspapers* are too expensive for a firm that services only a small part of the city (although local newspapers can be used, as we will discuss later). It is worthy of note that some large newspapers have attempted to cope with this problem by having special small firm advertising sections where a dozen or more individual small firm ads can be displayed on a single page. Attractive advertising rates have made such advertising possible for more small firms. Effectiveness of such ads has been demonstrated in many cases. *Magazines* usually cover too much territory for a small local firm. Metropolitan *radio* advertising has adjusted somewhat to the problems of the small firm through multisponsored programs. In smaller cities and towns, the local radio station and newspaper may do a good job of covering the market of the small firm.

© *Marjorie Pickens, 1980*

FIGURE 13-2
Billboard advertising can be effective for small firms as well as large firms.

Billboards are most effective when used near the actual site of the small business. The use of billboards in political campaigns has demonstrated their effectiveness, although their appeal in elections is usually to a much wider audience than that of the market of a particular small firm. Commercial billboards are quite expensive for individual firms, but they are often custom-made for sites such as on another of the owner's buildings, or a friend's vacant lot that are available on less expensive terms to the particular firm.

Effectiveness of *specialty advertising* has been proved by many small firms. Its appropriateness will vary with the type of business. It can take almost limitless forms. Pencils for children when school begins, calendars distributed in attractive shopping bags to neighborhood homes, matchpads, telephone pads for firms taking telephone orders, blotters, ball-point pens with company name inscribed, and even gummed labels for various uses have all been effective in particular cases. All should prominently show the firm's name, address, and phone number. Experience will demonstrate the effectiveness of any particular devices used.

Advertising in *public transportation* vehicles has become big business and can be effective for small firms if it is possible to coordinate the particular vehicles used and the firm's market. Local streetcars, buses, subways, and taxis are most popular.

Yellow-page advertising is recommended only where the firm is dealing in shopping goods or has a market where customers may be looking for a firm which is first contacted by telephone.

Despite its abuse over the years, *direct-mail advertising* remains the most effective advertising media for the great majority of small firms. It has the advantages of being selective in its coverage, less expensive, more flexible, adjustable to any size firm, and subject to measurement of its effectiveness. Because of past abuse, however, it must be done well to avoid being tossed into the nearest wastebasket.

MEASURING ADVERTISING EFFECTIVENESS

Whenever possible, every advertising program undertaken should be checked for its effectiveness. Some of the ways the small firm can do this are:

1 Advertise one item in one ad only. Have no references to the item on the sales floor. Then count the calls and requests that result.

2 Place separate identifying marks in an ad that appears in two places. The reader is asked to bring the ad to the firm to obtain a special price or prize. See how many ads come in from each source.

3 Omit a regular advertising project for intermittent periods and watch any change in sales.

4 Check sales results when a new advertisement is placed.

While the results of these and similar advertising programs cannot be measured precisely, they can give some indication of effectiveness. Timing, products advertised, weather, and attractions offered, such as valuable coupons, will affect results. If no results are observable, it can be said that the program is not effective as direct action advertising. However, it may have notified some people of the existence of the firm, and they may include it on future shopping journeys. It will thus have served an institutional purpose.

It should be obvious that the most important thing in designing an advertising program for any small firm is knowing your market—knowing where the present and potential customers you seek are located. The more owners know about their customers, the better they can devise ways to get their advertising messages to them. If many customers live in a condominium, for example, an ad in the local house paper may be most effective. If many live in private homes in a small town and take the local newspaper, newspaper advertising is recommended. These are only obvious examples. Time spent in studying the potential customer market will pay good dividends. Much of the wasted expenditures for advertising can be traced to careless preparation of the advertising, not knowing the market and hence misdirecting the advertising, and using the wrong media.

Once an advertising program has been decided upon, it must be consistent and continuous throughout the year. Special features or special events are appropriate for extra expenditures at certain times, but the basic program must

---

Are your judgments based on what you know or what you hear?

THE MAN WHO SOLD HOT DOGS

There was a man who lived by the side of the road and sold hot dogs.
He was hard of hearing so he had no radio.
He had trouble with his eyes so he read no newspapers.
But he sold good hot dogs.
He put up signs on the highway telling how good they were.
He stood on the side of the road and cried: "Buy a hot dog, Mister?"
And people bought and profits were good.
He increased his meat and bun orders.
He bought a bigger stove to take care of his trade.
He finally got his son home from college to help him out.
But then something happened.
His son said, "Father, haven't you been listening to the radio?
Haven't you been reading the newspapers?
There's a big depression.
The European situation is terrible.
The domestic situation is worse."
Whereupon the father thought, "Well, my son's been to college, he reads the papers and he listens to the radio, and he ought to know."
So the father cut down on his meat and bun orders, took down his advertising signs, and no longer bothered to stand out on the highway to sell his hot dogs.
And his hot dog sales fell almost overnight.
"You're right, son," the father said to the boy.
"We certainly are in the middle of a great depression."

be continuous, with both a long-run and a short-run objective in view at all times.

Publicity

Publicity has often been described as advertising that is not paid for. It includes such things as public news about the owner of the firm which tends to brighten the firm's image or make friends for the business. Notices of support given to community activities, awards won by employees for excellence in their industry, public citations for service rendered, election to office in community organizations, sponsorship of a team in the Babe Ruth Softball League, notices of new services or techniques available are examples. Such activities give the firm a reputation for being interested in and related to the community interests, for striving to give the latest and best services, for having competent people to serve its customers, or for just being a desirable place to do business. Their effect may often be more indirect than direct promotion, but, in any event, the potential of publicity should be exploited wherever possible.

Displays

Displays are an on-site method of sales promotion. Products which are not normally considered impulse items to most people are often sold through an effective display in the windows or on the sales floor. Displays enable the merchant to add changes, interest, and brightness to the standard layout, and

FIGURE 13-3
Displays can be effective sales developers.

© Lisl/Photo Researchers, Inc.

FIGURE 13-4
Competitive merchandise sales can be assisted by large displays of affected products.

when done well, can do much to increase sales. Even the occasional use of a display as an "obstacle course" item can be effective if not overdone. Windows can be used for sophisticated displays, such as in men's clothing stores, or for giving information about special sales or events, for example, in grocery stores. The use of home-made window signs to advertise prices on Saturday or week-end specials has become a vital activity in many consumer goods firms.

Special Event Sales

Using special events as direct sales promotion has become a well-established feature of most consumer goods businesses. They are sometimes used by industrial goods firms, but less often. The firm's anniversary, Lincoln's or Washington's birthday, the firm president's birthday, the addition of a new service for customers, the start of the spring and fall seasons, etc., can all be used as occasions to promote sales. Major holidays are ideal for sales. Making the most of such events may entail use of other direct promotion methods, such as advertising, but special events justify classification as a separate direct promotion method.

Manufacturers' Aids

Manufacturers' aids are any form of assistance provided by the manufacturer to small wholesalers and retailers for promoting sales. These aids may take the form of national advertising of the products involved, assignment of sales representatives to be in the particular store, provision of attractive window and floor displays, or actual contributions to an advertising program. Such products as home appliances, automobiles, television sets, and men's suits and shirts are often accompanied by such assistance from the manufacturer. Firms having franchises and/or distributorships are frequently aided by the parent firm in many of these matters.

Personal Selling

Personal selling means all those activities and characteristics of the individual salesperson which make for successful sales. If it is recognized that all people are not good salespersons, we can appreciate that there are certain things that make good ones. Some of these are the ability to discover potential customers, a knowledge of ways to acquaint potential customers with available merchandise, and the ability to close a sale. The types of skills required will vary with different kinds of firms and products. Personality, human psychology, and merchandise knowledge are always important.

Fundamental to all good personal selling is a thorough knowledge of the merchandise by the salesperson. The advantages, various uses, and special qualities of the merchandise must be thoroughly known. Discerning customers look to the salesperson for such knowledge. They know quickly if the salesperson is competent or incompetent in this regard. If a salesperson is only an order

FIGURE 13-5
Personal selling is a most effective tool in producing sales and customer satisfaction.

Donald Dietz, 1979/Stock, Boston

taker, this fact is soon obvious to such customers. If equipment or machinery is involved, the salesperson must be able to demonstrate the product efficiently. In retailing, such characteristics as pleasant personality, good appearance, knowledge of prices, and interest in finding a product to fill an expressed need become more important. Confidence in firms is developed through successful personal selling. A positive training program for all salespeople should be a must for small firms, just as it is in large firms. Advertising may produce a first inquiry from potential customers or bring them into a retail establishment, but unless the personal selling that follows is satisfactory, not only the first sale but all potential repeat business is in jeopardy.

The four basic steps in making any sale have often been summarized as follows:

1 Gaining the prospective customer's attention
2 Arousing interest
3 Creating desire for the product—overcoming objections
4 Closing the sale

The detailed sales plan in applying these four steps varies with the type of product and type of business. The drugstore salesperson will need to give less attention to these steps because the customers come in with an interest in a particular product. The person who is selling an electric saw to a prospective customer will need to pay attention to every detail of the sales plan.

INDIRECT SALES PROMOTION

We observed earlier in this chapter that indirect sales-promotional methods are usually classified as public relations, good customer relations, customer services, product styling, and packaging of products. These may all be applied to the established demand customers we have previously discussed, but they can also be applied to the development of new customers.

Public Relations

A firm's public relations determine its image, or popular reputation, in the general community. The nature of its public relations, good or bad, is reflected in the community's attitude toward the firm. Every business has public relations, either consciously or unconsciously, and a good image cannot normally be purchased. It is the responsibility of every person associated with the firm. Every act of the firm's representatives contributes to the overall image of the firm. Good public relations are a cumulative net result, which is more easily destroyed than built. Good public relations develop goodwill and sales. Every owner should be aware of the importance of good public relations and should be sure that each employee knows the importance of them and how they are built. Building good relations in the community is a never-ending project. Every proposed business policy should first be analyzed in terms of its effect upon the company image. Every crisis decision must always consider the possible effect upon the firm's image.

Customer Relations

Good customer relations build sales independently and also contribute to the total image of the firm. Satisfied, happy customers are the best form of advertising. Word-of-mouth advertising results from happy customers. Good customer relations are basically the result of past transactions with the firm. Such practices as speedy handling of complaints, assistance in emergencies, favors in obtaining items, and abiding by announced policies all assist in developing good customer relations. Courteous, competent, and pleasant treatment of customers is most important.

Customer Services

Customer services can be a part of both public relations and good customer relations. Many customers want special services and seek out firms that supply them. Examples are air-conditioned stores, night hours for shopping, credit accounts, delivery service, and lines of merchandise not generally available. Pricing policy may be adjusted to a particular customer group. Trading stamps may provide an attraction as a customer service. Effective administration of any services offered is essential to making them valuable as sales developers. Firms selling industrial products have found recently that the most valued customer services are on-time deliveries, conformity to specifications of products sold, and efficient accounting procedures.

Product Styling and Packaging

Product styling and product packaging are obvious aids in developing sales volume. Customers who desire to be first with the latest styles seek out the merchants who have them. When similar products are offered in various styles, they seek choices. Packaging can be an equal attraction. The cosmetics field is an excellent example of products which have been presented in all types of beautiful bottles and packages. Even choices in the packaging of bread have recently been of concern to some customers, some preferring a package which has either a detachable tie (device to reclose the package after opening) or the inner wrapper supplied by some bakers. Such customer preferences probably reflect a desire for uniqueness rather than utility in the product just discussed.

All the indirect sales promotion methods reflect a conviction that the customer is the most important part of any successful business. There can be no profit in the absence of sales. Efforts to keep present customers happy and to develop new ones constantly are essential to continued profits and growth.

QUESTIONS FOR CLASS DISCUSSION

1 Can you give an example of manufacturers' aids helping individual retailers make sales?
2 Does a neighborhood store in your hometown do any advertising? How? Would you recommend any other advertising?
3 How would you describe established demand as contrasted with promoted demand?
4 How would you define advertising?
5 Is advertising as important to small firms as to large ones?
6 How is the problem of choosing the advertising media different for small firms and for large ones?
7 What is specialty advertising? Give some examples.
8 Would you recommend advertising on the "Tonight Show" for a small-town department store? Why?
9 How do you recommend that direct-mail advertising be made effective?
10 What do we mean by "checking the effectiveness of advertising"? What are some of the methods by which this can be done?
11 What is meant by saying that creating an "obstacle course" with a display can increase sales of an item of merchandise?
12 What are the four basic steps in successful selling?
13 Do you agree that good public relations can normally not be purchased? Why?
14 What is meant by saying that product styling can be an indirect sales promotion device?

PROJECTS FOR HOME ASSIGNMENT AND/OR CLASS DISCUSSION

1 Do you know of a product you or your family prefer because of its packaging and styling? Explain such a case and why you prefer it.
2 List what you think would be the best advertising media for your own hardware store in a suburban area. Prepare a specific ad for the store.
3 Can you name some special events that could be the basis of special sales for a fast-food franchise? How would you advertise them and where?

CONTINUING PROBLEM:
The Kollege Klothes Shop

PART 13: ADVERTISING AND PROMOTION

Your clients admit a lack of knowledge as to how to proceed with a program of advertising and promotion of sales. They seriously desire your recommendations.

Assignment for Part 13

Prepare a report showing your recommendations for a program of sales promotion for the new college clothes shop. Will you rely on established demand or aggressively pursue newly created demand? How? Which promotions will you use? What advertising media, if any, do you recommend for this new shop? How will you suggest measuring the effectiveness of your advertising? What other suggestions will you make as recommendations to your clients?

REFERENCES FOR FURTHER READING

"Advertising Guidelines for Small Retail Firms," Small Business Administration Pamphlet No. SMA160.

"Do You Know the Results of Your Advertising?" Small Business Administration Pamphlet No. SMA169.

Steinhoff, Dan, *The World of Business,* McGraw-Hill Book Company, New York, 1979, chap. 15.

Tate, Curtis E. Jr., Leon Megginson, Charles Scott, Jr., and Lyle Trueblood, *Successful Small Business Management,* rev. ed., Business Publications, Inc., Dallas, Texas, 1978, chap. 16.

CHAPTER

PRICING POLICIES

When I first opened my business I figured my prices were my own business. Nobody was going to tell me what price to place on my merchandise. I set my own and people could buy it or leave it. Many didn't buy. Now I know my prices must reflect many things I can't control.

The Late Learner

FACTORS AFFECTING INDIVIDUAL PRICES

The prices that any firm can charge for its merchandise are subject to many influences. Some or all of the following considerations may apply in a particular case:

1 Fair trade laws
2 Nationally advertised prices
3 Desired customer clientele
4 Competitor price policies
5 Market strategy
6 Manufacturers' suggested prices
7 Type of merchandise handled

   8 Policy on loss leaders
   9 Seasonal nature of sales
  10 Demand factor for certain products
  11 Price lining
  12 Target return pricing

A word about each of these factors will introduce us to the total scene of setting prices. *Fair trade laws* still exist in many states. These laws allow the manufacturer of a product to make agreements with dealers who retail the product on the price it can be sold to the public. *Nationally advertised prices* must be recognized by small firms as at least an upper limit to the prices they place on items so advertised. *Competitor prices* on similar lines or merchandise with similar quality must be recognized when active competition exists between firms. *Market strategy* is a policy of setting prices and quality in a range not served by competitors.

Where a special clientele is served, its buying habits can be reflected in price policy. For example, if affluent people want special services and special merchandise, they are willing to pay for such service. In other cases, the desired clientele may be price-conscious and price policy will be directed to serve them.

Manufacturers' suggested prices are designed by the manufacturers to protect the quality image of their products and to protect profit margins for the individual retailer. Price policy is significantly affected by the *type of merchandise handled* by the firm, whether convenience, shopping, or specialty merchandise. This subject is pursued in detail in a later chapter. Novelties or special-interest items normally carry higher markups.

Loss leaders (products sold below cost) are still illegal in some states whose laws reflect an earlier attempt by independent firms to combat the increase of chain-store competition. *Seasonal nature of sales* can affect pricing policy by making it possible to alter prices with the high and low seasons of sales volume. The nature of *overall demand* is likewise a consideration in setting individual prices. Elastic demand suggests lower prices. Specialty goods, such as luxury items and style merchandise, carry higher prices. *Price lining* is a policy of keeping merchandise in fairly well-defined price ranges. Dresses at $19.95, $24.95 and $29.95 would be an example.

Target return pricing is a relatively recent development in the theory of pricing. It involves adding a desired percentage return on investment or a specific dollar amount return to total fixed costs in setting retail prices. This higher fixed cost total is then added to variable costs in setting prices. This method assumes a given volume of sales in terms of units of product against which the procedure is applied. For example, a factory plans to sell 10,000 units of its product in the coming year. Fixed expenses are $150,000, variable expenses are $300,000, and it is desired to earn a profit of 10 percent on its investment of $500,000 (or $50,000). Using a target return pricing principle, the owner would add the $150,000, the $300,000 and the $50,000 for a total of $500,000. This total is the amount which must be received in sales of the 10,000 units of product in order to produce the desired return on investment. This means that the unit price would be $50 (10,000 times $50 equals $500,000). We can only hope that the many other circumstances that affect pricing, including the competitor's prices, would not change this price calculation.

From this maze of influences on individual prices, some always present and some justifying irregular application, there are always basic considerations that take overall precedence in the determination of the price policy for the individual firm.

AVERAGE MARKUP AND INDIVIDUAL PRICES

Up to now, we have used average markup figures for our type of business in setting up the projected income statement. We have found that if a firm has sales of $100,000 and gross margin of $40,000, it has an average markup on total sales of 40 percent. This does not mean that every item in the store was marked up 40 percent of sales. (The principle of markup on sales, not on costs, will be explained later.) Some had more than this average markup and others undoubtedly had less than 40 percent markup. The total year's sales probably included some loss leaders, or items which were sold below actual invoice cost. Pricing policy in total must recognize these facts—while always bearing in mind that the overall average markup must be maintained to arrive at the planned profit.

Pricing policy can be expressed diagrammatically, as in Figure 14-1.

The days when many businesses operated on a basis of a standard markup on

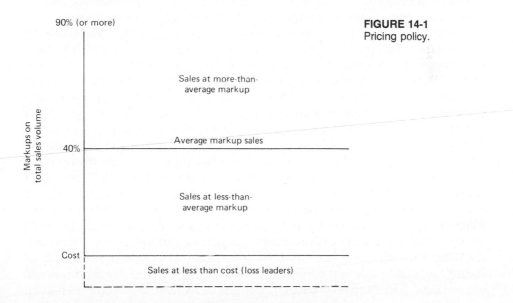

FIGURE 14-1
Pricing policy.

every item in the store are long past. Almost every firm today has sales in each of the four areas shown in Figure 14-1. Dynamic pricing policy demands that owners be aware of the aggregate sales volume in each area so that overall total sales will average out to the markup necessary to provide desirable overall profits. Individual prices will reflect the many points discussed above. If loss leaders are a desirable part or necessary condition of the total merchandising plan, they must be offset by extra profit margins on other items. As we have noted, loss leaders are still illegal or regulated in some states. Any merchandise sales in the less-than-average markup area must also be offset by sales in the above-average markup area.

Understanding this pricing policy will explain why the price of corn flakes may be $1.09 (its normal markup price) one day in a grocery store, 89 cents on another day, and $1.14 on still another. Wednesday specials, other sales prices, and special attractions will alter the price of the same product from time to time. These variations are intended to attract customers who are price-conscious and to compensate for the deficiencies in gross margin on other occasions. We can see this policy well applied in the Wednesday specials of grocery stores. It should be especially noted that the prices of many of these specials are subject to a "minimum order of $5 or $7 excluding tobacco items." The idea of attracting sales by using less-than-average markup items is practiced by retailers in almost every line of consumer goods. They may be used with equal effectiveness by sellers of many industrial goods.

THE NATURE AND COMPUTATION OF MARKUP

Markup represents the difference between what is paid for merchandise and the price at which it is sold to the customer. That markup, or gross margin, is the merchant's reward for rendering a social service in bringing the merchandise to the customer. The merchant has given the merchandise *place utility*. The basic justification for any profit is a reward for rendering this service.

The markup should always be computed as a percentage of the retail price, not as a percentage of the cost of merchandise. The most competent proprietor will compare sales records from period to period in terms of the percentage of sales and average markup represented for each department or type of merchandise. The total of all operating expenses, cost of goods sold, and profits must equal 100 percent of sales. Statement analysis is always facilitated when all items on the income statement are stated as a percentage of the sales figure.

We must recall here the proprietor who insisted that the accountant was wrong in stating that there was an operating loss for the period rather than a profit. The proprietor contended that there was a profit because "markup was 25 percent, while operating expenses were 23 percent, including my salary, and therefore I must have a net return on investment of 2 percent of sales." Of course, the accountant was correct; the owner's markup was based on cost and not on sales. A markup of 25 percent of cost is equivalent to 20 percent on sales.

TABLE 14-1 MARKUP EQUIVALENTS

Desired percentage of sales	Equivalent percentage of cost
10	11.1
13	15
15	17.7
20	25
25	33.3
30	42.9
33⅓	50
35	53.9
40	66.7
50	100

The firm had actually incurred a net loss from operations of 3 percent of sales (see Table 14-1).

To illustrate this situation, consider merchandise costing $100. Marked up at 25 percent of cost, the sale price would be $125 (25 percent times $100, added to $100). But operating expenses are 23 percent of sales. This amounts to $28.75 (23 percent times $125). Net result is a loss of $3.75 on each $125 of sales or $100 of cost of merchandise. (Markup of $25 is $3.75 less than operating expenses of $28.75). No firm can long endure under such circumstances. Obviously, this owner had to increase the markup or reduce operating expenses to get back into a profit position.

TABLES TO ASSIST IN SETTING PRICES

To ease the problem of retail pricing and still assure that markups are based on sales prices, tables have been prepared to show what percentage of cost is necessary to provide the desired percentage of sales price in the markup. A segment of such a table is shown in Table 14-1. Most office supply stores have them available.

It can be seen from Table 14-1 that 20 percent of sales, for example, is equivalent to 25 percent of cost. If a 20 percent markup on sales is desired and if it is easier for persons pricing merchandise, they can just take 25 percent of the cost and add it to the cost to arrive at sales price. The important thing is to quote the markup as 20 percent of sales price and use this figure in statement analysis.

SETTING INITIAL PRICES

Initial prices on merchandise must cover all these items:

1 Markdowns

2 Shortages
3 Damaged merchandise
4 Employee discounts
5 Operating expenses
6 Cost of goods sold
7 Profits

The new firm may not know how to estimate the volume of some of these items. Data gathered for comparable firms in the planning stage can assist in making realistic estimates. None can be neglected. It is much safer to use a generous estimate than to be short in the calculations. Operating expenses and desired profits are clearly set forth on the budgeted income statement. The other items will be reflected in a lessened net sales figure and will not normally appear in the expense accounts. It is always hoped that markdowns, shortages (like shoplifting losses), and damaged merchandise will be kept to a minimum. Employee discounts are usually desirable as a basic part of personnel policy but do not appear on the income statement. A popular figure used in retailing to represent the first four items listed above is 3 percent of net sales. This will vary, of course, with different firms and different policies.

INITIAL PRICE: MARK-ON VERSUS AVERAGE MARKUP

It is because of the implications of the preceding paragraphs that marketing experts draw a distinction between *mark-on* and the *average markup,* as the latter term is computed from the year-end income statement. The distinction is based on the fact that many of the items just discussed (markdowns, shortages, damaged merchandise, and employee discounts) are normally not shown on the income statement as such. In most cases it would be impossible to put a dollar amount on these items. Markdowns are recorded at lower sales prices; shortages like shoplifting are not sales at all, but the merchandise lost is still included in the cost of goods sold; damaged merchandise sold at a discount is merely a lessened sales item; and employee discounts are usually recorded as sales at lessened prices. *It is important, however, that all of these items be covered in the initial price set upon the merchandise.* Hence the term mark-on denotes the total amount added to the cost of merchandise in setting the *initial price.*

In contrast to this, when we refer to average markup shown on an income statement (gross margin divided by sales), we are using the net sales which resulted after all of the above items have had their effect on the sales figure, or have been included in the cost of goods sold when they were shortages instead of sales. The average markup reflected on the income statement may be 38 percent, but if the items of markdowns, damaged merchandise, shortages, and employee discounts amounted to 4 percent of net sales, a mark-on of 42 percent would be necessary in setting the initial price.

The fundamental lesson to be learned by small firm operators is that if you wish to maintain an average markup on net sales of a given percentage, you must use a somewhat higher percentage of sales in setting the initial price.

PRICE CALCULATIONS

If 25 percent of net sales is required to cover operating expenses, if 3 percent is required to cover markdowns, shortages, damaged merchandise, and employee discounts, and if 12 percent is the desired profit, then an average total mark-on of 40 percent of sales must be applied to maintain the planned profit. The income statement at the end of the year will still show an average markup of 37 percent if the 3 percent allowance for markdowns, shortages, damaged merchandise, and employee discounts is utilized according to plans. Thus, mark-on is 40 percent and average markup is 37 percent.

Looked at another way, the initial price of any merchandise offered for sale can be computed as follows:

> Initial price in dollars must equal cost of merchandise, plus operating expenses, plus markdowns, plus shortages, plus damaged goods, plus employee discounts, plus profits.

How is the retail price of a particular item computed when the markup as a percentage of sales is known? Let us take a case which illustrates our figures above. Mark-on is now 40 percent of sales. If mark-on is 40 percent of sales price, the cost of the item is 60 percent of sales price. An item—a dress, say—costing $25 would retail for $41.67. Computations can be made in two different ways:

1

$$\frac{.4167}{60\,)\,25.0000} \times 100 = \$41.67$$

24 0
1 00
  60
 400
 360
 400
 420

Explanation of computations:

1 The cost of the dress equals 60 percent of sales price. We divide the cost ($25) by 60 to find 1 percent of sales price. Then multiply this 1 percent by 100 to find 100 percent of sales price.

2

$$\frac{41.67}{.60x\,)\,25.0000} = x$$

2 By algebraic formula we would use: $.60x = 25$ and then solve for x to find retail price of $41.67.

If the item involved in this calculation were to be sold in various price ranges, it would be placed in the next price range above $41.67. Dresses, for example, might be sold at $35, $45, or '55. The $25 dress would likely be put on the $45 rack.

We should stress here what the retail price would have been if the markup had been computed on cost rather than sales price. We would merely take markup percentage, 40 percent, of $25 ($10), and add it to cost ($25) to establish a retail price of $35. It is this ease of calculation which had made this method more popularly understood and also has contributed to the errors in statement analysis previously mentioned.

QUESTIONS FOR CLASS DISCUSSION

1 What is a table of markup equivalents?
2 What is the difference between "average markup" and "initial price setting"?
3 What does market strategy mean as a price policy?
4 What does price lining mean as a price policy?
5 What is a loss leader? Would you ever recommend its use?
6 Does average markup mean that every item in a store has the same markup?
7 What items must be covered by markup other than normal operating expenses and planned profits?
8 How would you compute the sale price for an item which costs $8 and is to be marked up 20 percent of sales price?
9 Do you believe employee discounts are justified for most types of business firms?
10 How does a store owner achieve an average planned markup on total sales for the year?
11 If an item sells for $10 and has been marked up one-third of selling price, what did it cost the firm?
12 Do inventory losses usually show up as a specific operating expense on the income statement? If not, how is this expense accounted for?
13 How does target pricing work?

PROJECTS FOR HOME ASSIGNMENT AND/OR CLASS DISCUSSION

1 Prepare a pricing determination for a firm which buys a particular product for $35, desires a 40 percent average markup, and needs 10 percent of sales to cover markdowns, employee discounts, and damaged merchandise.
2 As part of pricing policy for your own firm, would you ever condone the use of "loss leaders"? Explain in a brief essay what your policy would be and why you would have it.

CONTINUING PROBLEM:
The Kollege Klothes Shop

PART 14: SETTING PRICE POLICIES

Our clients are admittedly in the dark as to establishing an overall pricing policy for the merchandise they will sell. They again want your recommendations. They desire to have a quality image for the shop yet realize that they must have regular, perhaps weekly items which are attractively priced to bring old and new customers into the shop to make purchases.

Assignment for Part 14

Prepare a list of your recommendations and why each is important to maximize sales while keeping the quality image that your clients desire. You will probably include all or some of the following thoughts. Will outside influences affect the setting of some prices? What general price policy is essential to keeping a quality image, and still have "specials" to lure in old and new customers? Which merchandise would you recommend for more-than-average markup, which for average markup, and which for less-than-average markup? Perhaps certain items would vary in price from week to week. Would you ever recommend a loss leader? How will you maintain the desired average markup during the year when some merchandise is sold at less-than-average markup? Will you recommend special sales events? When? What other recommendations would you make?

REFERENCES FOR FURTHER READING

"A Pricing Checklist for Small Retailers," Small Business Administration Pamphlet No. 158.

Fox, Edward J., and Edward W. Wheatley, *Modern Marketing*, Scott, Foresman and Company, Glenview, Illinois, 1978, chaps. 14, 15.

"What Is the Best Selling Price?" Small Business Administration Pamphlet No. 193.

TYPES OF MERCHANDISE SOLD AND MERCHANDISING IMPLICATIONS OF EACH

.

I never did understand that stuff about convenience, shopping, and specialty products. If the same product can be a convenience good to one customer, a shopping good to a second customer, and a specialty good to a third, why should we bother to study details about each?

The Late Learner

The particular type or types of merchandise sold by the individual firm should be reflected in the total nature of the operation.

All products can be classified into two major groups: (1) consumer goods and (2) industrial goods. Within these broad classifications, many further characteristics should be noted. We will first examine consumer goods and then turn our attention to industrial goods.

CLASSIFICATION OF CONSUMER GOODS

Consumer goods are those products purchased at retail by customers for their own use. They may be generally separated into three groups:

1 Convenience goods
2 Shopping goods
3 Specialty goods

FIGURE 15-1
Firms selling convenience goods should stress displays of impulse items.

1 *Convenience goods* are products that the customers desire to buy with a minimum of effort. The more convenient their purchase, the better. Price is not a major factor when customers seek such a product in a hurry. They do not search around or shop in different stores for convenience goods. Most convenience goods are purchased when the customer makes a special trip to obtain them. Other convenience goods may be purchased on impulse, perhaps in response to an attractive display. Most convenience goods are staple items of low value.

Examples of convenience goods are tobacco, drugs, gasoline, soft drinks, newspapers, and ice cream. These are obviously items which, when wanted by customers, are wanted as quickly as possible.

2 *Shopping goods* are those items that most customers buy after comparing price, fashion, quality, and service of several different sellers. Buyers shop around before making a final decision on the particular item to be purchased. Most shopping goods are relatively high in value and are not bought frequently. This is why comparisons are so important to most people. Husband and wife usually consult the family budget first when considering the purchase of shopping goods. Individual buyers may place different relative values on price, fashion, quality, and service. Only when they are satisfied that they have found the best value for what they want do they make the final decision to buy.

Examples of shopping goods, for most people, are furniture, rugs, suits, shoes, jewelry, chinaware, automobiles, and television sets. Each can represent a substantial item in the family budget and demands close comparison before purchase.

Sybil Shelton/Monkmeyer

FIGURE 15-2
Firms selling shopping goods need well-trained salespersons.

FIGURE 15-3
The ability to explain the advantages of merchandise over competing goods is essential when selling shopping goods.

Sybil Shelton/Peter Arnold, Inc.

3 *Specialty goods* are items that the individual buyer believes have special qualities that make them preferable. They are usually items of high value. Price is not of major concern to most specialty goods customers. Their preference is usually expressed for a particular brand. They insist on this brand to the exclusion of all others.

Examples of specialty goods, for many people, are stereo sets, expensive shirts, television consoles, tires, antiques, or even brand-name chocolates. People who believe that they should have only an RCA or Zenith television console, or Goodyear or Firestone tires, for example, will not be concerned that these goods may not be available conveniently in their neighborhoods. They will go out of their way to find a merchant in town who carries their desired brand.

It should be observed that not all people fall into these general buying-habit categories. Knowing your market is crucial to successful business operation.

The classification of consumer goods and the examples within each classification represent what is considered the majority view of most consumers. If firm owners find, from studying their market, that it is in accord with these classifications, then they can turn their attention to the management implications for each type of consumer merchandise. Any notable exceptions found in the market can be adjusted for in merchandising policies.

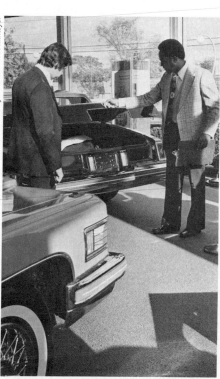

Sybil Shelton/Monkmeyer

FIGURE 15-4
Firms selling specialty goods need attractive, comfortable selling space.

Merchandising Implications for Different Types of Consumer Goods

The three types of consumer goods generally influence merchandising in the following ways:

1 Convenience goods
   a Less capable sales persons are needed.
   b Nearness to competitors is undesirable.
   c Store hours can usually be longer and still be profitable.
   d Variety of products in one line is not of prime importance.
   e Displays of impulse items are important.
   f Location in store is important.
2 Shopping goods
   a Location should normally be near competitors so that customers can compare goods.
   b High-rent areas are not essential.
   c More capable and higher-paid sales people are necessary.
   d Ability to explain advantages of merchandise over competing products is essential.
   e Assistance to customers in value determination is important.
3 Specialty goods
   a Attractive, comfortable selling space for customers is important.

FIGURE 15-5
Our affluent society demands costly marketing services and will support such things as air-conditioned shopping malls.

Stock, Boston

    b Advertising can cover wider areas of the city productively.
    c Efficiency in installations is important.
    d Customer services are a premium item.
    e Special sales may be less important.
    f Publicity emphasis is on location and brands more than on price.

INDUSTRIAL GOODS

Industrial goods are those products that are sold to other business firms, either for their own consumption or for use in their own manufacture of other products. These goods, too, are extremely varied. They may be classified as follows:

    1 Raw materials: oil, grain, logs, unprocessed tobacco, wool, fresh fruits, etc.
    2 Semimanufactured goods: sheet aluminum or steel, leather, ores, pig iron, etc.
    3 Parts: blades for cutting machines, automobile wheels, bearings, ax handles, etc.
    4 Supplies: cleaning compounds, plastic bags, wrapping paper, fuel, office stationery, etc.
    5 Machinery and equipment: all machines and equipment items used in the factory, office, or store.

Note that the same product can be both a consumer good and an industrial good. The customer's purpose in buying the good will decide the classification of the particular item. For example, coal purchased for a factory is an industrial good, whereas coal purchased for the home is a consumer good.

Small firms do engage in the manufacture of many industrial goods. Individual firms may both sell their product to industrial firms and distribute them through wholesalers to retailers to consumers. The selling process in these two areas has distinct differences.

Special Features of Industrial Goods Selling

Any small firm selling to industrial users should recognize these special characteristics of industrial sales:

    1 Industrial goods buyers are better informed about the products they buy. They buy products on the basis of performance and not because of advertising or emotion.
    2 Many industrial goods are sold directly by the factory to the user without the use of any intermediaries.
    3 There are fewer customers for industrial goods but the average sale is usually much higher.
    4 Factories will often request products made to their own specifications.
    5 Many industrial goods are sold with the seller providing installation and repair service.

6 Industrial goods prices are more sensitive to changing business conditions.

The implications of these characteristics for small firm manufacturers are that they must have salespeople capable of demonstrating the performance of the product; they must be prepared to call on business customers rather than await buyers at the business; they must know where the potential users of the product are located (which relates to their own locations) and be prepared to offer installation and repair service either by their own staffs or through competent agents. And they must recognize the sensitive nature of industrial prices by keeping aware of business conditions.

All these factors will not apply in every case. The normal procedure in the particular line of products must be understood, however, and then the organization and services that apply must be arranged.

COST OF DISTRIBUTION

It is never too early in business education for students, small firm owners, and informed citizens to address themselves to the often-heard complaints about "the excessive costs of distribution." It is generally contended that efficiency in distribution has not kept pace with the economies of mass production. The facts bear investigation. Our best marketing studies show that up to 50 percent of the consumer dollar goes for distribution costs and about 50 percent of the consumer dollar goes for manufacturing costs. Marketing costs have increased over recent years but only as a percentage of the retail price. In true dollar cost, marketing costs have also declined. There are reasons why they have not declined as much as manufacturing costs. An example of the retail cost of a popular consumer good today will illustrate the facts.

Let us consider the price of a popular line of radios or coffee makers.

It will be seen that manufacturing cost has been reduced from $20 to $12—a reduction of 40 percent. Distribution cost has been reduced from $16 to $12— a reduction of 25 percent. Retail price has been reduced from $36 to $24—a reduction of 33⅓ percent.

Former price and its breakdown	Today's price and its breakdown
$20 for manufacturing cost	$12 for manufacturing cost
16 for distribution cost	12 for distribution cost
$36 former retail price	$24 present retail price

If these percentages are seen in isolation, it would appear that distribution efficiency has not kept pace with manufacturing economies. It is this first impression that has caused most of the complaints that are heard.

Some of the less-known facts are the following:

1 Distribution costs have actually been reduced. In this example they are cut 25 percent. New ideas in distribution are constantly being tried. Distribution markets are open to everyone in a free economy, and anyone who can save money can corner a large percentage of the market. Some of the new ideas that have been applied include piggyback trucks, carload rates, area distribution centers, large-size order requirements, and attractive discounts for large orders.

2 Mass-production economies necessitate wider markets in which to distribute the increased production. The wider the market served, the greater the expenses of distribution. Thus, mass production itself has added expense factors to distribution costs.

3 Consumers today have established a demand for products with high costs of distribution. As a society becomes more affluent, its increased purchasing power is reflected in a demand for more expensive consumer goods. Frozen foods entail greater distribution costs than do fresh local vegetables. Imported products, which customers are demanding in rising quantities, carry extra distribution costs. Heinekin is more expensive than Schlitz, largely because of the distribution costs. We did not have frozen bakery goods until relatively recently. They demand refrigeration and expensive handling throughout the distribution process.

4 Some customers, in fact an increasing percentage of them, have demanded costly marketing services. They are willing to pay for them and want them in expensive shopping centers. These services include delivery, free parking, evening shopping hours, air-conditioned stores and shopping centers, and sales on account. Such services are expensive and add to the total costs of distribution.

When these facts are considered, it is obvious that without great ingenuity in distribution activities, little or no reduction in distribution costs could have been achieved.

QUESTIONS FOR CLASS DISCUSSION

1 Do you believe that less capable sales people are needed to sell convenience goods than shopping goods? Explain.
2 Why can advertising for specialty goods usually cover a wider area than for the corner drugstore?
3 When you buy a shirt or blouse, do you consider it a convenience, shopping, or specialty item? How do you distinguish between these three types of consumer goods?
4 Why should shopping goods firms generally be located in the same area of town?
5 Do you agree that factories should be located close to their markets?
6 When should a factory be located close to its source of raw materials? Why?
7 How could the same product be both an industrial good and a consumer good?
8 "Industrial goods are bought on a basis of performance and not on emotion." What does this mean to you? Give examples.
9 Are there more or fewer customers for industrial goods than for consumer goods? Explain.
10 How has an affluent society increased distribution costs?
11 Have distribution costs per unit of product really increased with the increase in mass production? Explain.

PROJECTS FOR HOME ASSIGNMENT AND/OR CLASS DISCUSSION

1 a Prepare in one column a list of 10 products that you or your family regularly purchase. In an adjacent column indicate whether you consider each a convenience good, shopping good, or specialty good.

b Explain how different people might place some of those same products in a different category.

2 Write a short paper defending middlemen against the charge that distribution costs have not declined as much as manufacturing costs.

CONTINUING PROBLEM:
The Kollege Klothes Shop

PART 15: TYPES OF MERCHANDISE SOLD AND MERCHANDISING IMPLICATIONS

After lengthy discussions with your clients, they agree that most of the "high ticket" items to be sold in the store are really shopping goods to most of your customers. This means that most customers will probably compare price, quality and service, and fashion before making purchases. This is not to say that we won't have many items in the store that may be bought on impulse, such as neckties and scarfs. We will also find that some customers will consider a particular kind of suit, dress, or shirt a specialty good. But to the vast majority of our potential customers most of our products are found to be shopping goods.

Assignment for Part 15

Prepare a report for Jones and Gomez on the merchandising implications of selling shopping goods. Follow those that were reviewed in this chapter or others you may suggest. Then show how you would apply each of these implications in making operating policies for the store.

REFERENCES FOR FURTHER READING

"Are Your Products and Channels Producing Sales?" Small Business Management Pamphlet No. MA203.

Fox, Edward J., and Edward W. Wheatley, *Modern Marketing,* Scott, Foresman and Company, Glenview, Illinois, 1978, chap. 15.

"Learning About Your Market," Small Business Administration Pamphlet No. SMA167.

SEASONAL VARIATIONS IN SALES: A KEY TO BETTER MANAGERIAL DECISIONS

If you can't show a profit in March or October, why not just close the store during these months? And if you don't have enough customers on Tuesday and Wednesday each week, why not keep the store closed on those days?

The Late Learner

Most small firm owners acknowledge that not every month in the year has the same amount of sales. They also know that not every day in the week produces a similar total of sales. Even such relatively stable firms as grocery stores generally report that their monthly sales are heaviest in September, November, and December. The beginning of school in September and the holidays in November and December account for this difference. Summer months when schools are closed or when people are off on vacation or moving to another city show a decline in sales. In resort towns, firms obviously do their biggest business in the months that are vacation time for other people.

These differences in sales volume have produced the concept of seasonal variations. Seasonal variations means those differences occurring in certain months of the year. But variations in sales during different days of the week have become known as daily sales variations. A complete knowledge of the detailed

TABLE 16-1 AVERAGE MONTHLY
SALES FOR THE ABC
DEPARTMENT STORE

January	$ 60,000
February	50,000
March	40,000
April	40,000
May	45,000
June	45,000
July	30,000
August	30,000
September	40,000
October	40,000
November	60,000
December	120,000
Total sales for year	$600,000

variations in both categories is important to making the best cost control decisions for any firm, large or small.

At Miami Beach until about 20 years ago, the seasonal variation in business was so great that most hotels closed up completely from April until December. Today, because of huge expenditures by tourist development boards and airlines to encourage year-round vacations, most of the hotels stay open. Great increases in travel from South America and Europe to Florida in the summer months has been another stabilizing factor. But even here the seasonal factor has another aspect. In the summer, a different income group is served and policies are different. In the peak season of January, February, and March, room rates are very high and many additional services are available for the "carriage trade. In the summer months, hotel managements frankly seek to produce just enough income to cover cash outlays and make some contribution to fixed expenses and renovations necessary for the following peak season. Room rates are lower, services are more limited, and the extras available in winter, such as golf privileges and expensive dinner shows with top name entertainers, are greatly reduced. Thus we see a different application of management decisions to cope with the seasonal factor in income. A few small hotels in Miami Beach still close in the summer months because their operators own or operate other hotels in the Catskills or other northern summer-resort areas where the season is just the opposite of that in South Florida.

Most retailers and manufacturers do not have such a clear choice in adjusting to their seasonal variations in total income throughout the year. It is still important, however, that they know the extent of the variations. There are other things they can do in the best interests of their business firms.

CHARTING SEASONAL VARIATIONS: A GOOD STARTING POINT

Without actual sales data for the period of a year, the new small firm may have difficulty in measuring the extent of its seasonal variations in sales. But even here industry statistics offer data for many types of firms. Once variations have been noted it is always valuable to place those variations on a simple graph or chart to assist management in designing policies to adjust expenses to those variations.

Since students seem to find the case method helpful in understanding concepts, then we may best approach this subject with a review of an actual case with which your author is familiar. Its facts are as follows:

AN ACTUAL CASE STUDY OF SEASONAL VARIATIONS

The case involves a small department store in a southern city with a population of approximately 60,000. When its monthly sales for the past several years were confirmed, the variation was consistent as shown in Table 16-1.

These monthly variations were plotted on graph paper. The results are shown in Figure 16-1.

FIGURE 16-1
Monthly variation in sales for the ABC Department Store.

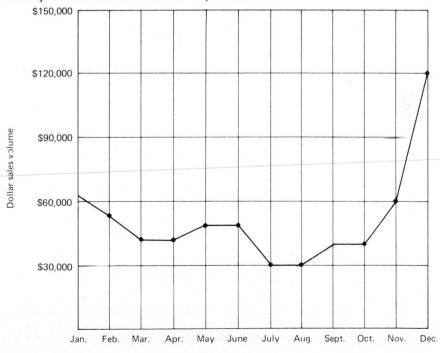

ANALYSIS OF THE SEASONAL SALES CHART

When the results of the analysis of seasonal variations were discussed with the owner of the store, several very interesting facts came to light. Some of them were:

1 The owner had been using only an annual break-even chart based upon annual sales of $600,000. This suggested that an average monthly sales volume of $50,000 was needed. A monthly break-even chart that would reflect the actual differences in sales volume in the summer months was never made.

2 Although sales dropped badly in the slack season, no special action to adjust expenses accordingly was taken.

3 The fact that 40 percent of annual sales were made in the three months of November, December, and January was not noted. The three slack summer months provided only 17 percent of annual sales.

4 Inventories had been kept at normal levels during the year, but some extra orders were made for the holiday trade.

5 Employees each had several years' service with the store, and their loyalty was well established. As a reward, they were allowed to take their vacations any time during the year. Because of this, part-time employees were hired in the spring and fall months, as well as in the December rush, to handle customers.

6 The owner was reluctant to make policy changes because "after all, we did show a profit for the year.

DECISION MAKING FROM SEASONAL SALES ANALYSIS

The consulting report sent to the owner listed the errors in some of the situations cited. It recommended several positive steps to improve the firm's profitability. These included:

1 Part-time employees should be hired only during November, December, and January.

2 All employee vacations should be granted only in July and August.

3 Inventory policy should reflect the lower sales in the summer months by reducing purchases of year-round merchandise in the spring and early fall.

4 A positive program of sales promotion for the slack periods should be studied. Perhaps special sales, attractive prices, or other ideas could increase sales in the slack months.

5 Monthly break-even charts and income statements should be made.

When it was pointed out to the owner that several thousand dollars was the estimated saving from applying the first three suggestions, the reaction was most enthusiastic about them and possibly about other decisions that could be made. In his last meeting with the consultants, consideration was being given to closing the store entirely during July and August and reopening when school began in September, when a community-covering, dynamic advertising program would be launched. That idea was discouraged by the consultants.

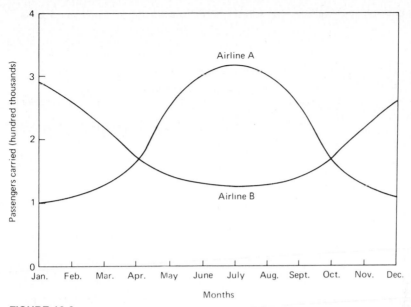

FIGURE 16-2
Comparison of seasonal variations for two airlines.

   This case is recited in detail mainly because its implications are appropriate for so many small firms. Even in the planning stage of a new small firm, seasonal variations for the type of business at hand can be determined within reasonable limits. Decisions like those recommended in the case just described can be enacted from the beginning. Existing firms should study their situation for possible policy changes.

   Many students have probably heard of the two small airlines that accidentally compared their monthly revenues and found the peak season for one was the slack season for the other. The result was an agreement between them to lease planes to each other during their respective peak seasons rather than have planes idle for one season. Each obtained leasing revenue without buying additional equipment, and maintenance costs were reduced for both lines. Their seasonal variations are shown in Figure 16-2.

   In summary, all small firm owners should know their seasonal variations in as much detail as possible. When these variations are significant, every attempt should be made to adjust operating expenses and inventories accordingly. We have noted with the case study some of the ways this may be done.

QUESTIONS FOR CLASS DISCUSSION

1 We have heard that even a doctor's office has seasonal variations in its income. Do you agree? Explain.
2 What is the danger in "resting on one's laurels" and neglecting seasonal variations in sales volume?

3 What could cause seasonal variations in the sales volume of a neighborhood grocery store?

4 Are there any variations in the monthly sales of most small department stores? What could cause them?

5 How drastic do you think the seasonal variations are for a resort restaurant in a far-north village?

6 Is the fact that "we made a profit last year" a good reason to neglect a study of seasonal variations? Explain.

7 What are some of the things an owner can do to aid profits when significant variations in seasonal business are normal?

PROJECTS FOR HOME ASSIGNMENT AND/OR CLASS DISCUSSION

1 Prepare a written report on the values or risks of hiring part-time employees.

2 Explain what your policy would be on granting employee vacations in periods of your highest sales volume.

CONTINUING PROBLEM:
The Kollege Klothes Shop

PART 16: SEASONAL VARIATIONS IN SALES

We have seen from the study of this chapter that important differences in profitability can be achieved by knowing what the seasonal variations in sales are and making management decisions to adjust operations to these variations. Jones and Gomez believe your explanation of these facts. Now they request that you advise them about those variations and what they should do with that knowledge.

Assignment for Part 16

Break down the annual sales on the budgeted income statement previously prepared into monthly amounts. If you cannot find industry statistics on these variations, you can make your own breakdown based upon your knowledge of business. We know, for example, that most college shops do more business in September, December, and before the Spring Ball than in other months. Summer months in most college towns usually show a much lower sales volume each month. You may assume that the busier months do twice the sales volume of the lighter months. In any event, show the portion of your total sales expected each month. Use any other information you may have on this matter.

Chart your monthly sales on a chart similar to the one in this chapter.

What management decisions does your chart suggest on such matters as the hiring of extra help, vacation policies for full-time employees, inventory control, or others.

REFERENCES FOR FURTHER READING

"Danger Signals in a Small Store,"   Small Business Administration Pamphlet No. SMA141.

"Keep Pointed Toward Profit," Small Business Administration Pamphlet No. MA206.

"Marketing Checklist for Small Retailers," Small Business Administration Pamphlet No. SMA156.

CHAPTER 17

PURCHASING AND INVENTORY CONTROL

I have only one policy on purchasing and inventory control. Keep the warehouse full, and you never lose a sale. I know it costs money to carry inventory, but it also costs profits to lose sales. If you always keep the warehouse full, your inventory will take care of itself.

The Late Learner

The term "merchandising" is used very broadly in business. It usually covers all facets of the business that have to do with merchandise: acquiring it, handling and displaying it, seeking out potential customers for it, selling it, and rendering services to customers who have bought it. These activities can be divided into at least the following subjects:

1 Purchase of inventories
2 Inventory control
3 Sales promotion and advertising
4 Publicity
5 Displays of merchandise
6 Selling activities
7 Pricing policies
8 Customer service

Each of these subjects is a large one, and many books have been written on the theory and practice of each. For the student or new firm planner, we can attempt here only to summarize some of the key considerations in each area. Such a summary can also be used to check the actual performance of an existing firm. This chapter will cover purchasing and inventory control.

PURCHASING MERCHANDISE

The key questions that small firm owners must ask themselves are: Am I buying through the established channels of distribution for this type of business? Is there another source that would give me the same dependability and service? Am I getting the best prices available for comparable quality? In what quantities should I be buying merchandise?

Most small retailers have wholesale houses available in their own locality that are eager and willing to serve them. Most consumer goods are normally distributed from manufacturer to wholesaler to retailer. In addition, there are sales people from out-of-town suppliers who will call on the merchant to present their products. Job-lot dealers may operate in the area and have special quantities of merchandise for sale. A basic decision the new owner must make is whether to buy only from established wholesalers who serve the area or to buy wherever needed types of merchandise are available. If the firm has a distributorship for a particular line of merchandise, the source of supply is assured as part of the distributorship arrangement. Most small firm retailers carry similar merchandise in different price lines. Each price line may be served by a different wholesaler or distributor. Experience will soon tell the owner which are the most popular lines with their customers, and they will buy accordingly.

The inventory investment is usually the largest investment in the new small firm. Because of this, the owner must constantly be concerned with making this investment as profitable as possible. This can be done using the following strategies:

1 Determining how much to buy on each order
2 Taking advantage of all purchase discounts offered
3 Combating the constant problem of slow-moving merchandise

The object is to have the proper merchandise turnover.

DIFFERENT TYPES OF WHOLESALERS

New retailers are often confused by the various types of wholesale establishments which may be available to serve their procurement needs. New wholesalers are often not sure of how their planned firms fit into the generally accepted organization of the wholesale function. The following comments should clarify the situation for both groups.

Wholesalers are generally classified as:

Full-service wholesalers (also called merchant wholesalers)
Limited-function wholesalers
Agent middlemen (also called intermediaries)

Full-service wholesalers are the most numerous in most lines of consumer goods. They usually buy their inventories directly from the manufacturers and thus take title to the merchandise. They store the merchandise in their own warehouses, deliver and/or assemble the products involved, and maintain a location where customers may inspect the products and place orders. They do not work on commission, but rely upon their ability to sell their products at a profit to make their own operations successful. They are called *full-service wholesalers* because of the extra services they extend to their customers—such as granting credit on sales, providing delivery service, and supplying current market information.

Limited-function wholesalers render fewer marketing functions for their customers. *Jobbers,* who specialize in odd-lot sales only, are often placed in this category. Wholesalers who merely sell merchandise that is delivered by the manufacturer to the customer are another example. They are often called *drop shippers.* Wholesalers who do not grant credit to their customers but make cash sales only are similarly classified.

Agent middlemen are wholesalers who actually provide a procurement function for their customers. Most do not take title to the merchandise they buy or sell for their customers. They merely arrange for such sales through their customers and contacts. They usually work on commission only. Any extra services extended to their customers are the exception, not the rule. Examples of this group are *brokers* who arrange sales for their clients without ever taking title or possession of the merchandise products involved; *selling agents* who often contract to take the entire output of a small factory and sell it wherever the market may be; and *manufacturers' agents* who usually represent their manufacturer in only a certain specified territory and make sales of their product for delivery by the manufacturer.

Commission merchants are also usually classified as agent middlemen, but they operate somewhat differently. They do not take title but usually assume physical possession of the merchandise they are employed to sell. They often provide temporary storage until they have completed their sales. They usually provide delivery service of the merchandise when sold. Sometimes they grant credit to the firms to which they sell, but this is not uniform practice. They are paid for their services by a commission on the selling prices they develop. Special arrangements with the principal they represent may add other compensation.

HOW MUCH TO ORDER AND WHEN

How much of each item should be purchased on each order? The most important consideration here is to avoid stockouts while keeping the investment under control and the working capital active and available. Most retailers determine a minimum size in the inventory of any item as the reordering point. This minimum stock must take into consideration the time necessary to get a new order placed and delivered. Some allowance for contingencies in this regard is usually advisable. For example, if canned milk is sold at the rate of a case per week and it takes one week to get a new order placed and delivered, such an order could be placed when the stock is down to one case. Prudence suggests ordering a bit sooner.

But how many cases should be ordered? If local wholesalers with speedy delivery or pick-up service are easily available, if there is no price advantage in ordering more, and if storage space is limited, grocers cannot be accused of hand-to-mouth buying if they keep a reserve of one case and just have one case delivered each week. Such a situation does not usually exist. Even the problem of bookkeeping and totaling several invoices during the month would probably suggest that the grocers buy one month's supply each time. More likely, they have opportunities for purchase discounts for prompt payments of invoices, and lower prices for larger-quantity purchases. These factors would cause them to increase their ordering quantities. Larger orders would be encouraged by their wholesalers. Keeping track of every item in a large inventory is a big job, and some system should be established for keeping information available. Some small firms use tags taken from each item to post against inventory on hand. Others determine monthly usage and order just that amount each month until a physical inventory is taken.

THE ECONOMIC ORDERING QUANTITY (EOQ): THE SQUARE ROOT FORMULA FOR INDUSTRIAL BUYING

Industrial buyers have several basic square root formulas which apply more effectively to their type of buying. Modern minicomputers make the calculations easy. One formula computes the economic ordering quantity in dollars. We will illustrate this formula first here.

For each item being purchased, the formula considers the dollar amount of the product used in the previous year, the cost of issuing a purchase order; and the cost of storing, insuring, protecting, and maintaining inventory on hand. When these factors are known, the formula is as follows:

$$\text{Economic ordering quantity} = \sqrt{\frac{2AB}{i}}$$

where A = the annual usage in dollars
  B = the cost of issuing a purchase order, in dollars
  i = the cost of carrying inventory, expressed
    as a percentage of the inventory value

We can illustrate the use of this formula with an actual example: If a factory used $75,000 of a product last year, the cost of issuing a purchase order was $6, and it cost 12 percent of the inventory value to store, insure, protect, and maintain the inventory (0.12 percent), we can insert these figures into the formula as follows:

$$\text{Economic ordering quantity (EOQ)} = \sqrt{\frac{2(\$75,000)\ 6}{.12}} = \sqrt{\frac{\$900,000}{.12}} = \sqrt{\$7,500,000}$$

The square root of $7,500,000, carried to four decimal points, is $2,738.6127.

The following calculation of that square root by long-hand methods will make us appreciate the value of computers. Minicomputers and even many pocket-size calculators have a square root button which will instantly give us the answer once the basic figure has been properly inserted.

The calculation of the square root of $7,500,000 is as follows:

$$\begin{array}{r} 2\quad7\quad3\quad8.6127 \\ \sqrt{7,'50'0,0'00.} \end{array}$$

	4
	350
47	329
	2100
543	1629
	47100
5468	43744
	325600
54766	328596
	700400
547721	547721
	15267900
5477222	10954444
	431345600
547,72247	383405729
	47939871

The most economic ordering quantity is, therefore, $2,738 each time an order is placed. If each unit costs $50, the number of units ordered would be 55 ($2,738 ÷ 50).

This formula uses a square root, but the time spent calculating it is worthwhile. It takes the guesswork out of the buying process. (Tables of square roots are available.) Different product groupings with similar usage patterns can be placed together so that calculations are minimized. The ordering quantity is recorded on each inventory sheet for future use. The formula does have some limitations, such as schedule changes, price changes, commercial practices, packaging limits, and the perishable nature of products, which will prevent strict adoption in some cases. These can all be handled as adjustments, however, in the initial calculation.

The foregoing example of computing the EOQ shows the order in total dollars. In the current period of rampant inflation which started in the late 1970s and has continued into the 1980s, it is often deemed best to compute the EOQ in terms of number of units because the prices are so subject to regular increases. Thus, we have another formula available that computes the EOQ in terms of units and that uses the current price at the time a new order is being placed. Under this plan the formula becomes:

$$\text{EOQ} = \sqrt{\frac{2 \times R \times O}{P \times i}}$$

In this formula R = Sales for past period (in units)
P = Price per unit (now)
O = Processing cost per order
i = Inventory carrying charge as a percentage of inventory value

When this formula is used with the current price inserted, it will give the number of units to be ordered in the ideal ordering quantity. Notice that it again involves the computation of a square root. This formula is often referred to as "the standard formula" for computing EOQ.

Beginning inventories for a new factory must be based upon close scrutiny of available industry statistics and planned production schedules. As experience is gained in operations, the techniques of the square root formulas can be applied.

As factories grow larger, management will usually find it desirable to utilize even more refined economic-purchase order formulas that can be operated on computers. Many of these formulas have as many as 15 variables to be considered in arriving at precise ordering quantities.

In small factories the responsibility for initiating new purchase orders for materials and supplies must be the responsibility of the person in charge of inventories. A minimum inventory is established that allows for the normal lead time in getting stocks replenished (the time necessary to get purchase orders issued and new materials received). When that minimum point is reached, immediate action is necessary. Notice that the minimum inventory reached can be given in different ways. One is to have the minimum stock in separate bins or shelves. Another is to post to a current inventory record all material issued to production. This record adds all incoming shipments, deducts material issued, and thus has a perpetual inventory of balances on hand. The size of that minimum inventory may be adjusted because of new business developments such as transportation strikes, supplier problems, etc. It may also be affected by attractive prices available or changes in the production demands due to new products or extra usage of particular items in the total inventory.

Regardless of which system is used to keep control of inventory, the most important thing is to work the system. Practicing the old idea of always having more than enough on hand to avoid stockouts or machinery shutdowns without regard to the adequacy of the inventory or the investment involved is prime evidence of inefficient management. Special circumstances may create exceptions. Too much inventory is wasteful. It ties up working capital unnecessarily, increases storage costs, and increases the risks of obsolescence and deterioration of the products.

INVENTORY CONTROL CONSIDERATIONS FOR RETAILERS

What is the ideal amount of inventory? For retailers, it is that inventory which does not lose profitable sales and can still justify the investment in each part of its total.

For manufacturing firms, it is that inventory which maintains production schedules with a minimum investment in inventory.

Let us quickly admit that the ideal inventory is easier to describe than to determine in particular cases. Some examples will serve to illustrate the rule. If a drugstore has repeated requests for an aerosol spray product but does not have this item on its shelves, it is losing profitable sales by not stocking that item. If the owner's reason for not carrying the item is that it is only bought seasonally, the reasoning is not good; such a policy is driving potential customers to competitors. If it is seasonal, the owner should arrange the stock so that little or no investment is tied up in the item during the off season.

Carrying too many brands or sizes in a particular item can easily produce a situation where the total investment is not justified. Stocking many brands of toasters in one drugstore would be an example. People who want to buy a toaster in a drugstore are not usually concerned with a particular brand. Brand-conscious customers in this case would likely go to the brand distributor. Other consumer items that can easily fall into this category for various types of retailers are dishware, shirts, hammers, men's suits, and dresses. A choice may be desirable but excessive brands are not usually necessary. The type of store and type of customer must, of course, always be considered, but the underlying principle of inventory control remains continually important. Knowing the customers you have or are seeking is the best information to have in this regard.

Some items that are not generally popular may still have to be carried in minimum quantities for other reasons. For example, few drugstores still carry bar shaving soap. In one case, the druggist admitted that his shelves always had one dozen bars in stock because of two customers who regularly made substantial purchases in the store and who demanded this product from time to time. Giving up the small investment in bar shaving soap would have driven those customers together with their profitable purchases to another store. A slow-moving item was justified here, even though its sales probably could not justify even the small investment.

Retail Inventory Control Techniques

The problems of inventory control are really more difficult for most retailers than for factories. The factory has a specific production schedule, and the inventory of raw materials is adjusted to that positively planned usage. Retailers, however, may have the demands on their inventories change with the whims of their customers, with style changes which are often unpredictable, or with the changing character of their market. They may drop or add new products or new lines of products at any time. Yet for most retailers the importance of efficiently managing this largest investment remains. Even if the ideal inventory has been approached, it is often subject to change on short notice. And the problems of different retailers vary in many ways. Some of the techniques that can be used to assist inventory control are:

1 Keep a constant surveillance of sales results and inventories. There is no substitute for this. All other techniques only assist actual experience.

2 Set minimum reordering point and maximum inventory on all basic stock items. Such basic stock is not susceptible to most frivolous demand changes.

3 Obtain data from modern cash registers to identify key items for sales. These will reflect increased or decreased sales of such items.

4 Have a detachable portion of sales slips that will record sales of particular items. A two-part price tab, half of which can be detached at time of sale, will accomplish the same purpose. Summaries of these data will provide sales information to govern purchases.

5 Rely on suppliers who regularly visit the store to maintain proper inventories without wasteful expenditure. (The bread truck driver knows how many loaves of each kind of bread to leave each morning.)

6 Use wholesaler or manufacturer recommendations if products represent a distributorship for certain brands.

PURCHASE DISCOUNTS

Good management demands that all purchase discounts should be taken. The excuse that cash is not available is not valid. A purchase discount is a reduction in the price on any invoice offered in return for prompt payment of the invoice. The most common discount offered by suppliers is 2/10, n/30. This means that if the invoice is paid within 10 days, 2 percent of the gross amount can be deducted, but in any event the entire amount is due in 30 days. An invoice for $1,000 of merchandise can thus be settled in full for $980 if paid within 10 days, instead of $1,000, which would be due on the thirtieth day. Net saving is $20. A saving of 2 percent for paying bills 20 days sooner is saving at the rate of 36 percent per year. (It is earned in 20 days and there are 18 periods of 20 days each in the year.) The often observed tendency to avoid paying such bills within the discount period represents neglect of good financial management. The typical drugstore must sell many units of shaving cream, cigarettes, or magazines to clear $20 in profit. One of the differences between efficient and inefficient firms lies in the attention given to this matter.

A study some years ago of over 1,000 small firms showed that most were lax in taking advantage of purchase discounts. It also showed that 2 percent of purchases was more than the majority paid in federal income taxes.

If adequate cash is not available, the competent proprietor with a good credit standing can borrow the necessary amount from his or her bank for the 20 days involved in the case above. At 12 percent interest, the $980 would cost $6.54 in interest. Even deducting this interest from the $20 saved, the proprietor is still $13.46 ahead by paying the invoice within the discount period. Such clear gains cannot be ignored.

While advocating taking advantage of all purchase discounts for prompt payment, and all quantity discounts where the quantities involved are justified by the company's inventory policy, we should also caution about ordering too large quantities in order to receive quantity discounts. One year's supply should be the maximum order placed regardless of attractive prices on larger quantities. In many cases, an order of this size cannot be justified.

THE PROBLEM OF SLOW-MOVING MERCHANDISE

One of the hardest lessons for new retailers to learn or to accept is the desirability of selling slow-moving merchandise at less than normal markup or, in some cases, at less than cost. Every firm faces this problem to some degree. Stores selling style merchandise are particularly vulnerable to the risk of being stuck with an inventory of slow-moving products that will lose value as the style fades. Bathing suits and fashion shoes are examples of products that should be marked down as seasons or styles pass. Merchants sell Christmas cards at half-price the day after Christmas to combat this problem. They don't want working capital tied up in the cards for a whole year. Other products are subject to deterioration, fading, or other defects when kept in stock too long. Wise merchants who find such items in their inventory act to sell them as best they can as soon as they can. Special sales, markdowns, and advertising are some of the devices employed.

The Department of Commerce and the Small Business Administration have prepared several aids for small firm owners. They include long lists of ideas on how to move such products and generally reduce the problem. All proprietors should take advantage of these services. The typical report includes the following suggestions for liquidating slow-moving inventory:

1 Make traffic obstacles of large displays of the items.
2 Offer special discounts for quantity purchases.

3 Put specially colored lights on displays.
4 Offer 1-cent sales.
5 Place slow-moving goods next to best sellers.
6 Have grab-bag sales.
7 Use specially colored price tags.
8 Offer "Special of the Day" items.

MERCHANDISE INVENTORY TURNOVER

Some attention was paid to inventory turnover in Chapter 4, where we needed to know the average turnover for our type of firm. We can now return to that concept with more experience.

We have found that the ideal merchandise inventory is the one which does not lose productive sales and can still justify each part of its investment. We have investigated many of the ramifications of achieving that happy state. We know that the turnover is computed by dividing cost of goods sold by the average inventory. It is also clear now that too much inventory can lessen the turnover and result in inefficiency in total operations.

A time-honored measure of efficiency in management has been this turnover figure. When comparing two firms, the one with the higher inventory turnover is usually assumed to be the more profitable. An erroneous conclusion has resulted in many cases. We are regularly reminded in these instances that a profit is made every time the inventory is turned. It is assumed, therefore, that the higher the turnover, the higher the profits. This is not always true. It does not measure profitable sales lost because no merchandise was available. To illustrate with an extreme case: Consider the hardware store with an inventory consisting of one hammer. No other merchandise is on the shelves. The owner sells a hammer each day. After the sale, the owner goes to the nearby supply house and buys another hammer. At the end of the month, there is a merchandise inventory turnover of 30 times per month, or 360 times per year. But has it been efficient? Many productive sales were lost through lack of inventory. A proper inventory with a turnover of 5 times per year would have produced much better results.

Experience has demonstrated that too much inventory is usually less harmful than inadequate inventory and stockouts. The ideal inventory as described earlier may never be exactly achieved. Nevertheless, it has great value as a principle and should always be pursued.

QUESTIONS FOR CLASS DISCUSSION

1 What is meant by saying that "the ideal inventory should be able to justify the investment in each part of its whole"?
2 Have you ever been the victim of a stockout? What was your reaction?
3 What are the advantages, if any, of buying regularly from the same wholesalers?
4 How can it be dangerous to buy very large quantities of a particular item in order to receive an extra discount?

5 How do distributorships assure steady supply of merchandise?

6 Do you agree that the merchandise inventory is usually the largest investment of small firms?

7 What is the ideal inventory for a retailer?

8 What is the ideal inventory of raw materials for a factory?

9 What is hand-to-mouth buying?

10 If a factory used $20,000 of one raw material last year, should it order this amount on January 1 next year? Explain.

11 What are the possible advantages of placing large orders if so doing is consistent with inventory needs?

12 How can carrying too many competing items adversely affect the inventory investment and consequent profits?

13 Why can an efficient merchant not afford to neglect purchase discounts?

14 A saving of 2 percent in 20 days represents an annual rate of 36 percent. Explain how this is true.

15 Can the merchandise turnover ever be too high? Explain.

PROJECTS FOR HOME ASSIGNMENT AND/OR CLASS DISCUSSION

1 Make up your own problem on economic ordering quantities for a factory and solve it with each of the formulas in the chapter. Do you get the same answer with each?

2 In your own firm, which type of wholesalers would you prefer to do business with? Are there advantages in dealing with different ones? Explain.

CONTINUING PROBLEM:
The Kollege Klothes Shop

PART 17: INVENTORY CONTROL

We have studied the importance of good inventory control and good purchasing procedures in this chapter. Because we are writing about a retail type of business we cannot use most of the industrial buying procedures we have studied. However, inventory control in our college clothes store will remain an important item for our clients to be aware of. We have reviewed in this chapter several methods of inventory control for retail stores.

Assignment for Part 17

Prepare a report for your clients with your suggestions on how they should plan to control inventories. Will you adopt one of the plans reviewed in this chapter? How will your plan work? What protection will you have against stockouts and the resulting loss of sales? Will you plan on the same minimum inventories on every item you sell? Will you assure that excessive investment in inventories is avoided because of the cost of working capital? How?

REFERENCES FOR FURTHER READING

Deitzer, Bernard A., and Karl A. Shilliff, *Contemporary Management Incidents,* Grid Publishing Company, Columbus, Ohio, 1977, Incident No. 4.

Musselman, Vernon A., and Eugene Hughes, *Introduction to Modern Business,* 8th ed., Prentice-Hall, Inc., Englewood Cliffs, N.J., 1981, chap. 9.

Tate, Curtis E. Jr., Leon Megginson, Charles Scott, Jr., and Lyle Trueblood, *Successful Small Business Management,* rev. ed., Business Publications, Inc., Dallas, Texas, 1978, chap. 14.

PART **FIVE**

MERCHANDISING AND SALES DEVELOPMENT

THE BREAK-EVEN CHART: FIXED AND VARIABLE EXPENSE ANALYSIS

I don't see the need for studying whether expenses are fixed or variable. They are all expenses, and they all have to be paid. No small business owner likes expenses, and he always tries to keep them down as much as possible.

The Late Learner

A business that has only variable expenses, all varying directly and proportionately with sales, cannot possibly operate at a loss. Such a business would be very unusual. Yet the idea is more than an academic or theoretical concept. Such firms are known to the author.

The foregoing statements are offered here in the hope that they will stimulate the student's interest in a study of the nature and consequences of fixed and variable expense relationships in any business firm.

Basic to such a study should be the recognition of the fundamental law of business: the greater the risk, the greater must be the potential profits. It follows that when the risk of loss is removed or even lessened, the potential profits must be less. Some sacrifices must be made in exchange for the protection against loss. In the case of the firm which has only variable expenses that vary directly and proportionately with sales, the sacrifice is that the profit margin on the first dollar of sales is the same as the profit margin on the last dollar of sales. Such a firm which has total expenses of 85 percent of sales will have a profit of 15 cents on the first dollar of sales and a 15-cent profit on the one hundred-thousandth dollar of sales. Many small firm owners of long experience would likely welcome such an arrangement in exchange for this protection against loss if, indeed, it was possible to attain such an expense position. Although such a position is extremely rare, in fact impossible in almost all cases, the facts involved can be useful in making decisions for any business.

WHAT ARE FIXED EXPENSES?

By definition, fixed expenses are those that do not change with the sales volume. No matter what the sales are, the expense stays the same. A good example is the set monthly rent paid for the store or factory premises. The rent may be $400 per month. This is known as a flat rental, and it has no relation to the volume of sales made by the business during the month. It must be paid every month whether sales are good or bad. This is a true fixed expense. Other fixed expenses in a typical small firm are depreciation on fixed assets, and most insurance premiums. In all these cases the expense goes on at the same amount without reference to sales made.

WHAT ARE VARIABLE EXPENSES?

By definition, variable expenses are those that change with the sales volume of the business. One type varies directly and proportionately with sales, the best example being commission expense. If all salespersons, for example, receive commissions only and no sales are made, there is no commission expense. As sales grow larger and larger, the commissions grow accordingly. If all salespersons receive commissions of 10 percent of sales, the commission expense account grows directly and proportionately to total sales. Such expenses are the exception.

Most variable expenses do *not* vary directly and proportionately with sales. In fact, there are all degrees of variability. As a result, most variable expenses are really *semivariable*. Let us examine some of the typical variable expenses to determine how closely they vary with sales.

1   Cost of Goods Sold   Normally, the expense of cost of goods sold will bear a close relationship to sales made. But it may vary somewhat if there are increases in the price paid for merchandise which cannot be offset by increases in sales prices, or if special bargain purchases are made which increase profit margins. These situations seldom make a large percentage change in the relationship between cost of goods sold and sales. Strong competitive pricing situations may force owners to adjust their prices unwillingly in order to maintain average margins. Cost of goods sold can, therefore, be considered in most cases as bearing a direct and almost proportionate relationship to sales.

2 Utilities Expenses Utilities expenses cover the cost of such items as telephone, electricity, water, and gas. If these expenses are billed on a flat per-month charge, they are truly fixed expenses. If they are charged on a usage basis and the use varies from period to period during the fiscal year, a distinct variable factor is involved. Telephone and telegram expenses usually have a tendency to rise with increased sales volume. Heating in the winter by electricity or gas, or cooling in summer may bring variability into these utility charges. Many firms have a policy of charging the basic telephone bill as a fixed expense and the extra charges for long-distance calls and telegrams as variable expenses. Where the variations are small from month to month in total utilities expense, most firms consider the total as a fixed expense.

3 Advertising and Promotion Expense If a specified amount is set aside for these items in the yearly budget and if it is spent on a regular program or at specified periods, the total can be considered a fixed expense. If the policy of the firm is to increase or decrease its expenditures for advertising and promotion on a basis of monthly decisions, for example, it becomes a variable expense. Many firms have a policy of planning a specific advertising budget but remain open to extra advertising for special occasions. In these cases, the planned budget could be considered a fixed expense and the extra expenditures would be considered variable when analyzing the total operation for a specific period.

4 Salaries for Sales Staff A common mistake is failure to analyze the expense of salaries for sales staff and to assume that it is a 100 percent variable expense. This neglects the concept of a skeleton staff. By skeleton sales staff we mean the minimum number of salespersons who must be on hand to keep the doors open for business. Salaries for these people are a fixed expense. The variable portion of sales salaries is all salaries that will be expanded or contracted with changes in the sales volume. Competent managements study the need for adding salespeople as sales grow. Often they find the need for part-time people in certain seasons or on certain days of the week, or even during certain hours of the day. Sales salaries still do not vary directly and proportionately with sales volume. As sales increase, new salespersons are added to the payroll so that four people are doing the work in a leisurely way that three persons were doing last week under considerable pressure. Thus sales and sales salaries do move in the same direction but not proportionately at any given time. Figure 18-1 illustrates the relationship of sales and most semivariable expenses. Points *A, C, E,* and *G* might represent the addition of a new salesperson, a new bookkeeper, or a second person making deliveries. At these points there is a vertical increase in the dollar total of the variable expenses. Between points *B* and *C, D* and *E, F* and *G,* and *H* and *J,* the variable expenses stay the same. As sales increase, each semivariable expense tends to increase also.

5 Rent Expense and Percentage Lease Rentals Landlords have long demonstrated that they are more competent in knowing the value of store or factory

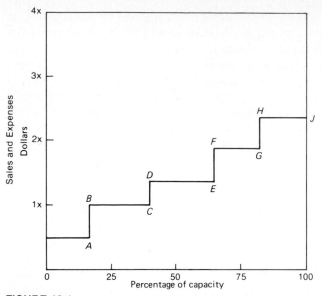

FIGURE 18-1
Relationship of sales and semivariable expenses.

space than are most small firm owners. In most big cities especially, the percentage lease rental arrangement is replacing the flat rental previously mentioned. A percentage lease provides a minimum flat fee plus an additional charge made on sales above certain amounts. For example, the total rental charge may call for a minimum of $400 per month plus 1 percent of sales over $100,000 annually and 2 percent of sales over $200,000. In such a case, the $400 flat charge is a fixed expense and the additional charge is a variable expense. Small firm planners must be prepared to evaluate the type of lease they are offered. Under the flat rental plan, the proprietor has a chance to retain more profits when business is very good. Under the percentage lease, the proprietor shares the profit of extra sales with the landlord. It would be most unusual for the landlord to give the firm a completely variable rental contract. Some instances are known. Requests for such rental arrangements may be appropriate.

6 Delivery Expenses Are they fixed or variable? Would the person making deliveries be discharged if sales were down 50 percent? Not if the same routes were to be covered but with fewer deliveries. Perhaps the deliveries would be less frequent each day. Perhaps the bookkeeper would operate the truck half the time. Gas, oil, and maintenance expenses should reflect some variation as a result of wide variation in sales volume. The policy of the owner on these matters will determine whether the total is considered fixed, variable, or divided into parts of each.

THE BREAK-EVEN CHART

Knowing what the total expenses are and how to make a break-even chart are essential to good management. A correct break-even chart is valuable as a supplement to budget making, pricing policies, decisions on sales policies, and expense control and expansion plans, among other things. The completely competent business person should know what sales volume is necessary to *break even* (the point where there is no profit and no loss). The break-even chart can indicate the profits to be achieved at different levels of expanded sales. It can tell the results of changes in price policies and the benefits of expense reductions that might be available.

A break-even chart shows the relationship of fixed, variable, and total expenses to sales at all volumes of sales. It measures all expenses and income from sales on the vertical axis, and the units sold or percentage of capacity on the horizontal axis. Profits at any level of capacity or at any volume of sales are measured by the vertical distance between the total expense line and the sales income line.

An accurately drawn break-even chart tells firm owners what sales volumes are necessary to reach the break-even point, and the percentage of their capacity this sales volume represents. It tells them the profits to be derived from any planned expansion of sales. These relationships are measured against a presently existing set of facilities and expense analysis. Any change of store space, for example, would call for the creation of a new chart made for the expanded facilities and expenses.

An example of a complete break-even chart is shown in Figure 18-2. It has been prepared for the Jones Department Store, which had sales for the year of $300,000, fixed expenses of $50,000, variable expenses of $150,000, and total expenses of $200,000. The firm operated at 60 percent of capacity during the year. Students should study this chart to see how each line is plotted, where the two connecting points for each line are, and the reasons for each. Be sure you can tell how to measure the profit for the year on this chart.

Making Your Own Break-Even Chart

Most students and most owners of small firms will understand the preceding example of a break-even chart and appreciate its usefulness. The actual construction of such a chart for a specific firm is not so widely understood. All small firm owners should know how to construct such a chart and how to use it for purposes of analyzing their own operations.

The following is a step-by-step explanation of how to construct a break-even chart for any business when the percentage of capacity is known. Each step is illustrated on the break-even chart shown in Figure 18-3.

Step 1 Analyze each operating expense on the income statement (or planned income statement) to determine whether it is fixed, variable, or divided

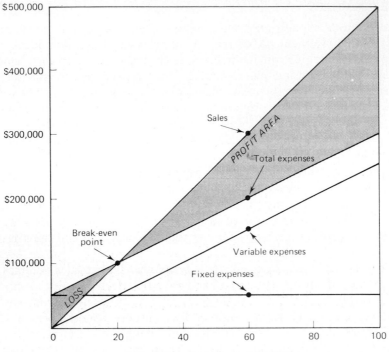

FIGURE 18-2
Break-even chart for the Jones Department Store.

between these two according to the policies of the owner. List the fixed expenses in one column and the variable expenses in another column. Total the columns and add the cost of goods sold to the variable expense column. *For this illustration we will use the ABC Company, which had sales of $100,000 for the year, costs of goods sold of $50,000, and operating expenses of $35,000, broken down into fixed and variable expenses as follows:*

Fixed expenses		Variable expenses	
Flat rental paid	$6,400	Sales salaries	$15,000
Taxes	1,200	Office salaries	8,000
		Percentage lease, extra	
Depreciation	400	payment	500
Delivery expense	1,400	Telephone & telegrams	500
Utilities expense	600	Advertising & promotion	1,000
		Subtotal	$25,000
		Cost of goods sold	50,000
Total fixed expense	$10,000	Total variable expense	$75,000

Step 2 On a blank sheet of paper (or graph paper), draw the vertical and

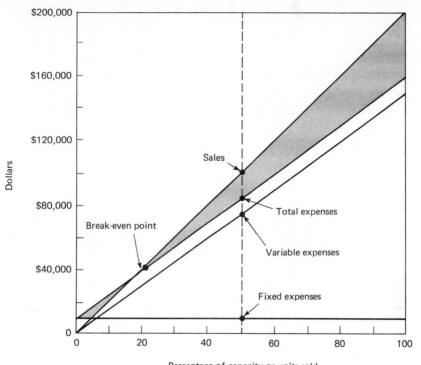

FIGURE 18-3
Break-even chart for 1981 for the ABC Company when the percentage of capacity is known.

horizontal axes for your chart. The chart should be about 5 inches *square*. Label the vertical axis "Dollars (sales and expenses)" and the horizontal axis "Percentage of Capacity" or "Units Sold." Divide each axis into equal parts and mark each division with a dot. Place dollar amounts on each dot on the vertical axis, beginning with zero at the lower left corner and increasing in equal amounts to the top of the vertical axis. The dollar amount at the top of the vertical axis should represent sales at 100 percent of capacity if known. This amount is broken up into 10 equal amounts. In our example, we will assume that *operations for the year were at 50 percent of capacity and use $200,000 as the top figure on the vertical axis,* with cumulative divisions of $20,000 each as the scale starts from the bottom.

Step 3 Draw a solid line from the lower left corner of the chart to the upper right corner. This will become the sales income line.

Step 4 Find the point of 50 percent capacity on the horizontal axis. Draw a vertical dotted line from the bottom of the chart to the top at this 50 percent capacity point.

Step 5   On the vertical dotted line, mark the points representing $10,000, $75,000, $85,000, and $100,000, all measured against the left axis. These points mark the total of fixed, variable, and total expenses and the sales volume at 50 percent of capacity.

Step 6   On the left axis, mark the point for $10,000. This is the total fixed expenses and total expenses at zero sales, or zero percentage of capacity.

Step 7   Every complete break-even chart should have four lines. We drew the sales line in step 3, which bisects the square chart. Now draw the other three lines. Fixed expenses, by definition, are the same regardless of sales volume. Therefore, connect the $10,000 mark on the left axis and the $10,000 mark on the vertical dotted line, and extend the straight line on across the chart. Variable expenses, by definition, are zero at zero sales and $75,000 at 50 percent of capacity. Therefore, connect the point zero on the left axis with the $75,000 mark on the vertical dotted line, and extend the straight line on across the chart. Total expenses are the combination of both fixed and variable expenses. That total is $10,000 at zero sales and $85,000 at 50 percent of capacity. Therefore, connect the $10,000 point on the left axis and the $85,000 mark on the vertical dotted line, and extend the straight line on across the chart.

We now have a break-even chart for the ABC Company. It tells us many things about the operations. Among these things are the following:

1 The break-even point for the firm is a sales volume of $40,000. This is the point in sales volume where neither profit nor loss will result. On the chart it is found at the point *where the sales line and the total expense line cross.* Any sales less than $40,000 would put operations in the loss area of the chart. As sales expand into the profit area, profits become larger and larger.

2 Only 20 percent of possible capacity is necessary to reach the break-even point. This is found by comparing the break-even point with the horizontal scale. It follows that $40,000 of sales represents 20 percent of capacity.

3 Profits on the $100,000 of sales for the year was $15,000—measured by *the vertical distance between the total expense line and the sales line,* read against the vertical dollar axis.

4 As sales volume expands, the profits on each succeeding dollar of income is greater than on the preceding dollar. A sales increase from 50 to 60 percent of capacity will not yield as much profit as an increase from 70 to 80 percent of capacity. The reason is that after we pass the break-even point, all fixed expenses are prorated over a greater number of units of sales.

5 We can measure the profit results of a 10 percent increase in prices, for example, by superimposing another sales line from the lower left corner across the chart connecting through the vertical dotted line at the point of $110,000 ($100,000 plus 10 percent). We can also observe the results of a 10 percent reduction in total expenses by superimposing a line from $9,000 ($10,000 less 10 percent) through the point $76,500 ($85,000 less 10 percent) on the vertical dotted line. This type of analysis may be necessary if the firm is faced with the necessity of increasing income or reducing expenses. In any event, it provides good information for decision making and study of the operation.

6 If sales could be expanded to 100 percent of capacity, profits would rise to $40,000—again the vertical distance between sales and total expenses on the right axis. As a practical matter, we can observe that if this point is even approached, most small firms have already made plans to expand their facilities.

The Problem of Measuring Capacity

The problem of determining at what percentage of capacity the firm operated has prevented many small firm owners from making maximum use of a break-even chart. We can easily overcome this problem.

A factory operation which has machines that can produce 100 units of its products a day can easily determine 100 percent of its capacity. It merely multiplies working days times 100 units to find what production will be if full production is maintained during the month or year. By then comparing actual production with this capacity, the percentage is determined. For example, if the plant operated 250 days per year and its capacity per day was 100 units, maximum production at 100 percent capacity would be 25,000 units. If actual production is 15,000 units, the percentage of capacity for operation during the year is 60 percent (15,000 divided by 25,000).

For retail and wholesale operations, the measurement of utilized capacity is not so easily determined. Some retailers use a flat amount of sales per salesperson (for example, $300 per day) to represent 100 percent of capacity. This method must include the number of salespersons who can conveniently operate in the available sales space. Others attempt to combine average sale, time required per sale, salespeople's time on the sales floor, and number of salespeople who can conveniently operate in the sales space, to arrive at a figure that would represent 100 percent capacity sales for a given period. Store hours must be considered in any such calculation.

How to Make a Break-Even Chart When Percentage of Capacity Is Not Known

It is not necessary to resort to these types of calculations to have the benefit of a break-even chart. The chart in Figure 18-4 has been constructed without reference to the percentage of capacity at which the firm operated. Its construction is explained in detail.

Figure 18-4 shows the break-even chart when the percentage of capacity or number of units is not known. The same ABC Company data is used.

Step 1   Find any convenient point on the vertical scale to insert the $100,000 sales volume. Any point about midway up the scale is normally used unless it is

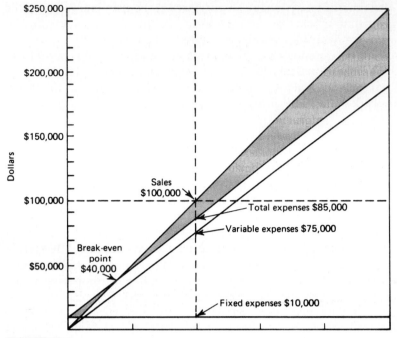

FIGURE 18-4
Break-even chart for 1981 for the ABC Company when the percentage of capacity is unknown.

felt that close-to-maximum capacity has been achieved. In that case, choose a higher point on the vertical scale.

Step 2 Bisect the angle on the grid at the lower left corner. Extend this line far enough across the grid so that it allows for the maximum length of the horizontal and vertical lines. This is the sales line on any break-even chart which uses a square grid.

Step 3 Scale the vertical axis in even units from the point where you inserted the $100,000 amount for sales.

Step 4 Draw a horizontal dotted line from the $100,000 sales point completely across the grid. Where the horizontal dotted line crosses the sales line, draw a vertical dotted line from bottom to top of the grid.

Step 5 On the vertical dotted line, plot the points for fixed, variable, and total expenses against the vertical axis scale.

Step 6 Draw the lines for fixed, variable, and total expenses from the left axis to the plotting points on the vertical dotted line. Remember, sales and variable expenses connect at the point zero on the vertical axis, and fixed expenses and total expenses connect at the point of fixed expenses ($10,000) on the vertical axis.

When we compare this chart with Figure 18-3, it will be seen that the scale is different, but all readings are identical. The break-even point calls for the same volume of sales, and profits are the same at all sales volumes. The only unknown is the percentage of capacity represented at each measuring point. The profit effects of an increase in sales can still be measured in the same manner.

COMPUTING THE BREAK-EVEN POINT BY FORMULA

Where the immediate objective is to find only the sales volume that is necessary to reach the break-even point, handy formulas are available. The following is a popular formula for this purpose.

$$\text{Break-Even Point} = \frac{\text{Fixed Expenses}}{1 - \frac{\text{Variable Expenses}}{\text{Sales}}}$$

If we insert into this formula the same figures that we used above for the ABC Company (fixed expenses $10,000, variable expenses $75,000, total expenses $85,000, and sales of $100,000), we will get the same break-even point for sales of $40,000 as follows:

$$\text{Break-Even Point} = \frac{\text{Fixed Expenses}}{1 - \frac{\text{Variable Expenses}}{\text{Sales}}}$$

$$= \frac{10,000}{1 - \frac{75,000}{100,000}}$$

$$= \frac{10,000}{1 - .75}$$

$$= \frac{10,000}{.25}$$

$$= 40,000$$

QUESTIONS FOR CLASS DISCUSSION

1 Do you believe that cost of goods sold is a variable expense of any business? Why?
2 Why is it better to compute a firm's percentage of capacity on a basis of actual business days, rather than using 365 days for the year?
3 Is it possible for any business to be immune to loss? How?
4 What sacrifices must a business make to reduce risk?

5 What types of expenses increase directly and proportionately with sales?

6 What expenses increase directly but not proportionately with sales?

7 If the rent is $400 per month plus 1 percent of sales over $50,000, how would you classify the total rent expense?

8 What do we mean by the "skeleton staff expenses"?

9 What are the three most important things you believe a break-even chart tells you?

10 Does an annual break-even chart reflect seasonal variations in sales volume?

11 Why is the cost of goods sold added to the variable operating expenses when making a break-even chart?

12 Is it true that the greater the fixed expenses, the further to the right is the break-even point? Why?

13 What other uses can an owner make of an accurate break-even chart?

14 Do you consider delivery expenses a fixed or a variable expense? Explain.

PROJECTS FOR HOME ASSIGNMENT AND/OR CLASS DISCUSSION

1 Write a short essay explaining the importance of an adequate inventory, the extra costs of having too much inventory on hand, and the dangers of having too little inventory on hand.

2 What would your policy be on markdowns in your firm? Explain the reasons for each part of your policy.

3 a Write a short paper on the value of a break-even chart for any small firm.

b How often do you think it would be wise to make a break-even chart? Monthly? Quarterly? Or annually?

CONTINUING PROBLEM:
The Kollege Klothes Shop

PART 18: THE BREAK-EVEN CHART AND EXPENSE ANALYSIS

As business students, we no longer have to be told of the importance of a break-even chart and its many valuable uses to small firm owners. The value of any business techniques studied, however, lies in our ability to apply them. This is what we want to do for our clients.

Assignment for Part 18

1 List every fixed expense on the budgeted break-even chart previously prepared in one column and every variable expense in another column. Add the cost of goods sold to the variable expense column. You decide which column each expense properly belongs in. You may decide to split some operating expenses between fixed and variable.

2 Using the column totals you have prepared, construct a break-even chart on a 5-inch grid. Assume that the store operated at 60 percent of capacity in the

first year of operation. Read the break-even point from your chart, both as to sales and percentage of capacity needed to achieve break-even.

3 Using the break-even formula in the chapter, compute the break-even sales volume to see that it gives you the same dollar of sales required to break even. You will need the same totals for fixed and variable expenses computed above.

REFERENCES FOR FURTHER READING

"Attacking Business Decision Problems with Break-Even Analysis," Small Business Administration Pamphlet No. MA234.

Niswonger, C. Rollin, and Philip E. Fess, *Accounting Principles,* 12th ed., South-Western Publishing Company, Inc., Cincinnati, Ohio, 1977, chap. 24.

Steinhoff, Dan, *The World of Business,* McGraw-Hill Book Company, New York, 1979, chap. 31.

"Simple Breakeven Analysis for Small Stores," Small Business Administration Pamphlet No. SMA166.

SELLING ON CREDIT: ADMINISTERING A CREDIT PROGRAM

When I started my business, I knew that people had to have credit to buy things when they wanted them rather than waiting for payday. But I always thought they would pay me on their next payday. Was I wrong! I had to borrow money to pay my own current bills while waiting for customers to pay their accounts. And some of them never *paid me. Thank goodness for credit cards.*

The Late Learner

CREDIT SELLING WILL INCREASE SALES

There are few axioms in the world of business, but one of them is "if you sell on credit you will increase sales, even to the same customers to whom you previously sold for cash only." This alluring proposition has great appeal to small business firms. Sales are the foundation of profits, and anything that will help to increase sales commands the attention of competent business owners.

But there is more to credit selling than meets the eye. Every retail business must first decide whether it will offer credit arrangements to its customers. The ability to finance credit accounts must be assured. If credit is to be available, a decision must be made about the kind of credit to be extended. Will the firm sell to its customers on open account and carry these accounts receivable on its own books until they are paid? Or will it sell only to credit card holders who have been approved for credit by one or more of the many credit-card companies now so active throughout the United States? In this chapter we will review the details of both types of consumer credit.

TRADE CREDIT VERSUS CONSUMER CREDIT

Trade credit is credit extended from one business firm to another. *Consumer credit* is credit given by retailers to their customers, who are the final users of the products or services sold. Sales by manufacturers and wholesalers are almost always made on a credit basis. Retail sales on credit are about half of the total retail sales in the country. Only the growing popularity of chain grocery stores and others that sell for cash only has kept retail sales on credit from growing larger.

Trade credit almost always carries a sales discount for prompt payment. We learned in Chapter 17 that "terms of sale 2/10, n/30," for example, means that 2 percent of the total amount may be deducted if the invoice is paid within 10 days, but the entire amount is due in 30 days. Such discounts are extremely rare in consumer credit. The trend is quite the opposite. Most retail sales on credit carry a charge to customers for the privilege of postponing their payment to a later date. Large firms have adopted this practice even more than small ones. Various types of consumer credit accounts will be discussed later in this chapter.

THE BUSINESS WORLD OPERATES ON CREDIT—OF NECESSITY

Our business world could not operate without credit. There is not enough currency and coin in the country to finance the business transactions carried on every day. Total bank deposits exceed the actual money in the country several times over. The key is credit extended throughout the economy. Without credit from banks, credit from other business firms, and the sale of securities, large and small manufacturers could not operate. Without credit from manufacturers, banks, and other sources, wholesalers could not operate. Retailers depend on credit from banks and wholesalers. Without credit terms available, the average family could not buy a home, an automobile, major appliances, or finance expensive vacations. The importance of the credit standing of the business firm and of individuals is obvious. Unless a reputation for prompt payment of obligations is developed, credit sources will not be available. A good credit standing is essential to business success. Business owners must look for good credit standing of firms or individuals to whom they grant credit.

OPEN ACCOUNT CREDIT

Open account credit means that the merchant allows customers to say "charge it" when they make purchases. A copy of the sales slip for each purchase is recorded on the firm's books. The total charges for each customer are added and shown on a statement, which is sent to the customer, usually on the first of the following month. Such unpaid balances appear on the firm's balance sheet as accounts receivable. Open account credit operates quite differently from credit-card credit, which we will investigate later in this chapter.

Great care must be taken in granting such open account credit. We learned in Chapter 8 that, even when such credit is carefully granted, the firm will soon have a total investment in accounts receivable of 45 to 60 days' credit sales when they are selling on a 30-day credit basis. Careless credit granting will greatly increase this amount. Accounts receivable tie up the working capital of the firm. We stressed in Chapter 8 the importance of the firms' having sufficient cash in the business to be able to invest in such accounts receivable.

The Costs of Open Account Credit

Whenever a business firm, large or small, makes open account credit available to its customers, it automatically assumes additional costs. These should be considered seriously before a business owner embarks upon a general credit policy. Too many new small firms fail to recognize some of these costs. They include:

Bookkeeping costs to record customer purchases and payments received
Printing of sales slips, statement forms, letterheads, envelopes, and credit memos
Postage costs for mailing statements
Interest on working capital invested in accounts receivable
Collection costs for delinquent customers
The inevitable bad debts that are never collected

Full recognition of these costs has caused more and more small firms to turn to credit-card sales rather than carrying customer accounts on their own books.

The seriousness of the credit problem is emphasized by the aggregate losses on debts incurred every year by American business firms. The most conservative estimates run into the millions. The most efficient firms are satisfied to keep their bad-debt losses below 2 percent of their credit sales. Studies show that small firms which exercise inadequate control over their credit extensions have often had losses on bad debts that exceed 5 percent of their credit sales. Profitability can be seriously affected in such cases. Such data point up the need for care in credit extension.

The longer a credit sale is carried on the books, the greater is the likelihood of its not being collected in full. This fact shows the necessity of close follow-up on accounts that become past due. Small firms too often have been lax in enforcing good collection procedures.

With the benefit of the foregoing facts about the world of credit, new firm planners can make choices for their firms. If they decide to sell on open account, either exclusively or in connection with credit-card sales, they must turn their attention to the question of which customers should be granted credit and on what basis.

ADMINISTERING A CREDIT PROGRAM

It has been seen that credit sales may increase total sales and profits. This is true, however, only if the increased sales do not cost more in administration expenses and bad-debt losses than the profits on the credit sales. Every firm should, therefore, have a procedure for granting credit. Any customer who asks for credit desires the use of the firm's capital. In exchange, the customer should be willing to comply with reasonable rules for the granting of that credit. No exceptions should be made.

The credit manager always wants to be sure that the account will be paid. The manager must find out the applicant's record for payment, capacity to pay, and how much credit the applicant can properly handle. Everyone is worth some credit; the question is how much. No business does its customers favors by granting them more credit than they can handle. Such a credit policy only invites ill will from the customers in the long run and might even force them to consider bankruptcy. Giving credit is a serious responsibility.

Well-managed companies take the following steps in granting credit:

1 Have the applicant for consumer credit fill out a credit application blank that calls for such basic information as name, address, age, present and past employment, length of employment, salary, home ownership details, past credit extended, payments now being made on other accounts, bank accounts, family status including dependents, and other asset information. An example of a credit application blank is shown in Figure 19-1. Applicants for trade credit should submit their companies' official financial statements.

2 Check the applicant's credit record with local credit bureaus and other credit agencies. Find out what limits were placed on the applicant's credit by other firms. Remember you are always looking for evidence of the applicant's possession of the "four C's of credit"—character, capital, capacity, and conditions. Trade-credit applicants are checked by credit bureaus and/or by Dun & Bradstreet, a general trade-credit agency. (See Figures 19-2 and 19-3.)

3 On the basis of knowledge gathered from an independent investigation plus confirmation of information on the application, determine the limit of credit you feel can safely be granted. If the investigation proves that an applicant is a high risk, the decision must be to deny any credit at all. Assuming that investigation proves an applicant worthy of credit, compare the desired merchandise purchase with the limit you have set. This will determine whether the applicant should be granted credit on an installment-loan basis, a revolving-account basis, a budget-account basis, or an open charge account.

4 Discuss your decision with all applicants. Explain the reasons for the decision if asked. Support your decision by explaining that applicants' payments must be in line with their available income and that you are protecting them from getting too far into debt.

Credit Application Form Suitable for Any Small Business Firm

				HOME PHONE
			AREA CODE	

PLEASE PRINT ALL INFORMATION REQUESTED

NAME FIRST INITIAL LAST	DATE OF BIRTH	SOCIAL SECURITY NUMBER
HOME ADDRESS APT. NO. CITY	STATE	ZIP CODE	NO. OF YRS.
LANDLORD OR MORTGAGE HOLDER ADDRESS	OWN □ RENT UNFURN. □	RENT FURN. □ OTHER □	MO. PAYMENT
PREVIOUS ADDRESS CITY STATE ZIP CODE	NO. OF YRS.	DEP. CHILDREN
PRESENT EMPLOYER BUSINESS ADDRESS (IF SELF-EMPLOYED GIVE NAME AND NATURE OF BUSINESS)	POSITION	NO. OF YRS.	BUSINESS PHONE
PREVIOUS EMPLOYER BUSINESS ADDRESS	POSITION	NO. OF YRS.	DATE LEFT
NAME AND ADDRESS OF NEAREST RELATIVE NOT LIVING WITH YOU	RELATIONSHIP	PHONE

IF CREDIT IS REQUESTED FOR CO-APPLICANT/SPOUSE, FILL OUT THE FOLLOWING:

NAME FIRST INITIAL LAST	DATE OF BIRTH	SOCIAL SECURITY NUMBER
CO-APPLICANT/SPOUSE'S EMPLOYER BUSINESS ADDRESS	POSITION	NO. OF YRS.	BUSINESS PHONE

CREDIT REFERENCES: (Banks, Stores, Credit Unions, Finance Co.'s) and Complete List of ALL Debts Now Owing. Attach Additional Sheet if Necessary.

NAME	ADDRESS	CITY	STATE	BAL. (IF ANY)	MO. PAYMENT	ACCOUNT NUMBER

MAKE/YR. OF AUTO	FINANCED BY ADDRESS	MO. PAYMENT	APPLICANT'S MONTHLY INCOME $
□ CHECKING ACCT. – BANK NAME			OTHER MONTHLY INCOME $
□ SAVINGS ACCT. – BANK NAME			
THE UNDERSIGNED ARE JOINTLY AND SEVERALLY LIABLE FOR ALL CHARGES INCURRED ON ANY ACCOUNT PURSUANT TO THIS APPLICATION.			CO-APPLICANT/SPOUSE'S MONTHLY INCOME $ IF CREDIT REQUESTED
SIGNATURE OF APPLICANT		DATE	TOTAL MONTHLY INCOME $
SIGNATURE OF CO-APPLICANT AND/OR SPOUSE IF CREDIT IS REQUESTED		DATE	

FIGURE 19-1
Typical application for credit used by large firms. Small firms should be equally careful in extending credit. This form complies with the newest regulations of the Equal Credit Opportunity Act.

5 Follow up on new credit accounts regularly. This can be done even before an aging of accounts receivable (to be expláined later in this chapter) is made. When payments are delinquent and notices and other steps taken have been ignored, it may be necessary to exercise right of repossession if it is available. If all has worked out well, it is desirable to inform the customer that better credit terms can be arranged in the future.

Types of Credit Accounts

There are at least four basic types of consumer credit accounts.

1 Open Accounts Open accounts are ordinary charge accounts. With this type of account the customer charges all purchases throughout the month and is expected to pay the total charges when a statement is sent by the firm. Most firms

NAME AND ADDRESS OF CREDIT BUREAU MAKING REPORT

| | SUMMARY REPORT | | SINGLE REFERENCE | | TRADE REPORT |

Credit Bureau of Anytown
2309 Fair Street, P. O. Box 765
Anytown, Anystate 67045
Telephone 265-7821 (936)

| | SHORT REPORT | | [X] FULL REPORT | | PREV. RES. REPORT |

DATE RECEIVED	DATE MAILED	CBR REPORT NO
11-26-73	11-29-73	
DATE TRADE CLEARED	DATE EMPLOY VERIFIED	INCOME VERIFIED
11-27-73	11-28-73	[X] YES ☐ NO

CONFIDENTIAL *Factbilt*® REPORT FOR First National Bank of Anytown

IN FILE SINCE:
7-70

This information is furnished in response to an inquiry for the purpose of evaluating credit risks. It has been obtained from sources deemed reliable, the accuracy of which this organization does not guarantee. The inquirer has agreed to indemnify the reporting bureau for any damage arising from misuse of this information, and this report is furnished in reliance upon that indemnity. It must be held in strict confidence, and must not be revealed to the subject reported on.

REPORT ON (SURNAME):	MR. MRS. MISS	GIVEN NAME:	SOCIAL SECURITY NUMBER	SPOUSE'S NAME:
DOE	Mr.	Robert Thomas	123-44-5678	Betty L.

ADDRESS:	CITY:	STATE	ZIP CODE:	SPOUSE'S SOCIAL SECURITY NO.:
921 Third Avenue	Anytown	Anystate	67046	134-66-9810

COMPLETE TO HERE FOR TRADE REPORT AND SKIP TO CREDIT HISTORY

PRESENT EMPLOYER AND KIND OF BUSINESS:	POSITION HELD:	SINCE	MONTHLY INCOME:
Anytown Morning Herald - Newspaper	Circulation Manager	7-1-70	$ 850.00

COMPLETE TO HERE FOR SHORT REPORT AND SUMMARY REPORT AND SKIP TO CREDIT HISTORY

DATE OF BIRTH:	NUMBER OF DEPENDENTS INCLUDING SPOUSE ► 3		[X] OWNS OR BUYING HOME	☐ RENTS HOME
5-15-28				

FORMER ADDRESS:	CITY:	STATE	FROM 8-55	TO: 6-70
606 Grove Street	Thattown	Thatstate		

FORMER EMPLOYER AND KIND OF BUSINESS:	POSITION HELD:	FROM 8-55 TO: 6-70	MONTHLY INCOME: $ 650.00
City Publishing Company - Book Publisher	Bindry Manager		

SPOUSE'S EMPLOYER AND KIND OF BUSINESS:	POSITION HELD:	SINCE: 1-1-71	MONTHLY INCOME: $ 350.00
Anytown Oil Company - U	Secretary		

CREDIT HISTORY (Complete this section for all reports)

KIND OF BUSINESS	DATE ACCOUNT OPENED	DATE OF LAST SALE	HIGHEST CREDIT	AMOUNT OWING	AMOUNT PAST DUE	TERMS OF SALE AND USUAL MANNER OF PAYMENT
F	7-70	7-70	21,300	20,277	0	1$120-1
D	8-72	8-72	1,724	1,193	0	1$60-1
F	9-72	9-72	232	101	36	1$18-3
C	4-71	11-73	46	27	0	R$12-1
H	8-70	10-73	130	0	0	0-2
B	7-70	Checking Account Opened				
	9-70	11-73	400	253	0	R-1
B	1-72	1-72	324	0	0	1$24-4
Trade Reported 9-8-73						
0	-	-	-	253	253	0-9
Trade Reported 1-10-73						
0	-	-	121	0	0	0-5

Public Records:
9-5-72 Judgment, Anytown Rentals vs Robert T Doe, $123.74, Satisfied 10-72
3-12-73 Release of Tax Lien, Internal Revenue Service vs R. T. and B. L. Doe, $475.00

INDICATE IF FILE CONTAINS

[X] Items of Public Record ☐ Any record of accounts placed for collection [X] Any reports received from other Credit Bureaus

IF ANY OF THE ABOVE ARE CHECKED, GIVE DETAILS

Trade from Thattown, Thatstate, 9-70, In File 8-55

F	1-67	1-67	300	0	0	1$12-1
D	1963	6-70	750	0	0	0-1
B	6-69	3-70	665	0	0	R-1

AFFILIATED WITH   PRINTED IN U.S.A.

Form 100 ◼ **Associated Credit Bureaus, Inc.** *CREDIT BUREAU REPORTS...*

7

FIGURE 19-2
Credit report. This type of report may be obtained from local credit bureaus when a business owner is checking on the eligibility of credit applicants. *(From Credit Bureau Reports.)*

send out statements monthly, but full payment each month is not insisted upon. No interest charges are normally made against such accounts.

2 Revolving Accounts It would appear that revolving accounts were designed for customers who live with eternal indebtedness. The firm sets an upper limit to the amount that may be charged, and any purchases below that limit are

Deciding What to Do!

1 Credit Bureau employees are instructed NOT to tell you to grant or reject an applicant for credit. Their job is to assemble facts so that you can make up your own mind.

2 If the record looks good and you wish to grant credit, you do so.

3 If the record clearly indicates the applicant does not meet your requirements for credit, you tell the customer the reason for your decision. If your denial was based on information supplied by the Credit Bureau, you are required under Public Law 91-508 to give the customer the name and address of the Credit Bureau.

Only refer to the Credit Bureau for credit consultation those consumers you have refused credit because of information you received from the Credit Bureau.

If your denial for credit was based on information obtained from sources other than the Credit Bureau, the consumer should not be referred to the Credit Bureau. The consumers should be told truthfully why they are being declined or why you are not extending them a line of credit.

FIGURE 19-3
Some ways to make use of a credit bureau. *(From Credit Bureau Reports.)*

automatically approved for credit sale. The customer must then pay a certain amount or a specified percentage of the total charges at the end of each month. Interest is charged on the unpaid balance each month, and credit purchases can continue to be made against the account up to its limit.

3 Installment Accounts Installment accounts were specifically designed to make possible the sale on credit of larger purchases. The customer makes a down payment, preferably at least 20 percent of the total purchase price, and the balance is spread over a monthly payment plan. Good business practice limits such payments to not more than 3 years. Many installment accounts are for a shorter period. Carrying charges are added to the amount due, usually up to 1 percent per month. Most such sales are protected by a chattel mortgage on the item being sold or a conditional sales contract, so that the merchant may repossess the item if payments are not made. The customer obtains title only when the payments have been completed.

4 Budget Accounts Budget accounts are designed to handle payments which ordinarily fall between short-term open accounts and longer-term installment accounts. No down payment is required and customers are normally given 3 months to remit the total price in equal payments. Customers are expected to make payments without reminders in the form of statements from the seller.

Service charges are made only when the original plan of payment is not maintained.

Each of these four types of accounts necessitates special forms and clear identification to the buyer. Payment plans for each must be explained and understood.

Accounts Receivable Turnover

The accounts receivable turnover is the relationship of the credit sales made during the year and the average amount of accounts receivable carried on the books. It is computed by dividing the total credit sales for the year by the average accounts receivable. It tells management if credit customers are paying their accounts on time.

$$\frac{\text{Credit sales for the year}}{\text{Average accounts receivable}} = \text{Accounts receivable turnover}$$

When seasonal variations in credit sales are normal during the year, it is especially important to average the accounts receivable to obtain a more accurate measure of their turnover. Firms selling to one another on a basis of trade notes receivable should include the balance of any such notes receivable in their receivables in computing the turnover.

Every good management keeps a close check on the turnover figure and makes decisions based on the trend of this turnover. This figure also serves as a check on the paying habits of the firm's credit customers and on the credit-extension policies of the credit department. Increasing turnover indicates that customers are paying their accounts more quickly. If the turnover is decreasing, customers are paying more slowly, and/or the credit department is granting unjustified credit.

An example will illustrate computation of the accounts receivable turnover and its significance in evaluating performance.

The AAA Company is a small department store that sells to many customers on a 30-day credit basis. In 1981 its credit sales were $300,000. The average accounts receivable on the first of each month was $50,000. Its accounts receivable turnover, therefore, was six times per year. In other words it took one-sixth of a year (60 days) to collect the average amount of receivables carried on the books. But the firm was selling on a 30-day credit. If all customers paid their account balances on the first of the month, the turnover would have been 12 times per year. Management considerations in such a situation involve answers to questions such as the following:

1 Can the company carry these receivables without impairing its cash position?

2 Has credit been granted unwisely to customers who average 60 days to pay 30-day accounts?

3 Is this account-paying schedule normal for this type of business?

4 Has the loss on bad debts been increased because customers take 60 days on the average to pay current charges?

5 If bad-debt losses are not out of line, would it be desirable to arrange financing to enable the firm to carry its accounts receivable for this longer period?

6 Can anything be done to encourage more prompt payment of credit accounts by customers?

7 Would an interest charge on past due accounts stimulate more prompt payment?

Circumstances will vary from firm to firm as answers to these questions are sought. The important thing is to know the facts in regard to the accounts receivable turnover and to make policies accordingly. New restrictions may have to be placed on credit granting. Or perhaps credit will be granted only through credit cards. On the brighter side, a turnover of 12 times per year for the AAA Company may suggest that profits could be expanded by further granting of credit. Such a turnover rate indicates that customers are paying their bills on schedule and that losses on bad accounts are at a minimum.

AGING OF ACCOUNTS RECEIVABLE

To combat the problem of delinquent accounts, an *aging of accounts receivable* should be made regularly by the small firm owner. An example of such a statement is presented in Table 19-1. The first two columns show the customer's

TABLE 19-1
ABC COMPANY
Aging of Accounts Receivable
October 1, 1981

Customer Name	Current Balance	Number of days on books				
		0–30	31–60	61–90	91–120	Over 120
M. Jones	$375	$ 75	$300			
H. Harris	160	60	50	$50		
G. Salzman	50	50				
P. Miller	500	300	100	100		
G. Geipel	50	—	—	—	$50	
B. Thompson	75		75			
H. Strauss	35	10	—	25		
J. Hegner	125	100	—	—	—	$25
T. Nathan	400	100	100	100	100	
A. Cohen	425	25	200	200		
G. Young	75					75
J. Osborg	200				100	100
Totals	$37,000	$22,000	$8,000	$5,000	$1,000	$1,000

name and current balance. In the other columns, that balance is broken down into what portion of it was charged in the last 30 days, what portion has been on the books 30 to 60 days, what portion 60 to 90 days, and what portion over 90 days. As we observe our axiom that the longer an account is on the books the more likely is its failure to be paid in full, we can see that prompt action should be taken via an established collection procedure whenever a balance becomes past due. The exact point and exact steps will be decided by firm policy. Alternatives are presented later.

In this case, $37,000 represents the balance of the accounts receivable account for the firm. The total of all the other columns is also $37,000. This statement shows the proprietor that $22,000 is current month charges, $8,000 is less than 60 days old, $5,000 is less than 90 days old, but $1,000 is more than 90 days old and $1,000 is over 120 days old. When the proprietor estimates the bad-debts expense for the year, serious consideration should be given to charging off the last $2,000. Its collection is definitely in doubt when it has been on the books so long. Accounts once charged off as a loss must always be reported as income if their unlikely collection should occur.

Number of Days' Sales in Receivables

An even more precise measure of customer paying habits is the number of days' sales represented in the accounts receivable on a given date. This figure is found by dividing the total accounts receivable at the end of the year by the average daily credit sales. The latter figure is found by dividing the credit sales for the year by 365. If the firm has $50,000 of accounts receivable on December 31 and the average daily credit sales are $1,000, the receivables represent 50 days of credit sales. If selling is on 30 days' credit, it is clear that customers are late in paying. This calculation can also be made in terms of business days rather than calendar days by dividing the credit sales for the year by the number of business days the firm is open for operation rather than by 365, as shown above.

We should note that the example of the AAA Company's selling on 30 days' credit and having 50 days of credit sales on its books is not farfetched. You will recall that in the planning of an opening day balance sheet (Chapter 9), it was recommended that we be prepared to finance 1½ to 2 times the credit sales in the maximum credit period. Most new firms which carry their own receivables will reach such a position within the first or second year of operation.

HANDLING DELINQUENT ACCOUNTS

Credit customers who do not pay on schedule cause the firm several problems. The firm must cut off their credit so that they are lost as future customers even if their finances improve. Also the old balances restrict liquidity of the working capital, and the net result is usually an uncollectible account that becomes bad-debts expense. Partial collection by attorneys or collection firms involves more expense. No merchant likes to make credit sales in good faith and then have the sales cause these problems. The best course of action when accounts become overdue is to minimize the eventual losses by taking the following steps:

1 Send a second statement in 60 days from purchase. This could include a note to the effect that "Perhaps our first statement was not received or was mislaid. We know you would not want your credit status impaired. Please advise us if there is any complaint about our products or service."

2 Telephone the customer or send a telegram in 70 days, asking the reasons for nonpayment.

3 Send a third statement in 75 days. Include a note to the effect that "Your credit status is at stake. We are forced to turn over accounts 75 days old to our collection agency or attorney."

4 Send a registered letter in 80 days, including a certified copy of the statement, saying that the account is being referred to the collection agency.

5 Turn the account over to the agency or the firm's attorney for legal action in 90 days.

Small firm owners usually have an advantage over large firm owners in this situation, since they know their customers better. If this is so, they can usually accomplish more through personal contact with the customer than by resorting to the steps just described. If they find that a genuine customer complaint exists, they may open the door to making a fair adjustment and keeping the customer. But the possible delinquent situation should always be anticipated by picking the right credit customers in the first contact.

PERSONAL AND COMPANY CHECK CASHING IS ANOTHER FORM OF CREDIT

Credit extension is normally thought of as allowing customers to charge their purchases to the firm at the time of purchase, with the balances due to be paid at least once a month. Cashing checks for customers and companies, however, is another form of credit extension. Few merchants will not confess to having cashed checks for customers that came back from the bank marked "NSF" (not sufficient funds) or "no account here." One major airline reported to the author some time ago that it had accepted more than $2 million in bad checks in one year. It now encourages the use of credit cards whenever possible. These facts point up the necessity of a policy on check cashing. The natural result has been an increasing reluctance to accept checks.

Devices are now available to aid in this problem. "Debit cards" have been introduced. These are plastic cards, held by customers, which may be inserted into an electronic box by the merchant to confirm that check-writers have funds in their accounts to cover their checks. Check guarantee companies, which will guarantee personal checks to the merchant, now exist. Many banks have machines available 24-hours a day to enable their card holders to get cash from the machines by inserting their cards. These machines not only make it easier for customers to get cash; they also reduce the use of personal checks. Merchants must be cautious in cashing checks for people they do not know. We will see more and more evidence in this chapter that the small firm should restrict its credit sales to credit cards and not attempt to carry many open accounts receivable on its own books. Neither should it accept personal checks without substantiation of the customer's identification and/or assurance that the check is good.

CREDIT-CARD CREDIT

The huge increase in the use of credit cards in the United States in the past ten years has been one of the major merchandising and financial developments of the century. In 1980 it was estimated that there were more than 75 million individual credit cards outstanding. Many families have as many as ten cards in effect. Outstanding dollar balances exceed $60 billion, or almost $600 for every family in the country. More than 10,000 banks offer credit-card services.

Credit cards are being used today for ever-increasing types of purchases. They originally were designed to assist travelers with the problem of cashing personal checks when they were away from home. They were used most often for purchasing airline tickets and paying hotel bills, auto rentals, and gasoline purchases. *Today retail purchases of consumer products and services represent their widest use.* In California credit cards can be used to pay property taxes, to buy auto tags, and even to pay state income taxes. Other newer uses include payments to doctors and dentists, political parties, churches, and even mortuaries. Most credit cards were originally issued free of charge for approved applicants. These included the most popular: Master Charge (now MasterCard) and VISA. Each card specifies the maximum credit the holder may charge. Since 1980, however, an important development has been the charging of an annual fee to holders of most credit cards, including American Express, Diners Club, VISA and MasterCard. These charges ranged up to $20 per year in 1981.

The cards named above are all issued by general credit-card companies. Many can be used around the world. But we should also observe that many individual service and product companies still issue their own credit cards. These are called *single-firm credit cards.* Oil companies, department stores, hotels, and chain restaurants are most prominent examples. The objective is to stimulate sales of the firm's own products or services while avoiding the costs of the general credit-card companies. Some oil companies even honor the credit cards of other oil companies. Oil companies charge no fee to service stations, garages, or other firms using their cards. Most of these individual company cards carry no service charge to customers who pay their monthly balances promptly. When such cards are issued by smaller firms, the effect is usually comparable to open account selling. They may still have good advertising and sales development value.

How Credit Cards Operate for the Customer

When a cardholder wishes to make a purchase against a credit card, he or she must first ascertain whether the firm honors that card. Most small firms that accept credit cards have signs displayed in their front window or door indicating the types of cards accepted. To make a purchase, the customer merely shows the merchant the credit card. The merchant, who may phone the credit-card company or a credit bureau to confirm the customer's credit limit, processes a multiple-copy bill called a *charge notice*. The customer signs the notice and keeps one copy. The merchant files the other copies and returns the credit card to the customer.

At the end of the month the credit-card company sends the cardholder a statement of the total charges and the minimum payment required on the total. A due date for the payment, in full or in part, is indicated on the statement. If the cardholder decides to make the minimum payment only, he or she is charged interest at the rate of 1½ percent per month, or 18 percent per year, on the unpaid balance.

Credit-card companies prefer customers who do not pay in full each month— but who do pay in full, with interest, some time in the future. In 1976 one large credit-card company in the New York area established a flat service charge to customers who paid their bills in full each month. This charge was subsequently declared illegal and it obviously was not popular with credit-card holders.

How Credit Cards Operate for the Merchant

When sales are made on credit cards, the business is assured of full collection of those sales, less the credit-card company charge, each month. The owner merely tallies the total credit-card sales slips and takes them to the credit-card company. The settlement date is usually the fifth of each month. With some credit cards, sales slips may be deposited in a commercial bank in the same manner as currency or checks. Credit-card charges to large and small business firms vary from 1 to 6 percent. The rates are lower now than when credit cards were first introduced.

The charge to the specific firm will vary with two basic factors: (1) the total volume of credit-card sales and (2) the average dollar sale. Thus, an airline which discounts $2 million per week with a credit-card company and has an average sale of $100 may receive a charge of 1 percent. The average charge for a small volume of credit sales and a much lower average sale is 5 or 6 percent. For an additional 1 percent discount merchants may cash in their slips sooner. Most small firm owners do not know that the rate they are charged is negotiable. Competition between credit-card companies is keen, and small firm owners should always take advantage of this fact in requesting a lower rate from their credit-card companies.

Are Credit-Card Companies' Charges Too High?

Credit-card companies are not philanthropic organizations. We would not wish them to be. They render positive services to business firms, small and large, and are organized to make a profit. They have large administrative costs. One credit-card company executive reports that the average cost of each computerized entry is 28 cents.

Susan Berkowitz

FIGURE 19-4
Small firms should give customers early notice about which credit cards they accept.

The companies suffer losses from misuse of stolen cards and when accounts for which they have advanced funds to the individual merchants are not paid. Credit-card companies "buy" accounts without recourse to the merchant. This means that unpaid accounts are losses to the credit-card company. They cannot collect losses from the merchants to whom they advanced money.

The companies' only past sources of income were the discounts charged to merchants when accounts were bought and the interest charged to cardholders who did not pay in full each month. The inadequacy of this income made the annual charges to cardholders necessary. In addition, the major general credit-card companies face stiff competition. Their reported profits have not been out of line with the services rendered, and many companies report that any profits were long in coming.

Should Small Firms Encourage Credit-Card Credit?

The predominant answer to this question that we have gathered from successful small business owners is yes. There may be communities where customers still demand open account credit. In such circumstances the individual small firm must satisfy the customers and meet the competition. However, the general trend throughout the country is obviously toward wider and wider consumer use of credit cards. Manufacturers and wholesalers who supply small firms must abide by the prevailing trade credit terms. As we have noted, little if any business between firms is done on a credit-card basis.

The small retailing firm which is adequately financed to carry its own open accounts receivable must measure its costs of open account credit against the cost of credit-card credit. Experienced firms can do this most effectively. If the total costs of bookkeeping, printing, postage, interest, collection costs, and bad debts are less than the discount paid to the credit-card company, it pays to have open accounts available. If the individual firm is inadequately financed to carry its own receivables, if the owner does not want the bother of the bookkeeping and other aspects of administering a credit program, and if no community demand exists for open account credit, a program of credit-card credit seems preferable. The cost differences between the two plans of credit are often slight. Many small firms still offer both open account and credit-card credit, but the trend is definitely toward more credit-card selling.

New Laws Governing Consumer Credit Practices

The great current interest in consumerism in our country has been accompanied by new federal legislation designed to protect customers. Chief among these are:

1 The Consumer Protection Act
2 The Equal Credit Opportunity Act
3 The Truth in Lending Act
4 The Fair Credit Billing Act

It is most important for all business firms which extend credit carried on their own books to become familiar with these regulations. Much has been written to interpret the new regulations for business firms. Space prohibits even a condensed summary here, but we can observe some of the main provisions.

1 All credit applicants must receive the Equal Credit Opportunity Act Notice, which appears in the lower right column of Figure 19-5. This notice advises creditors that they cannot discriminate against credit applicants on the basis of sex or marital status.

2 All newly approved applicants and existing customers with credit accounts must be informed of their rights and the procedures in case of billing errors or inquiries.

3 Merchants must disclose the names of credit bureaus providing credit reports on the applicant if those reports were the basis for denying credit.

4 Credit refusals cannot be based on such statements as "You fail to meet our standards," but must be explained with a list of specific reasons.

5 Women may use their birth names, married names, or hyphenated surnames, if they choose, on applications.

6 Merchants must hold all applications and credit evaluation working papers for at least 15 months.

7 Separate accounts must be granted to all creditworthy applicants when they wish it, whether or not they are married.

IN CASE OF ERRORS OR INQUIRIES ABOUT YOUR BILL

The Federal Truth in Lending Act requires prompt correction of billing mistakes

1. If you want to preserve your rights under the Act, here's what to do if you think your bill is wrong or if you need more information about an item on your bill
   a. Do not write on the bill. On a separate sheet of paper write (you may telephone your inquiry but *doing so will not preserve your rights under this law)* the following
      i. Your name and account number
      ii. A description of the error and an explanation (to the extent you can explain) why you believe it is an error.
         If you only need more information, explain the item you are not sure about and, if you wish, ask for evidence of the charge such as a copy of the charge slip. Do not send in your copy of a sales slip or other document unless you have a duplicate copy for your records
      iii. The dollar amount of the suspected error
      iv. Any other information (such as your address) which you think will help the creditor to identify you or the reason for your complaint or inquiry
   b. Send your billing error notice to
      Customer Service Department
      P.O. Box 523500
      Miami, FL 33152

   Mail it as soon as you can, but in any case, early enough to reach the creditor within 60 days after the bill was mailed to you. If you have authorized your bank to automatically pay from your checking or savings account any credit card bills from that bank, you can stop or reverse payment on any amount you think is wrong by mailing your notice so the creditor receives it within 16 days after the bill was sent to you. However, you do not have to meet this 16-day deadline to get the creditor to investigate your billing error claim

2. The creditor must acknowledge all letters pointing out possible errors within 30 days of receipt, unless the creditor is able to correct your bill during that 30 days. Within 90 days after receiving your letter, the creditor must either correct the error or explain why the creditor believes the bill was correct. Once the creditor has explained the bill, the creditor has no further obligation to you even though you still believe that there is an error except as provided in paragraph 5.

3. After the creditor has been notified, neither the creditor nor an attorney nor a collection agency may send you collection letters or take other collection action with respect to the amount in dispute, but periodic statements may be sent to you, and the disputed amount can be applied against your credit limit. You cannot be threatened with damage to your credit rating or sued for the amount in question, nor can the disputed amount be reported to a credit bureau or to other creditors as delinquent until the creditor has answered your inquiry. However, you remain obligated to pay the parts of your bill not in dispute

4. If it is determined that the creditor has made a mistake on your bill, you will not have to pay any finance charges on any disputed amount. If it turns out that the creditor has not made an error, you may have to pay finance charges on the amount in dispute, and you will have to make up any missed minimum or required payments on the disputed amount. Unless you have agreed that your bill was correct, the creditor must send you a written notification of what you owe, and if it is determined that the creditor did make a mistake in billing the disputed amount, you must be given the time to pay which you normally are given to pay undisputed amounts before any more finance charges or late payment charges on the disputed amount can be charged to you.

5. If the creditor's explanation does not satisfy you and you notify the creditor *in writing* within 10 days after you receive his explanation that you still refuse to pay the disputed amount, the creditor may report you to credit bureaus and other creditors and may pursue regular collection procedures. But the creditor must also report that you think you do not owe the money, and the creditor must let you know to whom such reports were made. Once the matter has been settled between you and the creditor, the creditor must notify those to whom the creditor reported you as delinquent of the subsequent resolution.

6. If the creditor does not follow these rules, the creditor is not allowed to collect the first $50 of the disputed amount and finance charges, even if the bill turns out to be correct

7. If you have a credit problem with property or services purchased with a credit card, you may have the right not to pay the remaining amount due on them, if you first try in good faith to return them or give the merchant a chance to correct the problem. There are two limitations on this right
   a. You must have bought them in your home state or if not within your home state within 100 miles of your current mailing address, and
   b. The purchase price must have been more than $50
      However, these limitations do not apply if the merchant is owned or operated by the creditor, or if the creditor mailed you the advertisement for the property or services

Equal Credit Opportunity Act Notice

The Federal Equal Credit Opportunity Act prohibits creditors from discriminating against credit applicants on the basis of sex or marital status. The Federal Agency which administers compliance with this law concerning this bank is Comptroller of the Currency, Consumer Affairs Division, Washington, D.C. 20219

FIGURE 19-5
Statement of disclosures required by the Equal Credit Opportunity Act. The above statements must be a part of the application for credit.

8 All credit applicants must be notified of the decision, orally or in writing, within a reasonable time.

9 Creditors may not close an account because the customer refuses to pay an amount which he or she has indicated to be in error.

10 The creditor may not request information about birth-control practices or childbearing capacity of the customer and may not consider statistics or assumptions relating thereto.

It is important to observe that other new legislation provides that consumers can legally refuse to pay their credit-card balances if they have a complaint about products purchased from independent merchant firms. The credit-card company cannot pursue claims against such customers for their purchases or charge interest on such balances while the claims are being settled. Any legal action the company may take must be against the merchant firm if the claim is sustained.

All this new legislation has contributed to the increasing use of credit cards by customers and the increasing encouragement of credit-card sales by small business firms. Only large firms and credit-card companies can normally stand the expense of staff experts to administer credit programs and to make sure the firm complies with the abundant rules and regulations. Key details and forms may be obtained through trade associations or bankers or other friends of small firms.

Credit-card sales now give the customers more protection than ever. As one credit-card company executive reports, "The consumer who doesn't use credit cards today is short-changing himself." It seems a fair prediction for the decade of the 1980s that more and more credit programs will be under the jurisdiction of credit-card companies which have the expertise to make their programs comply with the abundant legislation which now governs credit granting. This same expertise may also help to protect people from using excessive and unwarranted credit.

It may still be worthwhile for customers to pay cash. Another new feature of the current wave of consumer legislation makes it legal to give a discount of up to 5 percent to retail customers who pay cash. This law was deemed necessary to avoid charges of price discrimination.

SUMMARY

The business world operates on credit. From the growers of raw materials to manufacturers, distributors, transportation companies, or retailers, business operations necessitate the use of credit. Consumer credit to buyers of all products is a vital part of the entire credit system in this country. Trade credit is credit that is offered by one business firm to another. Consumer credit is that offered by retailers to buyers of consumer goods. Without credit most families would be unable to purchase their homes, their cars, their major appliances, and many other items.

Granting of credit must always be based upon the applicant's ability to repay debts incurred within a specified schedule. For the small firm, this necessitates careful granting of credit in the first place and careful administration of a credit program, once it is established. The costs of a credit program are significant. They include bookkeeping costs, postage, supplies, interest on investment in receivables, costs of collection, and eventually bad-debts expense for those accounts which are never collected. Some loss on bad debts should be anticipated whenever a general program of credit is undertaken.

Small firms usually have a choice of carrying their own receivables on open accounts or restricting their credit sales to credit cards. More and more small firms are finding it desirable to accept credit cards, even though the average charge is still about 5 percent of all credit-card sales discounted with the credit-card companies. It is a genuine service to small firms to be able to collect their credit sales in full by the fifth of the following month, less the credit-card company charge, and avoid the expenses and losses of their own program. New credit legislation suggests that businesses of the future will have even more credit based on credit cards and administered by experts in the field.

QUESTIONS FOR CLASS DISCUSSION

1 Do you agree that if a customer desires credit from your store he or she should be able to get an established credit card? How should this fact govern credit policies for small retailers?
2 What is meant by the phrase "the number of days' credit sales in receivables"?
3 Would you sell on credit and carry the accounts on your own books if you owned a dress shop? Why?
4 What are the advantages to small firm owners of selling on customers' credit cards? The disadvantages?
5 What is an "aging of accounts receivable"? How often would you recommend that one be made for small firms?
6 What is the difference between trade credit and consumer credit?
7 How would you explain the statement, "The world operates on credit"?
8 Do you believe the statement that "a firm will sell more merchandise, even to its present customers, if credit accounts are made available"? How do you explain this?
9 How does a revolving account work?
10 Is an installment account different from a revolving account? How?
11 When would you recommend use of a budget account?
12 How is the credit reputation of an applicant checked?
13 Do you agree that you do not do a person a favor by granting credit that he or she cannot likely afford? Explain.
14 What kind of a policy would you establish to handle delinquent accounts?

PROJECTS FOR HOME ASSIGNMENT AND/OR CLASS DISCUSSION

1 Explain how you would handle the matter of granting credit to customers in your retail business. Would you carry your own accounts, insist on credit cards, have no credit at all, or a combination of all methods?
2 Do you agree that the expenses of operating an accounts receivable ledger could exceed the 5 percent charge of a credit-card company? If so, explain how this could happen.

CONTINUING PROBLEM:
The Kollege Klothes Shop

PART 19: SELLING ON CREDIT: ADMINISTERING A CREDIT PROGRAM

We can assume here that our well-planned and well-financed business will have trade credit available from most of its suppliers. We also know the importance of credit in all phases of the business world. Our clients are particularly interested in what types of consumer credit they should make available to their customers. They request your recommendations.

Assignment for Part 19

Prepare a report showing the type of consumer credit program you would recommend for the Kollege Klothes Shop. What are the advantages and disadvantages of selling for cash only, for selling on credit cards, and for selling on open accounts receivable which the firm will carry on its own books? Perhaps you will recommend a combination of these three basic types of consumer credit. Would you also consider revolving accounts, installment accounts, and budget accounts for the store? Why or why not? How would you handle delinquent accounts if, indeed, you decide to carry customers on your own books?

REFERENCES FOR FURTHER READING

"Credit and Collections," Small Business Administration Pamphlet No. MA232.

Macfarlane, William N., *Principles of Small Business,* McGraw-Hill Book Company, New York, 1977, chap. 15.

"Retail Credit and Collections," Small Business Administration Pamphlet No. SBB31.

RISKS AND HOW TO DEAL WITH THEM

All those risks the experts talk about could scare a person out of starting a new business. Once you realize that most of these risks apply to all of us every day in our personal lives, you get smart and figure out how to protect yourself in the best manner.

The Late Learner

Risk can be defined as the chance of damage, injury, or loss. Every business firm operates with daily risks, and the small firm is no exception. The total dollar costs incurred from risks may be much greater for large firms, but they are relatively more important for small firms. The small firm is characteristically less able to absorb losses from risks. These facts make it very important that every small firm understand the risks to which it is subject. Once these are known, a policy can be established on how best to handle the risks so as to keep losses to a minimum.

Risk is a vital part of everyday life. Each of us takes chances in driving to work, crossing the street, owning a house, traveling on public transportation, buying food, attending the movies, and eating in restaurants. Accidents happen in the best-regulated routines, and they may result in injury, damage, or loss to the person affected. Individuals, like businesses, take steps to protect themselves from many of these risks. People install burglar alarms and window guards in their homes as protection against risk of loss from robbery. Generally, they tend to guard themselves and their families by shifting the chance of loss to an insurance company. They purchase life insurance policies to protect their families in case of death; they buy title insurance on their homes to be sure that they are protected against any defects in the title which may be discovered later. Most automobile owners buy insurance to protect themselves in case of collision damage, bodily damage, and property damage to others. Almost any type of risk can be insured against, but the question is, how much can one pay in insurance premiums? If every possible risk in an individual's life were insured against, the cost of insurance would be prohibitive for most people.

The small business owner has all the previously mentioned risks and many more. For small firm owners, competence demands that they give serious attention to what risks they assume when they start operations. They face the same losses, damages, and injuries that are faced by individuals, and the losses, damages, or injuries to the business may be even more serious to the success of the business. Most common risks are generally recognized, but a serious investigation may reveal some that are not usually noted.

RISKS FACED BY THE SMALL FIRM

1   Damage to Property   The property of most small firms is represented by its inventory and its building if it is owned by the firm. The building and the inventory are constantly subject to the risks of damage and loss from fire, theft, floods, hurricanes, and riots. Cars and trucks owned by the firm are also open to loss through theft or damage.

Property damage to business firms in the United States is estimated to be as high as $1 billion yearly, placing it at the top of the list of possible risks for most firms.

2   Liability to Employees   All employers are responsible for the health and safety of employees while they are performing their duties for the firm. Legislation giving employers such responsibility has been one of the greatest developments in social responsibility in recent years. The employer's liability is no longer left to individual court action but is assured by the requirement that workers' compensation insurance be carried by employers to provide this protection to employees.

3   Liability to the Public   This type of risk is often illustrated by the proverbial slip on a banana peel by a customer in the store. Store owners are liable for injuries received by persons on their premises. This liability applies to apartment houses, factories, and wholesale establishments as well as to retail establishments. This risk includes not only physical injuries, but also damage to the property of others. It further covers liability for defects in merchandise that the firm has sold. Readers may recall cases in which cosmetics firms have been sued for alleged harmful results when people have used their products; cases where canned food companies have been sued because people were made ill by

Dick Hanley/Photo Researchers, Inc.

FIGURE 20-1
The risk of fire damage is so great that all small merchants should insure the firm against damage to property.

spoiled contents; restaurants sued for a customer's illness resulting from eating on the premises; airlines and railroads and bus companies sued for injuries incurred by travelers; or theaters sued for patrons' injuries sustained in a theater fire or accident. All these risks are examples of possible liability to the public.

4 Death of Key Employees Valuable employees are a firm's best asset. Real losses could be sustained if they should die suddenly. This is a possible loss which can be insured today.

5 Excessive Loss from Bad Debts We have noted in other chapters the importance of extending credit carefully and on the basis of a well-established procedure. Losses due to inability to collect accounts receivable can be severe. Protection against such losses can be expensive, as we shall see later in this chapter.

6 Faulty Title to Real Estate Students may not recognize the importance of being sure that real estate purchased does, indeed, have a clear title that cannot be challenged at law. Innumerable cases are on record where such titles were not conveyed even though the purchasers thought they had such a title. In areas such as Florida, which has existed under five national flags, and where such events as the real estate boom and bust of the 1920s created many uncertainties about land titles, the problem is especially significant. A recent case established that fire insurance premiums did not cover an owner because he had unknowingly been paying insurance premiums on adjacent property rather than on his own.

7   Shoplifting   This serious management problem seems to be growing in our society. It cannot be dismissed, because no firm seems free from the attendant losses. Legal action is expensive and difficult to administer. We will consider management ideas on the problem later in this chapter.

8   Loss through Dishonest Employees   No business people like to admit they have dishonest employees. However, countless cases of employee theft are reported every year. Such losses can be in the form of cash, securities, or merchandise. This is another real risk that must be recognized and coped with.

9   Financial Hardship   Financial hardship has probably caused more small firms to go out of business than any other single risk. It is especially sad to see a firm with otherwise excellent prospects suffer because illiquidity has been allowed to dominate its financial condition.

10   Marketing Risks   Marketing risks cover such things as having an inventory of merchandise suddenly fall in value because the market price has dropped. The risk of having a location lose its value is also a marketing risk. In

FIGURE 20-2
Shoplifting by the public and store personnel have created great expenses for business firms today as they attempt to minimize resulting losses.

George W. Gardner/Stock, Boston

style merchandise, situations occur where the style has fallen out of favor, and the remaining merchandise on the owner's shelves has lost most of its value. The small miller may have bought a large supply of wheat, for which he paid the market price 2 months ago. His finished product, flour, will bring a price which reflects the price of wheat when he sells the flour. All merchants face some of these types of marketing situations and should know about their existence. When all prices are rising, as in a period of inflation, the risk will not be present. In a period of declining prices, the risk becomes greater.

The above risks are 10 of the more prominent types faced by many small firm owners. Individual cases may produce other risks that should be recognized.

WHAT TO DO ABOUT RISKS

When the existing risks are known, business owners may turn their attention to the matter of what to do about them. They will realize that some risks are easier to control than others. In all cases, good management will do some of the following:

1 Eliminate risks
2 Minimize risks
3 Shift risks
4 Absorb risks

The action taken will vary with the desired policy, services, and circumstances of the individual firm, and the business owner has several choices.

DEVICES AVAILABLE TO COPE WITH RISKS

1 Remove the Cause   If losses are being incurred from injuries to workmen handling dangerous equipment, install safety guards on the machinery. Replace equipment that has proved to be defective. Faulty wiring should not be tolerated. Employ an outside delivery service if necessary to remove the risk of keeping your own delivery equipment.

2 Create Self-insurance   Under a self-insurance plan, a specified amount is set aside in a reserve fund each year to be available to cover any losses incurred. Rather than the owner paying premiums to an insurance company, the cash is held in this reserve fund. Unfortunately, this plan has been used with bad results by many one-store small firms. This self-insurance plan can be recommended only when the business has several geographically separated units. School systems and small chains of hamburger shops or grocery stores are ideal candidates for self-insurance. A small loss on one will usually be covered by the reserve fund. A significant loss for a one-store firm usually results in a net loss for the firm because the reserve fund has not yet become large enough to cover losses. Unless the reserve fund is well built up, the risk remains and protection is inadequate.

3 Purchase Outside Insurance An insurance policy shifts the risk to the insurance company. Insurance can be purchased from established insurance firms to cover many of the risks listed here. These are considered normal business risks. In addition, Lloyd's of London will insure almost any nonbusiness risks—for a price.

It would appear that there is no alternative to buying insurance to protect the inventory and building against various possible losses such as fire, theft, floods, or hurricanes. Owners are required by law to carry workers' compensation insurance to cover their employees. They surely should carry public liability insurance to cover risk of liability to people on their premises. If key personnel are sufficiently valuable to the business, owners may buy life insurance on their lives, payable to the company.

For loss from excessive bad debts, only the loss in excess of what is normal for the particular line of business can be insured. Credit insurance is not available to cover what are considered normal losses. The cost of such insurance is very high, and it is not recommended for most small businesses. Proper administration of a credit program, as outlined in Chapter 19, is preferable.

Fidelity bonds may be purchased to protect any firm from losses incurred by employee thefts. Only established losses are reimbursed, and such establishment is often difficult. In business practice these bonds have been used much more to cover cash losses than merchandise losses. Too many firms buy such protection only for those employees who operate cash registers or handle money in other operations. It is common knowledge today that the losses incurred by business firms from merchandise stolen by employees far exceed losses in the form of cash. This situation suggests that fidelity bonds should be used more widely to cover losses of both cash and merchandise.

Surety bonds which will protect the firm for losses incurred as a result of the failure of others to perform on schedule may be purchased. Failure of a contractor to complete an important addition to the store in time for the Christmas trade under the terms of a contract would be an example. In such a case the insurance company would pay the firm for the established loss incurred.

Title insurance is available on all real estate purchases for a small sum, and it should always be requested.

Insurance is either not economically available or not usually recommended to cover the other risks on our list.

4 Hedging Any small firm that buys quantitites of products quoted on the nation's well-established commodity exchanges should know about hedging and should practice it to protect normal profits. Hedging is often misunderstood as a device to make profits, but it is only to protect normal profits.

A few of the commodities regularly traded on the commodity exchanges are sugar, wheat, corn, citrus fruits, soybeans, soybean oil, cocoa, wool, oats, rye, silver, and copper. Whenever merchants buy large quantities of a product listed on the exchanges for use in manufacturing and sell it later as a part of their final product, they can protect themselves against losses in the price of the commodity by *hedging*. On the day they purchase the material, they also sell a futures contract on the exchange. The difference between the price paid for products delivered today (spot price) and the price in the futures market is roughly the cost of insuring and storing the same commodity for the period of time from today to the date of the futures contract. When the merchants sell their manufactured products, they will neutralize any loss in the price of the raw material commodity by buying a futures contract. The profit or loss on the commodity (spot) sales will be offset by the profit or loss on the purchase and sale of the futures contracts.

5 Good Management Good planning and good management are probably the best protection against most of the other risks we have considered. Price fluctuations of any normal retail inventory may be upward or downward. Good management will keep itself informed of price trends. Study of population trends and business activity will warn merchants early if their location is losing its value. Good accounting records and study of operations against a budget will warn of any developing adverse trends.

To handle the risks of shoplifting and dishonest employees, good management will provide devices such as internal security guards and signal systems for detecting shoplifters. A reputation for prosecuting shoplifters and training all employees to be alert to the problem will help to reduce shoplifting. Tags in merchandise which set off alarms at the entrance unless removed by the sales person are now common. These methods are often expensive but necessary. Personnel policies will provide means of checking employees whose honesty is questioned. Inspection of employees at checkout time is being used by manufacturing firms, some airlines, and other types of firms. It is recommended for wholesalers and retailers when losses in this area are deemed a high risk. As we have seen, fidelity bonds may be purchased to protect the firm from losses by dishonest employees.

The risk of financial hardship can best be coped with by proper financial planning and financial management. This common risk has caused the downfall of many firms which otherwise had a most profitable future. Good planning along the lines we have reviewed in this text, watching the key financial ratios in the financial statements, the cash adequacy rule, and investment in receivables, and having a cash flow statement are devices to protect against this risk. Having a good performance record for honesty and fair dealing will help the business person secure financial help when it is needed.

Chapter 30 is devoted to managing the daily operations of the firm. It will demonstrate how danger signals appear that may affect the financial standing of the firm. Thus warned, the owner can quickly apply corrective action.

COINSURANCE FOR BUSINESS FIRMS

Small firm owners should know how coinsurance works. It is a subject often misunderstood. For example, a building owner who has a $20,000 building insured against fire loss for $10,000 would not collect in full for an $8,000 fire loss.

Insurance companies are not in business for charity, nor should they be. As business organizations, their function is to pool the risks of many and pay those who incur losses. Their premiums must provide them with adequate income to cover these losses, their operating expenses, and a profit.

They know from experience that fire damage to business buildings, for example, rarely results in complete loss of the building. To protect themselves and the client against having to pay insurance on the total cost of a building only partially destroyed, for example, they offer a coinsurance clause in their policies. *Coinsurance* means that owners of a building can literally share the potential loss with the insurance company if they are willing also to share the premium cost.

Business buildings, like residential buildings, may be protected against losses in varying degrees under such coinsurance clauses. This means that potential losses may be shared by the owner and the company while major protection is still given to the owner.

For example, a building owner may wish to insure his or her building at 50 percent of its market value. The savings in annual insurance premium costs may be considered as an offset to any potential losses incurred. This does not mean, however, that any losses incurred up to 50 percent of the building value will be paid in full by the insurance company. The owner becomes subject to the coinsurance clause in his or her policy.

The most common percentage of market value of buildings used in coinsurance is 80 percent. If the building is insured at 50 percent of its value and 80 percent is the coinsurance percentage, the owner will recover fifty-eightieths of losses incurred. If there is an $8,000 loss, the owner will recover $5,000. Coinsurance truly means a shared risk.

Let us review a more detailed illustration of how coinsurance works.

ABC Manufacturing Company has a small factory building valued at $40,000. It is insured under a coinsurance policy at 80 percent of market value, or $32,000. This amount is the face value of the owner's policy ($32,000). The insurance company will be liable for the full amount of any losses up to $32,000. A complete loss on the building, or $40,000, would result in the owner's bearing an $8,000 loss and the insurance company's paying to the owner $32,000.

The formula for computing insurance company liability in such cases is as follows:

$$\text{Insurance company liability} = \frac{\text{face value of policy}}{80\% \text{ of property value}} \times \text{amount of loss incurred}$$

As we apply this formula, we can see that if the ABC Company had insured its $40,000 building for only $16,000 (less than 80 percent of market value) and then incurred a $16,000 loss, it could collect only $8,000 ($^{16}/_{32}$, or $^1/_2$, times $16,000). This is true even though the face value of the policy was $16,000.

If a building is insured for more than 80 percent of its market value, the insurance company pays any losses in full up to that of the face value of the policy. This type of coinsurance never pays more than the face value of the policy.

OTHER FACTS ABOUT CASUALTY INSURANCE FOR SMALL BUSINESSES

The small firm owner should be aware of the following facts:

1 A regular (standard) fire insurance policy pays the policyholder only for losses that are directly due to fire. Other indirect losses, known as consequential losses, may be even more important to the small firm's welfare. Some of these consequential losses are:

a Loss of use of the building

b Continuing expenses after a fire such as salaries, rents paid, and interest obligations

c Loss of rental income on buildings owned and rented out

d Extra expenses of obtaining temporary quarters

Most fire insurance policies have available a consequential loss clause to cover such losses. An extra premium is charged for such a clause, of course.

2 Fire losses caused by windstorms, tornadoes, or hurricanes are not covered by a standard fire policy. To have protection in such cases, it is essential to have a windstorm policy, or an endorsement known as the Extended Coverage Endorsement, which covers windstorms, plus eight other specified perils.

3 Flood insurance is designed to protect buildings and inventories against such risks as overflowing rivers and tidal waves. Water damage insurance, which is distinct from flood insurance, covers such risks as roof leaks, bursting water tanks, and leaking pipes.

4 Marine insurance covers merchandise while it is in transit. There are two types:

a Ocean marine insurance, covering transportation of merchandise and products on water.

b Inland marine insurance, which covers both land and water transportation.

5 Automobile collision insurance is considered a must by prudent business people. Business cars and trucks, as well as personal cars, should be insured. This insurance can be purchased under both a full-coverage policy (which pays all losses from collision damage in full) or a deductible policy, which carries a lower premium but provides that the owner is responsible for the first $50 to $100 in damage from each accident.

6 Comprehensive policies are available to cover fire and theft losses on automobiles. They can protect the owner against any risks of damage or loss, including flood, windstorm, riot, glass breakage, robbery in the car, theft of the car, fire damage, or even hail damage. Collision damage is not included in these policies. Rates on policy premiums vary from state to state in accordance with the loss record for the particular area.

7 The *relative incidence of loss* means the likelihood of the risk's causing a loss to the firm. The relative chance of an automobile collision, for example, is greater for most people than the risk of losing a limb. Thus, collisions are said to have a higher incidence of risk. It follows that the higher the incidence of loss, the more important it is to have insurance protection.

8 An *insurable interest* means that the person buying insurance is subject to a financial loss if the property or person insured should be damaged or deceased. Such an insurable interest is a prerequisite to the purchase of any insurance policy. Key-man or key-woman insurance, the right of a company to insure the life of valuable employees, is a relatively recent large development in the business field. A business firm, large or small, has an insurable interest in the lives of its key employees when the business would suffer should those persons be removed by death. Under usual conditions, group life insurance policies on the lives of employees may be charged as expenses to the firm. Benefits from these policies are payable to the families of the deceased employee.

BASIC FACTS ABOUT LIFE INSURANCE FOR BUSINESS AND FOR BUILDING PERSONAL ESTATES

We have seen the importance of having adequate protection against casualty risks in business management. Whenever the incidence of such risks as fire, theft, and other damage is high, most business owners shift the risks to insurance companies. But the matter of life insurance is of growing interest and value to small firms as well. Small firms, like large ones, can carry key-man (or woman) life insurance on the lives of valuable employees to protect them against the loss of such employees. The fact that a company can carry a group life insurance policy on all of its employees up to $50,000 each and charge the premiums as business expense can be a major part of a personnel policy and help retain good employees.

Because life insurance can be used for business purposes or for the building of personal estates, it should be important for all informed citizens to know the basic facts about different kinds of life insurance policies. But first we should be sure we understand the basic terms used in connection with such policies. Some of these follow.

Terminology of Life Insurance

Face amount of the policy	The amount paid by the insurance company in the event of the death of the insured, for example, $1,000.
Premium	The amount paid annually to maintain the face of the policy in force, for example, $20 per year.
Beneficiary	The person designed to receive the face amount of the policy in the event of the death of the insured.

Insured	The person whose life is covered in the policy.
Cash value of policy	The amount the insurance company will pay if the policy is cancelled.
Loan value of policy	The amount the insurance company will loan to the insured if he or she wishes to borrow against its cash value.
Paid-up policy	A policy on which no further premiums are required, or a new policy for less than the face value, given to an insured person who desires to cancel the original policy, take a policy for less than the original face, and pay no more premiums.

Types of Life Insurance Policies

There are four basic types of life insurance policies. Some special policies may include features of more than one of these types. If we understand the basic types, we can evaluate special policies which may be under consideration at any time. These four basic types, their characteristics, and their uses, plus a word of explanation about each, are as follows:

    1 Term Life Insurance Policies   This is the least expensive type of life insurance (see Table 20-1). It can be written for short periods, such as one year, or for longer periods of years—even for life. It provides full payment of the face of the policy to the designated beneficiary if the insured dies during the life of the policy. Term insurance is unique in that no payment of face value is ever made if death occurs after the stated expiration date of the policy. This very feature, plus the inexpensive premiums, have made the policy extremely valuable in the business world.

    Such term policies are increasingly used to provide collateral security for firm or personal obligations. Bank loans or mortgage debts on plant and equipment can have a provision that the borrower take out a term policy on his or her life payable to the creditor, that will assure full payment of the obligation in the event of his or her death. It is often called *credit life insurance* when used in this manner. Only a small addition to regular payments on such obligations is needed

TABLE 20-1 APPROXIMATE ANNUAL PREMIUM COSTS OF DIVIDEND-PAYING LIFE INSURANCE POLICIES AT AGE 22

Type of insurance	Annual premium per $1,000 face value
Term (5-year renewable to age 65)	$ 3.40
Straight life	15.00
Limited pay (20 years)	22.20
20-year endowment	45.70
Endowment to age 65	19.00

in most cases to pay for the insurance. Creditors thus are not forced to interfere with the business firm's operations to collect the debt.

Financial advisors recommend to all young married couples with a mortgaged home or condominium that they take out a term life policy on the life of the breadwinner of the family to assure that the mortgage will be paid in full in the event of the insured's death. The home is thus fully paid for and the remaining spouse is not longer faced with this debt. Many mortgage companies and other financial institutions are encouraging, if not requiring, such insurance protection for both the borrower and the lender. Family protection and estate building usually suggest that the amount of any life insurance carried should be proportionate to the current debts and present versus future earning power of the family.

Term life insurance is unique in other ways. Historically it has no cash value, no loan value, and no paid-up policy is available. These features are also part of the price paid for the inexpensive premiums required.

2 Straight Life Insurance Policies This is the type of life insurance on which the great American insurance industry was built. Premiums are based on actuarial figures of life expectancy, as in all insurance. When a policy is once taken out on the life of an individual, that person normally pays the annual premium until death. The face amount of the policy is then paid to the designated beneficiary. In recent years many insurance companies have introduced provisions that no further premiums are to be paid after some ripe old age, such as 85 or 90, is reached, if the policy has been in effect a minimum number of years. The policies are considered paid up for the full face value at that time. Face value, plus any accumulated dividends or interest, are paid to the beneficiary at the death of the insured.

Most straight life policies may be cancelled after a minimum time period, and the insured may then be given a paid-up policy for a lesser face value than the original policy. The insured may also borrow against active policies up to the amount of the cash value or cancel the policy if desired and receive the cash value. Straight life insurance is more expensive in the short run than term insurance but less expensive than the following types.

3 Limited Pay Plan Life Insurance The very fact of longevity and the continued payment of premiums on straight life policies motivated the development of limited pay plans. The most popular pay period is 20 years, but other periods of time may be used. Premiums are higher than straight life policies. Many people are willing to pay a higher premium in exchange for limiting the number of years the premiums are to be paid. The insurance becomes a fully paid-up policy at the end of the designated years. This insurance is similar in all other ways to straight life insurance.

Limited pay policies have the features of cash value, loan value, and a paid-up policy of lesser value if cancelled prior to payment of the premiums for the specified years.

4 Endowment Life Insurance Policies Endowment policies have the unique feature that when the premiums have been paid for the specified number of years, the insured may collect the face value. Endowment policies are sold on a basis of premiums being paid only for the number of years specified in the policy. In exchange for the right to collect the face value in full at maturity, premiums are higher than for any other form of life insurance. Full protection on the insured's life for the entire life of the policy is assured. A beneficiary must be named who will collect the face value if the insured's death occurs before maturity. This type of insurance has been dubbed by some "the insurance for people who want to take it with them."

Endowment policies have all the characteristics of loan value, cash value, and an available paid-up policy.

Loan Value of Life Insurance Policies as a Source of Temporary Working Capital

When any life insurance policies, except term, have been in force a few years they build up a loan value, as we have noted. This loan value may be used to assist business owners in times of cash shortages or special needs. The interest rate charged on such loans against life policies is not as high as that charged by most financial institutions. Such loan value can be counted on to be available without risking a refusal on a loan application elsewhere. The full face value of life insurance policies remains in effect during the period of such loans, subject to the outstanding loan.

From this brief review of the fundamentals of casualty and life insurance it should be clear to students and the experienced small firm owner that *every business needs a good insurance agent.* Competent business owners today *buy* insurance to fit their needs and do not have to be *sold* insurance protection. They analyze the relative incidence of each risk to which they are subject and plan their casualty insurance accordingly. They then decide how they can use life insurance for business purposes or for personal estate building, and choose appropriate policies. A thoroughly competent and conscientious insurance agent who specializes in the problems of small firms can be an invaluable asset to any small firm owner.

QUESTIONS FOR CLASS DISCUSSION

1 What is meant by saying that we all live with risks every day of our lives? What are some of these risks?
2 What risks are incurred by ownership of a building?
3 If you rent a building for your store, should you still insure the inventory of merchandise? Why?
4 What is workers' compensation insurance? How does it work?
5 What kinds of risks does the owner of a department store incur as far as the general public is concerned?
6 How do risks of a restaurant vary from those of a department store?

7 What is title insurance? Do you think it is important?

8 How would you cope with the risk that your location may lose its value?

9 What is the best way to protect a business against the risk of financial hardship?

10 What do we mean by "shifting the risk" as a means of coping with possible loss?

11 When is self-insurance a practical idea?

12 Have you considered a term life insurance policy on your life with your parents as beneficiaries? Why?

13 Should you protect against all risks by buying insurance?

14 If your answer to question 13 is no, give an example of risks you would not insure against. How would you handle them?

PROJECTS FOR HOME ASSIGNMENT AND/OR CLASS DISCUSSION

1 If you were the owner of a business that was subject to all of the risks listed in this chapter, which ones would you try to eliminate, which ones would you be willing to absorb, and which ones would you transfer to an insurance company? Prepare a written report explaining your answers for each.

2 Write a short report explaining to some business friends how much fire insurance they should carry to be protected on all fire losses up to 80 percent of the value of their $150,000 building.

3 Explain the difference between cash value, loan value, and a paid-up policy as these terms relate to life insurance.

CONTINUING PROBLEM:
The Kollege Klothes Shop

PART 20: RISKS AND HOW TO DEAL WITH THEM

Now that we hopefully have recovered from the shock of learning the huge risks faced by every business and by every individual, we must take an intelligent approach to the problem. This means we should identify for Jones and Gomez the various types of risks to which their new firm will be subjected, and then plan how we will advise them to deal with each of the risks. This chapter will guide us in doing this job.

Assignment for Part 20

Prepare a list of the various risks you feel that their firm must face. The chapter list may not be all-inclusive as you study the situation. You may eliminate some of the risks listed in the chapter if you feel they do not apply to this firm.

Then explain how you would advise coping with each of these risks. Would you recommend that they eliminate them, minimize them, insure them with outside insurance companies, create self-insurance, or hedge them? Explain the relative incidence of each risk as you plan your recommendation for meeting it.

REFERENCES FOR FURTHER READING

Lasser, J. K., *How to Run a Small Business,* 4th ed., McGraw-Hill Book Company, New York, 1974, chap. 10.

Macfarlane, William N., *Principles of Small Business,* McGraw-Hill Book Company, New York, 1977, chap. 14.

Steinhoff, Dan, *The World of Business,* McGraw-Hill Book Company, New York, 1979, chap. 20.

CHAPTER

PERSONNEL POLICIES
AND ORGANIZATION FOR
SMALL FIRMS

When jobs are less plentiful, personnel appreciate their employment more. But it seems that our personnel policies today must recognize that good employees have more opportunities to transfer to other companies. We had to study means of reducing labor turnover.

The Late Learner

College students today usually have positive ideas about the personnel policies of business organizations. Their opinions and attitudes have been largely influenced by the decades of the sixties and seventies, when employers sought employees in what was a seller's market. The demand for workers usually exceeded the supply of able people. Now in the eighties, when unemployment in many areas has become high, employers are unwilling to hire people without proper training and ability. Jobs are harder to come by during such periods, and applications are scrutinized more closely.

Successful business firms, however, have always recognized the difference between finding and retaining good employees. In big business we have seen extensive programs of on-the-job employee training, sensitivity training, opportunities to try different positions, merit raises to provide regularly increased income for productive workers, and supervisory and executive programs of various types. All are designed to improve employee productivity, encourage creativity, and generally to make workers happy and convinced that they have an attractive future with the firm.

At the same time, the past decade has seen an increasing percentage of trained people going into business for themselves in preference to working for large corporations. One large midwestern university reports that regular studies of its graduates show that those who went into business for themselves have the highest average income. This is a healthy indication for the state of the small business firm today, but it also means that small business owners must fully understand the problems of obtaining and retaining good employees.

It is a refreshing experience for students to consider these problems from the employer's viewpoint, and to sit for a while on the other side of the desk. They must devise a personnel program for their contemplated firms, and it must be a good one if the business is to be really successful.

Everyone recognizes that good employees are a firm's most valuable asset. Many customers are "turned off" and do not come back to a business where employees have been discourteous, incompetent, or have given other bad impressions. It is often said that a retailer can lose established customers much more easily than he can gain new ones. Customers are the lifeblood of any business. Their continued patronage is essential to the firm's profit objectives. Good employees can do much to assure this objective. Even those not in contact with actual sales contribute much to keeping the entire organization efficient and able to render proper service to customers.

With this in mind, small firm owners can start their personnel programs with a review of those things that are important to employees. The degree of importance may not be in the order presented here, but all of these factors are influential.

THE FRAMEWORK FOR PERSONNEL PROGRAMS

Before taking a look at what employees usually want from their jobs and suggesting ways to achieve the goal of an efficient, happy, and productive staff of employees for any business, we should recognize the legal framework in which all personnel policies operate. In the modern business world, personnel programs are not left to the sole discretion of business owners. Even well-meaning policies that have proved successful in the past may run into conflict with the barrage of legal regulations that all employers must abide by today.

Chief among the governmental regulations for employers today are minimum wage laws, fair employment regulations, the right of employees to collective bargaining and to form their own unions, requirements for withholding income taxes and other items from employee paychecks for the federal government, and public policy relative to being an equal opportunity employer. It is not our purpose here to evaluate such regulations but only to indicate to new firm planners that it is important to check the current status of regulations at the time they are starting new firms.

Fringe benefits, health and safety programs, profit-sharing plans, pensions, and vacation policies are all part of a complete personnel program. Surely all successful business owners must recognize today that fair wages that are competitive, fringe benefits that are attractive, desirable working conditions, and a sense of concern for employees are important parts of building a staff of dedicated and efficient employees.

WHAT DO EMPLOYEES WANT FROM THEIR JOBS?

1 Fair Wages Wages must be more than enough to buy the essentials of life. Employees want sufficient money to have adequate insurance, to be able to educate their children, and to provide for their old age. They want real wages to increase from year to year so that they can enjoy an improving status. They want to feel that their wages bear a relation to their contribution to the firm.

2 Continuous Employment Even when wages are quite satisfactory in all respects, employees still want to know that their employment is assured into the future. They will often take other positions at less pay, only because the outlook for permanent employment is better. Yearly earnings are more important than weekly earnings for most employees.

3 Reasonable Hours of Work Even employees who truly want to work for a living still want the hours of work to be reasonable. When the 8-hour day was established, it was hailed as a great achievement for all wage earners. Today we are on the threshold of a further reduction in the workday and/or workweek, and small firms must abide by the rules of society. They can often adjust their working hours more easily than large firms because their employees usually live close to their work and because of the closer rapport possible between staff and employers. For example some employees may be willing to work split shifts.

4 Pleasant and Safe Working Conditions Factory workers want minimum risk from industrial accidents, occupational diseases, and fatigue-creating factors such as noise, disturbances, and vibration. Factory, wholesale, service, and retail employees all want healthy working conditions in a pleasant environment.

5 Sense of Improving Status Employees expect to achieve status improvement over a period of time with the firm. This may take the form of opportunities to use talents other than those that first got them their job, a chance to participate in decision making for the firm, or a chance to demonstrate improved status through a title that their friends will respect.

6 Feeling of Contribution Despite any contrary impressions that appear in the newspapers during labor strife, most employees want to feel that they are making a contribution to the firm. Nothing is more frustrating to good employees than not knowing where their jobs fit into the total operation, not knowing the value of the work they do, and, even more, not having anyone display interest in what they are doing. Here again, the small firm has advantages over the larger firm because of the relative size of the business.

7 Respect for Management Employees are much happier and better workers when they respect the management of their firm and think that it is competent, fair, and alert to employees' contributions.

Small business has often been accused of being unable to provide all these conditions for employees. Competent owners refuse to accept such an accusation. The numerous small firms whose employees have many years of service with them demonstrate that small business can successfully compete for and keep good employees.

ADVANTAGES OF SMALL FIRM EMPLOYMENT

Among the advantages of employment in a small firm are the following:

1 The small firm can provide employment for people who want to work in the area where they live.

2 Employees are often neighbors and enjoy social life and sporting events together, with or without the owner, thereby creating spirit and harmony among the group members.

3 The firm is small enough so that employees can be close to the employer at all times. Therefore, complaints and irritations can be solved at once, rather than sent to a committee.

4 Small firms can readily observe and compliment any exceptional achievements of employees.

5 Employees have greater opportunities to try different jobs in small firms because employers can pay close attention to their talents and desires.

6 Employees can more easily take part in decision making and be made to feel they are a part of that process because of their highly regarded and sought-after opinions.

7 Wages can be comparable to the wages paid by large firms while the wage earner maintains the advantages of working for a small firm.

8 Group benefits, such as life insurance and company-supported activities, are equally available in small firms.

9 Profit-sharing plans which aid firm growth and profitability can be set up.

10 Employees can become stockholders if the legal form of organization is a corporation.

These advantages do not exist automatically. They must be the result of a deliberate personnel policy. Some suggestions for such a policy follow.

PERSONNEL POLICY SUGGESTIONS

The small firm owner can take certain steps to assure a good personnel policy.

1 Create an image that the firm is good to work for. Word of mouth from employees can do much to aid this objective.

BLAKELY ELECTRONICS, INC.
"An Equal Opportunity Employer"
Application for Employment

Personal Data

1. Name _____

2. Address _____   3. Phone Number _____

_____

4. Marital Status _____   5. Dependents _____

Employment Status

6. Type of employment sought _____ Full-time _____ Part-time

_____ Permanent _____ Temporary

7. Job or position sought _____

8. Date of availability, if hired _____

9. Are you willing to accept other employment if the position you seek is unavailable?

_____ Yes _____ No

10. Approximate wages/salary desired $ _____ per month.

Education and Skills

11. Circle the highest grade completed :

8 9 10 11 12   13 14 15 16   Graduate School
High School   College

12. Please provide the following information about your education. (Include high school, trade or vocational schools, and colleges.)

a. School name _____ Degree(s) or diploma _____

School address _____

Date of admission _____ Date of completion _____

b. School name _____ Degree(s) or diploma _____

School address _____

Date of admission _____ Date of completion _____

13. Please describe your work skills. (Include machines, tools, equipment, and other abilities you possess.) _____

_____

Work History

Beginning with your most recent or current employer, please provide the following information about each employer. (If additional space is needed, please use an additional sheet.)

14. a. Employer _____ Dates of employment _____

Employer's address _____

Job title _____ Supervisor's name _____

Job duties _____

Starting pay _____ Ending pay _____

b. Employer _____ Dates of employment _____

Employer's address _____

Job title _____ Supervisor's name _____

Job duties _____

Starting pay _____ Ending pay _____

Military Background

If you were ever a member of the Armed Services, please complete the following:

15. Branch of service _____ Rank at discharge _____

Dates of service _____ _____ to _____

Responsibilities _____

Type of discharge _____

Memberships, Awards, and Hobbies

16. What are your hobbies? _____

17. List civic/professional/social organizations to which you have belonged. _____

_____

18. List any awards you have received. _____

_____

References

In the space provided, list three references who are not members of your family :

19. a. Name _____ Address _____

b. Name _____ Address _____

c. Name _____ Address _____

20. Please feel free to add any other information you think should be considered in

evaluating your application. _____

_____

_____

By my signature on this application, I:

a. Authorize the verification of the above information and any other necessary
inquiries that may be needed to determine my suitability for employment.

b. Affirm that the above information is true to the best of my knowledge.

_____ Date _____
Applicant's Signature

FIGURE 21-1
Application for employment. (*From* Personnel Management and Human Resources *by Wm. B. Werther, Jr. and Keith Davis. Copyright © 1981 by McGraw Hill, Inc. Used with permission of McGraw-Hill Book Company.*)

2 Don't limit employee applications to people who happen to stop in and ask for a job. Go out and recruit employees. This can be done at schools and universities which maintain job placement bureaus for their students, at established government and private employment agencies, and through referrals from friends and other business firms. Advertising in newspapers or other media can also be very effective.

3 Establish applicants' capabilities before hiring them. Physical examinations are a must, including tests of vision, movement, strength, stamina, and hearing, as appropriate to the job. Psychological tests are also recommended. Hiring the handicapped for appropriate jobs is a fine thing to do, but you should not do handicapped persons a disservice by expecting them to fill positions they cannot handle.

4 Have all applicants fill out a detailed application form and give references. See the sample form in Figure 21-1. Check references carefully, including credit references and other personal data. Check further than references whenever possible.

5 Always have an extended interview with the applicant, in pleasant surroundings, and have his or her application in front of you. The interview should enable you to rate the applicant. The interviewer should direct discussion into various channels to find out as much as possible about the applicant: background, previous employment experience, ambition, sincerity, likes and dislikes, hobbies, sporting interests, responsibilities, etc. The applicant's self-evaluation is important also. Discuss past salaries and expected future salaries.

6 Even small firms should have job descriptions[1] available to discuss with applicants. These should be carefully explained, including salaries. The normal sequence of advancement, including opportunities for such advancement, salary ranges, and average time at each level, should be described. If the firm has an organization chart, it should be shown and explained to the applicant.

7 A positive program of orientation of new employees should be established, preferably in writing. When new employees first come to work, a supervisor should be assigned to introduce them to fellow employees, the company layout, the facilities of the firm, and their own positions. Any printed material for employees should be given to them.

8 Have regular meetings with employees to discuss matters of mutual interest. Invite opinions, even contrary ones.

9 If training programs are desirable or necessary, establish them for regular presentation. No exceptions should be made for employees deemed able to benefit. Most small firms will do actual job training on the job.

10 Have a specified trial period for each new employee. Be sure that he or she knows about it. Do not hesitate to terminate a new employee whose work is unsatisfactory during this period. Weak employees hurt the morale of all who carry their share.

11 Provide at least an annual review of each employee's progress and productivity. Such reviews should be discussed with employees, so that they know how they stand with the firm.

12 Keep salaries in line with the competition, or better than elsewhere—if

---

[1]Personnel managers have three techniques to assist them in getting people into appropriate jobs:

Job analysis   A detailed study of jobs, including identification and examination of the elements and characteristics of each job and the requirements of the person assigned to the job.

Job description   Description of the objectives of the job, the work to be performed, responsibilities involved, skills needed, working conditions, and relationship to other jobs.

Job specification   Description of the special qualifications required to fill a particular job including experience, special skills, and any physical requirements.

These are parts of a total job-evaluation program.

Sepp Seitz, 1981/Woodfin Camp & Assoc.

FIGURE 21-2
It is important to determine the applicant's capabilities to the fullest extent possible before hiring.

Cary Wolinsky/Stock, Boston

FIGURE 21-3
Most small firms will do actual job training on the job.

this can be justified. Have a merit system of pay raises within a rank to be put into effect if they are earned. Be sure that all new and current employees know the salary ranges available to them if they are promoted.

ORGANIZATION WITHIN THE SMALL FIRM

The organization of a firm is usually reflected on an organization chart. That chart formalizes the relationship of all positions. Authority flows from the top down—responsibility from the bottom up.

Most small firms do not make a formal chart of their organization, but this may become necessary if the firm grows and additional delegation of authority and responsibility becomes appropriate. A typical organization chart for a drugstore is shown in Figure 21-4. The owner may perform one or more of the functions shown. The size of the firm will determine when more people are assigned to other functions, that is, how many additional functions will be carried out by the owner and how many will be delegated. Even small factories will have separate divisions for production, sales, finance, and personnel. Responsibility for each is normally delegated to a department head who reports to top management.

In any small firm, even one without a formal organization chart, it is important that each employee know precisely his or her responsibility and authority. If the owner works with the business each day, the owner is the top authority. If he or she is confident of the abilities of the employees, then certain authority will be delegated to them to facilitate getting things done and to

FIGURE 21-4
Organization chart for a drugstore.

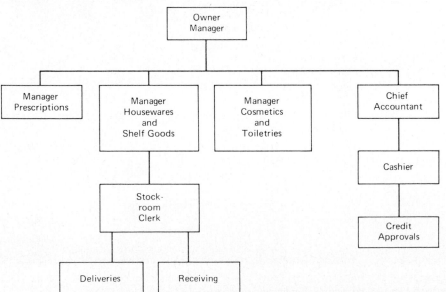

expedite the many routine decisions that must be made every day. For example, the company may have a policy for customer exchanges of merchandise sold. All competent salespersons should normally be able to handle most steps in this procedure. Approval of credit applications is a different matter. This authority can be specifically delegated, but it carries a responsibility that requires special analytical ability. One person should be assigned final authority for this function.

All employees, from the stockroom workers to the sales manager, should know what is expected of them and the scope of their authority in performing their assigned tasks. It is an old principle of organization that authority must be commensurate with responsibility. This is another way of saying that if you give a person a job to do, you must also give the authority necessary to do it. When policies are established for the firm, all employees should know what the policies are and who is responsible for their administration.

While we have emphasized the small firm in our discussion here, it should be noted that as firms grow they also have to add more division managers, personnel managers, and other staff members to meet their expanding staff needs. All of the staff members mentioned here are straight-line employees. Line employees report directly to a superior above them and direct those below them on the organization chart. Growth may bring the need for other staff members, such as legal counsel, who reports only to a senior official of the firm. Such persons have no line authority over other employees in the firm.

QUESTIONS FOR CLASS DISCUSSION

1 Would you like the responsibility for keeping a large group of employees happy and productive? Why?
2 Do you believe in a six-month trial period for all new employees? Why?
3 If "good employees are a firm's greatest asset," how would you assure good employees for your business?
4 How can employees do harm to a business?
5 Do you agree that it is easier to lose customers than to develop them?
6 What do you think employees really want from their jobs?
7 Would a 50 percent increase in all salaries solve the personnel problems of all American business firms?
8 Do you agree that most employees really want to feel they are contributing in their jobs? How can this need be achieved?
9 What are some of the advantages which small firms have in assuring that they have happy and productive employees?
10 Would you recommend a profit-sharing plan for your own small firm? How would you devise such a plan?
11 What features would you build into your personnel policy?
12 What is a formal organization chart? Do you think such a chart is appropriate for small firms?
13 What do we mean by "making authority commensurate with responsibility"?
14 What should be the relationship of the warehouse manager and the floor manager in a modest-sized department store? Can this relationship be shown on the typical organization chart?

PROJECTS FOR HOME ASSIGNMENT AND/OR CLASS DISCUSSION

1 Prepare a short report on why "the boss must be the boss" in business and how he or she can retain authority and still have good relations with all employees of the firm.
2 Some companies encourage relatives to become employees of their firm and others positively prohibit having more than one member of a family employed by the firm. What are your thoughts about this?
3 Explain in one paragraph why "personal references" on an application form are normally less significant than a check of credit references and reports from former employers.

CONTINUING PROBLEM:
The Kollege Klothes Shop

PART 21: PERSONNEL AND STAFF ORGANIZATION

It is always a good experience for college students to put themselves in the owner's chair and devise a program of personnel management and staff organization for their own firm. It is valuable for students to face the problems and complaints so often aired by employees to see how they themselves would handle them. Our clients, Jones and Gomez, realize the importance of having happy and productive employees. They have requested that you tell them how to achieve this happy state of affairs.

Assignment for Part 21

(1) Prepare a report outlining the personnel program you would recommend for the firm and, (2) fit the various positions you would recommend into an organization chart. Perhaps you will want to draw up an outline of an organization first and then fit the various employee positions into that chart. In drawing up your program for personnel, demonstrate your understanding of employee desires. Explain what policies you would establish concerning salaries, fringe benefits, training programs, handling of employee complaints, recommendations for job descriptions and classifications, if needed, and hours of employment for each position. Jones and Gomez hope that you will assure them that their employees will perform productively and will think the firm is a good place to work.

REFERENCES FOR FURTHER READING

Baumback, Clifford M., Kenneth Lawyer, and Pearce C. Kelley, *How to Organize and Operate a Small Business,* 5th ed., Prentice-Hall, Inc., Englewood Cliffs, N.J., 1973, chap. 16.
Corley, Robert N., Robert Black, and O. Lee Reed, *The Legal Environment of Business,* 5th ed., McGraw-Hill Book Company, New York, 1981, chap. 14.
"Measuring Sales Force Performance," Small Business Management Pamphlet No. MA190.

CHAPTER

INVENTORY VALUATION
METHODS AND
DEPRECIATION METHODS

When I heard that I could value my inventory in different ways or take depreciation charges at different rates, I was sure that something crooked was going on. How is this possible? Is it legal?

The Late Learner

Students who have had a 1-year course in accounting, business owners who have become familiar with accounting for their own businesses, or students who understood the preceding chapters, should now be ready for a more detailed look at the problems associated with valuation methods that may be applied to inventories, and with depreciation rates that may be applied to fixed assets.

The subjects of valuation and depreciation are particularly appropriate for new firms because the owners have a completely free choice of methods available for both. Final decisions can be postponed until the end of the first year. Operations for the first year can affect the choices made. New firm owners can make better decisions if they know the various methods.

Historically, inventories were always valued at the *lower of cost or market*. This method is still popular, and it has advantages in many cases. Its chief disadvantage for the small firm is that if the market value is lower than cost, the firm actually takes inventory losses before they have been incurred through sale of the merchandise. This will be explained fully in the following examples and discussion.

METHODS OF VALUING INVENTORIES

Today the small business firm has a choice of at least five major methods of valuing its inventories. Expediency, tax considerations, operation results, and the outlook for the future are some of the considerations which will affect the choice made in the particular case. These five methods are:

1 Lower of cost or market
2 First in, first out (FIFO)
3 Last in, first out (LIFO)
4 Weighted average cost
5 Retail price method

To illustrate the application of each of these methods to a specific inventory, let us consider the small firm which sells a relatively high-priced product. This could be a piano store or a firm selling block-making machines. We will supply full data to value its inventory, using the first four methods. A separate example is given showing the retail price method.

Company X sells product A. Its purchases of this product during 1981 were as follows:

January—10 units at $6,000 each
March—5 units at $6,500 each
June—15 units at $7,000 each
September—10 units at $8,000 each
December—10 units at $8,500 each
On December 31, the market price from the supplier was $9,000 per unit.

Inflation had continued. On December 31, company X has 22 units of its product on hand as the year-end inventory. Of these 22 units, 8 were purchased in December, 8 in September, 4 in June, and 2 in January.

The company is interested in knowing how these 22 units could be valued under each of the five cited methods of valuation.

Detailed computation of the value of the inventory using each of the methods follows.

Lower-of-Cost-or-Market Method

This method necessitates computing two values, cost and market, and then using the lower of these two figures. The market value is easy. Market value on December 31 was $9,000 per unit. Therefore, market value is 22 times $9,000, or $198,000. Computing cost value of the 22 units in the inventory necessitates finding the invoices for each purchase, separating the value of those particular units in the inventory, and totaling the result. In our problem, that is done as follows:

8 units purchased in December × $8,500	=	$ 68,000
8 units purchased in September × $8,000	=	$ 64,000
4 units purchased in June × $7,000	=	$ 28,000
2 units purchased in January × $6,000	=	$ 12,000
Total cost of the 22 units	=	$172,000

When we compare market value of $198,000 and actual cost value of $172,000, under the lower-of-cost-or-market method the value of the inventory would be $172,000.

First In, First Out (FIFO) Method

This method coincides with the normal movement of merchandise in most inventories. At least, almost every small firm owner hopes that inventory will move smoothly through the process of acquisition to sale. Exceptions are, of course, to be recognized in some special types of firms.

FIFO means that the first inventory received is the first sold and, therefore, the remaining inventory is assumed to be the last merchandise purchased. In our problem, the 22 units in the inventory would be the 10 purchased in December, the 10 purchased in September, and 2 of the units purchased in June. The student will immediately recognize that this statement probably does not conform to the facts of the firm. No doubt some of the units purchased in September and December have been sold. Nevertheless, FIFO is an approved method of evaluation, and its calculation would be as follows:

10 units purchased in December × $8,500	=	$ 85,000
10 units purchased in September × $8,000	=	$ 80,000
2 units purchased in June × $7,000	=	$ 14,000
Total FIFO value of the 22-unit inventory	=	$179,000

The student will see that we already have some variation in value. Lower of cost or market gave us a value of $172,000, while FIFO indicates a value of $179,000. The importance of the valuation method should begin to unveil itself. But other values are available under the remaining methods. Let us continue.

Last In, First Out (LIFO) Method

As the name of this method indicates, the method assumes that the last units purchased were the first ones sold. Normal retailing activities would not suggest this movement of the inventory in most cases. Yet, in such lines as style merchandise, this may be true more often than suspected. Nevertheless, this too is an approved method of inventory valuation. Existing firms must have approval of the Internal Revenue Service to change to this method for purposes of income tax returns. New firms in their first year of operation may adopt this method from the beginning.

Under LIFO, the 22 units in the inventory would be the earliest units purchased—the 10 units purchased in January, the 5 units purchased in March, and 7 of the units purchased in June. Calculation of a LIFO value would, therefore, be as follows:

10 units purchased in January × $6,000	= $ 60,000
5 units purchased in March × $6,500	= $ 32,500
7 units purchased in June × $7,000	= $ 49,000
Total LIFO value of the 22 units in inventory	= $141,500

This LIFO value, arrived at under the circumstances of rapidly increasing purchase prices, is substantially less than either of the preceding two value computations. The significance of its potential use will be seen later in this chapter.

Weighted Average Cost Method

This method is more than merely an average cost. It demands that the average cost be weighted to reflect the number of units purchased at different prices. This necessitates that we compute the total cost of units at each price and divide that total by the number of units bought during the year to find the weighted average cost of one unit. This figure is then multiplied by 22 to arrive at the inventory value. That calculation is done as follows:

10 units in January at $6,000	= $ 60,000
5 units in March at $6,500	= $ 32,500
15 units in June at $7,000	= $105,000
10 units in September at $8,000	= $ 80,000
10 units in December at $8,500	= $ 85,000
Total cost of 50 units	= $362,500

First, $362,500 divided by 50 (units purchased) equals $7,250, the weighted average cost of one unit. Then, 22 times $7,250 equals $159,500, the weighted average cost of the 22 units in the December 31 inventory. Inventory value under this method is, accordingly, $159,500.

Retail Price Method

This method of inventory valuation is particularly appropriate for retail firms that carry hundreds of items in their inventories. Its application involves gathering all costs and expected retail prices on the beginning inventory and the purchases during the year. Freight-inward charges are then added to the cost total and additional markups are added to the original expected retail price total. Markdowns would be deducted from total expected sales price.

The dollar difference between these totals (markup) is then computed in dollars and as a percentage of the sales total. Actual sales are deducted from this sales value of all merchandise handled during the year to give a retail value of the inventory remaining. By deducting the average markup from this figure, we arrive at the inventory value.

For example, if total invoice costs of beginning inventory, purchases, and freight-inward charges during the year total $60,000, and normal retail prices plus additional markups or less any markdowns total $90,000, the planned markup is $30,000, or 33⅓ percent of retail. Then, if actual sales at retail are $45,000, the remaining inventory has a retail value of $45,000. By deducting the markup percentage (33⅓ percent) from $45,000, we arrive at a cost value of the inventory of $30,000.

Adjustments can be made in this method for employee discounts, inventory shortages, etc., in computing the cost percentages. An advantage of this plan for retailers is that employees need only list retail prices when taking inventory counts from the shelves. All cost data and summary work can be quickly completed in the office.

To apply the retail price method strictly to our same problem with company X and the data used in the previous valuation methods, we must set a retail price on the 50 units purchased during the year and record actual sales of the 28 units sold (50 purchased less the 22 in the ending inventory), as shown in Table 22-1.

TABLE 22-1   COMPUTATION OF INVENTORY VALUE
USING RETAIL PRICE METHOD

	Cost	Retail
Beginning inventory This was a new firm; all units were purchased during the year.	0	0
Purchases during year (50 units) The difference between this cost and retail is $155,350, which is the gross margin or markup percentage of 30% of retail. Cost is, therefore, 70% of retail.	$362,500	$517,850
Actual sales for the year (28 units)		$289,350
Inventory value at retail (22 units)		$228,500
70% of retail value is the cost of the inventory (30% is markup)		.70
Inventory value under retail price method		$159,950

WHICH VALUATION METHOD TO USE

Using our various methods, we have seen that the value of the 22 units in company X's inventory ranged from $141,500 to $179,000. How is the new small firm owner to make a choice? Several factors may be important in the decision.

First, profits and inventory value vary directly. The higher the inventory, the higher the resulting profit. Taxes may therefore be an important consideration in the choice made. The firm owner should also consider the outlook for sales in the immediate oncoming years. Will they be as good as this year? Were there windfall profits or other unexpected profits this year, so that profits exceeded expectation? Can such profits continue? Are there some antagonistic stockholders scrutinizing operations to be sure that the firm earned sufficient profit to pay their preferred stock dividend? Will the firm show a profit regardless of which valuation method is used?

When all these factors are considered, the firm owner will choose the method that will be best for all concerned.

It should be pointed out that in the purposely inflationary market example we used in this chapter, LIFO showed the lowest inventory value and FIFO the highest. In a declining wholesale market, the opposite would be true. The other methods illustrated show a greater tendency to reduce wide variations in resulting values.

The uninitiated are often shocked to learn that a specific inventory of products or merchandise can have different values. Critics often think of this as an inherently evil situation. But who is to say what is the true value of merchandise which is yet unsold or has been on the shelves for a long period? Just as we recognize that there can be no profit in the absence of its sale, so it would seem unfair to take an inventory loss in the absence of its sale. Using a consistent method will usually even out the value variations over time. Merchants cannot choose the method which favors their own purposes each year. As mentioned earlier, if a new firm wishes to change an adopted method for purposes of federal income taxes, it must get the written approval of the Internal Revenue Service; this approval may be given if the reasons for changing methods are sound.

METHODS OF DEPRECIATING FIXED ASSETS

The investment that any business has in its fixed assets must be recouped. Fixed assets wear out, or become obsolete, out of style, or technologically inadequate. Their costs are as true a business expense as the gasoline for the delivery truck. To provide the firm with capital to replace them, their costs must be charged to operations by way of depreciation expense. At the end of each fiscal period, a charge should be made to a *depreciation expense* account (debit) and a credit made to a minus asset account entitled *allowance for depreciation*. Each fixed asset should have such accounts in the records. These depreciation expenses are noncash expenses. No checks are written for them. But the depreciation expense accounts appear on the income statement as expenses, and the allowance for depreciation accounts are shown on the balance sheet as deductions from the cost value of the appropriate fixed asset accounts. These depreciation charges do not result in the creation of a cash fund to replace the assets, but they do provide a cross section of assets from which demands may be made for necessary capital to replace the assets.

The question for good management is how to charge off the assets as depreciation expense. How much should be charged each year? How long will the asset last before it must or should be replaced? Small firm owners must make decisions on these questions. When they decide on answers, they can turn to a method of depreciation.

There are at least four major methods of computing depreciation charges. Each has merit in particular cases. Small firm owners should be familiar with the details of each. They are known as:

1 Straight line
2 Use or production
3 Declining balance
4 Sum of the years digits

It may surprise the new student to know that the depreciation charges on a particular asset can also vary, just as an inventory can have different values. We will illustrate this variation in charges by computing the annual depreciation charge on a specific machinery and equipment fixed asset. The data we will use to illustrate all four methods follow:

> A small factory has machinery and equipment that cost $150,000. Its estimated life is 10 years. It is estimated that its salvage value at the end of 10 years will be $20,000. Best estimates indicate that it will turn out 100,000 units of the company's product. During the firm's first year of operation, it produced 15,000 units of its product.

What is the depreciation charge for the first year under each of the four methods listed?

Straight Line Method

This method provides for an equal charge in each year of the life of the fixed asset. It necessitates knowing the *depreciable value*. Depreciable value is *cost less salvage value*. In our problem, the cost of $150,000 and the estimated salvage value of $20,000 result in a depreciable value of $130,000. Straight line depreciation then spreads this $130,000 evenly over the 10 years of estimated life of the asset. This means an annual depreciation charge of $13,000.

Straight line depreciation is expressed as a formula as follows:

$$\frac{\text{Depreciable value}}{\text{Estimated life}} = \frac{\$130,000}{10 \text{ years}} = \$13,000 \text{ annual charge}$$

Under this method the adjusting entry at the end of each fiscal period would be a debit to depreciation expense, machinery, $13,000. Profits will accordingly be reduced by this amount for the year, and the asset account value will be modified to this extent by the allowance account, which will be deducted from the cost value on the balance sheet.

Use or Production Method

This method seeks to ascertain what proportion of the total production was achieved in the subject year. This percentage of the total is applied against the same depreciable value used above. In our illustration, the machinery produced 15,000 of the estimated 100,000 units in the first year, or 15 percent of the total. Accordingly, this method would charge off as depreciation expense in the first year 15 percent of $130,000, or $19,500.

Expressed as a formula:

$$\frac{\text{Annual production}}{\text{Total estimated prod.}} = \frac{15,000}{100,000} \times \text{depreciable value } (\$130,000) = \$19,500$$

Under this use or production method, the depreciation charge will vary from year to year. If only 10,000 units are produced in the second year, for example, the charge would be 10 percent times depreciable value, or $13,000. If 20,000 units are produced in one year, the depreciation charge would be $26,000.

Declining Balance Method

This method of computing depreciation has the distinction of being the only one that ignores salvage value. It is particularly suited to firms or assets that merit speedier depreciation of the total cost. It uses an accelerated rate and applies it to the cost of the asset. The most commonly used rate is twice the straight line rate which would normally apply. That is why it is often called the "double declining balance" method. In our problem, this would be 20 percent (two times the 10 percent straight line rate). Applying 20 percent times cost, $150,000, this method produces a first-year depreciation charge of $30,000.

Expressed as a formula:

$$2 \times \text{straight line rate } (20\%) \times \text{cost } (\$150,000) = \$30,000 = \text{first year charge}$$

It is called the declining balance method because in subsequent years the annual charge is always computed against the new book value of the asset. In our example, the book value of the asset after the first year is $120,000 ($150,000 less $30,000). In the second year, the charge for depreciation would be 20 percent times $120,000, or $24,000. The book value is then reduced to $96,000, which is the basis for the depreciation charge in the third year. The book value of any asset is its cost less its accumulated depreciation.

Sum of the Years Digits Method

This method also recognizes that assets normally give more service in their first years of operation than when they grow older and require more maintenance or repairs. The method possesses arithmetical neatness in that its total charges reduce each year, but the total charge neatly fits the exact amount of the depreciable value at the end of the asset's estimated life.

By "digits," we mean the years of the estimated life. In our example, the years are 1, 2, 3, 4, 5, 6, 7, 8 9, 10, . . . , one digit for each year of estimated life of the asset. The sum of the digits is the total of these year numbers, 55. This total, 55, becomes the denominator of a fraction which is applied to the number of years of estimated life remaining at the beginning of the year in which the charge is being computed.

In our example, there are 10 years remaining at the beginning of the first year, so the numerator is 10 over the denominator, which always remains at 55. In the first year, ten fifty-fifths ($22,636.36) of the depreciable value ($130,000) is charged off. In the second year, nine fifty-fifths would be charged off, in the third year eight fifty-fifths, etc. In the tenth year, only one fifty-fifth of the depreciable value remains in the asset account and it is then charged off, reducing the asset account to its estimated salvage value.

As a formula, this method appears as follows:

$$\frac{\text{Years remaining at beginning of year}}{\text{Sum of the years digits}} \times \text{depreciable value} = \text{annual charge}$$

$$\frac{10}{55} \times \$130,000 = \$23,636.36$$

WHICH DEPRECIATION METHOD TO USE

The best authorities in the field usually admit that depreciation methods are only intelligent guesses at best. No asset is going to fall apart on New Year's Eve because that date marks the end of 10 years of service. Most business people agree that new assets render more service at less expense when brand new. Even a new delivery truck carries a better image in its first years of service. Yet who is to decide the exact schedule for recouping the investment in any of a firm's fixed assets?

As noted earlier, all the methods illustrated are available to a new small firm in its first year of operation. Government officials insist that the same method be used consistently for taxing purposes unless permission is granted in writing to change it.

Using one method approved by the Internal Revenue Service for income tax purposes and another method for the firm's bank, its creditors, or its stockholders is not illegal or immoral. Full disclosure as to methods used via footnote on the balance sheet is recommended for both depreciation methods and inventory valuation methods.

The tendency of many small firms to ignore depreciation charges altogether in an attempt to maintain apparent profitability is seriously frowned upon. Any "window dressing" of financial statements usually results in the owner's being more misled than the creditors.

The decision as to which method to use will depend on the same factors cited earlier in this chapter when we discussed choosing an inventory valuation method. A projected gloomy outlook for the next 2 or 3 years suggests the use of a faster method of depreciation. Heavy taxes and/or technological obsolescence both suggest using faster rates of depreciation. Straight line depreciation is still the most popular method among small firms, but it may not always be the best for the particular case. Knowing the facts about the major alternatives should help the new firm owner to make the decision best suited to the situation.

Just as uninformed critics of business sometimes mistrust different valuations of the same inventory, they usually respond with mistrust to knowing that different amounts may be charged as depreciation on a specific asset and suspect that something crooked must be going on. Let us clarify that situation. *In any of the methods illustrated, no firm can ever charge more depreciation than the cost of the asset.* Whether that cost is charged off faster or more slowly, the total depreciation is limited to the firm's investment. In this modern age, no one has yet found an exact answer to serve the economics involved. It would indeed be a rarity if a fixed asset were sold or salvaged for exactly the amount of its estimated salvage value. Business people know that fixed assets do depreciate. They use the best methods known to measure when that asset value is used up. They never recover more as depreciation expense than they have invested.

QUESTIONS FOR CLASS DISCUSSION

1 Using the straight line method for computing depreciation, what would be the first year's depreciation on a delivery truck which cost $9,000, has an estimated life of 6 years, and a trade-in value of $1,500?

2 What would the depreciation be on the same delivery truck if the firm used the double declining balance method?

3 How would you describe the lower-of-cost-or-market method of evaluating an inventory at the end of the year?

4 What do the letters LIFO stand for in accounting methods? Do you believe there is any logic in this method of valuing an inventory? Does it apply to any business firm you know?

5 What is a weighted average? Can you think of any uses for a weighted average other than inventory valuation?

6 Do most firms you know move their inventory in the exact order in which it is purchased? Name such firms.

7 If market price is lower than its cost and you are using the lower-of-cost-or-market method for inventories, do you feel the firm should take an inventory loss before sale of the goods?

8 Where would the loss in the preceding question show up in the income statement?

9 Should a physical inventory be taken regularly by all business firms? Why?

PROJECTS FOR HOME ASSIGNMENT AND/OR CLASS DISCUSSION

1 The Jones Grocery Store purchased a new delivery truck for $3,500. It was estimated that the truck would render good service for 75,000 miles, have a trade-in value of $600 in 4 years, and have an estimated life of 4 years. The first year the truck was driven 20,000 miles. What would be the first-year depreciation on this truck using each of the four major methods of depreciation?

2 If a piano store purchased five pianos at $600 each, eight pianos at $500 each, and three pianos at $900 each, what is the weighted average cost of all its purchases?

3 Which inventory valuation method would you recommend for your neighborhood independent grocery store? Why?

4 Do you believe that new showcases render better value to a store in their first year than in their tenth? Why?

REFERENCES FOR FURTHER READING

"Checklist for Profit Watching," Small Business Administration Pamphlet No. SMA165.

"Inventory Management," Small Business Administration Pamphlet No. SBB75.

"Marketing Checklist for Small Retailers," Small Business Administration Pamphlet No. SMA156.

OTHER PHASES OF SMALL FIRM MANAGEMENT

CHAPTER

23

FRANCHISING

Gosh, I thought the only way to have your own business was to rent a store and buy merchandise to resell, or rent a factory, buy raw materials and make a product to resell. Do you mean there are other ways?

The Late Learner

The recent growth of franchising as a major factor on the business scene merits our giving the subject serious attention in our study. It is true that the vast majority of small firms started in our country every year (more than 100,000) are newly established, independent firms. A small percentage of new firm owners have purchased existing firms. Although the basic emphasis of this book involves the creating of a new firm, the concern of *this* chapter is franchising.

Good planning, financing, and management are essential to any type of small firm. This is true whether the firm represents a franchise, a newly created firm, or the purchase of an existing firm. That franchises have a lower failure rate than other new small businesses is due in most cases to the managerial assistance provided by franchisors. Failures can occur in any type of small firm when management does not apply continued good practice in the operation of the firm.

THREE BASIC METHODS OF ACQUIRING SMALL FIRM OWNERSHIP

The three basic methods of becoming a small firm owner are:

1 To buy a franchise
2 To buy an established business
3 To create a new business firm

Persons desiring to go into business for themselves will often find all three methods available in the particular location they have decided upon. Availability varies with the type of business involved. Each method has advantages and disadvantages in a particular situation. When all three possibilities exist, the prospective owners should carefully evaluate the facts they have discovered before making their choice among the alternatives. We will take a look here at the details of franchising, along with its advantages and disadvantages.

FRANCHISING

Franchising became very popular in the decade of the seventies, and this growth has continued in the eighties. Most people recognize such names as Kentucky Fried Chicken, Holiday Inn, or Howard Johnson as firms that have many units around the country which represent individually owned franchises of the parent firm. But franchising has now reached into many other types of business activity.

Franchising is basically a system for distributing products or services through associated resellers. The franchise gives rights to the franchisee to perform or use something that is the property of the franchisor. The parent company (Lum's, for example) is the franchisor. The small business owner (Harry Jones) who buys a franchise is the franchisee. Lum's gives rights to Jones to operate a Lum's restaurant in accordance with the terms of the contract which is signed. This franchise agreement (contract) is a contractual relationship with the rights and privileges of both parties defined. Most franchises specify a time period of operation which may be renewed.

The objective of franchises is to achieve efficient and profitable distribution of a product or service within a specified area. Both parties contribute resources. The franchisor contributes a trademark, a reputation, known products, managerial know-how, procedures, and perhaps equipment. The franchisee invests capital in the purchase of the franchise and provides the management of the operation in accordance with rules set down by the franchisor. Marketing procedures may be specified and a common identity is established.

Growth of Franchising

The recent popularity of franchising might indicate that the idea is relatively new. That is not true. In the fields of fast food, restaurants, and motels this growth has been steady since World War II. But American business had practiced franchising in other fields for many years before this. Firms like the Ford Motor Company, General Motors, Singer Sewing Machine, Rexall Drugs, and Coca-Cola have had franchises outstanding for many years. Some have existed since the turn of the century.

The Small Business Administration has drawn a distinction between the "older franchise groups" and the "new industry groups" that have gone heavily into franchising. The older group includes auto and truck dealers, service stations, soft-drink bottlers, and tire supply shops. The newer industry groups that have entered into franchising are almost endless. They include car wash, auto parts, repair services, restaurants, motels, hotels, convenience stores, drive-ins, employee help services, water conditioner services, hearing aids, swimming pools, and many others.

As long ago as 1969 the SBA estimated that more than a half million franchises existed in the United States. Their forecasted growth figures have been vastly exceeded. Incomplete studies estimate that there may be as many as 2 million franchises, and franchise sales may exceed $200 billion. These estimates may be conservative.

Different Types of Franchises

As franchising expanded into so many different fields of business activity, it was natural that different arrangements had to come forth for their contractual agreements. Most franchises can be classified into one of the three categories that follow:

1 Straight-Product-Distribution Franchises Under this type of franchise, which is the most popular today, franchisors merely supply the franchises with their products in saleable form and the franchises sell them in that same form. Auto agencies and appliance shops are prominent examples. With this type of arrangement the franchises operate under their own name, usually pay no franchise fee, and earn their profit from resale of the products. The franchisors earn their profit from the price at which they sell to the franchisee.

2 Product-License Franchises These are typified by Burger King or Pizza Hut franchises. In these cases the franchises use the franchisor's name but manufacture their products to comply with the franchisor's requirements. The franchisors provide brand identity and usually specify methods of manufacturing and/or distributing the product. Many franchisors in this category may also require that certain materials and supplies be purchased from the franchisor. A new franchise may be very expensive, and costs to the franchisee continue throughout the period of the franchise.

3 Trade-Name Franchises Under this type of franchise, the franchisor licenses its trade name to the franchisee but seldom exercises any control over the product or service being marketed. Equipment distributors often use this

FIGURE 23-1
Franchise firms have become popular in many lines of business.

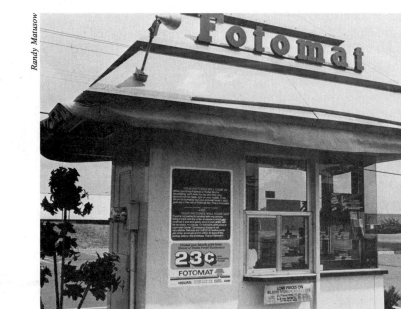

Mimi Forsyth/Monkmeyer

method of franchise. Costs to the franchisees are usually limited to a monthly fee for use of the trademarked equipment. Equipment for a car wash is an example of this type of franchise.

Advantages of Franchising

Franchising offers its maximum advantages when undertaken with due consideration to the interests of the franchisee as well as the franchisor. Under such circumstances we can point out in the following table, advantages to both parties.

To the franchisor	To the franchisee
1 Expanded distribution without increased capital investment.	1 Sound management procedures training, and decision-making assistance made available by franchisor.
2 Community acceptance of product enhanced when local franchisee ownership is held.	2 Less risk with market-tested products and popular products.
3 Marketing and distribution costs shared by franchisees.	3 Preestablished promotion and advertising programs provided.
4 Some operating costs may be transferred to franchisee.	4 Being part of large system of retailers.

5 Flat fees often collected each month from franchisees.	**5** Possible financial aid for part of purchase price at low interest.
6 Selling supplies or materials to franchisees can be profitable.	**6** Credit available in buying inventory and supplies.
7 Retains quality control of product via franchise agreement.	

Disadvantages of Franchising

Although it would normally appear that most of the advantages accrue to the benefit of the franchisor, a close look at many of our nationally franchised operations will indicate that there are still some disadvantages applicable to both parties to the franchise contract. These include the following:

To the franchisor	To the franchisee
1 Long distance control over franchisees.	**1** Usually gives up much freedom in management decisions.
2 Undue involvement in credit extensions to the franchisees for both investment and supply and inventory purchases.	**2** Obligatory purchases from franchisor, even if better prices elsewhere available.
3 Expenses of training and keeping on the road travelling supervisory personnel.	**3** Profits always shared with franchisor, either as a percentage or a flat fee.
	4 Franchises have become very expensive.

Franchises Need Planning Too

Despite the great growth and popularity of franchising in recent years, it should be noted that not all franchises have been successful. There are cases on record of huge prices being paid for a popular name franchise that folded because the market had been misjudged by both the franchisor and the franchisee. Great care should always precede any decisions to buy a franchise. Hundreds of buyers of franchises for a newly proposed fried-chicken outlet lost their entire investment when the parent firm went into bankruptcy before the first unit was opened.

Prudence suggests that those planning to enter into a franchise agreement should carefully investigate the franchisor firm, the composition of the contract, and confirm the market to be served. Sincere and honest people may be the targets of fraudulent business practices, false promotion schemes, and claims of exaggerated profit potentials. The Federal Trade Commission has attempted closer regulation and punishment of such abuses. The International Franchising

Association is doing good work in organizing ethical franchisors and establishing standards and codes of ethical procedure.

It is obvious that franchising has taken an important place in the small business field in our country. Many American franchisors have extended their franchises to Europe, Asia, and around the world. This significant development when handled with proper consideration for both parties can provide real advantages to both franchisors and franchisees.

BUYING AN ESTABLISHED BUSINESS

We noted at the beginning of this chapter that another way to become a small business owner is to purchase an existing business. This method, too, may have distinct advantages and disadvantages in any particular case. There are many things to be noted in evaluating a small business firm that is considered for purchase. But it is one thing to note the general advantages of buying an existing firm—it is quite another thing to confirm the existence of those advantages. Even more important is the true evaluation of the business—to confirm the value of its assets, confirm its past profitability, and determine how to overcome any inherited disadvantages that may come with the firm. The final step in this process is to arrive at a fair purchase price. Too often, ambitious small firm buyers have become victims of the "small business opportunities" racket. This racket involves those who would profit from selling existing firms at inflated prices under a camouflage of exaggerated claims, exaggerated profits, and exaggerated values for assets of the firm.

This whole procedure is considered so important that we have devoted all of Chapter 24 to the subject of buying an existing firm versus starting a new one, and the determination of a fair purchase price. After having studied the chapters up to this point we are ready to investigate the subject in detail.

QUESTIONS FOR CLASS DISCUSSION

1 How would you define a franchise?
2 What does the franchisor give to the franchisee under a franchise arrangement?
3 What does the franchisee give to the franchise arrangement?
4 Is the current popularity of franchises something really new on the total American business scene?
5 How does the Small Business Administration draw a line between the older franchise groups and the current trend toward franchising?
6 How can we distinguish between straight-product-distribution franchises and product-license franchises?
7 What is a trade-name franchise?
8 What do you think is the chief advantage of franchising to the franchisor?
9 What is the chief advantage of franchising to the franchisee which justifies the usually large investment in a franchise?
10 Do you agree that long distance control, credit involvement, expenses of training, and keeping auditors on the road are true problems and disadvantages to the franchisor?

11 If the franchisee gives up freedom in decision making, makes obligatory purchases from the franchisor, and always shares profits with the franchisor, are these items always disadvantages?

12 How can a potential franchisee check the company from which a franchise might be purchased?

PROJECTS FOR HOME ASSIGNMENT AND/OR CLASS DISCUSSION

1 After having studied Chapter 23, which method of becoming a small firm owner appeals most to you? Why?

2 If you owned a franchise for a fast-food chain organization, explain how your "giving up much freedom in management decisions" might be an advantage rather than a disadvantage. Explain how your answer would draw a distinction between well-trained owners with prior experience and the owner just entering into business for the first time.

3 If you or your instructor can obtain a copy of a franchise agreement, study it and report to your class on its provisions.

REFERENCES FOR FURTHER READING

Lasser, J. K., *How to Run a Small Business,* 4th ed., McGraw-Hill Book Co., New York, 1974, chap. 4.

Musselman, Vernon A., and Eugene Hughes, *Introduction to Modern Business,* 8th ed., Prentice-Hall, Inc., Englewood Cliffs, N.J., 1981, chap. 6.

Steinhoff, Dan, Bernard Deitzer, and Karl A. Schilliff, *Small Business Management: Cases and Essays,* Grid Publishing Co., Columbus, Ohio, 1975, Essay No. 12.

BUYING AN EXISTING FIRM VERSUS STARTING A NEW ONE

I bought this business and later found out that I had paid too much for it. I guess it is all right to buy one, but I wish I had started a new one instead. I had no way of telling a fair price for the firm I bought. Thank goodness we have ways available now to measure fair prices.

The Late Learner

For persons who want to own and operate a small firm, there are several ways to achieve their wish. They may follow all the steps we have covered in the process of planning and establishing a new firm, they may buy a franchise, or they may purchase an existing firm in their desired line of business. Many students of management may even inherit a business from their parents or relatives. Our discussion here concerns buying an existing firm.

The case for buying an existing firm as opposed to setting up a new one is not clear-cut. Each case must be decided on its own merits. There are advantages and disadvantages to each. The hard world of reality in business suggests caution and competence when considering either route to ownership.

ADVANTAGES OF BUYING AN EXISTING BUSINESS

If an existing business can be purchased at the proper price (a matter we will discuss later in this chapter), it usually has the following advantages:

1 A going concern with a good history increases the likelihood of successful operation for the new owner.

2 It has a proved location for successful operation.

3 The time, cost, and energy required to do a thorough planning job for a new firm are eliminated. Profits can be earned sooner.

4 It already has an established clientele.

5 Its inventory is already on the shelves, and suppliers are established.

6 Its equipment is already available, and its resources and capabilities are known in advance.

7 Financing is restricted to a single purchase transaction.

While these advantages appear at first reading to be very significant, each must be studied very carefully in the individual case.

DISADVANTAGES OF BUYING AN EXISTING BUSINESS

Even if the preceding advantages stand the test of careful study, they should be weighed against some important disadvantages:

1 The buyer inherits any ill will of the existing firm.

2 Lines of merchandise are already established and may not conform to the buyer's best judgment.

3 Certain employees may be inherited who are not assets to the firm.

4 The inherited clientele may not be the most desirable, and changing the firm's image is usually difficult.

5 Precedents set by the former owner are well established and may be difficult to change.

6 The building itself and the layout inside the firm may not conform to modern standards and may entail substantial expense in modernization.

7 The landlord's attitude and practices may not be conducive to a pleasant and profitable relationship.

8 The purchase price may not be justified and may therefore create a burden on future profits.

9 The value claimed for the current inventory may include slow-moving or obsolete merchandise.

Buying an existing firm does not *always* have disadvantages, but potential ones must be investigated thoroughly in every firm being considered for purchase.

EVALUATING AN OPPORTUNITY TO BUY

The problem for prospective buyers is how to confirm the advantages and the disadvantages in order to make a sound evaluation.

Any evaluation should begin with the potential buyer asking very specific questions and finding very specific answers. The list of questions and suggestions for finding the answers is as follows:

1 What has been the trend of profits for the firm? By trend of profits we mean more than merely the past year. At least 5 years should be reviewed. To find the answer we should (a) ask for copies of accounting audit reports, (b) review the firm's books, (c) study copies of bank deposits for the period, and (d) study copies of income tax returns for the past 5 years. If the seller (or business broker who has the firm listed for sale in his office) is not willing to provide these items, the buyer should be suspicious of the claimed profitability.

2 Is the business growing, declining, or relatively stable? The prime measure here is sales volume. Authenticity of sales claims should be verified. Audit reports are most valuable. Sales records, both cash and credit, are essential.

3 Are profits consistent with sales volume? We know now about comparative statistics which are available for almost every line of business. Several sources of such statistics were listed in Chapter 5. Any significant variation, up or down, from standard profits for this type of firm should be investigated.

4 Why does the present owner wish to sell? There may be entirely legitimate reasons for the decision, such as health, age, or a desire to move to Florida or California. The potential buyer must be sure that the current owner is not merely looking for a chance to sell at an inflated price or because of serious problems in the firm's operation.

5 Does the balance sheet for the firm reflect a sound current financial condition? By applying our basic current ratio, quick ratio, and proprietorship ratio rules (Chapter 3), we have a first approximation of financial soundness. From this point we must confirm the soundness of the assets. Are the accounts receivable current or a collection of long past due accounts? Is the inventory composed of fresh, modern merchandise, or does it include much obsolete merchandise which will be hard to sell? Only investigation of the accounts receivable ledger and inspection of the inventory will find the answers here.

6 Are the fixed assets properly valued, considering their cost and depreciation charges? Are they modern? Are they in good condition? The answers are to be found in purchase invoices, amounts of depreciation charges for past years, recognition of modern versus old equipment, and thorough checking of its condition by inspection and operation.

7 Are expenses in line with average statistics for this type of firm? The answer here is to refer again to comparative statistics while recognizing that there may be reasons for variations in the particular case.

8 If the store is rented, what is the nature of the lease? Can it be renewed? For what periods of time? Is it a percentage lease? What are those percentages? What is the landlord's attitude toward the business? If one of the chief advantages in buying the firm is the location involved, the lease and an option to renew become of great importance. Options should be in writing.

9 What is the competition in the area? By buying instead of organizing a new firm, one competitor has been eliminated. The nature of remaining competition is still important. It should be known. Chances for successful competition with other firms should be reviewed as carefully as if a new firm were planned.

10 What are the present owner's plans after the sale? Too often new buyers find that the seller is in competition with them soon after the sale. The best assurance against this is a clause in the sales agreement stating that "the seller agrees to not engage in the same business within 10 miles for five years." Such a clause is widely used today.

11 Will I need any of the present employees? Are they satisfactory? Honest sellers will usually give a prospective buyer an honest evaluation of their personnel. They may even assist in choosing only superior employees if they are going out of business for good. Interviews with employees and observations of their activities on the job can assist the potential buyer in making any necessary decisions.

12 What are the prospects for increasing profits? Even though the business has been profitable in the past, the competent buyer will analyze the floor space, the layout, the lines of goods carried, the market area, and the services now rendered in terms of whether or not a greater volume of sales and profits would be possible. Chain stores which purchase one-unit firms have a remarkable record of increasing sales after purchase. Individual buyers of such firms can do the same thing.

13 What is the customer and neighborhood attitude toward the firm? Interviews with customers within or outside the store and door-to-door neighborhood surveys are vital ways to find answers to this question. Some ill will may be discovered, but ways to overcome it may be devised. The important thing is to know what customers and neighbors think of the firm.

14 What is the reputation of the firm among business people in the area? Visits to surrounding firms, the chamber of commerce, or service clubs will provide answers. The seller may be known as a "poor payer" in the trade, a dealer in shoddy merchandise, a "sharpie," or one who is lacking in community support or renders too few services. Again, if any sort of negative reputations like this are discovered, they do not in themselves cancel the idea of purchasing the firm, but ways should be devised to change the firm's reputation if possible. Gathering information is important.

15 Are there any nationality, religious, or political factors in the area which would discourage purchase? Despite advances made in promoting goodwill among all peoples, it remains true that if a community is predominantly of one religious group, one nationality group, or even one political group, business people who are not members of that group may have a tougher time in developing successful business firms. Check the facts.

16 Do suppliers regard the seller favorably? Although any critical attitudes you discover may be overcome, relations with suppliers are a measure of business competence. On the other hand, if the firm owns valuable distributorships, it is important that their maintenance be assured. The same is true for franchises.

17 Is the community that the firm will serve a growing one? Population growth means new potential customers. It also means new competitors in most cases. Also, if there are newly planned shopping centers in the general area this may lessen the value of existing firms in long-established locations. Being established, though, gives existing firms the chance to maintain preeminence.

18 Are all liabilities correctly stated on the balance sheet? Individual contracts and other obligations may be checked in detail. The best protection for the new buyer is a clause in the sales agreement providing that any other claims or liabilities are those of the seller. Purchase of the specific assets and stated claims by a separate legal entity may be appropriate.

19 Would the investment make as high a return as could be made by starting a new firm? The answer usually is found in the purchase price, to which we will now turn our attention. We know that profits can be realized sooner, but we must also consider the future situation.

HOW MUCH IS A BUSINESS WORTH?

When the desirability of buying an existing firm has been confirmed, the important question becomes, "What is the price?" Business brokers, even more than the seller, will bandy about such terms as goodwill value, capital earnings basis, and replacement cost of assets. The majority of sales of small firms are made on the basis of asset value less liabilities, with some possible adjustment for profits in excess of a good salary for the owner plus a satisfactory return on his or her investment.

Goodwill as a Basis of Value

Goodwill may be described as the asset value of established patronage and an established name or image which is publicly recognized. It is usually assumed to give a firm profits above the average. The product names Jello and Beechnut have great asset, or goodwill, value. Smitty's Drugstore has very little in comparison. Most small firms have little or no goodwill as an asset of sale. Their goodwill usually derives from the owner's personality, which is not part of the sale. They may have special assets, such as a long-term lease on a prime location or a coveted distributorship that can command high prices.

Capitalized Earnings as a Basis of Value

Capitalized earnings as a basis of value are sometimes used alone for determining the value of a business. For example, if a firm regularly earns an annual net profit of $20,000 after the owner's salary and interest on the investment have been deducted, and the rate of capitalization is 20 percent, the value of the business is said to be $100,000. The computation involves finding the amount, 20 percent of which is $20,000. In this case, $20,000 divided by 20 equals 1 percent which, when multiplied by 100, equals the firm's value on this basis. Or, by formula, we would solve the equation .20x equals $20,000 and solve for x to find it is $100,000.

The rate of capitalization varies with the riskiness of the particular type of business. If risks are believed to be normal, the rate of 20 percent is popularly used. Firms considered to have less risk, such as a local water company, may use a lower capitalization rate with a consequent higher value. For example, a water company earning net profits of $20,000 capitalized at 10 percent would be valued at $200,000. (The $20,000 is 10 percent of $200,000, computed as shown above.)

When the risk is considered to be very high, the rate of capitalization is higher. Many neighborhood beauty shops, service stations, or dry-cleaning firms facing rough competition may be capitalized at a rate as high as 100 percent. This would mean that the value is equal to 1 year's profits.

When only capitalized earnings are used as a basis of value, the net value of assets is ignored in finding value. It is recognized that adequate assets exist to produce the earnings. Liabilities are, of course, confirmed, as is the value of the assets and other items which have been reviewed in analyzing the firm to be purchased, but these do not enter into the determination of sales prices when this method is used exclusively.

It should be emphasized again that only the profits in excess of what the buyer expects as salary for the time and effort involved in operating the firm and a desired rate of return on invested capital are the basis for using the capitalized earnings method of determining value.

Replacement Cost as a Basis of Value

Replacement cost of assets is a poor basis on which to determine their value for purposes of sale of the firm. Only in very rare circumstances, such as an extremely scarce supply situation, would assets ever have nearly the value of new assets to replace them. *Book value* (the original cost less reasonable depreciation) is often a sound basis for sale value. This is the value used for many small firm sales. Straight line depreciation is assumed here. Chapter 22 discussed alternative methods of depreciation.

Even the new student will recognize from these remarks that goodwill value, capitalized earnings, and replacement values usually leave something to be desired in arriving at a precise price for a particular business. It will also be seen why the purchase prices of most small firms represent an agreed net asset value (assets minus liabilities assumed), with possibly some adjustment for profits in excess of the desired profit for the buyer, plus a satisfactory rate of return on the investment.

Current market prices of assets of all types have dominated firm values in the eighties with its unheard-of inflation.

A Practical Way of Finding Value

Using a realistic example, let us see how the value of a small firm can be determined. A business has $60,000 net assets, with reasonably expected profits of $30,000 per year. The potential buyer values her time and energy at $20,000 and desires 10 percent as a return on her investment. She would be willing to pay a premium for the profits in excess of the amount sufficient to cover her salary and interest. If a purchase price of $80,000 is offered, she would need $28,000 to cover salary ($20,000) and interest ($8,000, or 10 percent of $80,000) if she invested the entire amount on the date of sale. This would be an attractive price because she can still contemplate $2,000 of extra profits. If the price is still being negotiated, she would be prepared to capitalize this extra $2,000 at 20 percent, or $10,000, if risks are only normal. She would have a maximum price of $90,000 in mind during the negotiating sessions.

SUMMARY

It is hoped this chapter has clarified for students and for business planners the primary problems involved when considering the purchase of an existing firm and the alternatives in finding fair purchase prices for such firms. It should be clear that positive rules are not available to apply to all cases. The art of negotiation can be very important in all phases of buying an existing firm.

QUESTIONS FOR CLASS DISCUSSION

1 What is meant by determining the value of a business on the basis of capitalized earnings?
2 If a business earns $25,000 per year consistently and has only normal risks, how much would it be worth on a basis of capitalized earnings?
3 If you are considering the purchase of an existing firm, why would you be interested in seeing its tax returns for the past 5 years?
4 What are some reasons for saying, "Buying an existing business increases the certainty of successful operation for the new owner"? Is this necessarily always true?
5 Can time be saved by purchasing an existing firm, rather than by doing a thorough job of planning and establishing a new firm?
6 Can the ill will of an existing firm be overcome if you purchase the firm? How?
7 What are the advantages of an official audit report, in comparison with an owner-produced report, when evaluating a firm for purchase?
8 How can bank-deposit records be useful in firm evaluation?
9 What ratios would you look for on the books of a firm you planned to purchase?
10 Would you be interested in the cost and depreciation charged off on fixed assets by a firm you wished to buy? Why?
11 Would you want to know the details of the lease if you were buying an existing firm? Why?
12 Do you believe in protecting yourself when buying a firm by having the seller agree in writing not to be in competition within 10 miles for 5 years? Is this a violation of the seller's civil rights?

PROJECTS FOR HOME ASSIGNMENT AND/OR CLASS DISCUSSION

1 If you were contemplating the purchase of an existing small business, do you think it would be too drastic to ask to see bank deposit slips and income tax returns for the past 5 years? Explain how these items could assist in determining a fair purchase price. Would you be demanding in your requests for other information and records?

REFERENCES FOR FURTHER READING

Baumback, Clifford M., Kenneth Lawyer, and Pearce C. Kelly, *How to Organize and Operate a Small Business,* 5th ed., Prentice-Hall, Inc., Englewood Cliffs, N.J., 1973, chap. 5.

Broom, H. N., and J. G. Longenecker, *Small Business Management,* 5th ed., South-Western Publishing Company, Inc., Cincinnati, Ohio, 1973, chap. 5.

Tate, Curtis E. Jr., Leon Megginson, Charles Scott, Jr., and Lyle Trueblood, *Successful Small Business Management,* rev. ed., Business Publications, Inc., Dallas, Texas, 1978, chap. 5.

CHAPTER

COMPUTERS AND ELECTRONIC DATA PROCESSING FOR SMALL FIRMS

Oh, yes, I know all about computers. They are expensive to buy and expensive to operate. My small department store has sales of less than $800,000 a year with an inventory of less than 500 items. My business just couldn't afford computer service. If I am wrong I wish you would clarify the facts for me.

The Late Learner

The above statement from our friend, "The Late Learner," seems to reflect the attitudes of many small firm owners, even in the eighties. The probability is that this entrepreneur cannot much longer ignore the need for some kind of computer service. The firm's operating costs, basic decision making based on up-to-date information, and resulting profits can most likely be improved with the appropriate use of computers.

This is not to say that anyone would recommend rushing out to purchase a large computer with multiple capacities for a small firm. It doesn't necessarily mean the purchase of any equipment at all. It *is* meant to say that this particular owner is probably unaware of the new techniques and services available to serve smaller firms. Such services are available today at a much lower cost than most people would believe. Recent technological developments and Electronic Data Processing (EDP) services bring to small firms greater opportunities than ever before to have data available that can make the firm more efficient and more profitable. In the management of successful firms, the departments with responsibility for presenting data to management too often succumb to the avalanche of paper work and the time required to process it. As these firms grow, the need for some sort of computer assistance grows—either the assistance of its own computer, that of a service bureau, or a time-sharing plan.

If we can discern the differences among these alternatives—their procedures and their costs—proprietors like "The Late Learner" can make correct decisions about them.

CHOOSING A COMPUTER OR ELECTRONIC DATA PROCESSING SERVICE

Once the small firm owner understands that the words "computer" or "computer service" are no longer scare words with impossible price tags attached, investigation of the alternatives to provide service needed by the firm can begin. As in all business decisions, this process should start with a clear statement of the services desired. Up to now, a majority of small firms using electronic data services have emphasized the production of payrolls and inventory control as their chief objectives. But so much more data can be made available if desired. Many firms have a complete basic accounting system produced in this manner. In fact, it is possible for all of the following functions to be conveniently programmed for easy reporting to management: The accounting functions (from inventory and payroll control to financial statement production); the finance functions (cash flow analysis, auditing, and government reporting); the marketing functions (advertising, market analysis, and development and market research); personnel functions (training, placement, insurance, wage schedules, and recruitment programs); the production functions (procurement, production control, quality control, and schedule maintenance); and even distribution functions (routing, shipping, and business logistics). No single small firm would need all of these possibilities. The needs vary with the type of firm—retailers don't have production functions, manufacturers emphasize production control, and so on.

When the individual management has determined what it needs from any electronic data processing system, the firm's management can look at the following alternatives to find the best system for providing information for those needs.

Mr. John D. Caley, Senior Consultant to the CPA firm of Laventhol, Krekstein, Horwath and Horwath, designed this chart to help small firms decide if they can truly benefit from using some form of electronic data processing. This chart is part of the Small Business Administration's series of Small Marketers' Aids (No. 149). Notice that this is only a suggested aid. Specific circumstances of the firm will alter the final decisions. Firms with less than 100 points on this chart may still need EDP. Others with more than 100 points may not. Notice the

DOES YOUR FIRM NEED ELECTRONIC DATA PROCESSING???

	How many of these do you have each month?	Give yourself these points	Your points
Number of checks written	_____	10 points for each 100	_____
Number of employees (in cluding salesmen)	_____	1 point per employee	_____
Number of customers' accounts receivable	_____	10 points for each 100	_____
Number of invoices you prepare	_____	10 points for each 100	_____
Number of purchases or purchase orders	_____	10 points for each 100	_____
Number of different items you carry in inventory	_____	10 points for each 1,000	_____
Do you have very large items in inventory, such as trucks?	_____	10 points is answer is yes	_____
Do you need help in keeping track of your inventory?	_____	10 points if answer is yes	_____

Total points for your business _____

If you fill in the blanks honestly and your total comes to 100 or more, you would probably benefit from using a service bureau. Even if your total is less than 100, you might be able to benefit. But no simple test such as this can make the decision for you. Look into it carefully. Remember that EDP should reduce costs or increase income enough to repay every dollar you put into it. Other points that will help you decide will be discussed later.

FIGURE 25-1
Does your firm need electronic data processing?

warning that "EDP should reduce costs or increase income enough to repay every dollar you put into it."

THE THREE BASIC ALTERNATIVE SYSTEMS

Three alternatives are widely used by small firms today:

1 Service bureaus
2 Time sharing
3 Firm operated computers

Each of these alternatives must be discussed in detail from the standpoints of their services, costs and benefits, advantages and limitations, and their adequacy to meet the specific needs of the individual firm. Let us take a closer look at each. They are discussed in order of their average expenses, with service bureaus being the most economical.

SERVICE BUREAUS

Service bureaus are designed to relieve the individual firm of the cost of buying computer equipment. The bureau sells its service to many firms: that service is to process the data of the firm into reports. Most service bureaus have a computer of their own on which the work of the clients is processed, although some lease time on computers owned by still a third party. Most have trained programmers and computer operators on their staff. All cities with a substantial business community have such bureaus.

Small firms using this alternative arrange with the bureau to have the desired data available at specified periods. This involves an arrangement whereby the firm delivers *transaction data* (such as receipts, check payments, sales slips, and journal entries not covered otherwise) to the bureau on a specific schedule. The bureau staff then produce the keypunched cards or tapes from these documents. Their computer processes this *input* and prints the reports desired by the client firm. This procedure is comparable to the "Mail-Me-Monday" service that was popular when all accounting was done manually. Merchants at that time could send the same transaction papers to an accounting service firm for recording.

The specified reports, of course, vary with the individual firm, but a fairly comprehensive system for fulfilling most basic accounting needs is now quite popular. This can include deriving reports from all transactions involving a cash receipts journal, a cash register, payroll register, sales journal, and general journal plus ledgers for receivables, payables, and property accounts. Where financial statements are a part of the system, the reports produced most often include balance sheets, income statements, inventory status, and payroll reports for government agencies. Accounts receivable reports and even budget reports and operating ratios may easily be added.

It should be noted that the earliest use by small firms of service bureaus in the seventies included chiefly the preparation of payroll checks and/or inventory control data. Because even this limited service successfully provided a real cost saving to small firms, the wider use of service bureaus for additional services today has been encouraged.

What Do Service Bureaus Cost?

Small firms expecting to use this type of electronic data processing can expect two charges:

   1 One charge for designing system
   2 A monthly processing charge

The service bureau will design and program a specific custom-made system for the individual small firm, or they can also offer a standard system that is adaptable to the needs of most small firms.

A specifically designed system will cost from $500 to $1,200 for most small firms that require the usual reports to which we have referred. This is a one-time charge. If an available standard system is adopted, the design charge is eliminated or greatly reduced. Some service bureaus provide such systems at no charge but then have a slightly higher monthly processing charge to compensate. It is recommended that a firm have an adequate system made available at the very beginning, since changes in the system involve additional design charges.

Monthly processing charges vary with the volume of transactions, of course. The normal monthly charges range from $200 to $500 for small firms recently interviewed in the south Florida area. Use of Figure 25-1 will assist firms in determining their volume of transactions and make possible an estimate of monthly processing charges involved.

Summary Thoughts on Service Bureaus

Service bureaus were the first companies to make available the wide use of electronic data processing for the average small firm. They remain a large and significant service to thousands of small firms in our country and abroad. Their costs remain the most economical for small firms which have limited their data needs to basic accounting data. They easily record all types of accounting transactions and can easily produce basic accounting statements. If desired, service bureaus can introduce analyses of particular items into the basic program.

Service bureaus first proved their cost effectiveness in producing payrolls and inventory records, but the economies they can now provide for producing general accounting systems for the typical small firm are well established. They involve no investment in equipment by the firm, they can eliminate routine clerical and accounting jobs, and they guarantee consistent, accurate reporting. They offer their customer clients the option of doing their own keypunching if they want—this may be economical when the volume of transactions becomes large. They ideally fit the plans of small firm owners who wish to avoid any direct involvement or investment in computer hardware or software. They have proved their cost-benefit merits in most cases when their services have been sought after the customer has made a careful scrutiny of costs and the firm's needs.

TIME SHARING

Since the late sixties small business firms have had the services of time sharing generally available to them. It is called time sharing because the individual firm shares the time of a computer which is owned by someone else. It requires that the small firm using this service have a terminal device installed in its place of business. This can be a terminal into which information is keypunched or a

FIGURE 25-2
A terminal for use in a modern business. *(Courtesy of Wang Laboratories, Inc.)*

teletype machine on which basic data is inserted. See Figures 25-2 and 25-3 for examples of terminals. The terminal is connected to a computer in another location via telephone lines. The basic computer may be many miles from the individual customer using the time-sharing service.

The customer firm must have a trained operator to enter the basic information into its terminal. The terminal transmits the information to the computer over the telephone wire. When the basic computer is available, it can return final

FIGURE 25-3-A small business computer is a valuable tool. *(Courtesy of Wang Laboratories, Inc.)*

results back to the customer firm's terminal in a matter of seconds. The average time for lengthy reports is usually less than two hours. This is known as *turn-around time*. With time sharing, there is no wait for messenger delivery or mail delivery of reports.

Time sharing reached its maximum utilization in the seventies before technological developments made possible the very popular minicomputers of today. Some business analysts believe that minicomputers may largely replace time sharing. However, it is clear that thousands of small firms today still use time sharing in preference to either service bureaus or owning their own computers.

What Does Time Sharing Cost?

Total costs of a time-sharing system involve the cost of a terminal and the price of the actual amount of computer time used. Terminals similar to those shown in Figures 25-2 and 25-3 may be rented in most cities at a charge of $75 to $150 per month. Teletype machines may usually be rented or purchased. Costs may exceed $1,000. Computer time charges are fairly well standardized in most cities. Lengthy reports are more expensive than one-page reports because of the time involved in recording and processing the data. It is not unusual, however, to find a cost as low as $5 to $8 per standard sheet including specified calculations.

Summary Thoughts on Time Sharing

A big advantage of time sharing is the speed with which reports can be produced. The author's experience indicates that this is not a major concern of the typical small retailer, wholesaler, or service firm. Two-day service from a service bureau seems quite satisfactory in most cases. It is true that the cost of time sharing is moderate when the vast computer power it is capable of supplying is recognized. The individual small firm must consider what its basic data needs are—rather than get carried away by the complete facilities offered by connecting with enormous computer capacity. Time sharing can be most efficient for special jobs, when the firm has a need for such special reports. Firms operating on a closely regulated budget system, for example, can have ready access to any variances from that budget. Any computer service eliminates much clerical time involved in making rough drafts, making involved calculations, and typing and reproducing reports.

Unless the customer firm is able to use a predesigned system, it will have to design its own. This involves the need for a programmer on the staff of the firm. Our experience has been that most small firms can use a "canned" system well. A programmer will need to know a basic computer language, but this is no longer a difficult task. Some people object to the noise of the terminals, but this has been greatly reduced with newer models.

Time sharing has no limit as to the type of data it can produce for the individual firm. Check writing, sales analyses, cost analyses, inventory controls, purchase order production, receivables and payables control and analyses all can benefit from the advantages of time sharing. We can only repeat that the special system adopted by any firm should be based on an authoritative analysis of its data needs. Trade associations, bankers, accountants, service bureaus, time-sharing firms, and computer firms are all available to help the individual small firm owner in making the best decisions. Small firm owners are well advised to confirm the costs of the alternatives that are presented. Historically, the service bureau arrangement has been more economical in providing for the basic accounting needs for the typical retailer, manufacturer, wholesaler, or service firm. Today, however, firms make a wider use of EDP possibilities using time sharing, and even more with their own computer.

FIRM OWNED COMPUTERS

The most significant EDP development in the decade of the eighties has been the wide availability of minicomputers. These have often been called small business computers, but their uses cover an even wider service to large firms and to individuals. Thus, today we can visit our stockbroker and find that he or she has a minicomputer on the desk that can show much detailed information immediately with the punch of a few keys. A small firm may have the computer connected to its cash register and thus have totals of all types immediately available. Perpetual inventories can be maintained with such an arrangement. Grocery stores have computers that can automatically ring up the price of items by merely moving the computer-marked prices over an attachment to the cash register.

The ability of minicomputers is awesome. Small firms can now program an entire accounting system into a small computer which does not need special atmospheric conditions or floor strength to operate efficiently. Minicomputers are available to small firms today that have all the features of their predecessors. These include the basic components of (1) an input unit, (2) a control unit, (3) a memory unit, (4) the arithmetic and logic unit, and (5) the output unit.

It was only in the latter years of the seventies that technological developments made these modern machines available. Their wide acceptance, combined with the economies of size, has brought their cost within the reach of many small firms which never contemplated such a development. Their wide acceptance is reflected in their rapidly expanding sales. Sales of minicomputers passed the billion dollar mark in 1980 and are expected to exceed 5 billion in 1982. New manufacturers are appearing all the time and selling their machines nationwide. There are still wide variations in design and recommended uses.

While the market today has been described by some experts in the field as "fragmented" (meaning that other products such as desk-top calculators and copiers and various designs of minicomputers are also in the field), it is clear that the general use of minicomputers is bound to become an important part of more and more small firm operations.

Which Small Firms Can Afford Minicomputers?

Precise measurements are not available to answer this question. But we can note the rule of thumb used by many vendors of minicomputers. That rule says that commercial users of minicomputers should have sales revenues of between $1 million and $3 million. When we consider that the Small Business Administration considers retailers small who have sales of up to $2 million (and in some industries up to $7.5 million), it is clear that the rule of thumb truly brings the minicomputer within the consideration of many small firms. We must quickly add that this doesn't mean that every small firm with sales of $2 million should hurry to the minicomputer vendor and buy the unit. We must also repeat that a close cost-benefit analysis should be made before every purchase. EDP should reduce costs or increase profits sufficiently to repay every dollar put into it. Firms owning their own computers must absorb any costs of repairs or computer downtime as well.

What Does a Minicomputer Cost?

In 1980 IBM announced a general-purpose computer with capacity to do all the things previously done by its predecessors at a cost of $18,000. IBM has approximately 30 percent of the computer market but does not dominate it as much as in previous years. Competitors offer comparable computers in the same price ranges, and computers with fewer capabilities are available at lower cost.

What Is Involved in Owning a Minicomputer?

The small firm undertaking this type of electronic data processing must have trained programmers and computer operators. A normal requirement for the firm which first installs a complete computer system usually involves changes in the forms and procedures of the accounting system. Computers may replace some jobs in the firm, but they will create other jobs for their operation. It is hoped that existing employees can be trained in the new system or that they may find other employment within the firm. Minicomputers have the advantage of fitting into existing office space without requiring special rooms, they are relatively simple to use, they are more reliable than their predecessors because of their simpler design, they require little or no scheduled maintenance, and their costs are coming down as manufacturers share the economies of scale.

Summary

As small firms are finding the economies of electronic data processing more and more necessary to maintain competitive positions, they have three alternatives to consider: (1) service bureaus, (2) time sharing, or (3) purchasing a minicomputer. There are no precise rules for answering which of these alternatives the individual firm should pursue. Many small firms have admitted to buying machines or services which they could not justify on a cost-benefit basis. Yet the need for reducing costs and getting better information for decision making is more and more pressing. The best procedure to follow is a close study first of the needs of the firm and then of the relative costs and savings provided by the three EDP alternatives we have studied in this chapter.

QUESTIONS FOR CLASS DISCUSSION

1 What does the term "electronic data processing" mean to you?
2 As a small firm owner, what alternatives would you have available if you decided to turn to electronic data processing?
3 How should a small firm proprietor decide among the alternatives available in electronic data processing?
4 How do service bureaus render their service to the individual firm?
5 How are service bureau charges determined?
6 Can a service bureau maintain a complete accounting system for a small-firm client?
7 How does using a time-sharing plan for electronic data processing vary from using a service bureau?
8 How do minicomputers differ from their predecessors?
9 What is the rule of thumb used by salesmen to decide when a small firm can afford a minicomputer? What limitations can you see to that rule?
10 From your study of this chapter how would you summarize the relative costs of the three options available for obtaining electronic data processing?

PROJECTS FOR HOME ASSIGNMENT AND/OR CLASS DISCUSSION

1 Discuss with your instructor the possibility of having a minicomputer available for a class period. Classmates will appreciate a chance to have its operations explained during the class period.

REFERENCES FOR FURTHER READING

"Accounting Services for Small Service Firms," Small Business Administration Pamphlet No. SMA126.
"Can You Use a Minicomputer?" Small Business Administration Pamphlet No. MA250.
"Computers for Small Business—Service Bureau or Time Sharing?" Small Business Administration Pamphlet No. 149.

EXPORTING AND IMPORTING: A CHALLENGING OPPORTUNITY FOR SMALL BUSINESS

Do you mean that with my little factory I could possibly sell my products abroad? Gosh, I thought only very large firms exported their products. And you say the government encourages and assists exporting? Tell me more.

The Late Learner

Exporting domestic products abroad and selling foreign products in the United States have always held a special fascination for many small firm owners. The lure is apparently based upon a number of things: the satisfaction derived from comparing the cultures and products of various countries; the uniqueness of the products involved; the general satisfaction that comes with travel; and the handling of international transactions. Being the sole distributor of special products in a certain market also has sound business attractions.

Along with this fascination for foreign business, however, there is a popular misconception that only very large firms are able to engage in the exporting and importing of the vast number of goods that are sold regularly in foreign markets. It is not generally recognized that the great majority of firms that export domestic products to foreign countries or import foreign goods for sale in the United States are very small firms from the standpoint of capital invested, number of employees, or total sales within a year. A lack of understanding of these facts has deterred many small firm owners from seriously investigating the possibilities of exporting their products or services, or importing other merchandise for domestic sale. Others have been discouraged by the unfamiliar procedures involved in dealing in foreign currencies; obtaining foreign markets; bills of lading; consular invoices and regulations; dealing through letters of credit issued by banks; investigating buyer or seller reliability and financial soundness; and concern for some foreign governments' stability.

Competent businesspeople look upon these features of the export and import business only as a challenge. They properly prepare themselves for the conduct of foreign business in order to gain the potential profits. Familiarity with all the features cited is essential to successful conduct of such business. Authoritative information on these procedures is easily available. Some of the sources will be cited in this chapter and others will be listed as references at the end.

It is to be emphasized that two major departments of the United States government, the Department of Commerce and the Small Business Administration, are heavily committed to the development of exporting American products abroad. They have invested much time, energy, and money in preparing publications and other aids for those who are in the exporting business or who are planning to enter into this field. Most of these publications are available free or for a very small charge by writing to the U.S. Department of Commerce, Washington, D.C., or the Small Business Administration, Washington, D.C., or by visiting a local office of these departments. Our Secretaries of Commerce regularly point out in their public addresses the importance of developing export trade of our products and services in an effort to balance exports with the vast imports we make every year. Developing our exports is in the national interest.

Because of the seemingly insatiable demand of Americans for goods of all types, foreign imports of consumer goods have vastly exceeded the volume of American consumer goods sold abroad. Much of this can be traced to the fact that it is easier to import foreign goods than it is to establish markets and sell domestic goods abroad. And that is why the American business community has been challenged to expand its exports.

The nature of the foreign markets for American products is succinctly described in an excellent brochure published by Trans World Airlines entitled "The Basics of Export Marketing." The following quotations, used by permission, bear repetition:

> Most companies are thoroughly familiar with the requirements for success in their industry in the United States. In many companies, however, little is known about the conditions for success in foreign markets, even though this knowledge can be gained quite easily.

> We do not hold that everything made in the United States is automatically a good candidate for export. We believe, however, that a large percentage of those firms who do not now export could do so with profitable results. We also believe that many firms whose products seem specially tailored to U.S. markets could find satisfying overseas volume, and that for many firms the existing product line is quite marketable as is.

All that is required, in most cases, is a better knowledge of the basics of export marketing.

While the reference here is to established firms, the same considerations would apply to new firms.

The emphasis in this chapter will be on developing export business because export operations are admittedly more demanding. The chief concern of importers is finding desired products, determining their landed cost, and setting prices to cover overhead and profits. Full knowledge of customs duties and tariffs on specific products is, of course, a part of determining the landed costs in this country.

SPECIAL REQUIREMENTS FOR ENTERING EXPORT TRADE

Export selling often has paper work requirements from foreign government regulations as well as from rules of our own government. Special emphasis, for example, is placed upon the shipping documents that accompany every shipment abroad. Packing lists and domestic bills of lading are essential. A shipper's export declaration is needed. This statement facilitates movement of the shipment through U.S. Customs and also provides statistical information which is used to provide summary information on total export trade. Detailed invoices are essential, just as they are in domestic transactions. Some foreign countries have special requirements for such documents as consular invoices, certificates of origin, inspection certificates, certificates of manufacturer, dock receipts, warehouse receipts, and insurance certificates. The list looks more awesome than it really is. The consuls of the various countries will clarify the requirements in a particular situation and assist in their preparation and handling.

Export licenses are required by the U.S. government except for goods not subject to government export administration laws. The great majority of consumer and household goods are not subject to these laws, but it is considered good policy to have an appropriate license nevertheless. Export licenses are of two types:

1   Validated Export Licenses   Our government controls the movement of certain goods if they are commodities of strategic importance, in short supply, or in support of foreign policy. A validated export license is required from the Office of Export Administration when products are so listed. Items that fall in this category are certain chemicals, plastics, highly technical electronic and communications equipment, and scarce materials such as copper. The Department of State handles special licensing for articles of war.

2   General Licenses   These licenses are of several types. They are published authorizations that are used to cover the export of commodities not subject to validated license requirements. It is in this category that the majority of exported merchandise falls. It is not necessary to submit a formal application or receive written authorization to ship these products. They can be shipped by merely inserting the correct general license symbol on the export control document known as the Shipper's Export Declaration. This declaration gives full details on the shipment.

It always makes good sense to check with your local Department of Commerce office before an order is quoted to see what special requirements are appropriate for the country involved. When a validated license is required, an order must be received before the license can be applied for. Your Department of Commerce will always have first-hand information on the latest developments regarding new rules and regulations that apply both here and abroad.

IS FINANCIAL ASSISTANCE AVAILABLE FOR EXPORTING FIRMS?

Yes, there are many types of financial assistance available, especially to established firms with a record of successful business performance. As in all business firms, there is no substitute for having your own working capital. All credit is dependent upon the proper infusion of an adequate amount of investor capital in any firm. Your own line of credit at your bank is always a bulwark of strength to support international operations. Banks with international banking departments can be of great value, since they maintain relations with their own branches or with other correspondent banks throughout the world.

In addition to these basic and traditional sources of financial assistance, the United States government cooperates with our commercial banks through the Export-Import Bank of the United States. This bank provides different financial arrangements to help U.S. exporters grant credit to their foreign customers. This help consists essentially of granting loans to approved foreign buyers of American exports. The policy is that no exporter should be denied his or her sale if the credit of the potential buyer is sound.

The Commodity Credit Corporation, an agency of the government, has the responsibility for encouraging export sales of agricultural products. It makes substantial credits available for such exports. The Private Export Funding Corporation is a private banking group owned by U.S. banks and industries designed to gather private capital to finance U.S. exports. It represents a closely knit group of domestic and foreign banks and local correspondents that bring advice and financing assistance to almost every city in the country through the local bank.

Both the Morgan Guaranty Trust Company (23 Wall Street, New York, New York 10015) and the Export-Import Bank of the United States (811 Vermont Avenue, Washington, D.C.) have prepared attractive and detailed brochures on the financing of exports which will be sent free to those in exporting or planning to expand in this direction. A brief summary of various methods of financing exports and agencies that are available to help with the financing is also available from the Department of Commerce, Washington, D.C. 21230.

IS ANY HELP AVAILABLE IN DEVELOPING FOREIGN MARKETS?

Emphatically, yes. There are no limits to creative individual ways of finding customers, or to the use of intermediary representatives to sell American products in export trade. Many firms develop their foreign markets completely on their own. However, if you desire assistance, it is as close as your nearest Department of Commerce office. The people there will gladly reply to mail inquiries if personal visits are difficult. This department has developed various programs to assist American firms in locating representatives or markets.

A key aid is the Agent/Distributor Service (ADS). A potential export firm need only file an application for agents or distributors of their products in a specific country with the Department of Commerce. International trade specialists will assist with the details of the application and assure that the relationship has no problems. With the details of the proposal and the cooperation of the U.S. Foreign Service, a list of business firms interested in representing the subject company will be sent to the potential exporter in the United States. The foreign firms contact the U.S. firm, and negotiations proceed between them. This valuable service is rendered for a fee of $25.

A further plan is the Trade Opportunities Program (TOP). Exporters, or would-be exporters, can subscribe to membership in TOP for $25. The firm then specifies the products it would like to sell and the countries it desires as markets through representation. Representation opportunities are matched with subscriber requests via computer. When a match appears, the computer prints out the opportunity notice which is then mailed to the subscriber. There is a charge of 50 cents for each matched account.

A third aid is the Export Contact List Services of the Department of Commerce. The department has a computerized list of more than 125,000 dealers or potential users of American products and services in more than 100 countries. This list, known as the Foreign Trader's Index (FTI), is updated regularly and is available to U.S. exporters in three different forms:

1 Export Mailing List Service (EMLS) For $15 the person making a request can receive up to 300 names of users of specific products in specific countries. Where possible, detailed information such as size, sales, employees, officers' names, and so on, is included. Additional names given above the 300 are charged at 5 cents each.

2 Data Tape Service This service provides magnetic tapes to people making requests. The tapes give full information on all users of products in any countries desired. The tapes are put on a person's own equipment for analysis.

3 Trade Lists This service provides target industry trade lists, state-controlled trading company lists, or lists of all commercial firms in developing countries.

Additional assistance for exporters is provided through specialized U.S. government trade missions. These are actually groups of American businessmen who have been recruited by the Commerce Department from a specific industry to promote the sale of the products of their industry or at least to establish local representatives in specific countries. The department provides marketing information and pays the expense of missions operations. Members pay their own expenses and conduct business for the firms they represent.

Other sources of assistance for market development are trade shows or other types of commercial exhibitions in which the government of the United States may be participating. These usually offer wide exposure for products and services of participating firms. The government also aids exporters who travel abroad by giving them information about local markets. Our embassies and consulates publish newsletters and other sources of information for the use of prospective exporters.

In the private sector of the economy there are also many efforts made to promote foreign sales. Industry-organized, government-approved trade missions are frequently sponsored by private groups who wish to promote their own sales or develop reliable representation abroad. Trade associations, chambers of commerce, industry groups, or single large firms often sponsor or finance promotions of foreign sales. Small firm operators will find that their local banks can be valuable in gathering data through their international departments or through correspondent banks. Airlines, ocean freight carriers, and port authorities also have significant data to assist potential exporting plans. Many of them publish booklets of data for potential customers. Business and travel magazines from abroad, often privately sponsored, are another source of market information.

It is important to point out here that finding the names of potential agents or distributors to represent an American company is one thing. As in all domestic business, it then becomes important to investigate the reliability of such representatives before entering into detailed and obligatory contractual relationships. This can best be done with assistance from commercial credit reporting firms, the *World Traders Data Reports* that are available from the Department of Commerce, or from your local bank and its affiliated banking institutions.

ARE THERE DIFFERENCES IN PRICING GOODS FOR EXPORT TRADE?

In the sense that all prices must be set to return a profit, there are not differences. But there may be philosophical or psychological policies that will accrue to the benefit of both buyers and sellers if adopted. American goods are generally expensive in foreign currencies, and sales can be greater if the product can be sold at lower than domestic prices. Some of the recommendations which have been made by international trade experts in this regard include:

1 Omit domestic marketing costs such as advertising and sales expense from

the price of that portion of the output that is sold abroad. This is not usually done but has much to commend itself to American exporters.

2 Determine marginal costs of the increased production that goes into foreign trade. Then use this figure, rather than full average costs, to compare with competitive prices to determine profits.

3 Modify your product so that it can meet consumer demand levels in a specific market. This may mean packaging it in smaller-sized packages or making a simplified product that serves the basic use.

4 Be sure that the customer understands the full landed cost of your goods in his or her city. If freight charges are not clear, be sure the customer knows they are to be added to the prices you have quoted.

Many well-intentioned foreign relationships are severed early because of a lack of understanding of some of the business terms used in correspondence. The great majority of present American exporters merely send their shipments under a "c.i.f." designation. This means price plus cost, insurance, and freight. The final cost under these circumstances may have little association with the invoice price quoted. It is absolutely essential that any terms used are clear to both buyer and seller. There are other terms used in the terms of sale which are often not understood thoroughly by domestic business people, to say nothing of foreign citizens. Some of these are "c. & f." (cost and freight) to named overseas port; "f.a.s." (free alongside ship) at named U.S. port; "f.o.b." (free on board) to which is added the point of origin, the port of exportation, or the vessel employed. Time spent in clarifying these terms of sale will preserve good friendships established in export trade.

HOW ARE SPECIFIC MARKETS CHOSEN?

Despite all the data presented in the preceding section, it is recognized that most small firm exporters are not interested in attempting coverage of more than 100 foreign countries as export markets. They would prefer to know which foreign markets have evidenced demand for the particular types of products or services which they offer for sale. Unless they already have information about how to choose the particular markets to be pursued, they can find assistance from both government and private sources. Some of these sources are the following:

The Bureau of Census issues the monthly *Foreign Trade Report FT 410— United States Exports Commodity by Country*. This highly significant publication provides a statistical record of the shipments of all merchandise from the United States to foreign countries. It includes both the quantities and dollar values of these exports to each country during the subject month. Cumulative statistics for the calendar year are also included. This report shows which of more than 160 countries have bought any of more than 3,000 American products. Comparing these reports for recent years will show market trends in each area, and designate the largest and most consistent markets for particular products. This report is on file at the Department of Commerce district offices, or available by subscription on an individual basis.

Market Share Reports is another publication of the Department of Commerce. It summarizes international trade in manufactured products and includes more than 75 percent of the total exported output of the factories in the free world. Imports of more than 90 countries including over 1,100 commodities are included. The American share of each market is indicated.

The Department of Commerce can also supply existing and potential exporters with extensive foreign economic data, including such factors about a specific market as age, income, literacy levels, auto ownership, appliance use, industries, and types of manufacture. Trade and tariff regulations, quotas in existence, licenses, and exchange permit information are also available for each country.

The Bureau of International Commerce of the Department of Commerce regularly issues many other reports on topics of interest to exporters. Such subjects as background for certain markets, economic trends in specific areas, growth within developing countries, and foreign market reports are covered in depth.

From the private sector of the economy additional information can be obtained from trade associations, foreign freight forwarders, international bankers, local chambers of commerce, and from other firms in the exporting business.

Foreign markets are extensive. They are dynamic. They are often changing and challenging. Those who would actively pursue them should take advantage of all information available to keep current on developments in the markets they choose to share.

GETTING PAID FOR YOUR EXPORTS UNDER VARIOUS FINANCING PLANS

One of the reasons some firms have neglected foreign market possibilities is that they are concerned about getting paid for their merchandise once it has been shipped. Exchange rates are considered an added risk that must be undertaken. Again, only a bit of study is required to remove these concerns and assure payments from any of a variety of plans. The problems of collection of amounts due is not a peculiarity of the export trade. As experienced businesspeople will testify, that problem is important for domestic firms as well. It is an axiom of business that careless extension of credit is bound to result in some losses from uncollectable accounts.

There are at least six different methods used in securing payment for export sales. A brief word of explanation for each is appropriate here.

1 Letters of Credit This is the traditional method for handling foreign shipments. The letter of credit is issued by a bank at the buyer's request in favor of the seller. It promises to pay the seller the agreed amount when documents covering the sale are received. Such letters of credit are usually irrevocable so that once the credit has been accepted by the seller it cannot be altered without his or her permission. The bank pays the seller in full upon proper delivery of the merchandise and presentation of the documents to the bank. Bank charges and government regulations abroad have made this method unpopular with buyers.

2   Sight Drafts   Whenever the seller wishes to retain control of the goods, or title thereto, shipment is made on a negotiable bill of lading. This bill must be properly endorsed by the bearer and given to the carrier before the cargo can be released. A sight draft is sent to the buyer's bank, along with the other documents. The bank notifies the buyer that the documents have been received and that as soon as the amount of the sight draft is paid, he or she may have the bill of lading and obtain receipt of the merchandise.

3   Time Drafts   These drafts operate in the same manner as sight drafts except that they are drawn for 30, 60, or 90 days in the future. When the buyer signs the draft he or she can receive the merchandise, but payment is not made until the due date of the time draft. The signed draft becomes a note payable.

4   Consignment Sales   Such sales operate the same for export as for domestic sales. The merchandise is delivered to the buyer, but title is retained by the seller. When the buyer sells the merchandise, then payment is made to the seller. The added risks of buyer responsibility and economic and political stability of the foreign government are assumed. Political risk insurance is available.

5   Open Accounts Receivable   When selling to buyers of unquestioned integrity, some exporters sell to foreign accounts just as they do to preferred customers in this country. The normal risks of collection are assumed. The exporters' capital is tied up in such receivables until payment is received. This method is least complicated.

6   Cash in Advance   This happy state of affairs is seldom available to exporters. Buyers usually object to this method because their capital is unavailable until the merchandise is received and resold. Small sales are still made this way in many cases.

It can be noted that factoring firms exist that specialize in collecting foreign accounts receivable. This method is not recommended in most cases, not only because of the fees involved but because of the importance of maintaining customer goodwill.

CHANNELS OF DISTRIBUTION FOR EXPORTED PRODUCTS

In the vocabulary of modern marketing the term *channels of distribution* refers to the paths taken by merchandise and/or its title as it moves from the manufacturer to the ultimate consumer. In exporting circles, *direct selling* means that the American manufacturer deals with foreign firms and is usually responsible for shipping the products overseas. *Indirect selling* means that the manufacturer deals with another American firm which acts as a sales intermediary, and this firm will normally assume the responsibility for moving the products to their foreign destination.

DIRECT SELLING

There are various methods of direct selling. The American firm may operate with a foreign representative (or agent), a distributor, or a foreign retailer; it may sell directly to ultimate consumers, or sell to state-controlled trading companies.

Sales Representatives In export selling sales representatives are comparable to manufacturer's representatives in this country. They have product literature or samples to present the products to potential buyers. They usually work on commissions, assume no risk or responsibility, take no title, and are under contract with the manufacturer for a specified but renewable period of time. They need not be exclusive representatives. Orders received are sent to the manufacturer for delivery.

Foreign Distributors These are merchants who purchase their products from the American manufacturer at the best prices they can get and resell such purchases at a profit. Title to merchandise is assumed at once. This method is particularly suited to products that need servicing, if the distributor will stock necessary parts and provide the service for a fee. This is also a highly popular method for selling household and consumer products.

Foreign Retailers Direct selling in this case is largely limited to consumer goods. There is much reliance upon travelling salespersons, but catalogs and brochures can be useful as well.

Selling Directly to Ultimate Consumers This has been a small part of the total export business in this country. Difficulty is often encountered when a foreign buyer places an order based upon an advertisement in a magazine which reaches foreign cities. The buyer often does not know foreign trade regulations that may impair delivery.

State-Controlled Trading Companies These exist in various countries in the world. The chief activities of these companies in recent years has been in the purchase of raw materials, agricultural machinery, and manufacturing and technical equipment. Countries which use such firms are primarily concerned with improving their self-sufficiency. Only a few have purchased consumer and household goods.

INDIRECT SELLING

These other American firms, or intermediaries, to whom manufacturers sell their products in indirect selling can be commission agents, country-controlled buying agents, export management companies, export merchants, or export agents. Exporting manufacturers have to choose the type of operation that seems best suited to their needs. These firms can be distinguished as follows:

Commission Agents   These firms are also known as buying agents. They are hired by foreign firms as "finders" of American products which are desired by the foreign firms. It is their function to find the requested merchandise at the lowest possible prices. Their remuneration is a commission paid by the foreign firm.

Country-Controlled Buying Agents   These firms are agencies or quasi-governmental firms representing foreign governments. They are given power to find desired products of all types for those countries.

Export Management Companies (EMCs)   These firms are of special value to small manufacturers endeavoring to promote foreign sales. The EMCs act as the export department for several manufacturers of noncompetitive products. Through their foreign contacts they solicit and transact business sales in the name of the manufacturer they represent. They do not buy or sell for their own account, they never take title to specific merchandise, and they do not finance any of the transactions. They may be paid on a straight commission basis, on a salary basis, or have a retainer fee plus commissions. They can be of exceptional value to a small firm which hasn't the time, personnel, or money to operate its own export department.

Export Merchants   These merchants purchase products directly from the manufacturer, take title, and have the packaging done to their own specifications. The merchandise is then sold overseas through their own contacts and in their own name. They assume all risks involved.

Export Agents   These agents operate like manufacturer's representatives in the United States. Title to merchandise and risks are retained by the seller.

The firm desiring to do export business must first make a decision as to whether it prefers and can manage direct selling or indirect selling. A second decision involves the choice of alternatives we have reviewed in each category. Small firm owners should recognize that in some of the marketing methods outlined they do not have direct control over the marketing and promotion of their product abroad. They should clarify their method and the timing of payment under each method to be sure that the financing is compatible with their financial resources. These decisions merit close study by those desiring export business. Circumstances will vary for each firm.

SUMMARY

Export business is good business. Its challenges can be met with good management. Abundant assistance is available from government agencies and private organizations for those who wish to enter the field. This assistance ranges from finding customers to giving financial assistance in completing transactions. It is national policy in the United States to encourage our private business firms to consider more export business. The potentials of export marketing represent a very real opportunity to expand sales and profits for many American firms.

Small firms may engage in importing and exporting at the same time. Importing has been well developed in the United States, in fact, so well that national policy is concentrating upon expanding exports instead.

REFERENCES FOR FURTHER STUDY

Most of the information contained in this chapter about how to proceed in the export business has been taken from or verified by government or private publications. These are regularly updated and should be reviewed by students and businesspeople interested in the export-import business. The following publications will be found most helpful:

1 "A Basic Guide to Exporting." Developed by the U.S. Dept. of Commerce, Domestic and International Business Administration. For sale by the Superintendent of Documents, U.S. Government Printing Office, Washington, D.C. 20402. Price 70 cents.

2 "Export Marketing for Smaller Firms," 3d ed., issued by the Small Business Administration. For sale by the Superintendent of Documents, U.S. Government Printing Office, Washington, D.C. 20402. Price 50 cents.

3 "The Basics of Export Marketing." A bibliography of information on sources with descriptive material. Produced by Trans World Airlines. Available from any district office of TWA. Free.

4 "An Introduction to Doing Import and Export Business." A manual for organizing and conducting foreign trade firms. Developed by and available from Chamber of Commerce of the U.S., 1615 H Street, N.W., Washington, D.C. Free.

5 "Export Control—Quarterly Report." Details licensing operations and actual shipments of commodities and security export conditions. For sale by the Superintendent of Documents, U.S. Government Printing Office, Washington, D.C. 20402. Price 25 cents.

6 "Expand Overseas Sales with Commerce Department Help." Small Business Administration Management Aid No. 199. Available from the Superintendent of Documents, U.S. Government Printing Office, Washington, D.C. 20402. Free.

QUESTIONS FOR CLASS DISCUSSION

1 What factors have drawn small firms into the import-export business?
2 What are the differences in the licenses required for the export of American products to other countries?

3 What is the chief way in which the Export-Import Bank assists American exporters?

4 What is the main purpose of the Commodity Credit Corporation in serving total export trade in our country?

5 Can a small firm receive any help in developing new foreign markets which it desires to develop?

6 Does the private sector develop foreign markets on its own?

7 How can foreign prices for American markets differ from domestic prices?

8 What do the terms "c. & f."; "f.a.s."; "f.o.b."; and "c.i.f." mean as they are used in export trade?

9 Which of the various methods for getting paid for exports would you prefer? What are the other methods?

10 How do foreign distributors operate in the buying and selling of American export products?

11 Is direct selling to foreign consumers a large part of American export business?

12 How can commission agents assist the development of export trade for American products?

PROJECTS FOR HOME ASSIGNMENT AND/OR CLASS DISCUSSION

1 With your instructor's assistance you can probably arrange for a guest speaker to visit your class from the Department of Commerce or the Small Business Administration, or a local business owner who sells abroad or imports products for sale. He or she will be glad to explain the details of engaging in exporting or importing products.

REFERENCES FOR FURTHER READING

"Market Overseas With U.S. Government Help," Small Business Administration Pamphlet No. MA237.

Musselman, Vernon A., and Eugene Hughes, *Introduction to Modern Business,* 8th ed., Prentice-Hall, Inc., Englewood Cliffs, N.J., 1981, chap. 21.

Steinhoff, Dan, *The World of Business,* McGraw-Hill Book Company, New York, 1979, chap. 30.

ESSENTIAL ACCOUNTING RECORDS AND A SIMPLIFIED ACCOUNTING SYSTEM

I never took a course in accounting and believed that I would always be dependent on my accountant for every bit of information from the records. I know now that I can operate a simplified accounting system for my business and keep myself better informed between accounting periods.

The Late Learner

Telling owners or planners of small firms that they must keep good accounting records seems to cause a reaction of bewilderment, and they have visions of countless hours spent on ledgers, journals, and posting. A good double-entry bookkeeping system is too often thought of as something requiring at least one full-time employee who makes decisions under divine guidance. Nothing is further from the truth.

At the same time, in many small firms the owners do not understand accounting and fail to keep proper records. It is amazing that many proprietors do not know whether their business has operated at a profit or a loss until many weeks after the close of their fiscal year because they are waiting for an outside accountant to come in and summarize their operations for the year. Audit reports are valuable, but timely knowledge on operating results is even more important to successful business management.

The objective of small firm owners should be to find ways to get essential accounting information economically, quickly, and with a minimum of desk effort. Unless the owners are completely unable to record figures, they can easily obtain the basic information using the methods outlined in this chapter. We studied basic accounting statements in Chapter 3. Now we must devise ways to obtain the underlying information for those statements. Minicomputers and other electronic data services for securing this data were covered in Chapter 25. This chapter explains the accounting involved in a manually operated double-entry accounting system.

By now it should be obvious to the student that if the firm kept records of at least its daily cash and credit sales, its cash receipts and payments, its invoices for purchases of merchandise, and all expenses paid or owed, the basic information for making an income statement could be obtained. Likewise, if purchases, sales, and exchanges of fixed assets are recorded at least in memorandum form, a balance sheet could be produced. Accountants employed to prepare these statements often have little else to work with.

It is nevertheless surprising to see how many firms do not keep even this basic information readily available in their files. Substantial guesswork is often necessary to produce the barest details for annual statements. Even when this basic information is available, however, the owner does not have the benefit of an analysis of operations from month to month or week to week. It is this type of owner who doesn't know the firm's profit position until long after the fiscal period has ended. Such neglect of good accounting information is a prime measure of management incompetence.

Day-to-day decisions in any business must depend upon the financial condition of the firm. Adverse income/expense relationships cannot be corrected, or even detected, without good accounting information. The sooner financial problems or undesirable trends are detected, the more quickly corrective action can be taken.

The simplified record keeping and the basic accounting system outlined in this chapter are designed particularly for retailers and wholesalers, but they can easily be adjusted for manufacturing firms. The discussion is divided into three parts:

1 Minimum information needs
2 How to gather the required information
3 Operation of a combined journal-ledger and a summary worksheet

MINIMUM INFORMATION NEEDED FROM ACCOUNTING RECORDS

1 **Sales** The owner should know not only the total sales by day, week, month, quarter, and year, but also should be able to break these sales down easily into departments, products, or types of merchandise as may be appropriate to the particular business. A grocery store usually divides its sales into meats,

produce, dairy, and staple groceries. A separate division may be needed for a delicatessen, if one is part of the store. Drugstores may divide sales into prescriptions, housewares, shelf medicines, tobacco, and magazines, and they may even have a separate category for gift cards.

These divisions of sales are necessary for the owner to be able to decide on the profitability of each department or line and to make decisions about it.

2 Operating Expenses Information is needed for total expenses, departmental expenses, product expenses, and any other appropriate divisions of expense. Retailers' expenses may be classified as selling expenses and general expenses. Owners of factories will want to divide total expenses into manufacturing, selling, and administrative expenses.

3 Accounts Receivable Records of total sales for cash and total sales on account must be available. A current record of balances owed by credit customers is fundamental. Sales to be charged to credit-card companies must be accessible so that statements may be submitted to those companies for payment.

4 Status of Accounts Payable Every debt incurred must be recorded, and the total debts outstanding at any time must be easily accessible. The records must provide a way to pay invoices within discount periods. Other due dates must be known and observed.

5 Inventory The accounting records must provide ways to give the owner regular information on the total inventory and its major divisions. We discussed inventory control in Chapter 17.

6 Payroll Records Payrolls involve much more than the issuance of weekly, bimonthly, or monthly checks to employees. The requirements of withholding taxes, FICA contributions (Federal Insurance Contributions Act, which provides health and welfare, disability, and pension benefits to employees), and other payroll deductions must be noted in detail for each payday.

7 Taxes Local, county, state, and federal taxes are an unavoidable part of managing any business. Details, except for federal income taxes, will vary from one location to another. Requirements must be determined, and then provisions for getting the proper information can be arranged.

HOW TO GATHER INFORMATION

1 Cash Register Use a modern cash register. This essential piece of business equipment can be invaluable in assuring accuracy in recording transactions. But it can do much more. Modern cash registers can provide classification of sales and expenses paid in cash into almost any groups desired. Sales can be divided into departments, products, or lines of merchandise. The register will then provide daily subtotals for each classification, as well as total sales for the day. It will also provide subtotals for cash sales and credit sales. Representatives of companies selling these machines will teach the individual firm how to utilize them to their greatest advantage.

2 Accounts Receivable and Accounts Payable Set up records for accounts receivable and accounts payable. If sales are made on credit and the company is carrying its own receivables, a record for each customer is essential. Such a record need not be elaborate. Many small firms use a 5- by 8-inch card for each customer on which each credit sale and each payment on account is recorded. A simple book of lined paper with a separate sheet for each customer will also suffice. Copies of sales slips are necessary to post each sale. This book is known as an *accounts receivable ledger.*

When sales are made on credit cards, it is necessary only to keep all such sales slips together by credit company to form a basis for sending statements to the company for collection.

A record of accounts payable operates similarly to the accounts receivable record explained above. In both cases, it is important to be able to tell immediately the current amount owed by a customer or the amount owed to a creditor. The record of amounts due to others is known as an *accounts payable ledger.*

3 Payroll Sheet Devise an adequate payroll sheet. Before each payday a complete payroll sheet must be completed. This sheet must have columns for employee identification, pay rate, overtime worked, taxes withheld, FICA contributions, and other authorized deductions. Once the form has been devised, it can be completed easily for each succeeding payday. Standard payroll sheets are available in stationery stores (see Figure 27-1).

4 Inventory Control Establish an inventory control procedure. The procedure will vary with the type of firm. Many retailers keep inventory records by accumulating price tags from merchandise sold. Accumulated tags show when reordering is appropriate. Other firms set minimum inventories and regularly check shelves and the warehouse to see that stocks are above that minimum. Alert cashiers can report when sales of particular items suggest an inventory check. Analysis of sales records shows which items are getting more or less popular and whether inventory size needs checking. Physical inventories should be taken regularly, never less often than once a year. A perpetual inventory may be appropriate for some kinds of firms—which means checking each item sold as a deduction and each item received in stock as an addition to the inventory. Owners should devise their own plans for keeping themselves informed on the adequacy of their inventories. Computers make provision of inventory data much easier in today's business world.

5 Office Supplies Provide the firm with a businesslike set of supplies. Any

Payroll period ending _____

Name	Hours worked	Earnings			Taxable earnings	
		Regular	Overtime	Total*	Unemployment compensation	FICA
H. Jones	40	$ 200.00	—	$ 200.00		$ 200.00
P. Sibley	48	200.00	$24.00	224.00	$ 224.00	224.00
J. Barlow	40	180.00	—	180.00		180.00
R. Rivets	40	150.00	—	150.00		150.00
Ms D. Smith	30	200.00	—	200.00	200.00	200.00
H. Strong	40	220.00	—	220.00	220.00	220.00
J. Miller	40	250.00	—	250.00	250.00	250.00
Totals†		$2,150.00	$24.00	$2,174.00	$1,350.00	$1,100.00

*A separate record of cumulative totals for each employee must be kept throughout the year for tax purposes, etc.
†The totals of the columns are the basis for the journal entries for the payroll illustrated.

FIGURE 27-1
Sample payroll sheet (or payroll register).

firm's image, its public relations, and its accuracy in record keeping are all served by using attractive and businesslike supplies. These include sales books, statements to be sent to customers, invoice forms, receipt forms, letterheads and envelopes, and wrapping and packaging supplies.

6 Business Papers Carefully preserve all underlying business papers. All purchase invoices, receiving reports, copies of sales slips, invoices sent to business firm customers, all cancelled checks, all receipts for cash paid out, and all cash register tapes must be meticulously retained. They are not only essential to maintaining good records, but they may be important if legal action involves any of these items.

7 Accounting Records Install a basic set of accounting books in a combination journal-ledger system. Such a system is explained in the latter part of this chapter. This is the heart of the accounting records. This basic record, plus a worksheet to summarize operations at the end of the month or fiscal period, will enable the owner to make formal balance sheets and income statements regularly. Any student who has had a high school course in bookkeeping should be able to handle both easily. Others can teach themselves by reviewing Chapter 3 and studying this chapter.

TIME REQUIRED TO MAINTAIN GOOD RECORDS

If the foregoing system still sounds as if it requires too much time and expertise to maintain, the following statements may help to dispel such thoughts. A men's clothing store that installed a similar system reports that less than 30 minutes a day of uninterrupted time was all that was needed to maintain daily records. A small department store with annual sales in excess of $700,000, with an average

	Deductions				Paid		Accounts charged		
FICA tax	Federal income tax	U.S. savings bonds	Misc.	Total	Net amount	Check number	Sales salaries	Office salaries	Other
$ 4.00	$ 35.00	$ 17.50	UF $ 5.00	$ 61.50	$ 138.50	623	$ 200.00		
6.00	38.00	17.50	UF 5.00	60.50	139.50	624	224.00		
4.00	30.00		AR 10.00	44.00	136.00	625	225.00		
5.00	25.00		UF 3.00	33.00	117.00	626		$150.00	
10.00	30.00	37.50	UF 2.00	79.50	120.50			200.00	
4.00	35.00	37.50	—	76.50	143.50	696		143.50	
15.00	40.00	—	—	55.00	195.00	697			$250.00
$83.00	$440.00	$225.00	$60.00	$808.00	$1,306.00	—	$1,250.00	$700.00	$250.00

of 18 credit sales per day and 20 purchase invoices per month, reported that less than 1 hour per day was sufficient. The owner handled this work herself as the system was established. She then trained one of her salespeople to do the work, and she did it during his slack periods on the sales floor or before the store opened each morning. Monthly summaries involving completing a worksheet, preparing formal statements, and preparing and mailing customer statements do require additional time. Many small firms engage a student as a part-time employee to handle the accounting details. Owners should not be occupied with these details when their time can be spent more profitably on other things.

THE JOURNAL-LEDGER ACCOUNTING SYSTEM[1]

Figure 27-2 is an example of a segment of one page of a journal-ledger. It illustrates most of the possible types of entries that a small firm will have during the course of a month. The entries and their explanation follow. The column headings can be arranged according to the owner's desires. For example, we have combined operating expenses with a column of brief explanation to facilitate finding subtotals for each type of expense.

Explanation of Journal-Ledger Entries

October 1:   H. Jones opened a retail store, investing $2,000 in cash, fixtures valued at $1,500, and an inventory of merchandise valued at $2,000. All assets were paid for in full, so no liabilities existed on opening day.

---

[1]It should be noted that simplified self-guiding accounting systems are available in most stationery stores.

Debit Cash (for increases) $2,000, debit Fixed Assets (for increases) $1,500, debit Merchandise Inventory $2,000, and credit H. Jones, Capital (for increases) $5,500. The assets invested are explained in the description column so that any transaction can be traced later.

October 2: Paid rent on the store building for October, $200, by check. Debit Operating Expenses (for increases) $200, credit Cash (for decreases) $200. The description column notes that the expense was for October rent so that all the items in the Operating Expenses column can be subtotaled at the end of the month.

October 3: Cash sales for the day, $300.
Debit Cash (for increases) $300, credit Sales (for increases) $300.

October 4: Sales on account for the day, $350, as follows: Consuelo Hernandez, $100; Alan Cook, $150; Marie Smith, $100. Debit Accounts Receivable (for increases) $350, credit Sales, $350. It is then necessary to go to the accounts receivable ledger and post debits

FIGURE 27-2
A segment of one page of a journal ledger.

H. JONES COMPANY
Journal-Ledger
October, 1978

Date	Description or Explanation	Cash and Bank		Accounts Receivable		Sales
		Debit	Credit	Debit	Credit	Credit
1978 Oct. 1	Jones opened business with $2,000 Cash; $1,500 Store Fixtures, and $2,000 Merchandise -Total $5,500	2000 —				
2	Paid Oct. Rent -Check #1		200 —			
3	Cash Sales	300 —				300 —
4	Credit Sales			350 —		350 —
5	Merchandise purchased from Fincher Co. on account					
6	Store Supplies -Rex Co- Ck.#2		200 —			
8	Cash and Credit Sales	600 —		200 —		800 —
9	Purchased Insurance on Inventory from Acky Ins. Co. - Ck #3		75 —			
10	Collections on Acct. (Hernandez)	100 —			100 —	
11	Jones withdrew cash		100 —			
12	Paid Fincher Invoice 206 - Ck #4		600 —			
13	Merchandise received from ABC Co.					
15	Sales Return (from Cook)				25 — (DR 25)	
16	Payroll - Checks 5-8		480 —			
23	Paid ABC Co. Invoice of 1/13 -less disc.		980 —			
	Omitted Transactions					
31	Sent gov't. checks for withholding FICA -United Fund- Cks.10,11,12		440 —			
31	Purchased showcases -XYZ Co-Ck.13		100 —			
		9300 —	6500 —	4100 —	3000 —	11 600 —

to Ms. Hernandez's, Mr. Cook's, and Mrs. Smith's individual accounts. This ledger is a supplemental record and does not require equal debits and credits.

October 5: Purchased merchandise for the inventory, $600, on account, from the Fincher Wholesale Company.

Debit Merchandise Inventory $600, credit Accounts Payable $600. It is then necessary to record the liability owed in the accounts payable ledger by opening a sheet for Fincher Wholesale Company and crediting it for $600. This record is also a supplemental record and does not require equal debits and credits.

October 6: Purchased supplies for the store, $200. Gave check in full payment.

Debit Supplies $200, credit Cash $200. The description column will indicate what was bought and from whom to enable the owner to analyze details at the end of the month.

October 8: Sales for the day, $800, of which $600 was for cash and $200 on account (Mrs. Cowart).

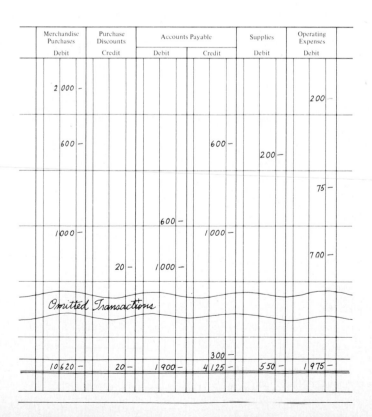

Merchandise Purchases	Purchase Discounts	Accounts Payable		Supplies	Operating Expenses
Debit	Credit	Debit	Credit	Debit	Debit
2 000 –					
					2 00 –
600 –			600 –		
				2 00 –	
					75 –
		600 –			
1 000 –			1 000 –		
					7 00 –
	20 –	1 000 –			
Omitted Transactions					
			3 00 –		
10 620 –	20 –	1 900 –	4 125 –	5 50 –	1 975 –

Debit Cash $600, debit Accounts Receivable $200, credit Sales $800.

Then charge Mrs. Cowart's sheet in the Accounts Receivable Ledger $200.

October 9:   Purchased insurance policy covering the inventory and fixtures in the store. Premium, $75, paid by check.

Debit Operating Expenses $75, credit Cash $75.

If insurance coverage extends beyond the period when the books are normally closed, the premiums may be charged to a Prepaid Expense account, which is an asset. Then, at the end of each period, the amount used up may be taken from this account and placed in the Expense account.

October 10:   Received check for $100 from Consuelo Hernandez to pay for her credit purchase on October 4.

Debit Cash $100, credit Accounts Receivable $100.

Then go to the accounts receivable ledger and credit Ms. Hernandez's account for $100.

H. JONES COMPANY
Journal-Ledger October. 1978

Date	Description or Explanation	Due to Government Agencies		Fixed Assets	H. Jones Withdrawals	H. Jones Capital
		Debit	Credit	Debit	Debit	Credit
1978 Oct. 1	Jones opened business with $2,000 cash; $1,500 Store Fixtures, and $2,000 Merchandise-Total $5,500			1500 —		5500 —
2	Paid Oct. Rent- Check #1					
3	Cash Sales					
4	Credit Sales					
5	Merchandise purchased from Fincher Co. on account					
6	Store Supplies-Rex Co.-Ck.#2					
8	Cash and Credit Sales					
9	Purchased Insurance on Inventory from Acky Ins. Co.-Ck.#3					
10	Collections on Acct.(Hernandez)					
11	Jones withdrew cash				100 —	
12	Paid Fincher Invoice 206- Ck.#4					
13	Merchandise received from ABC Co.					
15	Sales Return (from Cook)					
16	Payroll - Checks 5-8		220 —			
23	Paid ABC Co. Invoice of 9/13- less disc.					
	Omitted Transactions					
31	Sent gov't checks for withholding FICA-United Fund-Cks. 10,11,12	440 —				
31	Purchased showcases-XYZ Co. Ck.13			400 —		
		440 —	440 —	1900 —	400 —	5500 —

FIGURE 27-2
A segment of one page of a journal ledger (cont.).

October 11: Mr. Jones withdrew $100 from the business for personal expenses. Debit Mr. Jones, Withdrawals $100, credit Cash $100.

October 12: Sent check for $600 to Fincher Wholesale Company to pay for invoice covering merchandise purchased on October 5.
Debit Accounts Payable $600, credit Cash $600.
Then go to accounts payable ledger and debit (for decreases) the account for Fincher $600.

October 13: Purchased and received merchandise from ABC Company. The terms of sale are 2/10, n/30. Invoice for $1,000.
Debit Merchandise Purchases $1,000, credit Accounts Payable $1,000.

October 15: Alan Cook returned merchandise, $25, which was part of his credit purchase on October 4. Merchandise was defective. We gave him full credit on his account.
Debit Sales Returns $25, credit Accounts Receivable $25.
Then credit Mr. Cook's account in the accounts receivable ledger for $25.
If such transactions are infrequent, it is not necessary to open a special column for sales returns. Such entries can be placed in the Sales Credit column and circled to indicate that they are debits. The circled items can be totaled at the end of the month to find sales returns for the income statement.

October 16: Issued paychecks for employees covering the bimonthly payroll. Gross pay was $700, but withdrawals were made as follows: Withholding taxes, $175; FICA, $30; United Fund, $15. Take-home checks, therefore, totaled $480.
Debit Operating Expenses $700, Credit Cash $480, credit Due to Government Agencies $220.
All this information will come from the payroll sheet (see Figure 27-1). The amounts due various governmental agencies will be kept current from the payroll sheets and sent on due dates to those agencies.

October 23: Sent check to ABC Company for $980, covering invoice for $1,000, dated October 13, less 2 percent discount for payment within 10 days.
Debit Accounts Payable $1,000, credit Cash $980, credit Purchase Discounts $20.
In accounts payable ledger debit the ABC Company for $1,000.

October 31: Sent checks to government agencies for withholding taxes collected for the government out of employees' paychecks, $350, FICA payments of $60, United Fund payments, $30.
Debit Due to Government Agencies $440, credit Cash $440.
The amounts due will be taken from the payroll sheets since the last payment to the agencies.

October 31: Purchase new showcases for the store, $400. Paid $100 cash and signed contract for $300 to be paid in 3 months to XX Company. Debit Fixed Assets $400, credit Cash $100, credit Accounts Payable $300.

In accounts payable ledger credit XX Company $300.

Again the description column will identify what was bought and from whom, so that analysis of the Fixed Assets column can be made whenever desired.

QUESTIONS FOR CLASS DISCUSSION

1 After studying this chapter, does bookkeeping still seem a great mystery to you? Explain.

2 Can you think of situations where small firm owners could make wrong decisions because they lacked good accounting information? Name them.

3 Why should the owner of a drugstore want to have sales broken down by departments?

4 Have you ever closely observed a modern cash register? What things can it do for firm owners to help them have good accounting information available?

5 What is an accounts receivable ledger? How does it work?

6 What is an accounts payable ledger? How does it work?

7 If you hadn't taken a course in accounting, would this chapter have helped any in understanding basic accounting? Explain.

8 How would you describe a "journal-ledger" accounting system?

9 What types of inventory control system would you recommend for a business firm you would like to own and operate?

10 Are withholding taxes taken from employee salaries an expense to the business or a part of its total salary expense? Explain.

11 Why are attractive supplies important to any business firm?

12 Why can underlying business papers, such as invoices, become important in case of legal involvement?

13 Could you post 18 credit sales and 1 purchase invoice to a system such as outlined in this chapter in 1 hour? Explain.

14 If you had not taken a course in bookkeeping, do you think you could learn to operate a journal-ledger system as outlined here? Explain. How much study would it take?

REFERENCES FOR FURTHER READING

"Keeping Records in Small Business," Small Business Administration Pamphlet No. SMA155.

Niswonger, C. Rollin, and Philip E. Fess, *Accounting Principles,* 12th ed., South-Western Publishing Company, Inc., Cincinnati, Ohio, 1977, chap. 2.

"Recordkeeping Systems—Small Store and Service Trade," Small Business Administration Pamphlet No. SBB15.

WORKSHEETS, FORMAL STATEMENTS, AND CASH FLOW STATEMENTS

Accounting can be fun after you get the worksheet completed. I was so proud of myself when I first achieved that goal. It didn't take long to teach myself, either.

The Late Learner

Experienced bookkeepers can prepare a balance sheet and an income statement directly from the totals of the columns in the journal-ledger. They will make the necessary adjustments in the process. Keeping a worksheet as a permanent record is recommended.

The worksheet has been described as the best friend a bookkeeper ever had. On this one multicolumn sheet there is a complete summary of operations for the period, from a trial balance through the adjustments to the formal statements. A *trial balance* is merely a listing of all accounts in the journal-ledger with their balances.

All accounts in the journal-ledger are listed in the left column. In the first set of dollar columns, the totals of each account are inserted. These are the totals at the bottom of the journal-ledger. If an account has a column for both debits and credits, the difference between these amounts is inserted. This is the *account balance*.

In the second set of columns, adjustments are made to bring the accounts up to date. This usually involves recording the new merchandise inventory, the

329

supplies used, and any depreciation expenses which are to be charged. Other adjustments may be necessary. Actual debits and credits are made to the specific accounts involved.

When the adjustments have been completed, the first and second sets of columns are combined to make an adjusted trial balance. All additions and subtractions are made as we read across the page to the third set of columns.

Completing the worksheet from the adjusted trial balance involves transferring the income statement accounts to the income statement column and the balance sheet accounts to the balance sheet column.

On the completed worksheet shown in Figure 28-1, adjustments were necessary for the following items:

1 New merchandise inventory $3,000
2 Depreciation expense on store fixtures $25
3 New inventory of store supplies $400

Each step in completing the worksheet and the method of preparing statements from it are explained in the following pages.

COMPLETING THE WORKSHEET

Trial Balance Columns

All accounts in the journal-ledger are listed horizontally in that record. Their names are listed vertically on the worksheet. Opposite each account name, insert the totals from the bottom line of the journal-ledger in the trial balance columns. Four of our accounts (cash, accounts receivable, accounts payable, and due to government agencies) had both a debit and a credit column. In these cases, insert the difference between the debits and credits (the account balance) in the trial balance column. Be sure to list the balance on the appropriate side of the trial balance. When all accounts are inserted, add the debits and credits to be sure that the books are in balance.

Where a summary account title has been used, such as Operating Expenses, the trial balance can break the total down into any classification desired. By inspecting the individual items in our Operating Expense column, we have broken the total of $1,975 into: Rent, $200; Employee Salaries, $1,400; Advertising, $200; Delivery Charges, $50; Insurance, $75; and Miscellaneous Expense, $50. The Fixed Assets total of $1,900 has been similarly divided into Store Fixtures, $1,500 and Showcases, $400. If this amount of detail is not desired, only the totals need be used.

Adjusting Entries

Adjusting entries are necessary to update trial balance figures. For example, the Merchandise Inventory account shows a balance of $10,620. But we have an inventory, taken as of October 31, which tells us that the merchandise actually on hand is $3,000. The difference in these two figures must be the cost of the

H. JONES COMPANY
Worksheet
Oct. 31, 1978

Account	Trial Balance Debit	Trial Balance Credit	Adjustments Debit	Adjustments Credit	Adjusted Trial Balance Debit	Adjusted Trial Balance Credit	Income Statement Debit	Income Statement Credit	Balance Sheet Debit	Balance Sheet Credit
Cash	2 800 —				2 800 —				2 800 —	
Accounts Receivable	1 100				1 100 —				1 100 —	
Sales		11 600 —				11 600 —		11 600 —		
Merchandise Purchases	10 620 —			(1) 7 620 —	3 000 —				3 000 —	
Purchase Discounts		20 —				20 —		20 —		
Accounts Payable		2 225 —				2 225 —				2 225 —
Supplies on Hand	550 —			(3) 150 —	400 —				400 —	
Operating Expenses ($1,975)										
Rent	200 —				200 —		200 —			
Employee Salaries	1 400 —				1 400 —		1 400 —			
Advertising	200 —				200 —		200 —			
Delivery Charges	50 —				50 —		50 —			
Insurance	75 —				75 —		75 —			
Miscellaneous Exp.	50 —				50 —		50 —			
Due to Gov't. Agencies	0	0			0 —	0				
Fixed Assets ($1,900)	1 500 —				1 500 —				1 500 —	
Store Fixtures	400 —				400 —				400 —	
Show Cases	400 —			(4) 400 —	0					
H. Jones, Withdrawals			(4) 400 —							
H. Jones, Capital		5 500 —				5 100 —				5 100 —
Cost of Goods Sold			(1) 7 620 —		7 620 —		7 620 —			
Deprec. Exp.-Store Fix.			(2) 25 —		25 —		25 —			
Accum. Deprec-Store Fix.				(2) 25 —		25 —				25 —
Supplies Used			(3) 150 —		150 —		150 —			
	19 345 —	19 345 —	8 195 —	8 195 —	18 970 —	18 970 —	9 770 —	11 620 —	9 200 —	7 350 —
Net profit for month (before income taxes)							1 850 —			1 850 —
							11 620 —	11 620 —	9 200 —	9 200 —

FIGURE 28-1
A completed worksheet.

331

merchandise sold. Therefore, we make an adjusting entry in the second set of columns to take $7,620 out of the merchandise account and put in a new account, Cost of Goods Sold. This new account, and any others needed for the other adjustments, is opened at the bottom of the worksheet, below the Trial Balance totals. It is a debit to Cost of Goods Sold because such expense accounts are increased by debits, and a credit to Merchandise Inventory because assets are decreased with credits. The Merchandise Inventory account now shows a debit balance of $3,000, which is the value of the current inventory. This amount will be carried over to the Adjusted Trial Balance. This adjustment is marked (1) in the Adjustments column.

The second adjusting entry is to record $25 of depreciation expense on the store fixtures. We open a new account, Depreciation Expense—Store Fixtures, and debit it for $25. The credit is to an account entitled Accumulated Depreciation—Store Fixtures for $25. This is technically known as a *minus asset account* and is deducted from the Store Fixtures account on the balance sheet. It is carried across the worksheet as a balance sheet account with a credit balance. This entry is marked (2) in the Adjustments column.

Adjustment (3) is necessary to bring the asset account Supplies up to date. On the trial balance it shows a balance of $550. But we have taken an inventory and know that only $400 of these supplies are still on hand. The difference of $150 represents the supplies used up during the month. Therefore, we credit Supplies on Hand $150 and debit a new expense account, Supplies Used, for $150. This entry reduces the balance of the Supplies on Hand account to $400, which is the value of supplies still in inventory.

Adjustment (4) is to close the owner's withdrawal account into his or her capital account. Withdrawals are not operating expenses but capital reductions. We therefore credit H. Jones, Withdrawals $400, and debit H. Jones, Capital $400. This removes any balance from the Withdrawals account so that no figures need to be carried across the sheet. The debits and credits in the adjustments column are added.

Adjusted Trial Balance

This set of columns is only a total of the first two sets of columns. Unless a debit or credit has been added in the Adjustments column, the same trial balance figure will be carried across to the Adjusted Trial Balance, as illustrated in the case of Cash, Accounts Receivable, and Sales. Merchandise Inventory has a debit in the trial balance for $10,620, but a credit in the Adjustments column for $7,620. The debit balance of $3,000 is accordingly carried over to the Adjusted Trial Balance column. Supplies on Hand has a $550 debit in the trial balance but a $150 credit in the Adjustments column. The difference of $400 is carried over to the Adjusted Trial Balance. Every account, including the new ones opened at the bottom of the Adjustments column, must be carried to the Adjusted Trial Balance.

Income Statement and Balance Sheet Columns

Once the Adjusted Trial Balance is complete, the remainder of the worksheet involves only transferring each account on across the sheet to its appropriate column. All income and expense accounts go into the Income Statement column, and asset, liability, and New Worth (capital) accounts go to the appropriate side of the Balance Sheet columns. When each account has been transferred, the columns should again be added.

Now notice that the difference between the debits and credits in the Income Statement columns ($11,620 less $9,770) is the same as in the Balance Sheet columns ($9,200 less $7,350). This difference ($1,850) is the net profit from operations for the month. Another entry is made below these totals to transfer this profit from the Income Statement to the Balance Sheet, where it will appear as part of the owner's new Capital account balance.

We can now prepare formal statements. Items needed are on the worksheet. Samples taken from the worksheet are shown in Tables 28-1 and 28-2.

To prepare the journal-ledger for the next month's operations insert the balance sheet account balances under the date of November 1.

TABLE 28-1
H. JONES COMPANY
Income Statement
October 1–31, 1981

Gross sales			$12,000
Less sales returns			400
Net sales income			$11,600
Cost of goods sold:			
Inventory, October 1		$2,000	
Purchases during month	$8,620		
Less purchase discounts	20	8,600	
Goods available for sale		$10,600	
Less inventory, October 31		3,000	
Cost of goods sold during month			7,600
Gross margin			$4,000
Operating expenses:			
Rent		$ 200	
Employee salaries		1,400	
Supplies used		150	
Advertising		200	
Delivery charges		50	
Depreciation expense		25	
Insurance expense		75	
Miscellaneous expenses		50	
Total operating expenses			2,150
Net profit from operations before income taxes			$1,850

TABLE 28-2
H. JONES COMPANY
Balance Sheet
October 31, 1981

ASSETS			LIABILITIES		
Current assets:			Current liabilities:		
Cash		$2,800	Accounts payable		$1,925
Accounts receivable		1,100	Contract payable		300
Merchandise inventory		3,000	Total current liabilities		$2,225
Prepaid expenses		400	Fixed liabilities:		
Total current assets		$7,300	None		0
Fixed assets:			Total liabilities		$2,225
Store fixtures	$1,500		NET WORTH		
Less accumulated			H. Jones, Capital		$6,950
Depreciation	25	1,475			
Showcases		400			
Total fixed assets		$1,875	TOTAL LIABILITIES		
TOTAL ASSETS		$9,175	AND NET WORTH		$9,175

CASH FLOW STATEMENTS

Because any firm's cash position is important to its economic health, firm managers should use all tools available to keep abreast of cash flow and current cash position. One of the best of these tools is the *cash flow chart*. It is designed to estimate future cash receipts, outlays, and balances and then compare actual results with the estimate at the end of each month of operations. Careful preparation and use of the chart provide a schedule of cash flow and a ready device for ascertaining whether or not the schedule is being met.

If cash shortages are anticipated, arrangements can be made to meet these shortages. Periods needing expanded credit from the bank, for example, can be anticipated and planned for. If surplus funds are anticipated, arrangements can be made for profitably investing such funds. An estimated cash balance and an actual cash balance at the end of each month is provided.

As Table 28-3 shows the cash flow chart provides two columns for each month. One is for the *planned or estimated* cash receipts, outlays, and balances. The second column provides for inserting at the end of each month the *actual* receipts, outlays, and balances. Disparities between the estimated and actual amounts merit close attention. Adverse trends can be detected early and management decisions can be influenced by studying the results.

The estimated columns should preferably be completed for a year in advance. Great care should be exercised in completing the estimates in each area. Many discrepancies between estimates and actual results are caused by failure to recognize lags in collecting accounts receivable and by failure to recognize all cash outlays.

It should be emphasized that we are dealing here only with actual cash flow.

TABLE 28-3
CASH FLOW STATEMENTS

(The estimated figures (typed) are projected for a full year; the actual figures have been inserted for 3 months only.)

CASH FLOW STATEMENT - MILLER'S AUTO SUPPLY - 1978

	JANUARY Estimated	JANUARY Actual	FEBRUARY Estimated	FEBRUARY Actual	MARCH Estimated	MARCH Actual	APRIL Estimated	APRIL Actual	OMITTED MONTHS	DECEMBER Estimated	DECEMBER Actual	YEARLY TOTALS Estimated	YEARLY TOTALS Actual
1. Cash on Hand, 1st of Month	5000	5,000	3400	3400	2400	2,625	1975	1,900		3700			
2. Cash Receipts During Month													
a. Cash Sales	3000	3,800	3500	4,000	4000	4,205	4000	4,000		8000		72,600	
b. Payments on Accounts Receivable	1800	2,000	2000	2,000	2400	2,195	2400	0		4000	0	32,000	
c. Bank Loans	0	0	0	0	0	0	0	0		0	0	6,000	
d. Other Sources (list)	0	0	0	0	0	0	0	0		0			
3. Total Cash Receipts	4800	5,800	5500	6,000	6400	6,400	6400			12000		110,600	
4. Cash Available During Month	9800	10,800	8900	10,025	8800	9,025	8375			15700			
5. Cash Outlays for Month													
a. For Merchandise	1200	1,500	1200	2,000	1500	1,800	1500			4500		49,000	
b. For Wages & Salaries	3600	3,600	3600	3,600	3600	3,600	3600			4600		31,000	
c. Payroll Expenses	100	105	100	105	100	100	100			150		1,800	
d. Rent	400	405	400	405	400	400	400			400		4,800	
e. Utilities	100	125	100	125	100	155	100			200		1,600	
f. Insurance	50	50	50	50	50	50	50			50		600	
g. Interest	0	0	0	0	0	60	0			0		100	
h. Repairs & Mtce.	100	50	100	100	100	100	100			100		1,000	
i. Advertising	0	200	75	200	100	100	100			200		2,000	
j. Supplies	75	75	75	100	100	200	150			200		2,100	
k. Delivery Expenses	150	150	150	150	150	155	150			250		2,200	
l. Taxes	25	25	25	25	25	25	25			25		300	
m. Misc. Expenses	100	150	200	125	100	200	100			200		1,800	
n. Other Expenses (list)	0	50	0	0	0	0	0			0		300	
Total Misc. & Opr. Exp.	5900	6,475	6000	7,100	6325	6,825	6325			10875		98,600	
Loan Repayments	0	0	0	0	0	0	0			0			
Withdrawals	500	300	500	300	500	300	500			500		6,000	
Equipment Purchases	0	0	0	0	0	0	0			0			
6. Total Cash Paid Out	6400	6,775	6500	7,400	6825	7,125	6825			11375		104,600	
7. Cash Balance End of Month	3400	4,025	2400	2,625	1975	1,900	1550			4325		6,000	

335

Credit sales are not cash receipts. Payments received against accounts receivable are. Bank loans represent cash received. Repayment of such loans are anticipated as a cash outlay. Starting from cash on hand at the beginning of the month, we add all cash received to find cash available during the month. All cash paid out is deducted from this amount to arrive at cash position at end of the month.

Improving cash position by ignoring liabilities and purchase discounts is not recommended. When all liabilities are paid as due and cash flow shows a healthy cash position, the firm has a healthy all-around condition.

QUESTIONS FOR CLASS DISCUSSION

1 How would you describe a cash flow statement?
2 How would a cash flow statement made a year in advance be of value to the owners of a substantial small business?
3 How would you describe the worksheet?
4 Do you think the worksheet can be called "the bookkeeper's best friend"?
5 Where do the figures for the trial balance columns come from?
6 Why are adjusting entries necessary? Give some examples of necessary adjusting entries.
7 Once the adjusted trial balance columns are complete, how does the worksheet proceed?
8 Can you explain why the difference between the debits and credits in the income statement columns and the balance sheet columns is the same?
9 How did Mr. Jones's capital account go from $5,500 to $6,950?
10 On what amount will Mr. Jones pay income taxes for October?
11 Is the entire $1,850 of profits for October still in the business?
12 Can you find every item on the formal income statement and balance sheet in the columns of the worksheet?

REFERENCES FOR FURTHER READING

"Cash Flow in a Small Plant," Small Business Administration Pamphlet No. MA229.
"Keeping Records in Small Business," Small Business Administration Pamphlet No. SMA155.
Niswonger, C. Rollin, and Philip E. Fess, *Accounting Principles,* 12th ed., South-Western Publishing Company, Inc. Cincinnati, Ohio, 1979, chap. 3.

SMALL BUSINESS AND THE LAW

I didn't think my substantial small business would ever need an attorney or a certified accountant until I learned about the vast number of laws and regulations that apply to all small firms. I am glad I was warned in advance.

The Late Learner

No small business management text could include a detailed coverage of all the laws and regulations that apply to small firm operations. In fact, the avalanche of laws and regulations themselves requires many volumes of government documents just to state them. Dealing with regulations and laws is one thing that small and large firms share equally. The universal complaint of small business groups is that their very existence is endangered by the endless numbers of required reports and regulations to which they are subjected. At the White House Conference on Small Business it was pointed out that some of the reports required by law were in violation of other required reports. Compliance with some put the owners in violation of others. These regulations are issued by the federal, state, and local governments. The most recent expansion has come from the endless bureaucracies at all levels of government. Compliance has involved endless costs, time, and legal entanglements. A first objective of President

Reagan's administration was to remove many bureaucratic regulations in order to give business a better chance to devote its energies to making profits and increasing employment and productivity.

Despite the frustration involved with all these regulations, it is important for small firm owners and planners to be familiar with the laws that apply to them, whether they come from national, state, or local government bodies.

Our approach here is to point out the various areas of business management that can involve legal entanglements if not properly handled, and then to review many of the major laws and regulations that apply to large and small firms. In this way it is hoped that small firm owners or planners will recognize when it is necessary to get professional advice and assistance from their attorneys or accountants.

SOME REGULATION OF THE BUSINESS WORLD IS NECESSARY

Most people agree that some regulation of the business world is desirable. As the state exercises its police powers to protect the health, safety, and welfare of its citizens, such laws as regulation of food ingredients, sanitary requirements, and protection against fraudulent or unscrupulous operators are deemed essential. Controlling legal forms of business organizations through corporate laws is generally accepted everywhere. The federal government's power to control exports and imports in the national interest is generally accepted. No one argues with laws to protect business firms and citizens from harm and the destruction or stealing of their property. Compliance with new social legislation of recent years has been accepted by the business world with some reservations since it is recognized as being in the best interests of the nation. We are a nation of laws despite all impressions to the contrary in the 1980s when crime in the streets, arson, and murder are setting all-time records. Tax laws are accepted as essential—the business world asks only for a better cost-benefit ratio for the vast amounts of taxes collected from the business world. Stability of government, the national defense, adequate law enforcement manpower, and tax funds are essential. The business world does object to government waste and meaningless reports and regulations.

THE AREAS OF MANAGEMENT WITH LEGAL IMPLICATIONS

The inexperienced small firm operator may well ask why or when legal knowledge or assistance is necessary. What phases of small firm management involve technical legal knowledge? A list of the many areas in which legal requirements must be met will be helpful to the small firm owner. Some of them are:

Real estate transactions
Payroll procedures and withholding taxes
Obligations under all types of contracts
Preparation of legal documents for use with lending institutions or landlords
Obligations under contracts with suppliers or consumers
Tax laws and their latest changes
Insurance claims
Need for audited statements of the firm
Tort or negligence actions for damages to property
Minimum wage laws and other personnel regulations
Sales contracts
Agency relationships
Branch and subsidiary relationships
Unemployment compensation laws and workers' compensation laws
Collective bargaining agreements
Product liability laws
Purchasing contracts and other types of contracts
Consignment, installation, and open account sales
Local laws governing licenses, competency, zoning, and land uses
Negotiable instrument transactions
Leases of real or personal property
Bankruptcy and insolvency proceedings
Occupational Safety and Health Act (OSHA)
Trademarks, copyrights, and patents
Libel laws and their ramifications
Conflict with social legislation

Before looking at some of the specific laws that apply to all business firms, we should note again that the above list includes only some of the areas with legal implications that the small firm owner should be familiar with. The list is almost endless.

SOME SPECIFIC LAWS AND REGULATIONS APPLICABLE TO SMALL FIRMS

1 Laws Governing Management-Labor Relations Most of the currently effective legislation in this area has been developed since the passage of the National Labor Relations Act of 1935, also known as the Wagner Act since it was named for the then U.S. Senator Robert F. Wagner of New York State. This act and three later ones have since been described as "the four basic laws governing management-labor relations." These laws and their provisions are summarized in Table 29-1. The NLR Act is the legal foundation of collective bargaining.

2 Workers' Compensation Law Every state now has a form of workers' compensation law to protect employees from disabilities incurred on the job and related medical costs. Benefits are usually expressed as a percentage of the regular salary of the injured employee. Burial expenses and family allowances are usually included when employees are killed on the job. Premiums paid by employers vary with the safety records they have developed.

3 Unemployment Compensation These laws exist to protect workers against complete loss of income for a specified period when work is not available. Unlike Social Security, the employees do not contribute to the tax which provides the unemployment funds. This is a combined federal-state

TABLE 29-1 THE FOUR BASIC LAWS GOVERNING MANAGEMENT-LABOR RELATIONS

The National Labor Relations Act of 1935 (Wagner Act)

Key provisions prohibited employers: from interfering with rights of employees to form, join, or assist labor organizations; from dominating or contributing to labor organizations; from discouraging membership by discriminating against union members, or making nonmembership a condition of employment; from refusing to bargain collectively with duly elected representatives of labor; and from discharging employees for filing charges against their employer.

The Labor-Management Relations Act of 1947 (The Taft-Hartley Act)

Key provisions made the union shop illegal; gave the President power to order 90-day "cooling off periods" and to issue injunctions when the national interest was involved in a threatened strike; outlawed jurisdictional strikes, featherbedding, refusal to bargain in good faith, secondary boycotts, and union contributions to political candidates; required union officers to certify that they were not Communists; required labor unions to file financial statements with the Secretary of Labor; allowed employers to sue unions for contract violations; and permitted employers to petition the National Labor Relations Board to conduct elections.

The Labor-Management Reporting and Disclosure Act of 1959 (The Landrum-Griffin Act)

Key provisions provided mechanisms to prevent employer bribing of union officials; strengthened the rules against secondary boycotts; confirmed the union's right not to handle goods of a struck company; required unions to file constitutions and bylaws with the Secretary of Labor; forced unions to publish financial records open to membership review; made union officers more responsible for union finances; made embezzlement of union funds a federal crime; limited loans of unions to officers; and denied convicted felons the right to hold office in unions for five years after release from prison.

The Civil Rights Act of 1964

Key provisions of Title VII of this act prohibit discrimination in employment based on race, religion, national origin, or sex. All employers who engage in interstate commerce and who have 15 or more employees are covered by this law. Title VII also makes provisions for enforcement of the Civil Rights Act.

system and the employer pays taxes based on payrolls to both government bodies.

4 Antidiscrimination Laws In addition to the basic civil rights legislation summarized in Table 29-1, antidiscrimination laws can and do take the form of executive orders from the President. They automatically apply to all firms doing business with the government. All prohibit discrimination by employers, labor organizations, and employment agencies because of race, color, religion, sex, or national origin. The Department of Labor enforces the executive orders.

5 Equal Pay Act of 1963 This particular act is part of the Fair Labor Standards Act. It specifically prohibits discrimination on the basis of sex within any firm for "equal work on jobs the performance of which requires equal skill, effort and responsibility and which are performed under similar working conditions . . .." It has no application to hiring, firing, promoting, or demoting employees. These items are covered in Title VII of the Civil Rights Act (see Table 29-1).

6 The Age Discrimination in Employment Act This is the popularly discussed law that prevents retirement of employees before age 70 if they choose to remain on the job. Workers between the ages of 40 and 70 are also protected against other forms of discrimination.

FIGURE 29-1
Women are holding an increasing number of important positions in both small and large firms.

Randy Matusow

7 The Rehabilitation Act of 1973 This act is designed to protect qualified handicapped people on the job. Federal procurement contracts in excess of $2,500 have a provision requiring the employer to "take affirmative action to employ and advance qualified individuals" who may be handicapped but otherwise capable.

8 Occupational Safety and Health (OSHA) This is the well-known and much maligned OSHA that has been modified since its first passage in 1970. It has stirred great objections in the business world, not because of opposition to safety but because of opposition to some of its rules. It is designed to prevent or reduce industrial accidents, illnesses, and death by establishing and enforcing safety standards. It says that the firm shall "furnish to each of its employees . . . a place of employment which is free from recognized hazards that are causing or are likely to cause death or serious physical harm to employees; and shall comply with occupational safety and health standards promulgated under OSHA."

9 Local Laws Governing Business Firms These laws are not uniform from city to city or from county to county. They cover a multitude of local requirements with which the small firm owner must be familiar. Many licenses are merely revenue producers for the local community. Occupational licenses for beauty parlors, butchers, and morticians are cases in point. Planning and zoning requirements are other examples. Zoning requirements often limit the use of certain premises to specified activities. Setbacks from sidewalks or property lines, square footage requirements, parking requirements, and sign restrictions are other local laws that often apply to business firms.

10 Fair Labor Standards Act This act was first passed in 1938 and is regularly amended by Congress. It is the basic wage and hour law of the country. Its two objectives are (1) to place a floor under the wage rates paid to employees covered, and (2) to provide overtime compensation for hours worked in excess of a standard number of hours in any workweek. It provides rules against oppressive child labor employment and protects females against discrimination in wages.

As this text went to press the minimum hourly wage was $3.35 per hour, with time-and-a-half pay required for all hours worked over 40 hours per week. It was this minimum wage law that caused now-retired General Motors Chairman Thomas A. Murphy to point out its ruinous effect on the hiring of teenagers for summer work. It was his opinion that industry would and could provide thousands of additional summer jobs for teenagers if a lower wage could be paid. This law is administered by the Department of Labor.

11 Employee Retirement Income Security Act of 1974 (ERISA) Abuses in the administration of private firm pension plans in the past, provided the basis for this legislation. President Gerald Ford signed this act into law in 1974. It is popularly referred to as ERISA. It provides for adequate controls over such plans and minimum standards for the operation of all employee benefit plans within its jurisdiction. Such plans are now "vested" so that employees are assured of receiving their benefits when due. The Internal Revenue Service shares administration of ERISA.

12 Consumer Product Safety Act It is clearly established in current law that the seller is responsible for defects in products that cause injury to the customer. The Consumer Product Safety Act is only one of the laws that cover product safety. Others include the Magnuson-Moss Warranty Act; the Federal Food, Drug, and Cosmetic Act; the Wool Products Labeling Act; the Fur Products Labeling Act; and the Flammable Fabrics Act.

13 Federal Trade Commission Regulation of Trade Practices Specific laws have been passed by the federal government governing such trade practices as advertising, pricing policies, credit methods, and sales methods. The Federal Trade Commission is the principal agency responsible for administering these laws. The so-called "truth-in-lending" act is one such law. The Fair Credit Bill Act is another. The Robinson-Patman Act, which prohibits discriminatory pricing, is another. All laws on the books in this area are designed to maintain a competitive society and to protect consumers from unfair practices. Even antitrust laws apply to small firms as well as to large ones.

14 Laws Governing Trademarks, Copyrights, and Patents Many small firms operate with the advantages of trademarks, copyrights, and/or patents on their products. Proper protection and registering of each is very important.

A *trademark* is a word, name, symbol, or device used to distinguish one firm's products from other companies. Examples are Kodak, Coca-Cola, and McGregor. Trademarks and brand names may be registered with the government to protect their exclusive use. Legal life of a trademark depends on continued use. Trademarks are administered by the Patent and Trademark Office of the Department of Commerce.

Copyrights can be secured to protect an owner's exclusive use and distribution of creative work such as literature, music, art, films, and drama. They are effective upon completion of such works. As of January 1, 1978 copyrights provide protection for a term through the life of the author, plus 50 years after his or her death. Anonymous works are protected for 75 years from publication. Copyrights are administered by the Register of Copyrights, Library of Congress, Washington, D.C. 20559.

Patents are designed to stimulate the development and use of new discoveries. Such discoveries protect the owner by issuance of a patent giving him or her exclusive use of the invention for 17 years. The patent may not be renewed after that period.

GOOSEMYER   by parker and wilder

Figure 29-2
Goosemeyer. *(By Parker and Wilder, © 1980 Field Enterprises, Inc. Courtesy of Field Newspaper Syndicate.)*

15   Tax Laws and Withholding Requirements on Employers   The statement of federal tax laws is a full-volume production known as the Internal Revenue Code. It reflects the eternal search for new sources of tax funds by the federal government. It covers all types of taxes from income taxes to property taxes, corporation taxes to sales taxes, payroll taxes to death taxes. We also have *ad valorem* taxes, tangible property taxes, import taxes, capital gains taxes, and many others. It is indeed a keen and capable small business owner who is able to become an authority on all the taxes that may be applicable to the firm. Unique to business firms is the requirement that they must withhold taxes from the paychecks of all employees and send them regularly during the year to the federal government to be applied to the individual employee's federal income tax for the current year. This procedure alone requires extensive bookkeeping expense and equipment. Death taxes and inheritance taxes only prove that if a person manages to accumulate some capital wealth in this life the government wants a share of that, too. Yet, again, the business community recognizes the government's need for revenue to maintain essential and desirable governmental functions. The objections are based only on the waste in government bureaucracies and on the very poor cost/benefit ratio that most government expenditures represent. The disproportionate contributions of all persons to government revenues is also a major concern of many citizens in our society. A serious look at Table 29-2 will reveal the price employers and employees are paying only for the Federal Insurance Contributions Act (FICA). Note that these amounts are paid by both the employer and the employee. It is this tax which finances our social security system.

The social security program is designed to provide financial assistance in old age, survivor's and disability insurance benefits, and hospital insurance (under the Medicare program). The law that governs the provisions of our social security system is the Federal Insurance Contributions Act (FICA). It requires equal payments from both employers and employees, based on a percentage of a basic portion of each employee's salary or wages. Both that percentage and the portion of earnings taxed have increased regularly over recent years. For example, in 1976 the tax was 4.95 percent for social security plus 0.9 percent for hospital insurance, or a total of 5.85 percent on the first $15,300 of earnings. This amount was paid by both employees and employers—a total of 11.7 percent. In 1978 the rate was 6.05 percent, and it applied to $17,700 of earnings. Table 29-2 shows how FICA rates have increased over the years. Workers who are self-employed can provide for their own social security benefits by making one payment based on earnings. Until now, such payments have been higher than the rates for other workers but less than the combined rates for employees and employers.

16 The Endless Reports Demanded by Innumerable Government Bureaus
By far the most serious objections of businesspeople are against the seemingly

TABLE 29-2 PAST AND PROJECTED
FICA PAYMENTS FOR EMPLOYERS
AND EMPLOYEES

Year($)	Percentage	Salary base
1937 *	1%	$ 3,000
1955 +	2	4,200
1975 +	5.85	14,100
1978 +	6.05	17,700
1979 *	6.13	22,900
1980*	6.13	25,900
1981*	6.65	29,700
1982 *	6.70	31,800
1983–1984*	6.70	++
1985 *	7.05	++
1986–1989*	7.15	++
1990–2010*	7.65	++
2011 and up*	7.65	++

*Source: U.S. Department of Health, Education, and Welfare, Social Security Administration, *Social Security Bulletin,* March 1978, pp. 17–18.
+Source: U.S. Bureau of the Census, *Statistical Abstract of the United States: 1977,* 98th ed., Washington, D.C. 1977, p. 326.
++ Subject to automatic increases.

endless requests made for special reports by so many different government units. Even a list of such reports and the bureaus that request them defies our space allotment here. One small firm reported at the White House Conference that it had received a total of 122 requests for special reports on the firm's operations during a single year. Fines and jail terms are threatened to those who do not or cannot comply. In most cases, much time and expense is needed in order to comply. Some reports are inconsistent with those of other bureaus, and compliance with some requests place a person in legal jeopardy with other bureaus. These requests for regulatory reports deal with energy, ecology, personnel composition, financial details, compliance with special laws, special reports for different branches of the Department of Health, Education, and Welfare (HEW) and its successor, and almost any other phase of business imaginable. While the federal government is the chief offender here, some states also have carried this practice to the point of rousing serious objections from the business community.

17   The Uniform Commercial Code—the Basic Law of the Business World
All business firms operate within the many provisions of the Uniform Commercial Code. This highly significant uniform code was developed in our country in the 1950s. It has now been adopted by almost every state in the union. It replaced several independent laws developed to govern particular segments of business transactions. Before its passage we had a separate set of laws governing sales, another governing agency, another governing negotiable instruments, etc. But the uniform code has provided in a single code the basic rules of law governing basic types of daily business transactions. It has specific provisions in such areas as contracts, sales, agency rights and obligations, commercial paper, other negotiable instruments, bank deposits, collections, letters of credit, bulk transfers, documents of title, investment security, chattel paper, and sales of account. Its basic provisions should be known to every owner of a small firm. It is available in all libraries and most bookstores.

SUMMARY

This brief survey of the matter of small business and the law could easily discourage new firm planners. Hopefully, it will not. But it should be clear that compliance with the many laws and regulations in effect demands professional assistance, at least in the stage of setting up compliance procedures. Owners cannot afford the time to meet all regulatory needs. Fortunately, professional assistance is easily available from the firm's accountants. Every small firm should also have a capable attorney available on a retainer basis, or, at least, definitely available when needed.

REFERENCES FOR FURTHER READING

Broom, H. N., and J. G. Longenecker, *Small Business Management*, 5th ed., South-Western Publishing Company, Inc., Cincinnati, Ohio, 1979, chap. 24.
Corley, Robert N., Robert Black, and O. Lee Reed, *The Legal Environment of Business*, 5th ed., McGraw-Hill Book Company, New York, 1981, chaps. 7 and 8.
Wyatt, John W., and Madie B. Wyatt, *Business Law: Principles and Cases*, 6th ed., McGraw-Hill Book Company, New York, 1979, chaps. 4, 15, 19.

DAY-TO-DAY MANAGEMENT
OF THE ONGOING
BUSINESS FIRM

Why should I worry about all those facts you can gather about past operations? I know that all I have to do to increase profits is sell more merchandise. And I don't pretend to be able to predict the future.

The Late Learner

Day-to-day management of any successful business demands that the owners have available data of all types which become the basis for making current decisions. The gathering of those data can be a time-consuming and expensive process, yet its importance cannot be exaggerated. Fortunately, today's developments in minicomputers and other electronic data processing techniques have made that data-gathering process available to and economical for many small firms which never suspected they could afford such "luxuries." In fact, true cost reductions are available in most cases of successful firms with a growth record.

There are a number of ways to gather the information necessary to run a business. Chapter 25 dealt with the various electronic data services now available to speed the gathering of those data. This chapter deals with the various types of information that entrepreneurs need in daily management.

It is appropriate in this final chapter that we take a look at the small firm owner's activities as daily decisions are made governing the total operations of the business. The dynamics of the business world call for decision making almost every day. Problems arise, priorities change, policies are questioned, market developments arise, and countless other things call for the exercise of judgment in arriving at sound management decisions. The "management of change" is often a daily process.

Experience is a great developer of wisdom. Experienced firm owners carry many facts in their heads, facts which help them make decisions on new developments, as well as facts governing daily operations. Owners with less experience should seek to learn key facts about the firm and the industry or about the total business scene in which operations exist. Better judgment will result.

If each step in a good planning procedure has been thoroughly completed, much time and effort has been expended. After the firm has begun operations, the owner cannot rely upon any automatic accomplishment of the firm's objectives. Management must keep itself aware of key items that affect or may affect the firm's welfare. The basic management function of control demands regular analysis of operational results involving all phases of the activities of the firm, as well as analysis of outside factors that may have an influence on operations.

The individual small firm owner must normally assume a wider responsibility for this management control than does the head of a particular division of a very large firm. In fact, this difference in total responsibility has caused many learned business authorities to say that more ability is needed to be a manager of a substantial small firm than to be a specialized vice president of a very large firm. For example, the vice president for finance of a large automobile manufacturing firm is responsible only for keeping advised on matters of finance. These would include cash flow, current cash position, advice on security markets, capital structures of the firm, financial ratios, dividend capability and policy, anticipated cash demands, and so on. The vice president for marketing is responsible for decisions and recommendations only in the area of marketing and distribution activities of the firm. The vice president for manufacturing handles problems of production and production schedules. Each of these senior executives carries heavy responsibilities, but each is concerned with only one general area of the total firm activities.

These duties and many more must usually be the responsibility of the small firm owner. Every phase of the business is the owner's responsibility. He or she must be concerned with matters of daily sales, personnel, inventory control, supply sources, credit policies, new products, policy changes, market studies, public relations, advertising, location and site reviews, balance sheet data, income statement relationships, economic trends, all financial details, and many other things. The owner's duties can call for the management of change as well as the effective control of established procedures.

It is a long-established truism in management that early detection of adverse developments provides speedier correction of them and thus involves a minimum loss of efficiency. With so many areas to control, it is obvious that the demands upon the small firm owner are most significant and time-consuming. Yet effective managerial control is essential.

TIME DEMANDS VERSUS ACHIEVING MANAGEMENT CONTROL

It should be recognized that the time demands upon the owner in conducting normal operations may be so great that time for gathering data and analyzing key controls may necessarily become overtime hours. We have all seen many small firms where the presence of the owner is a key part of the business. Fine restaurants often build their image around a well-known proprietor. Customers come to see and be greeted by the owner, and perhaps to have a visit with the owner at their table. If the owner is not available, the customers lose a good deal of the image they have of the firm and their desire to patronize the restaurant lessens.

If this owner is also one who wants to be at the produce market at five in the morning to pick out the freshest vegetables and fruits for the kitchen, even more time is consumed in normal operations. All these demands mean that analysis time for management control of the firm is further limited. Analysis must be performed when the business is not open to customers, probably very late in the evening.

Small firm owners have another problem in that most small firms cannot afford to hire personnel purely to study operational results. As firms grow larger, more delegation of authority becomes essential. If department heads have been appointed or a full-time bookkeeper employed, these people can be most helpful in getting information to the owner to assist in control analyses. The drugstore organization chart studied in Chapter 21 shows that the owner-manager could call upon three department managers and an accountant to supply much data on current operations. Many small drugstores do not have this degree of organization because the volume of business is too small to allow it. In such cases the entire responsibility for accumulating data for analysis falls upon the owner.

ESSENTIAL DATA FOR EFFECTIVE ONGOING CONTROL

Interviews with many successful small firm owners reveal that they usually divide their management information into two categories: (1) data which they analyze daily, weekly, or monthly, and (2) long-range data which they check less often or whenever the occasion presents itself.

In the first category they include:

1 Sales data and trends
2 Production records
3 Cash position and cash flow outlook

4 Inventory data and need for adjustments
5 Analysis of the accounts receivable ledger
6 Policy violations and need for change
7 Price policy questions which may have arisen
8 Effectiveness of procedures against shoplifting and theft
9 Suggested new products or new lines
10 Weekly results compared with weekly break-even chart
11 Public-relations effectiveness

In the second category they include:

1 Adequacy of accounting data
2 Personnel policies
3 Outlook for expanding or contracting operations (These aspects of planning and forecasting are a continuing concern at all times.)
4 Effective measures in adjusting to seasonal variations
5 Review of lease arrangements
6 Review of location and site values
7 Possible changes in legal form of organization
8 Additional asset needs that might improve efficiency
9 Adequacy of risk coverage
10 Efficiency in purchasing and possible new sources of supply
11 Study of broader economic data and local developments that might affect expectations for the firm

The priorities given to the various items on any owner's list will vary with the other demands upon his or her time and the circumstances of the particular firm. For example, a small private water company would not need to check income records often. A restaurant would need these data almost daily. A small department store would need regular data at least weekly on a new department that just opened. Owners would be more concerned with inventory movement and inventory control in style goods departments.

USE OF DATA

It is one thing to gather the management data to which we have referred in the preceding paragraphs; it is quite another to use those data in making day-to-day decisions for the firm. It took considerable time for the author to recover from the shock of hearing a small firm proprietor say, "Why collect all of those facts? They are history and you can't change them now." He was exactly like The Late Learner quoted at the beginning of this chapter. Many college students and experienced operators realize that business history is studied to make improvements in efficiency for the future. We can take a brief look here at each of the items on our data lists to indicate when a management decision might be appropriate.

Data Analyzed Daily, Weekly, or Monthly

Sales Data and Trends If sales are increasing steadily and are in accordance with budgeted income statement plans, they can be looked upon with pleasure. If they are increasing faster than had been expected, that fact may call for a look at inventory adequacy to support the increased sales volume. If sales are dropping below expectations, the owner should find out why, in what departments, in what lines, or if the decline is general. Decisions to be made would involve how to reverse the trend. Would more advertising help? Has advertising been effective? Have we measured that effectiveness? Is the market changing so that total purchasing power in our market will remain lower? When did this trend start? Are there any other reasons for it?

Production Records If the factory was expected to produce 5,000 units of the product in September and only 4,000 were finished, decisions must be made to correct the problems. The problems may involve inefficient use of new machines, inefficient employees, faulty maintenance, absenteeism, labor turnover, training methods, or other things. Management must find the reasons and make decisions to prevent repetition. Perhaps it was only a matter of poor timing of employee vacations.

Cash Position and Cash Flow Outlook Management's concern is with providing assurance that obligations of the firm can be paid on time—within the discount period if discounts are offered. We have seen the trouble that can result when the cash position is inadequate. Very few small firms have complete cash flow statements (Chapter 28), but experienced small firm owners have a pretty good idea of what cash receipts to expect in the immediate future. If it is found that the cash position is really hurting, the reasons for it must be found. Perhaps it is slow collection of receivables. Is a campaign to collect delinquent accounts appropriate? It may be the purchase of enlarged inventories to take advantage of special buys. If so, should we arrange an additional line of credit to carry the firm until that inventory is sold and funds replenished?

Inventory Data and Need for Adjustments Where departmentalization of a firm is established, inventories must be checked by departments and/or particular lines of merchandise. If sales are up, is the inventory adequate to support sales in each department and in each line? If sales are down, is the decline general or confined to specific departments? It is dangerous to order general inventory reductions if the sales variations are limited to certain departments. When sales are off for a particular department, the inventory of that department may need reduction. When requests for items not carried in the inventory have been received a few times, a decision to add such items to the inventory may be appropriate.

Analysis of Accounts Receivable Ledger Even if the firm does not have a cash position problem, it should still make a regular analysis of its total accounts receivable. This will reveal which customers are getting behind in their payments and suggest caution in further credit to some customers. An aging of accounts receivable (Chapter 19) is a regularly used current management device. Decisions which may result from its analysis may include a new campaign to collect delinquent accounts, cutting off credit for certain customers, a policy of expanding credit more widely if the accounts receivable turnover is more than 12 times a year on 30-day credit, terminating open accounts, and resorting only to cash and credit-card sales. Without the facts, any needed corrective action cannot be taken.

Policy Violations and Need for Change If it is found that there is public objection to some of the policies of the firm, a management decision to change certain policies may be called for. For example, a grocer has a policy of selling all soft drinks only in nonreturnable bottles. Public resentment is great, and some customers actually change patronage to other stores for this single reason. Decision: Bring back returnable bottles to shelves and change the policy decision against their use. Advertise the new policy change.

Price Policy Questions That May Have Arisen It may be found that customers are being driven away because the firm is selling one or two specific items a few cents higher than the competitor down the street. Should we lower those prices? Do we value that type of customer? Is the item purchased in isolation or as part of larger orders? A decision is important. Another possible decision might be to clean out slow-moving inventory of certain items at special prices, or even as loss leaders via obstacle-course displays.

Effectiveness of Procedures against Shoplifting and Theft This problem never ends, and the alert merchant is always looking for evidence of the effectiveness of procedures to combat both shoplifting by outsiders and employee thefts. Whenever an incident of this nature is discovered, a new look at established procedures is appropriate to see if greater effectiveness can be achieved.

Suggested New Products or New Lines Most merchants keep a record of calls for merchandise which they do not carry. Not all such calls merit adding the item involved. But if such requests are repeated, a decision is appropriate on the advisability of adding those goods to the inventory. If the firm sells dresses in two price lines or in two brands and receives numbers of requests for another price line or another brand, this may suggest that the inventory should be expanded to include them. This might be an indication that an original policy was not suited to the particular market and should possibly be changed.

Coincidence of Weekly Results with the Break-Even Chart If an accurate break-even chart has been divided into weekly, monthly, and quarterly periods as well as the annual measure of income-expense relationships, the manager-owner will always have in mind a sales total that will reveal whether sales for any period have placed the operation in the profit area. Many small firm owners have such a figure in mind even without formal break-even charts. This is why they can tell you, "This was a good week," or a good month, or even a good day.

Public Relations Effectiveness   Measures of good or bad public relations may appear at any time during any business day, or even at a social gathering. Compliments may be received over participation in a community project, a special service rendered, support of a good cause, or innumerable other things. Likewise, complaints may be received. A manager notes both compliments and complaints to measure total effectiveness and to help govern future decisions on public-relations activities.

We have taken this brief look at some of the key data managers must have at their fingertips to help in the many decisions they are regularly called upon to make. These were the priorities included in the first category of data we mentioned. Not all owners will agree with this division of priorities, but none will disagree with the importance of each item on the list. Any owner having all this key information readily available will make better decisions for the welfare of the firm.

Data to be Checked Occasionally

Adequacy of Accounting Data   If an owner is often faced with a decision requiring accounting data that is not readily available, the decision to add financial analysis to the present accounting records will usually be forthcoming. A decision to request a bank loan which demands supporting data on cash flow would be an example of this. Total accounting value involves more than routinely recording operations and preparing the basic statements at the end of a fiscal period. Daily decisions on matters such as the ability to make an attractive purchase may be dependent upon basic accounting facts. Expansion plans cannot be properly judged without detailed accounting data. Daily decisions are enhanced by analytical accounting information. There is no uniformity of accounting adequacy for all firms. Each owner must decide the extent to which he or she needs details to govern daily operations.

Personnel Policies   Excessive absenteeism and labor turnover are usually signs that something is wrong with the personnel policies of the firm. If unskilled labor requiring little training is being utilized, labor turnover is not as serious as absenteeism, as long as replacements are always available. The public image of the firm, however, is adversely affected by either excessive absenteeism or labor turnover. When these facts are true of the firm, a serious look at policies in effect is called for. Excessive absenteeism requires investigation into its causes, its legitimacy, and its incidence for particular employees. Because of their greater dependence upon fewer employees, small firms are usually less able than larger ones to absorb absenteeism. The ability of workers to fill in for absentees is usually severely limited in the small firm. For example, if two salespersons are handling the retail counter, one person would find it extremely difficult to serve all the customers. It is true that good organization should always anticipate replacements in any position, but opportunities to do so successfully are fewer in a small firm. After reviewing the facts of any personnel problem, it may be decided that certain persons must be terminated. Salaries may justify review to cope with the problem. Personal conflicts between employees may be uncovered, or other measures may be necessary. The important thing is that the manager know the facts and speedily apply corrective action.

Outlook for Expansion or Contraction of Operations Not all small firm owners want to expand, even if the possibilities for profit exist. Many are satisfied to keep the business at its present level. The optimists and true entrepreneurs (venture managers) are always looking for profitable ways to expand the firm to become an ever-enlarging part of the total scene in their industry. Basic planning and forecasting are continuous activities. Contracting operations is sometimes dictated by the facts of recent firm history. Market changes and market opportunities represent the kinds of facts needed to make the proper decisions about expansion. That is why the efficient manager wants to keep informed on total markets, competition, available locations, detailed costs, and financing possibilities to support any necessary decisions. These are truly long-range considerations, yet they can be of utmost importance to the eventual welfare of the firm.

Adjusting to Seasonal Variations It is most important to have a clear picture of just how important seasonal variations have been in the firm's recent history. Management decisions must then be made concerning the inevitability of these variations and whether they can be evened out through special sales, production policies, or other devices. Changes in buying policies, employee vacation schedules, part-time employment, and even inventory control may be indicated. Nothing can be done authoritatively, however, without detailed facts upon which to base those decisions.

Review of Lease Arrangements Most retailers and many manufacturers lease their business facilities. As a result, the continuation of the business at a particular location is dependent upon renewal of the rental lease. It is very sad to see a successful small firm forced to move only because of its inability to renew its lease at prices the firm can afford. Options for renewal may be written into an existing lease. Percentage leases (a flat rental charge plus a percentage of sales over a stated amount) provide additional rental income for landlords if business sales exceed normally expected totals. Effective management always has one eye on this matter, looks for options, and tries to ensure continued favorable locations for the firm's operations.

Review of Location and Site Values   Just as the least terms are important, so is a review of the value of an existing location and site. Those firms which rent their facilities have the advantage of not being forced to remain in an unfavorable location if that location is losing its true value. When the current lease expires, the owners may not want to renew it because they have found a more favorable location at the right price.

Possible Change in Legal Form of the Firm   With all the new legislation by the federal government designed to assist small firms, it is important that the owner know of these opportunities. Such possibilities as forming a Subchapter S corporation or a 1244 corporation merit serious attention. We covered details about these corporations in Chapter 7.

Additional Asset Needs   Experience in operations may often suggest that a new piece of equipment, a new showcase, a different type of cash register, or other assets would materially improve the efficiency of the firm. Daily observation of procedures will clarify such needs and indicate which acquisitions are necessary.

Adequacy of Risk Coverage   The eternal problem of risks and how best to cope with them must be continually under review. New types of insurance protection appear often. The manager may see that the incidence of loss from certain types of risk has increased and now demands insurance coverage, whereas in the past the firm had relied upon good management to absorb that risk. The limits of public liability insurance that the firm carries may be found inadequate, and a decision to increase such coverage may be in order. New features, such as those that cover inventory losses, are often written into some insurance policies. Costs and protection may be affected. Fidelity and surety bonds may become appropriate, even though they had previously been deemed unnecessary. Minimum losses in some areas of risk may suggest that they be coped with only by good management in the future. The facts of current operations will supply details to justify any appropriate decisions.

Efficiency in Purchasing and Need for New Sources   Study of results may reveal lapsed discounts, availability of new sources at better prices and improved quality, better transportation arrangements, or better terms of sale. These matters must also be noted by managers as they make decisions for the ongoing firm.

Economic Data and Local Developments   All the information available about general business trends nationally, regionally, and locally should be a concern of management. Trade associations, chambers of commerce, daily newspapers, and business periodicals are all sources of such information. A manager's ability to make decisions on the basis of such data may have a great effect on the firm's welfare. Changing styles, decreased purchasing power in the area, new plant developments and new payrolls, trends in population growth, and changes in buying habits are some of the items in this category. It behooves efficient managers to keep themselves apprised of as much information as possible on these matters.

SUMMARY

We have approached the subject of managing the ongoing firm from the standpoint of the key data which must be readily available to the manager and how the manager should use that information. It is hoped that this approach has given the student an appreciation of the many duties that fall upon managers' shoulders and how they prepare themselves to make the proper decisions. With all the planning and operating details we have covered in this text, we feel sure that new small firm owners who have studied with us will be better qualified as successful managers.

PART SEVEN

CASE STUDIES

CUSTOMER RELATIONS HAS MANY RAMIFICATIONS

Mrs. Royer's husband operated a small independent bakery in their hometown of 50,000 people. Mrs. Royer often worked with him during the rush hours. The bakery had been very successful in competing with the larger bakeries. His breads, cakes, and pastries were popular with everyone who tried them, and the bakery had consistently made a good profit for many years.

As small firm owners, the Royers encouraged patronage of small firms by all of their friends. They made their own purchases at small firms whenever possible. They truly believed that a prosperous small business community was in the best interests of the people.

One of their friends was the proprietor of a small independent paint store located two blocks from the bakery. They had made intermittent purchases of paints, brushes, wallpaper, and allied products there for many years. Service was usually very good. But one day Mrs. Royer stopped by to purchase an additional quart of red cement paint. They had used a full gallon to paint a back porch landing but needed just a bit more to finish one corner.

The first time she stopped at the store she found it was closed at 2:00 P.M., contrary to the business hours posted in the front window. The second time she stopped by she was stopped at the door with an explanation that a robbery had just occurred in the store and that the police were inside investigating. The third time she returned she asked for a quart can of the same paint. She was advised by a new clerk that they carried this particular paint only in gallon sizes and, therefore, she couldn't buy just one quart. When she said, "I'm surprised that you don't have quart cans," the clerk replied with a smirk, "So, you're surprised," and turned away to prepare another order for delivery.

Mrs. Royer felt deeply offended. She then went to another paint store which was a serious competitor of the one she had patronized for so long. As a stranger in the store, she was greeted warmly. She explained her desire to get one quart of this particular brand of red cement paint. The clerk there said, "We don't carry this paint in quarts but we will get one at the wholesale house this afternoon and deliver it to your house later today."

Quite happy to be assured that her needs were now taken care of, Mrs. Royer returned to the bakery. But she was most upset at the treatment received from the first store which she had patronized for so long. She recited all the details to her husband. Together they decided that the customer relations of their friend's store needed some attention.

What would be your reaction to this situation and what action would you take? Would you advise the owner of the incident? Would you return to the store as a customer? What does the term "customer relations" mean to you? What violations of good customer relations do you observe in this case?

ARE INDEPENDENT GROCERS DOOMED?

Bill Hafner was a proud man who established his own independent grocery store 30 years ago. In its early years it faced tough competition from many similar independent grocers who seemed to be located every few blocks from his location. Each provided all of the usual services of the neighborhood grocer in those days—delivery service, sales on open account, and personal counter service by competent clerks. Customers could call in their orders and have their groceries, fruit, meats, and produce delivered on either the 10:00 A.M. or the 4:00 P.M. delivery. Most payrolls were paid on the first of the month when he started, and customers often brought their paychecks to the store for cashing and payment of their monthly credit charges from the store. It was traditional for the owner to "send home a bag of candy for the children" free of charge when the accounts were paid each month, as a gesture of patronage appreciation.

Almost from the beginning Hafner made a good profit with his store. He was always among the first in the wholesale produce markets early in the morning. He picked the best products and proudly displayed them for the pleasure and purchase of his customers. Fresh bread and other bakery products were delivered to the store each morning. He carried various lines of canned goods, always including the nationally advertised brands and a lesser-known brand which was lower priced. He hired his own butchers and insisted upon good quality meats. They always had a free bone for the customer's dog.

He had a separate tobacco counter, a candy counter where young children could pick out their choices of penny items, and a long counter where customers could designate their purchases to the clerk either to take along or to be delivered.

During the past 20 years, Mr. Hafner has seen one after another of his independent grocer competitors go out of business. In most cases the buildings they had used were not purchased by other grocers but were turned into bicycle repair shops, garages, sewing goods shops, barber shops, or just torn down and the property converted to other uses.

The predominating factor in all of these closings was the complaint that the independent grocer could no longer compete with the ever-expanding chain grocery stores. Mr. Hafner watched these developments with a great deal of concern. He noticed that he was losing some of his customers to the new chain store competition. He also noticed, however, that he was picking up about as many customers from his former competitors who still wanted the special services which he rendered and which the chain stores did not. He read that several midwestern states, as a device to assist independent merchants in meeting their chain store competition, actually passed laws to prohibit stores from using "loss leaders." The chain stores sold for cash only, did not provide a free delivery service, and all customers were obliged to go around the store with a cart to pick up their purchases and then go through a cashier's line to check out their total and make payment.

Some of these developments were very new at that time, and some skepticism existed among remaining independent grocers that the idea would ever catch on with the American public.

After 5 years of the growing chain store competitions, Mr. Hafner found that his sales had held steady or increased each year. But now he faced retirement and hoped that his son would take over.

Among Mr. Hafner's employees was his only son, Jerry. Jerry had worked throughout his school years and had continued with his father into his middle 20s. Jerry wanted to have his own store, but a different kind of store from his father's, and still different from the large chain stores. He had in mind a convenience store that did not extend credit, did not have delivery service, and did not always carry the most expensive kinds of merchandise. He would have prepackaged meat and produce. His father was against the idea. However, he wanted to encourage Jerry to go out on his own and do his own thing. He had always hoped that the present store would be maintained under its present operation, with Jerry as its owner.

1 What would your advice be to Jerry?

2 Could Jerry be successful operating the store as his father had for so many years?

3 Do you think that the independent full-service grocery has a future?

INADEQUATE INVESTOR CAPITAL

ALL THAT GLITTERS IS NOT GOLD

Maxie Stein was a personable young man who graduated from a good business school with a major in management. He always felt that the principles of conservative financing he learned about in his business courses were just too restrictive.

Maxie was particularly critical of such ratios in an opening day balance sheet as a 50 percent proprietorship ratio; he didn't believe in paying a credit-card company 5 percent of his credit sales, even if doing so guaranteed him full payment of the balances by the fifth of the following month; and he had been told that it is foolish to invest too much of your own money in your business because it is difficult for owners to withdraw money from the business.

After working for another firm for 5 years to gain business experience, Maxie opened his own small department store. He didn't think it wise to pay incorporation fees, so he decided to operate as a proprietorship. Following his convictions about business, he prepared the opening day balance sheet in Table C3-1.

Maxie was smart enough to employ an accounting firm to keep his records and give him annual financial statements, but he instructed the accountant not to charge off any depreciation on the fixed assets because "after all, we don't write checks to anyone for that kind of expense."

TABLE C3-1
STEIN'S DEPARTMENT STORE
Opening Day Balance Sheet
January 1, 1977

Current assets:		
Cash	$ 5,000	
Merchandise inventory	10,000	
Prepaid supplies	1,000	
Total current assets		$16,000
Fixed assets:		
Store equipment	$ 8,000	
Office furniture and fixtures	2,000	
Delivery truck	3,500	
Total fixed assets		$13,500
Total assets		$29,500

Current liabilities:		
Accounts payable		
(for inventory)		$ 8,000
Fixed liabilities		
Notes payable		16,500
Total liabilities		$24,500
Net worth		
M. Stein, proprietorship		$ 5,000
Total liabilities and net worth		$29,500

From the day he opened the business, sales exceeded his planned sales volume. Maxie was careful about taking money from the business for himself and restricted himself to $100 per week to cover his own expenses.

The accountant prepared the annual income statement and balance sheet each year. In his optimism that he had proved his points about financing, Maxie looked only at the net profits from operation figure at the bottom of the income statement. During the first 4 years of operation the income statements showed that he had averaged net profits from operations somewhat in excess of $16,000 per year.

Maxie became conscious of an inability to take advantage of good inventory purchase deals in the third and fourth years. He borrowed $5,000 from the local bank to improve his cash position. He made regular payments on the long-term note with which he had started the business, but he was later forced to borrow $5,000 from his father to meet current obligations.

When he received his annual statements at the end of the fourth year, Maxie was furious. His balance sheet for this year is shown in Table C3-2.

Maxie made an appointment with his accountant for the next morning. He questioned the accountant's ability and accused him of being responsible for the fact that Maxie's vendors now sold him c.o.d. only and were pressing him for payment on his outstanding balances to them, for the fact that the bank was pressing him for payments on the bank loan, and for the fact that he was not able to keep his inventory up to date or large enough to support his declining sales volume.

Some of Maxie's specific questions included the following:

1 How is it possible that the firm could have earned more than $64,000 in 4 years and still be in such poor financial condition?

2 Where are those profits now? I only took out $100 per week.

3 Can I get a refund on the income taxes I paid because of my financial situation now? After all, I paid my income taxes with company checks.

4 Are those income statements correct for the first 4 years of operation? How can they be?

If you were the accountant, how would you explain the situation to Maxie? Can you explain where most of the profits have gone?

TABLE C3-2

STEIN'S DEPARTMENT STORE

Balance Sheet

January 1, 1981

Current assets:			Current liabilities:		
Cash	$ 200		Accounts payable	$17,000	
Accounts receivable	23,500		Note payable, bank	5,000	
Merchandise inventory	6,000				
Supplies on hand	200		Fixed liabilities:		
Total current assets		$29,900	Note payable		
			(original loan)	$10,000	
Fixed assets:			Note payable (father)	5,000	
Store equipment	$ 8,000		Total liabilities		$37,000
Office furniture and fixtures	2,000				
Delivery truck	3,500		Net worth:		
Total fixed assets		$13,500	M. Stein, proprietorship		$ 6,400
Total assets		$43,400	Total liabilities and net worth		$43,400

ADMINISTRATIVE PROBLEMS: PERSONNEL MANAGEMENT

A GOOD MARKET DOES NOT ASSURE SUCCESS

After the Vietnam war three young veterans were looking for a business in which to invest their savings and at the same time give themselves good jobs. All had good business experience and some college training. One was a personable sales type, one a factory supervisor type, and the third a good accountant and office manager. They greatly desired to own a business and preferred to make a product rather than own a retailing outlet.

While investigating possibilities in the orange country of California, they had a meeting with several growers of oranges and other fruits and vegetables. The growers liked the three young men and indicated the great need in their area for a factory which would manufacture crates in which to ship produce. They offered assistance in making a market survey of the reasonable demand for crates and even showed the veterans a small warehouse which could be used for setting up such a plant. The building was available on a long-term lease at a price which seemed reasonable.

The three men liked the idea, investigated the total costs, and found they could finance the business with their joint savings and a small amount of help from their families. They then went to work to get the business going.

The market survey, the growers practically assured them, showed that a total of 1,200,000 crates annually was a minimum they could sell. Only two types of crates were involved. Of the total, 75 percent would be one type, 25 percent the second type. But the seasonal variation in the demand for the crates was immediately noticed by the factory man. The total demand was broken down into months as follows:

January	200,000 crates
February	80,000
March	70,000
April	60,000
May	50,000
June	50,000
July	50,000
August	60,000
September	60,000
October	70,000
November	200,000
December	250,000
Total	1,200,000 crates

Obviously the demand called for five times as many crates in December as in the slack months of the summer. The proportion between the two types of crates stayed the same throughout the year.

When they purchased the necessary machines, work tables, and tools they found that their building could only handle enough of this production equipment to produce an average of 4,600 boxes per day, or a total of 1,150,000 in the 250-day work year. To cope with this shortage from the 1,200,000 sales expected, the owners decided that they would request all factory employees to work Saturdays and Sundays for 7 weekends in September and October to provide the extra 50,000 crates with an average of only 3,571 crates per day.

Fortunately the factory opened in June during the lighter demand season. The owners hired 8 supervisors and 24 bench workers from local employment agencies. Some workers needed training, which the owners were able to provide as on-the-job training. Hirees with the most experience were made supervisors when first employed.

Things went very well, profits were good, and the employees increased their efficiency to the point that the planned average daily production was approached. Each owner applied his special talent in selling, factory operations, and general management.

They easily filled orders and built up an inventory of crates on hand. This inventory began to be a problem almost immediately because of the lack of warehouse space.

When the 7 overtime weekends were announced, the owners had no idea the supervisors would not cooperate 100 percent. The bench workers were to receive time and a half, but the supervisors were expected to work without extra pay because they were management employees. This meant that for those 14 days the bench workers earned just about as much as the supervisors. Supervisors received monthly salaries, the workers hourly rates.

The first weekend only four supervisors showed up for work, and production fell off significantly. The owners talked to each supervisor the next week and advised them that strict action would be taken if they failed to show up the next weekend. The next weekend five supervisors showed up, but two who had been there before didn't report. Inventory was also very high by this time in anticipation of the very heavy November, December, and January demand. Crates were stored in every available spot. Even the loading docks and empty truck bodies were filled with crates. Rafter space was used. No other warehouse space was available in the town.

The three owners decided on Sunday afternoon to have a meeting to solve the two problems of employee dissatisfaction and storage space.

How would you advise them to solve these problems?

OPERATING EXPENSE ANALYSIS

HOW FAR DO YOU GO WITH STATISTICS?

Ms. Lucille Schwartz and Ms. Olga Olsen started a beauty supply business 8 years ago. Ms. Olsen handled public relations and concentrated on the sales end of the business. Ms. Schwartz was the businessperson who watched after the profits and losses and internal management of the firm. From the beginning they were very successful. They incorporated the firm and charged generous salaries for themselves to corporate expense. They divided the outstanding stock equally. Their commercial bank held a line of credit open for them, but they rarely used it. They paid their bills promptly and took advantage of all sales discounts offered by their suppliers.

Their income statement for the eighth year of operation was in line with the previous years and was as follows:

SCHWARTZ AND OLSEN
Condensed Income Statement
Year Ended December 31, 1981

Net sales	$936,000
Cost of goods sold	702,000
Gross margin	$234,000
Operating expenses	171,600
Net profits from operations	$ 62,400

Ms. Olsen was delighted when the accountant delivered the report for the year. Ms. Schwartz, however, felt that the profits should be higher, even though she recognized that both owners had been paid good salaries, which were included in the expenses.

She asked the accountant to prepare a break-even chart for the firm. It showed that their break-even sales volume was far below their present sales volume. But Ms. Schwartz didn't like making deductions from those lines of the chart, so she set about to study the operational figures with good, plain seventh-grade arithmetic.

She took each figure on the annual income statement and divided it by 52 to find the weekly results. She then divided those weekly figures by 6 to find the average daily results. She produced the following table to show Ms. Olsen.

	Yearly	Weekly	Daily average
Sales	$936,000	$18,000	$3,000
Cost of goods sold	702,000	13,500	2,250
Gross margin	$234,000	$ 4,500	$ 750
Operating expenses	171,600	3,300	550
Net profit from operations	$ 62,400	$ 1,200	$ 200

She showed this table to Ms. Olsen, whose reaction was, "Isn't that nice. We're making an average of $200 per day over and above our salaries. What an excellent return on our modest investment."

Ms. Schwartz wasn't satisfied yet. She decided to compare average daily sales with average daily margin and average daily expenses. She spent hours on the past records to find the daily average sales for each day of the week. She then computed the 25 percent average markup on average daily sales and compared these figures with the average daily expenses. She then produced the following table.

	Average daily sales	Average daily gross margin—25%	Average daily expenses
Monday	$ 1,800	$ 450	$ 550
Tuesday	1,200	300	550
Wednesday	1,800	450	550
Thursday	3,600	900	550
Friday	4,200	1,050	550
Saturday	5,400	1,350	550
Weekly totals	$18,000	$4,500	$3,300

Ms. Schwartz was very pleased now. She suddenly realized why she and Ms. Olsen had been able to play golf, enjoy the theater, and spend more time with their families on Mondays, Tuesdays, and Wednesdays. She triumphantly showed her figures to Ms. Olsen. She insisted that she had proved that the business was losing money on Mondays, Tuesdays, and Wednesdays and that the only way to avoid this loss was to close the business on those days.

Ms. Olsen was shocked. The idea of staying closed 3 days a week just didn't sound right to her. She asks you to evaluate the situation.

LAYOUT FOR FACTORIES

SAMMY'S JAMS AND JELLIES, INC.

When Sammy Westhoff started making jams and jellies in the kitchen of his home to sell to the public, he never expected that his products would be in such great demand. His success forced him to find larger and larger facilities to produce his excellent products. After 8 years he was determined to find a factory building that would make his production more efficient. The problems he currently faced included much cross hauling of raw materials, inadequate storage space, poor loading and unloading areas, and inability to use conveyor belts or horizontal escalators in the manufacturing process. He knew that his labor cost was higher than that of his competitors because of the inefficiency of his factory operations.

He found an available building which he believed would be ideal for his operations. The building was 150 by 250 feet and had a railroad sidetrack on the north side. It was set back 100 feet from the south side of a busy industrial street. On the east it reached to within 6 feet of a side street. On the west the property had open ground space of 200 feet by 250 feet. The north, west, and south sides of the building had a 10-foot loading platform covered with a roof which reached 4 feet beyond the platform. Ceilings in the building were 40 feet high and sliding partitions reached across the entire floor space from east to west at 50-foot intervals. Some doors were in those partitions, and others could be added.

His manufacturing operations consisted of cooking the fruit, cooling it, adding sugar and other ingredients, filling the jars, packing the cases, storing the finished cases, and getting shipments out to buyers. The labeling of jars was done by machine on the production line and the printing on the cases was done before purchase. Most of the fruit, sugar, and other materials were received in carload or truckload lots. Trucks could enter the loading platform area on the three sides of the building with loading docks. The jams and jellies were cooked in 100-gallon steel drums, which had to be moved from the gas stoves in the process of adding other ingredients to the fruit. Each operation required a maximum of 50 feet of operation area in width and varied in length down the line from 15 to 30 feet.

Sammy was satisfied that he could easily meet his production schedule of 600 cases of jam per day and still have space to expand if his demand continued to grow.

He provides you with a sketch of the building and surrounding area and requests that you make a layout for his new factory.

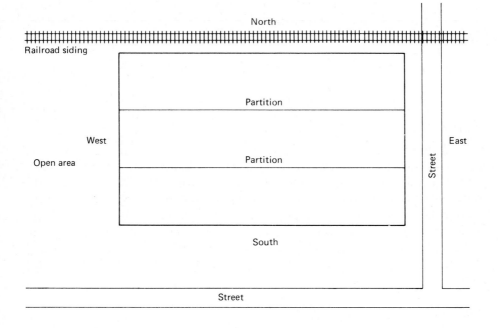

INVENTORY MANAGEMENT

SIMILAR FIRMS MAY HAVE GREAT DISSIMILARITIES

Barbara Bowens and Mary Hopkins each operated small business firms of the same type. Each had hired the same firm to make a market survey before they opened their respective businesses. The market surveys revealed that each was located in an area that should produce about the same sales volume at the same prices to similar customers. Because the women were fellow members of the Chamber of Commerce, they had occasion to meet quite frequently. They enjoyed comparing notes on their operations. They were not in direct competition, since their stores were in different parts of town, but they felt that their discussion of operations could be mutually beneficial.

Their discussions led them to the matter of their inventories. They were amazed to find a large discrepancy in the inventories each maintained in her store. They decided to compare income statements for the past year and see if they could account for the variations. Condensed income statements were as follows:

	Barbara Bowens' store		Mary Hopkins' store	
Sales		$200,000		$190,000
Cost of goods sold:				
Inventory, Jan. 1	$ 75,000		$ 15,000	
Purchases	150,000		150,000	
Goods available	$225,000		$165,000	
Inventory, Dec. 31	75,000		15,000	
Cost of goods sold		150,000		150,000
Gross margin		$ 50,000		$ 40,000
Operating expenses		20,000		25,000
Net profits from operations		$ 30,000		$ 15,000

The women knew how to compute average markups, inventory turnovers, and operating expenses as a percentage of sales. They compared all three. When they concentrated on the problem of why they had such different inventories, they turned to their trade association for comparative statistics. They found that the average inventory turnover for their type of firm was five times a year.

When they saw how far they each varied from this average inventory turnover, they decided to see if they could do something about the variations.

Barbara admitted that she had always figured it was better to have plenty of merchandise on hand rather than lose a sale due to "stockouts." Mary admitted her dislike for having too much working capital tied up in inventory. She was located close to a wholesale house, which made it easier to send one of her employees there or to drive there herself to get merchandise quickly. She paid for the gas for employee automobiles on such trips. She admitted that she had frequent "stockouts" and that, despite assurances to customers that the items would be available in a short time, those customers often did not come back.

Mary and Barbara decided to discuss the following questions, and they ask you to comment on each.

1 What was the average markup, inventory turnover, and profits as a percentage of sales for each store?

2 What are the disadvantages of having too much inventory on hand?

3 What are the disadvantages of having too little inventory on hand?

4 What is the ideal inventory?

5 In what ways can the profitability of the firm be affected by its inventory policy?

6 What recommendations would you make to each woman?

CASE **8**

THE OVERAGGRESSIVE SALES REP

The Specialty Shoe Store was a prosperous retail business in a large midwestern city. It sold both men's and women's shoes. Jack Jones, the owner, prided himself on the capabilities of his six salespersons, many of whom had been with him for several years. The three female and three male salespersons averaged 34 years of age, did not belong to the union, and often gave extra time to their work without extra pay when busy periods occurred. Jones instituted a profit-sharing plan, which was based on the earnings for the year and distributed at Christmas.

In June he was forced to replace one of the salesmen, who moved to another city to open his own store, Jones hired Byron Smith, who had just been graduated from the local junior college. Smith was clean-cut, 23 years old, had some previous selling experience, and appeared very personable. He was interviewed by the other five salespeople, as well as by Jones, before he was employed. All gave their approval.

Within 2 weeks Jones started receiving complaints from the other salespeople about Smith's overaggressive tactics on the sales floor, especially when Jones was not around. Young Smith rudely interrupted the others when they were making sales or considering choices of shoes with customers. He offered his positive opinions to the point that customers resented them. He sometimes took customers away from the other staff members. His favorite comment to the others was "Stick with me! Some day I will own this store." He interrupted the person assigned to balance the cash register at closing time. He insisted he could improve the established procedures because "After all, I've been to college."

At first the other salespeople tried to make kind suggestions to Smith, but they failed to change his method of operation. When Jones first became aware of the situation, he talked to Smith. He pointed out that Smith's sales record was good but that customer complaints and the complaints of his fellow salespeople had to stop. Smith said he would try to change his behavior. Jones felt particularly concerned about this situation because Smith's father was a personal friend and a fellow golfer at the local country club. As a result, he put off any final disciplinary action as long as possible.

In December Jones received a memorandum signed by the five senior staff members. It indicated that unless this aggravating situation were corrected immediately, they would not attend the Christmas party and would look for other jobs because they all planned to resign as of January 1. They also said that they would like an opportunity to have a full staff meeting to air their grievances. Jones knew he could no longer postpone action. He decided, in view of the total situation and his friendship with Smith's father, that he should have the requested meeting with the entire staff.

If you were Mr. Jones, how would you conduct the meeting and what decisions would you make?

CASE 9

THE HEARTACHES OF CREDIT MANAGEMENT

Mrs. Alice Billings is the credit manager for the ABC Department Store in Portland. Her duties include making the final decisions on applications for credit after her staff has concluded the regular investigation of formal applications. The ABC Department Store encourages open credit accounts for qualified applicants. It has maintained a good record of efficiency in administering its credit program. Losses on bad debts have been minimal. Few accounts get more than 90 days past due because of the store's effective program for handling delinquent accounts.

One morning Mrs. Billings found an application from Mr. Ned Albers on her desk. She knew Mr. Albers as a fellow church member, a regular contributor to charity, and a very kind and considerate person. He had four children in the public schools. His wife made most of the children's clothing and was also active in the church. They were known as people of modest means and limited income. None of these facts were known to the staff member who investigated the information and references on the application for credit.

The staff member had attached to the application a long, handwritten note for Mrs. Billings. It said that the application should not be approved, that the information given was inaccurate, the income was overstated, and the prior references reported that their credit experience was most unsatisfactory.

It was company policy that the credit manager must have a personal meeting with all credit applicants to advise them of the firm's decision to approve or reject credit and the limits placed on credit extended. Before setting up the appointment, Mrs. Billings learned from a mutual friend that the Albers application was made in the hope of buying a badly needed kitchen stove.

If you were Mrs. Billings, how would you handle the required meeting with Mr. Albers?

IF THERE IS A WILL, THERE MAY BE A WAY—TO GET STARTED

Bill Jacobs was a senior in college in New York. His best friend was Jack Evers, who operated a small sporting goods store in Bill's hometown. Both young men had always hoped and planned to move to California and establish a larger sporting goods store as partners. They planned their move for the following June when Bill would graduate with a degree in business administration. When Bill came home for his last spring vacation, he found Jack very downhearted. When he inquired, he found that Jack had figured out the investment they would need to open their California store. Jack saw no way they could arrange for sufficient capital. Together they went over the asset needs and came up with the following statement of assets to be used.

STATEMENT OF ASSETS TO BE USED

Cash	$ 3,000
Funds to invest in accounts receivable	3,000
Merchandise inventory	20,000
Prepaid insurance and supplies	1,000
Land and building	65,000
Store equipment	10,000
Office furniture and fixtures	2,000
Delivery truck	3,000
Total assets required	$107,000

Jack figured that he could net $15,000 from the sale of his present store. Bill had $10,000 available to invest. Bill had studied small business management in college. He knew that with certain constraints or decisions on providing needed assets they could open the business with their $25,000.

1 Set up your own constraints (decisions) and make an opening day balance sheet for the new California firm.

2 What are your basic ratios on the balance sheet? Can they be improved? How?

THE UNKNOWN PERCENT OF CAPACITY

When Harry Wong graduated from the university, he was employed as assistant office manager by the Supreme Auto Parts Company. Harry was a keen young man and was anxious to show in practice the many things he had learned in his college study. His first assignment was to establish a combined journal-ledger bookkeeping system for the young but fast-growing business. The owner was so pleased with the resultant saving in bookkeeping time and the efficiency of the system that Harry received his first raise after only 2 months with the firm. His next assignment was to establish a better system of inventory control. Again he did a good job; he installed a perpetual inventory system for the parts department which included signed receipts for every part issued, every part returned, and every part received from vendors. The system gave management a better control of the inventory and seemed to eliminate the unknown losses in inventory that had occurred in the past.

Over coffee one morning Harry asked the owner, Ms. Worlish, if she had ever considered the use of a break-even chart to analyze the results of operations. He pointed out the many uses that could be made of such a chart by showing the relationship of expenses and income at all levels of income of the business. Ms. Worlish replied that she would love to have such data available. She said the reason it had not been done in the past was that no one could establish a percentage of capacity at which the firm operated.

Harry saw a chance to further prove his value to the firm. He promised to make a break-even chart for the firm for the past year. Sales were $300,000; total expenses were $250,000 of which $50,000 was fixed. The percent of capacity was not known.

1 Can you prepare the break-even chart in a 5-inch grid?

2 How does your chart vary from one in which the percent of capacity is known?

OVERALL PERSONNEL POLICY

Mr. Baker, Mr. Carter, Ms. Garcia, and Ms. Johnson, are the equal owners, the board of directors, and the officers of the Bild Manufacturing Company. The company manufactures dishware and pottery products of various types, including a very popular line of dinnerware. The firm has been in business for 17 years and was started by the present owners and their relatives. It has 75 employees, including 50 factory workers, 12 salespeople who travel the sales territory, and 13 office employees. Profits are modest but steady.

One day the owners were called to a special emergency meeting to evaluate possible changes in their personnel policies. The day before, the National Labor Relations Board had conducted an election in the plant to decide upon a collective bargaining agent for the employees. The vote was close, but a 55 percent majority voted for no unionization and no formal collective bargaining.

The directors were shocked and saddened by the slim margin of their win. They had always prided themselves on the loyalty of their employees. They felt they had always rewarded their employees well and that surely they were happy and satisfied people who valued their jobs.

In a meeting with the employees this morning the directors requested information on the complaints which had motivated the election and its close results. They were pleased to learn that wages were not a chief complaint, although they did pay slightly less than their bigger competitors. The complaints revolved around fringe benefits. They can be summarized as follows:

1 Present vacation policy is 1 week after 1 year, 2 weeks after 5 years, and 3 weeks after 10 years' employment. The employees want 2 weeks after 1 year, 3 weeks after 5 years, and 1 month's vacation after 10 years' employment.

2 Employees want a guaranteed annual salary. They are willing to do other jobs, such as maintenance painting, if the factory does not have enough orders to maintain year-round full employment—which has rarely happened in the past.

3 Employees resented it when the management placed much routine accounting and inventory control on a terminal computer service. This eliminated two bookkeepers, who were later given other jobs. Net saving was $12,000 yearly.

4 Employees feel that the salespeople make too much money compared with factory workers. Salespeople work on a straight commission basis.

5 Employees complain that the company does not follow through on its policy of dismissing new employees whose work is not satisfactory after a 3-month trial period. They want a voice in the retention or dismissal decision. They feel that keeping weak employees is hurting plant efficiency.

6 Because a group life insurance policy for employees is a tax-deductible expense for the company, employees want their group policy increased to $50,000 for each employee. This is the legal maximum.

7 It is felt that some supervisors are not enforcing company work rules uniformly for all people under them.

Some of the employees who are known to have agitated for the union frankly indicated that their agitation will cease if acceptable answers can be found to these complaints. They indicated that the rank-and-file employees do not like a plan of union dues write-off from their salaries, and that they believe in the right-to-work laws, which remove the necessity of being a union member in order to work in their state.

At tomorrow's meeting the directors must recover from their disappointment and shock and take positive action on each of the employee complaints.

If you were a member of the board of directors, what would your recommendation be on each complaint? Can you defend your recommendations? How?

INVENTORY VALUATION

The grand piano department of Rizzo's Music Store showed the following purchases in 1981 after being completely sold out in the Christmas trade of 1980.

January—5 pianos at $2,000 each	July—5 pianos at $2,300 each
February—8 pianos at $2,100 each	August—6 pianos at $2,400 each
March—6 pianos at $2,000 each	September—8 pianos at $2,400 each
April—5 pianos at $2,200 each	October—10 pianos at $2,500 each
May—5 pianos at $2,200 each	November—10 pianos at $2,500 each
June—5 pianos at $2,300 each	December—15 pianos at $2,500 each

On December 31, 1981 the department had an inventory of 12 pianos on hand. The selling price then was $2,500. Of the 12 pianos on hand, 2 were purchased in January, 3 in May, 5 in November, and 2 in December.

1 How would the remaining 12 pianos be valued under LIFO, FIFO, weighted average cost, and lower of cost or market methods?

2 Which method would you recommend to minimize income taxes for 1981?

3 Which method would you recommend if the objective is to maximize profits in order to lure new investors?

AN EXISTING FIRM VERSUS A NEW ONE

Everett and Jeanie were childhood sweethearts who married after they graduated from high school. Jobs were scarce in their hometown so they opened a small restaurant of their own "on a shoestring." They were such a good team that they prospered from the beginning. As their finances improved, despite raising four children, their thoughts turned to their lifetime desire to move to Texas. When a chain offered them $75,000 for their restaurant, they decided the time had come to move south. They settled in a beautiful, large city called Dalworth, Texas, and immediately set about finding the location for a new restaurant.

They found an attractive suburban location and proceeded to plan the financing necessary to get underway. The building they planned to rent was new, and no equipment of any kind was available from the landlord. With careful planning they determined that they could equip the place and get underway with a minimum investment of $40,000. The market survey suggested a profit of $20,000 per year.

Jeanie came home from shopping a short time later and reported to Everett that she had found a "for sale" sign on "that cute little restaurant" they had visited some time before. She visited the owner and found that the business could be purchased for $35,000. The owner even showed her his bank deposits and income tax returns to prove that he had averaged between $18,000 and $21,000 net profit each year for the past 10 years. His desire to sell was explained as a wish to retire.

The ensuing discussion between Everett and Jeanie was the most bitter of their entire married life. Everett was screaming about the disadvantages of buying an established business and praising the advantages of starting a new firm in the fine location they had found. Jeanie favored buying the restaurant which had been established for years and was a proven moneymaker. She cautioned Everett about the additional risks undertaken in starting a new firm.

1 Can you help them resolve the dispute?
2 What specific factors should enter into their decision?

ETHICS VERSUS SHARP PRACTICE

Bill and Mary Davis have operated their small cosmetics factory for 5 years. Growth has been slow but steady. They were overjoyed in January of last year to have finally received a large order from the biggest department store in town.

The store's buyer was a shrewd negotiator who got the price for the order down to well below normal. The final feature of the order requested was sales terms of 2/10, n/30. Though this cut the small remaining profit on the order still more, Bill and Mary agreed. They convinced themselves that their working capital would be replaced within 10 days and the exposure of their products in the large store would result in more large orders in the future. The invoice totaled $2,000.

When they failed to receive a check within the next 30 days the Davises sent a duplicate statement to the department store. No response was received.

Three months later they received a check for $1,960 from the store. It was marked "invoice of January 10, paid in full." Obviously the 2 percent discount ($40) had been deducted from the original amount of the invoice.

Bill and Mary sat in their office pondering what action they should take, if any. What would you advise?

APPENDIXES

MANAGEMENT CONSULTANT'S CHECKLIST

The following pages give the student or small firm owner a basis upon which to evaluate an existing firm's effectiveness.

The last section shows some of the causes of business failure. The checklists show:

1 What an outside consultant looks for in evaluating an existing firm
2 What owners should check in evaluating their own business

The subjects covered are:

1 The firm's market
2 Asset adequacy
3 Adequacy and use of accounting records
4 Financial condition
5 Location analysis
6 Layout analysis
7 Proper legal form of organization
8 Sales development program
9 Pricing policies
10 Merchandising of lines of goods
11 Seasonal variations and their implications
12 Purchasing and inventory control
13 Expense analysis and break-even chart
14 Credit policies in effect for sales and purchases
15 Risks and protection provided
16 Personnel policies

1 FOR EVALUATING MARKETS

1 Is the firm's major problem a lack of sales?
2 What has been the trend of sales in recent years?
3 What factors can be determined as responsible for the trend of sales?
4 Was a proper market survey made when the firm started?
5 If so, what were the predicted results in sales volume?
6 If not, should such a survey be made now?
7 Have the basic sources of market survey data been studied?
8 Does population growth, new competition, or competitor change in methods justify new ways of serving this market?
9 Has the character of the population in the trading area changed, aside from general growth or decline? Has this affected sales?
10 Has the ratio of population to number of firms in this trading area changed since the firm was established? If so, what has been done by management to keep current with these changes?
11 Does the future look good, medium, or bad for this firm in this market?

2 FOR EVALUATING ASSET ADEQUACY

1 Does the firm lack any assets which would improve its capacity for service, its image, or its profitability?
2 Are its store fixtures, office fixtures, and/or machines modern? Would newer ones improve image, service, or profitability?
3 Are present fixed assets consistent with the floor plan, available additional space, and customer comfort?
4 Does the firm have the necessary capital to finance its own receivables? Should this be done?
5 Are cash balances and working capital adequate for the volume of business being done?
6 Do growth requirements of the immediate future suggest the need of any other current or fixed assets? If so, are plans satisfactory for their acquisition?
7 Could the firm expand sales and profits with more assets in its present operation? How?

3 FOR EVALUATING ADEQUACY OF ACCOUNTING RECORDS

1 Does the proprietor have monthly statements easily available?
2 Does a complete accounting system exist?
3 Does the present system involve excessive posting?
4 Would a combined journal-ledger system reduce the work of the system?
5 Can the owner tell quickly the amounts owed by credit customers? (Is there an accounts receivable ledger of some kind?)
6 Can the owner quickly ascertain the balances due to creditors? (Is there an accounts payable ledger of some kind?)
7 Can sales easily be broken down into departments, chief lines of merchandise, or special items?

8 Does the system in effect provide a means of telling the profitability of individual departments or lines of merchandise?
9 Do the monthly adjustments include properly the charges for depreciation, amortization, and new inventories?
10 What types of information, not now easily available, does an owner need?
11 Does the firm take advantage of purchase discounts? Do the records provide adequate notice of discount periods?
12 Do procedures include a regular aging of accounts receivable?

4 FOR EVALUATING FINANCIAL CONDITION

1 What is the relationship of assets and liabilities?
2 What is the relationship of current assets and current liabilities?
3 Are the current assets truly current?
4 Are the liabilities properly classified?
5 What is the working capital? Is it adequate?
6 What is the current ratio? What is the quick ratio? What is the proprietorship ratio?
7 Is the firm trading on too thin an equity?
8 Does it have trouble paying its current bills? Why?
9 Have the accounts receivable been aged recently? What is the firm's policy on charging off uncollectible accounts?
10 How much of current profits is going to pay for fixed assets?
11 Are any creditors withholding credit because of the company's debt-paying habits or its other financial problems?
12 Does the firm need additional investment capital? Are any sources available?
13 Is the inventory turnover a cause of financial stress? Has it been reviewed for slow-moving merchandise lately? Are there other problems?
14 Is the gross margin consistent with that of comparable firms? If not, why not?
15 Are operating expenses in line? If not, why not?
16 Do company policies indicate that the financial condition will be improved? How?
17 Are any other financial weaknesses apparent?

5 FOR EVALUATING LOCATION

A For Retailers

1 Is the firm located in a high-rent or a low-rent area? Should it be? Is the rent paid by the firm competitive?
2 If in a low-rent area and competing with firms in high-rent areas, how does it compensate in attracting customers?
3 Is the location good from the standpoint of meeting competition?
4 Is the total traffic in the area adequate?
5 Do neighboring stores draw potential customers?
6 Is there a parking problem for customers? Would it be worthwhile to pay for customer parking?
7 Is the location good for development of sales via promotion?

8 Is this location appropriate to the principles of location for convenience, shopping, and specialty stores?
9 Is there a better site available in the area?
10 Is the going-home side of the street or the sunny side of the street important to this firm? Does it have that advantage?
11 Do the community and general area suggest adequate payrolls, population trends, living habits, and attitudes to encourage firm development here?
12 Are any other disadvantages of this location observed?

B For Wholesalers

1 Is the location economically accessible to its market?
2 Are shipping costs in receiving inventory the lowest available? Would additional rail, truck, or air facilities improve efficiency and reduce costs?
3 Do competitors have advantages in costs of delivery to customers due to better location?
4 Do customers visit the plant in person or call in orders by phone? If they visit, is the accessibility and customer convenience satisfactory?
5 Does this location make possible the best layout of merchandise to expedite order filling and minimize labor costs?

C For Factories

1 Should this type of factory be close to its markets or to its raw materials? Is it?
2 Do the facilities at this location make possible the best use of the appropriate production layout?
3 Is the location appropriate to hiring the types of labor required? Is adequate labor of the desired type available?
4 Are utility costs consistent with those available at other potential locations?
5 Are adequate shipping facilities available at competitive costs? Would additional competition by shippers be helpful?
6 Are government attitudes and community facilities encouraging?
7 Do alternative locations offer reduced costs or better profits? Why?

D For Service Firms

1 Is customer visitation an important part of the business? If so, are facilities for customer comfort adequate?
2 Is the location consistent with the type of clientele sought and its habits in buying this service?
3 Does the firm need a high-rent location? Is it in one?
4 If efficient working conditions for employees are important, do they exist?
5 Is the firm paying an expensive rental for space when most of its business comes via telephone? Is this necessary?
6 Is drop-in business important? Does it exist in adequate quantity? Can it be developed by advertising?

6 FOR EVALUATING LAYOUT

A For Retailers

1 Is the present layout encouraging to sales because it reflects buying habits of customers?
2 Could it better reflect a good "selling machine"? How?
3 Is merchandise attractively displayed?
4 Is merchandise displayed to facilitate easy comparisons and easy examination?
5 Is customer comfort properly provided to meet the particular shopping habits of the firm's customers?
6 Are associated lines of merchandise displayed adjacently?
7 Does the layout reflect maximum use of light, ventilation, and heat?
8 Is maximum view of store space by customers, employees, and managers desirable? If so, is this view now possible?
9 Are selling and nonselling activities properly separated?
10 Are convenience, shopping, and specialty goods properly located in the floor plan?
11 Does the image of the store reflect colors, fixtures, and displays which are compatible with the type of customers sought?

B For Wholesalers

1 Does the layout make order filling easy?
2 Are most popular lines of merchandise located adjacently?
3 Is maximum use made of rolling equipment in filling orders?
4 Do customers visit the firm often? If so, is the image proper?
5 Are receiving doors convenient to inventory stacks? Are more doors needed?
6 Is the line of travel from merchandise collection for orders to location of loading deliveries direct? Could it be shortened to reduce costs of order filling?
7 Are aisles wide enough for efficient operation?
8 Can the height of merchandise stacks be reduced in the present space?

C For Factories

1 Does the firm now use a process or a product layout?
2 Is maximum use made of the advantages of the present layout?
3 Can the unproductive movement of raw materials, goods in process, or finished products be reduced?
4 Are testing and quality-control stations located in the best spots on the production line? Should there be more quality-control locations?
5 Are materials to be placed in production located close to the point of introduction into production?
6 Are material-receiving areas located as close to storerooms as possible?
7 Are luncheon areas, rest rooms, drinking fountains, and other employee areas located for maximum efficiency?

7 FOR EVALUATING LEGAL FORMS OF ORGANIZATION

1 Under what legal form of organization is the firm now operating?
2 What are the major risks to which the firm is subjected?
3 Does the legal form of organization give the firm proper protection against these risks?
4 Does the firm supplement its legal form of protection with public liability insurance? Is the amount adequate?
5 Is unlimited liability a serious potential problem for the owner(s)?
6 Has the present form limited financial needs in any way?
7 Has the owner considered changing the legal form?
8 What is the relative incidence of the major risks of the firm?
9 Are there tax advantages available by changing the legal form of organization?
10 Is the owner fully aware of the management advantages of the alternative legal forms available for the firm?
11 Are the features of a Subchapter S corporation known? Would you recommend them in this case?
12 Is the firm utilizing all the advantages of the present legal form of organization?

8 FOR EVALUATING SALES DEVELOPMENT

1 Has the firm properly distinguished between established demand and promoted or created demand for its goods?
2 Has the owner considered all the direct and indirect sales promotion methods?
3 Are the applicable sales promotion methods being used in effective quantities?
4 Is the present advertising program being checked for its effectiveness?
5 Is the present sales volume consistent with the potential for the firm in this trading area? If not, how could it be increased?
6 Do customers generally reflect a feeling of satisfaction in doing business with the firm?
7 What is the firm's image in the community which it serves?
8 How could it be improved if deficiencies are found?
9 Is personal selling by employees consistent with the best practices?
10 Do any suggestions seem apparent for improving sales promotion?

9 FOR EVALUATING PRICING POLICIES

1 Do prices now produce an average gross margin consistent with the sales volume for this type of firm? If not, why?
2 Is the firm's pricing policy influenced by fair trade laws, nationally advertised prices, or competitor prices?
3 Is market strategy employed in setting prices?
4 Is the owner reluctant to adopt less-than-average markup prices when good judgment dictates their use?
5 Do prices reflect attempts to sell slow-moving merchandise?
6 Are proper methods used in moving slow merchandise?
7 Is style merchandise a factor in markups and markdowns?
8 Does original markup policy reflect normal markdowns, employee discounts, damaged merchandise, and shortages?
9 Does the firm use adequate markups to produce desired results?
10 Are markups based on cost or retail prices?

11 Have loss leaders ever been used? Were they necessary or productive?
12 Does the firm's overall pricing policy reflect a dynamic management?
13 Do above-average markup sales cover the sales in less-than-average markup items?

10 FOR EVALUATING MERCHANDISING

1 Does the owner recognize the differences in convenience, shopping, and specialty goods?
2 Is the merchandise inventory arranged to reflect these categories?
3 If sales effort is primarily in one category, does the merchandising policy properly reflect this fact?
4 Is the merchandising policy generally in line with the majority of customers in the trading area?
5 Are selling policies and services in line with the products (credit plans, delivery services, etc.)?
6 If selling industrial goods, does the firm recognize the differences in merchandising its goods and consumer goods?
7 Is the location consistent with the type of merchandise sold and the price policies in effect?
8 Is employee capability consistent with the needs of the type of merchandise being sold?

11 FOR EVALUATING SEASONAL VARIATIONS

1 Does the firm have distinct variations in sales in different months and/or seasons of the year?
2 Is the management using accepted methods of adjusting operating expenses to these variations?
3 Is purchasing policy consistent with the noted variations?
4 Would the addition of different lines of merchandise or different products help to even out the seasonal variation in sales?
5 If seasonal variations are drastic, would it be better to close the business entirely for some period in the year?
6 If a manufacturing firm, would it be more profitable to use the slack periods to build up inventory and to cut down factory overtime in the busy seasons?

12 FOR EVALUATING PURCHASING AND INVENTORY CONTROL

1 Are the proper sources of supply now being used?
2 Is the firm taking advantage of all purchase discounts?
3 How are minimum inventories and ordering points determined?
4 Has the firm suffered from stockouts of finished merchandise or raw materials?
5 What is the record for quality, service, and price of its present suppliers? How about dependability and assistance in periods of sellers' markets?
6 How does the firm set its minimum ordering quantities?
7 Has buying policy been guilty of buying too large quantities which were not justified by carrying costs?
8 What is the cost of carrying inventories in stock until needed?
9 Does the firm owner know what the best average inventory is and use it to guide purchasing policy?

10 Could more effective purchasing contribute profits to the present results of operation? How?

13 FOR EVALUATING EXPENSES AND A BREAK-EVEN CHART

1 Have fixed and variable expenses been thoroughly determined?
2 Are there advantages to altering the present relationship of fixed and variable expenses? Is this possible?

What Caused 10,326 Businesses to Fail in One Year?
Classification Failures Based on Opinion of Informed Creditors and Information in Dun & Bradstreet Reports.

Percent Manufacturers	Wholesalers	Retailers	Construction	Commercial services	All	Underlying causes
1.3	2.6	1.9	1.7	1.6	1.7	Neglect
1.3	2.0	1.2	0.8	1.1	1.2	Fraud
9.8	9.1	16.1	10.1	15.5	13.3	Lack of experience in the line
11.2	13.4	15.9	20.8	16.3	15.6	Lack of managerial experience
18.6	14.1	19.3	19.5	17.1	18.4	Unbalanced experience*
54.6	55.0	41.3	43.0	44.3	45.7	Incompetence
1.1	1.6	1.6	0.8	0.6	1.3	Disaster
2.1	2.2	2.7	3.3	3.5	2.8	Reason unknown
100.0	100.0	100.0	100.0	100.0	100.0	Total
1,932	957	4,428	1,545	1,464	10,326	Number of failures
$368,846	$189,083	$100,290	$183,920	$243,800	$185,641	Average liabilities per failure

*Experience not well rounded in sales, finance, purchasing, and production on the part of the individual in case of a proprietorship, or of two or more partners or officers constituting a management unit.

† Because some failures are attributed to a combination of apparent causes, the totals of these columns exceed the totals of the corresponding columns on the left.

Source: Dun & Bradstreet, Inc., Business Economics Department, New York.

3 Has the firm produced a break-even chart for annual operations?
4 Has this chart been reduced to monthly periods?
5 Could the break-even point in sales be lowered? How?
6 Can any fixed expenses be made variable in order to reduce risks?
7 How would profits change with a 10 percent increase in sales?
8 How would profits change with a 10 percent reduction in fixed expenses?
9 Is the firm approaching 100 percent of capacity in its present quarters?
10 Is the present percentage of capacity known? Can it be increased?
11 Is each expense dollar providing a productive return to the firm?
12 Can semivariable expenses be controlled any better?

Apparent Causes		Percent	Manufacturers	Wholesalers	Retailers	Construction	Commercial services	All†
Due to	Bad habits		0.3	0.9	0.5	0.4	0.5	0.5
	Poor health		0.4	1.7	0.9	0.8	0.7	0.8
	Marital difficulties		0.1	—	0.2	0.2	0.2	0.1
	Other		0.5	—	0.3	0.3	0.2	0.3
On the part of the principals, reflected by	Misleading name		0.1	0.2	0.1	0.1	0.1	0.1
	False financial statement		0.4	0.7	0.2	0.3	0.1	0.3
	Premeditated overbuy		—	0.2	—	—	—	0.1
	Irregular disposal of assets		0.4	0.6	0.5	0.3	0.4	0.4
	Other		0.4	0.3	0.4	0.1	0.5	0.3
Evidenced by inability to avoid conditions which resulted in	Inadequate sales		47.0	42.7	45.4	40.1	48.4	45.3
	Heavy operating expenses		11.6	9.3	7.0	9.6	0.2	8.8
	Receivables difficulties		15.6	15.9	3.8	13.7	6.8	9.1
	Inventory difficulties		3.7	5.8	6.3	0.8	0.5	4.2
	Excessive fixed assets		5.8	1.7	2.4	2.5	6.9	3.7
	Poor location		0.8	1.5	6.9	0.6	2.7	3.7
	Competitive weakness		21.5	25.2	26.8	31.1	24.3	26.0
	Other		6.5	7.8	2.8	3.3	4.9	4.4
Some of these occurrences could have been provided against through insurance	Fire		0.3	0.7	0.6	0.3	0.3	0.5
	Flood		0.1	—	—	—	—	0.0
	Burglary		0.1	—	0.2	—	—	0.1
	Employees' fraud		0.1	0.5	0.1	0.1	0.0	0.1
	Strike		0.0	0.2	0.0	0.3	0.0	0.1
	Other		0.5	0.2	0.7	0.1	0.3	0.5
	Percent of total failures		18.7	9.3	42.9	14.9	14.2	100.0

14 FOR EVALUATING CREDIT POLICIES

1 Is the firm financially equipped to carry its own accounts receivable?
2 What types of credit accounts are available to customers now?
3 Should other types of accounts be made available?
4 What is the cost of administering the present credit program?
5 Would it be better for this firm at this time to discount all its receivables with a finance company or bank?
6 Are credit-card sales being collected efficiently? What is their cost?
7 Should the firm issue its own credit cards?
8 Does its credit policy reflect the fact that the company has both small and large credit sales?
9 Has an aging of accounts receivable been made lately? What does it show?
10 Has the write-off of bad debts been realistic, too low, or too high?
11 If the firm sells to business firms, has a sales discount been offered? Should it be?
12 Has the firm taken advantage of purchase discounts offered to it?

15 FOR EVALUATING PROTECTION AGAINST RISKS

1 Has the ownership truly analyzed all the major risks to which the firm is subject?
2 What protection has been provided against each of these risks?
3 Is the incidence of risk properly considered in the protective action taken?
4 Is self-insurance appropriate for this firm?
5 How many risks are being absorbed? Should they be?
6 Is coinsurance appropriate for this firm? How?
7 Are there any recommendations for reducing risks or getting protection more economically?

16 FOR EVALUATING PERSONNEL POLICIES

1 What has been the turnover of desirable employees?
2 Are any outstanding reasons for resignations to be observed?
3 Does the company provide training for new employees?
4 Are company policies regarding personnel known to all new and old employees?
5 Are there incentives in the personnel policy for employees to seek advancement?
6 Does the policy reflect the generally agreed-upon objectives of all employees?
7 Do opportunities exist for employees to work at different types of positions?
8 Is the company image one that suggests this is a good firm to work with?
9 Are pay scales and/or other advantages consistent with larger firms in the area?
10 Is there any problem of employees being overtrained or undertrained?
11 Are there any recommendations for changes in the present policies?

GOVERNMENT PUBLICATIONS TO AID SMALL BUSINESSES

Every citizen should know the extent to which the government tries to assist those who are planning a new firm and those operating a small firm. Both the Department of Commerce and the Small Business Administration have staffs available to help small firms in arranging financial assistance, in dealing with management problems, and in getting government contracts. The Small Business Administration has also issued innumerable small publications, usually in pamphlet form, which are either free or priced at only a few cents each. All small firm owners and planners should be familiar with these publications. They should also know the address of the closest SBA field office to which they can write to obtain any of the publications listed below. Addresses are given in Appendix Three. The list of available publications varies from time to time, and older ones may not always be available. Following is a list of those currently available.

FREE PUBLICATIONS

Management Aids

Series No.   170   The ABC's of Borrowing
             178   Effective Industrial Advertising for Small Plants
             186   Checklist for Developing a Training Program
             187   Using Census Data in Small Plant Marketing
             190   Measuring Sales Force Performance

Small Marketer's Aids

Series No.   71   Checklist for Going into Business
118   Legal Services for Small Retail and Service Firms
119   Preventing Retail Theft
123   Stock Control for Small Stores
126   Accounting Services for Small Service Firms
129   Reducing Shoplifting Losses
130   Analyze Your Records to Reduce Costs
133   Can You Afford Delivery Service?
135   Arbitration: Peace-Maker in Small Business
137   Outwitting Bad Check Passers
140   Profit by Your Wholesalers' Services
141   Danger Signals in a Small Store
142   Steps in Meeting Your Tax Obligations
144   Getting the Facts for Income Tax Reporting
146   Budgeting in a Small Service Firm
147   Sound Cash Management and Borrowing
148   Insurance Checklist for Small Business
149   Computers for Small Business—Service Bureau or Time Sharing?
150   Business Plan for Retailers
151   Preventing Embezzlement
152   Using a Traffic Study to Select a Retail Site
153   Business Plan for Small Service Firms
154   Using Census Data to Select a Store Site
156   Marketing Checklist for Small Retailers
158   A Pricing Checklist for Small Retailers
159   Improving Personal Selling in Small Retail Stores
160   Advertising Guidelines for Small Retail Firms
161   Signs and Your Business
162   Staffing Your Store
163   Public Relations for Small Business
164   Plan Your Advertising Budget
166   Simple Breakeven Analysis for Small Stores
167   Learning about Your Market
168   Store Location: "Little Things" Mean a Lot
169   Do You Know the Results of Your Advertising?
170   Thinking About Going into Business?

Small Business Bibliographies

Series No.   1   Handicrafts
2   Home Businesses
3   Selling by Mail Order
9   Marketing Research Procedures

10 Retailing
12 Statistics and Maps for National Market Analysis
13 National Directories for Use in Marketing
15 Recordkeeping Systems—Small Store and Service Trade
18 Basic Library Reference Sources
20 Advertising—Retail Store
29 National Mailing-List Houses
37 Buying for Retail Stores
53 Hobby Shops
55 Wholesaling
64 Photographic Dealers and Studios
66 Motels
67 Manufacturers' Sales Representative
72 Personnel Management
75 Inventory Management
79 Small Store Planning and Design
80 Data Processing for Small Businesses
85 Purchasing for Owners of Small Plants
86 Training for Small Business
87 Financial Management
88 Manufacturing Management
89 Marketing for Small Business
90 New Product Development

FOR-SALE PUBLICATIONS

The following publications can be purchased from the Superintendent of Documents, Government Printing Office, Washington, D.C. 20402. They vary in price from about 50 cents to $3. Some are 100 or more pages long. Almost every conceivable problem in small business has some coverage. Be sure to give the catalog number when ordering any of these publications.

Small Business Management Series

The booklets in this series provide discussions of special management problems in small companies.

No.   Stock No.

1 An Employee Suggestion System for Small Companies   045-000-00020-6
Explains the basic principles for starting and
operating a suggestion system. It also warns of
various pitfalls and gives examples of suggestions
submitted by employees.

9 **Cost Accounting for Small Manufacturers**   045-000-00162-8
Assists managers of small manufacturing firms,
producing a broad range of products, establish
accounting procedures that will help to document
and to control production and business costs.

15 **Handbook of Small Business Finance**   045-000-00139-3
Written for the small business owner who wants to
improve financial management skills. Indicates the
major areas of financial management and describes a
few of the many techniques that can help the small
business owner.

20 **Ratio Analysis for Small Business**   045-000-00150-4
Ratio analysis is the process of determining the
relationships between certain financial or operating
data of a business to provide a basis for managerial
control. The purpose of the booklet is to help the
owner/manager in detecting favorable or unfavorable
trends in the business.

22 **Practical Business Use of Government Statistics**   045-000-00131-8
Illustrates some practical uses of Federal
Government statistics, discusses what can be done
with them, and describes major reference sources.

25 **Guides for Profit Planning**   045-000-00137-7
Guides for computing and using the break-even
point, the level of gross profit, and the rate of return
on investment. Designed for readers who have no
specialized training in accounting and economics.

27 **Profitable Community Relations for Small Business**   045-000-00033-8
Practical information on how to build and maintain
sound community relations by participation in
community affairs.

28 **Small Business and Government Research and**   045-000-00130-0
Development
An introduction for owners of small research and
development firms that seek Government R and D
contracts. Includes a discussion of the procedures
necessary to locate and interest Government
markets.

29 **Management Audit for Small Manufacturers**   045-000-00151-2
A series of questions which will indicate whether the
owner-manager of a small manufacturing plant is
planning, organizing, directing, and coordinating the
business activities efficiently.

30 **Insurance and Risk Management for Small Business**   045-000-00037-1
A discussion of what insurance is, the necessity of
obtaining professional advice on buying insurance,
and the main types of insurance a small business may
need.

31 **Management Audit for Small Retailers**   045-000-00149-1
Designed to meet the needs of the owner-manager of
a small retail enterprise. 149 questions guide the
owner-manager in a self examination and a review of
the business operation.

32 **Financial Recordkeeping for Small Stores**   045-000-00142-3
Written primarily for the small store owner or
prospective owner whose business doesn't justify
hiring a full-time bookkeeper.

33 **Small Store Planning for Growth**   045-000-00152-1
A discussion of the nature of growth, the
management skills needed, and some techniques for
use in promoting growth. Included is a consideration
of merchandising, advertising and display, and
checklists for increase in transactions and gross
margins.

34 **Selecting Advertising Media—A Guide for Small**   045-000-00154-7
Business
Intended to aid the small business person in deciding
which medium to select for making the product,
service, or store known to potential customers and
how best to use advertising money.

35 **Franchise Index/Profile**   045-000-00125-3
Presents an evaluation process that may be used to
investigate franchise opportunities. The Index tells
what to look for in a franchise. The Profile is
worksheet for listing the data.

36 **Training Salesmen to Serve Industrial Markets**   045-000-00133-4
Discusses role of sales in marketing program of small

manufacturer and offers suggestions for sales force to use in servicing customers. Provides material to use in training program.

37 **Financial Control by Time-Absorption Analysis**   045-000-00134-2
A profit control technique that can be used by all types of business. A step-by-step approach shows how to establish this method in a particular business.

38 **Management Audit for Small Service Firms**   045-000-00143-1
A do-it-yourself guide for owner-managers of small service firms to help them evaluate and improve their operations. Brief comments explain the importance of each question in 13 critical management areas.

39 **Decision Points in Developing New Products**   045-000-00146-6
Provides a path from idea to marketing plan for the small manufacturing or R&D firm that wants to expand or develop a business around a new product, process, or invention.

40 **Management Audit for Small Construction Firms**   045-000-00161-0
Written to help top executives of small construction firms to make a self-appraisal of their management practices. Recommends ways to improve existing practices and introduce effective new ones.

Starting and Managing Series

This series is designed to help the small entrepreneur in the effort "to look before leaping" into a business. The first volume in the series—*Starting and Managing a Small Business of Your Own*—deals with the subject in general terms. Each of the other volumes deals with one type of business in detail, and their titles are designed to inform of their contents. Available titles are listed below.

No.   Stock No.

1 **Starting and Managing a Small Business of Your Own**   045-000-00123-7
20 **Starting and Managing a Small Retail Music Store**   045-000-00107-5

Nonseries Publications

Export Marketing for Smaller Firms   045-000-00158-0
A manual for owner-managers of smaller firms who seek sales in foreign markets.

U.S. Government Purchasing and Sales Directory   045-000-00153-9
A directory for businesses that are interested in selling to
the U.S. Government. Lists the purchasing needs of
various Agencies.

Managing for Profits   045-000-00005-2
Ten chapters on various aspects of small business
management, for example, marketing, production, and
credit.

Buying and Selling a Small Business   045-000-00164-4
Deals with the problems that confront buyers and sellers
of small businesses. Discusses the buy-sell transaction,
sources of information for buyer-seller decision, the
buy-sell process, using financial statements in the buy-sell
transaction, and analyzing the market position of the
company.

Strengthening Small Business Management   045-000-00114-8
Twenty-one chapters on small business management. This
collection reflects the experience which the author gained
in a life time of work with the small business community.

Small Business Goes to College   045-000-00159-8
Subtitled "College and University Courses in Small
Business Management and Entrepreneurship," this
booklet traces the development of small business
management as a college subject and provides samples of
courses offered by some 200 colleges and universities. It
should be useful to educators as well as to counselors
who seek sources to recommend for their clients'
self-development.

SBA FIELD OFFICE ADDRESSES

Boston	Mass.	02110	60 Batterymarch Street, 10th Floor
Boston	Mass.	02114	150 Causeway St., 10th Floor
Holyoke	Mass.	01050	302 High Street, 4th Floor
Augusta	Maine	04330	* 40 Western Avenue, Room 512
Concord	N. H.	03301	* 55 Pleasant Street, Room 211
Hartford	Conn.	06103	One Financial Plaza
Montpelier	Vt.	05602	* 87 State Street, Room 204, P.O. Box 605
Providence	R. I.	02903	40 Fountain Street
New York	N. Y.	10278	* 26 Federal Plaza, Room 29–118
New York	N. Y.	10278	* 26 Federal Plaza, Room 3100
Melville	N. Y.	11747	35 Pinelawn Road
Puerto Rico & Virgin Islands Hato Rey		00919	* Carlos Chardon Ave., Fed. Bldg. Rm. 691
St. Thomas	V. I.	00801	* Veterans Drive, Room 283
Newark	N. J.	07102	* 970 Broad St., Room 1635
Camden	N. J.	08104	1800 East Davis Street
Syracuse	N. Y.	13260	* 100 South Clinton Street, Room 1073
Bufialo	N. Y.	14202	* 111 West Huron St., Room 1311
Elmira	N. Y.	14901	180 Clemens Center Parkway
Albany	N. Y.	12207	* 445 Broadway-Room 236A
Rochester	N. Y.	14614	* 100 State Street, Room 601
Philadelphia	Bala Cynwyd, Pa.	19004	231 St. Asaphs Rd., Suite 646 West Lobby
Philadelphia	Bala Cynwyd, Pa.	19004	231 St. Asaphs Rd., Suite 400 East Lobby

Harrisburg	Pa.	17101	100 Chestnut Street, Suite 309
Wilkes-Barre	Pa.	18702	20 North Pennsylvania Avenue
Wilmington	Del.	19801	* 844 King Street, Room 5207
Baltimore	Towson, Md.	21204	8600 LaSalle Road, Room 630
Clarksburg	W. Va.	26301	109 North 3rd St., Room 302
Charleston	W. Va.	25301	Charleston National Plaza, Suite 628
Pittsburgh	Pa.	15222	* 1000 Liberty Ave., Room 1401
Richmond	Va.	23240	* 400 North 8th St., Room 3015, P.O. Box 10126
Washington	D. C.	20417	1030 15th St. N.W., Suite 250
Atlanta	Ga.	30367	1375 Peachtree St., N.E., 5th Floor
Atlanta	Ga.	30309	1720 Peachtree Road, N.W., 6th Floor
Statesboro	Ga.	30458	* 52 North Main Street
Birmingham	Ala.	35205	908 South 20th St., Room 202
Charlotte	N. C.	28202	230 S. Tryon Street, Suite 700
Greenville	N. C.	27834	* 215 South Evans Street, Room 206
Columbia	S. C.	29202	* 1835 Assembly, 3rd Floor, P.O. Box 2786
Jackson	Miss.	30201	* 100 West Capitol Street, Suite 322
Biloxi	Miss.	39530	111 Fred Haise Blvd., 2nd Floor
Jacksonville	Fla.	32202	* 400 West Bay St., Room 261, Box 35067
Louisville	Ky.	40201	* 600 Federal Pl., Room 188, P.O. Box 3517
Miami	Coral Gables, Fla.	33134	2222 Ponce De Leon Boulevard, 5th Floor
Tampa	Fla.	33602	700 Twiggs Street, Suite 607
West Palm Beach	Fla.	33402	* 701 Clematis St., Room 229
Nashville	Tenn.	37219	404 James Robertson Parkway, Suite 1012
Knoxville	Tenn.	37902	502 South Gay St., Room 307
Memphis	Tenn.	38103	* 167 North Main St., Room 211
Chicago	Ill.	60604	* 219 South Dearborn St., Room 838
Chicago	Ill.	60604	* 219 South Dearborn St., Room 437
Cleveland	Ohio	44199	* 1240 East 9th St., Room 317
Columbus	Ohio	43215	* 85 Marconi Boulevard
Cincinnati	Ohio	45202	* 550 Main St., Room 5028
Detroit	Mich.	48226	* 477 Michigan Ave.
Marquette	Mich.	49855	540 W. Kaye Avenue, Don H. Bottom Univ. Ctr.
Indianapolis	Ind.	46204	* 575 North Pennsylvania St., Room 552
South Bend	Ind.	46601	501 E. Monroe St., Suite 120
Madison	Wisc.	53703	212 East Washington Ave., Room 213
Eau Claire	Wisc.	54701	* 500 South Barstow St., Room B9AA
Milwaukee	Wisc.	53202	517 East Wisconsin Ave.–Room 246
Minneapolis	Minn.	55403	100 North 6th St.
Springfield	Ill.	62701	Four North, Old State Capital Plaza
Dallas	Tex.	75235	1720 Regal Row, Room 230
Dallas	Tex.	75242	* 1100 Commerce St., Room 3C36
Marshall	Tex.	75670	* 100 South Washington Street, Room G-12
Ft. Worth	Tex.	76102	501 West 10th Street, Room 527
Albuquerque	N. M.	87100	5000 Marble Avenue, N.E., Room 320
Houston	Tex.	77002	500 Dallas Street
Little Rock	Ark.	72201	320 West Capitol Ave., P.O. Box 1401
Lubbock	Tex.	79401	* 1205 Texas Avenue, Room 712
El Paso	Tex.	79902	4100 Rio Bravo, Suite 300
Lower Rio Grande Valley	Harlingen, Tex	78550	222 East Van Buren Street, P.O. Box 2567
Corpus Christi	Tex.	78408	3105 Leopard Street, P.O. Box 9253
New Orleans	La.	70113	1001 Howard Avenue, 17th Floor

Shreveport	La.	71101	*	500 Fannin Street, Room 5B06
Oklahoma City	Okla.	73102	*	200 N.W. 5th Street, Suite 670
Tulsa	Okla.	74103		333 West Fourth Street, Room 3104
San Antonio	Tex.	78206	*	727 East Durango Street, Room A-513
Austin	Tex.	78701	*	300 East 8th Street
Kansas City	Mo.	64106		911 Walnut St., 23rd Floor
Kansas City	Mo.	64106		1150 Grande Ave., 5th Floor
Springfield	Mo.	65803		220 E. Commercial Street
Sikeston	Mo.	63801		400 N. Main Street
Cedar Rapids	Iowa	52402		373 Collins Road NE
Des Moines	Iowa	50309	*	210 Walnut St., Room 749
Omaha	Neb.	68102		19th & Farnum St., 2nd Floor
St. Louis	Mo.	63101		One Mercantile Tower-Suite 2500
Wichita	Kans.	67202		110 East Waterman Street
Denver	Colo.	80202		1405 Curtis Street, 22nd Floor
Denver	Colo.	80202		721 19th Street
Casper	Wyo.	82601	*	100 East B Street, Room 4001, P.O. Box 2839
Fargo	N. D.	58108	*	657 2nd Ave., North, Room 218, P.O. Box 3086
Helena	Mont.	59601	*	301 S. Park Avenue, Room 528, Drawer 10054
Salt Lake City	Utah	84138	*	125 South State St., Room 2237
Sioux Falls	S. D.	57102		101 South Main Ave., Suite 101
Rapid City	S. D.	57701	*	515 9th St., Room 246
San Francisco	Calif.	94102	*	450 Golden Gate Ave., P.O. Box 36044
San Francisco	Calif.	94105		211 Main Street, 4th Floor
Oakland	Calif.	94612	*	1515 Clay Street–Room 947
Fresno	Calif.	93712		1229 "N" St., P.O. Box 828
Sacramento	Calif.	95825	*	2800 Cottage Way, Room W-2535
Las Vegas	Nev.	89101	*	301 E. Stewart, P.O. Box 7525, Downtown Station
Reno	Nev.	89505	*	50 S. Virginia St., Room 114, P.O. Box 3216
Honolulu	Hawaii	96850	*	300 Ala Mona, Room 2213, P.O. Box 50207
Agana	Guam	96910		Pacific Daily News Bldg., Room 508
Los Angeles	Calif.	90071		350 S. Figueroa St., 6th Floor
Santa Ana	Calif.	92701		2700 North Main Street
Phoenix	Ariz.	85012		3030 North Central Avenue, Suite 1201
Tucson	Ariz.	85701	*	301 West Congress Street, Room 3V
San Diego	Calif.	92188	*	880 Front Street, Room 4-S-29
Seattle	Wash.	98104		710 2nd Ave., 5th Floor
Seattle	Wash.	98174	*	915 Second Ave., Room 1744
Anchorage	Alaska	99501		1016 West 6th Ave., Suite 200
Fairbanks	Alaska	99701	*	101 12th Ave., Box 14
Boise	Idaho	83701		1005 Main St., 2nd Floor
Portland	Oreg.	97204	*	1220 S.W. Third Avenue, Room 676
Spokane	Wash.	99210	*	West 920 Riverside Avenue Room 651 P.O. Box 2167

INDEX